Karl Marx on India

From the *New York Daily Tribune*

(including Articles by Frederick Engels)

and Extracts from Marx–Engels

Correspondence 1853–1862

Karl Marx on India

From the *New York Daily Tribune*

(including Articles by Frederick Engels)

and Extracts from Marx–Engels

Correspondence 1853–1862

Edited by IQBAL HUSAIN

Introduction by IRFAN HABIB

Appreciation by PRABHAT PATNAIK

Aligarh Historians Society

 Tulika Books

Published by **Tulika Books**
35 A/1 (ground floor), Shahpur Jat, New Delhi 110 049, India

© Aligarh Historians Society 2006

First edition (hardback) 2006
Second edition (paperback) 2006
Third edition 2008
Fourth edition 2011
Fifth edition 2014

ISBN: 978-93-82381-40-2

Printed at Repro India Limited, Mumbai

Contents

Abbreviations

Av. or Avineri	Shlomo Avineri (ed.), *Karl Marx, On Colonialism and Modernization* (New York, 1969).
CW or *Collected Works*	Karl Marx and Frederick Engels, *Collected Works*, various volumes (Moscow, 1975–89).
FIWI	Karl Marx and Frederick Engels, *First Indian War of Independence* (Moscow, 1959).
FR	*The Fifth Report from the Select Committee of Parliament* (London, 1812).
NYDT	*New York Daily Tribune.*
OED	*Oxford English Dictionary*, Compact Edition, 2 vols (Oxford, 1971).
On Colonialism	Karl Marx and Frederick Engels, *On Colonialism*, fourth edition (Moscow, 1976).
Selected Correspondence	Karl Marx and Frederick Engels, *Selected Correspondence*, edited by Dona Torr (Calcutta, 1945).
Selected Correspondence, Moscow	Karl Marx and Frederick Engels, *Selected Correspondence* (Moscow, 1956).
Tribune	*New York Daily Tribune.*

Acknowledgements

This volume has been made possible by the help of many friends and colleagues. Professor Irfan Habib suggested the project and has vetted the entire final text. The Indo–US Education Foundation (with the collaboration of the University Grants Commission) made possible a trip to the US in 1990 and so enabled me to use the *New York Daily Tribune* files. In the US, I had the benefit of advice and help from Professor Emeritus Walter Hauser of the University of Virginia, Charlottesville, and the late Mrs Rosy Hauser, and from Professor Richard Barnett, also of the University of Virginia. I received much hospitality (and a great deal of care) from Mr and Mrs Sajjad Yusuf, Charlottesville. At the Alderman Library of the University of Virginia, where I worked on the *New York Daily Tribune* files and microfilms, the most courteous attention and help from members of the library staff was extended to me. At the Library of Congress, Washington, Mr Samuel Iftikhar, a Deputy Librarian, made all the requisite facilities available. I must also thank Ms Cassandra Pyle (Executive Director) and Ms Leila M. Benhow and Ms Lydia Z. Gomes (Senior Associates) of the India Programme, Council for International Exchange of Scholars, Washington, for much help and consideration. Certain editions of works quoted by Marx needed to be traced at the British Library, London, and Bodleian Library, Oxford, both of which extended me the requisite facilities. Dr Najaf Haider, then at New College, was my host at Oxford.

At Aligarh, I have made extensive use of both the Maulana Azad Library and the Research Library of the Department of History. For some volumes of the English version of the *Collected Works* of Marx and Engels, and some other books, I was able to draw on the personal collections of the late Mr Ali Ashraf, and Professors Sayera I. Habib, Irfan Habib and Pradeep Saxena. Dr Ramesh Rawat also gave me some references.

Professor Shireen Moosvi, Secretary of the Aligarh Historians Society, made available to me all the office facilities of the Society and gave much other help. Mr Muniruddin Khan and Ms Ushra set the initial text on the Society's computers.

Dr Rajendra Prasad and Ms Indira Chandrasekhar of Tulika Books have given me valuable advice and guidance. The index has been prepared at Tulika Books.

IQBAL HUSAIN

Editor's Note to this edition

This reprint corrects some printing slips and incorporates some additional information in the footnotes and in the reference material at the end of the volume.

The reader's attention is invited to the *Addendum* at the bottom of page 291, for in Marx's dispatch to *NYDT* here referred to, he draws an important inference about the effect of the Rebellion of 1857 on British exports to India.

June 2008   IQBAL HUSAIN

Prefatory Note

The American journalist and politician Horace Greeley (1811–1872) established the *New York Daily Tribune* (*NYDT*) in 1841. It was to be a serious paper, cheap enough to be read by ordinary Americans. The causes it espoused were Protectionism (and so hostility towards the economic pre-eminence of Free-Trade Britain), workers' right to combine, women's rights and, after 1850, slaves' emancipation. By 1860, it had become the paper with the largest circulation in the United States (the weekly *Tribune* selling about 200,000 copies). Charles A. Dana (1819–1897), Editor (later Managing Editor) of the paper from 1847 to 1862, was a follower of Fourier, the French Utopian Socialist, and had met Karl Marx on his trip to Europe in 1848. The nature of the newspaper made it possible for it to accommodate Marx's views in its columns; and nineteen articles on Germany under Marx's signature appeared in 1851–52, although these were, in fact, written at his request by his friend Frederick Engels. The first report actually written by Marx was submitted in August 1852, and was about England.[1] Marx's association with the *Tribune* waned when, with the American Civil War breaking out in April 1861, the *Tribune*'s interest in non-American matters declined; and Dana's own departure from the *Tribune* in 1862 practically synchronized with the publication of Marx's last article in it.[2] The *Tribune* itself survived until 1924.

Marx's articles published in the *Tribune* from 1852 to 1862 constitute a separate genre among his works, for two particular reasons. First, these constitute the major part of that body of his work which was originally published in English. In August 1852, when he submitted his first article to the *Tribune*, it was written by him in German and transformed by Engels into the English version that was actually published. This arrangement continued until February 1853, from which time onwards Marx wrote his pieces directly in English. Since his articles on India (or containing passages relevant to India) began to appear in the *Tribune* only from June 1853, all his articles in the present volume represent texts written in English by Karl Marx himself. One must, however, allow for some changes by the editors, including even insertions, which in many cases cannot be

---

[1] This was 'The Elections in England – Tories and Whigs', datelined 6 August 1852 and published in the *Tribune* of 25 August 1852 (*CW*, Vol. 11, pp. 327–32).

[2] 'The Mexican Imbroglio', datelined 15 February 1862, published in the *Tribune* of 10 March 1862 (*CW*, Vol. 19, pp. 172–77). On Dana's departure from the paper, see Engels's letter to Marx, 5 May 1862 (*CW*, Vol. 41, p. 359).

located, for the original drafts have disappeared. Second, the general assignment was for him to write on events outside America, which meant that Marx was pressed to read material on various countries and parts of the world where notable events were then taking place. This irritated him considerably because it represented a major distraction from his theoretical studies and practical work in the European working-class movement. Financial reasons were mainly why he put up with the distraction; the payments the *Tribune* made were modest, but Marx, with hardly any other source of income and except for some steady support from Engels in Manchester, was hardly in a position to choose.[3]

In the event, there is no doubt that the work Marx undertook for his *Tribune* articles not only influenced his later theoretical work (one major result being his incorporation of colonialism as a factor in the genesis and expansion of capitalism), but also gave him an opportunity to apply the general principles of his method of historical materialism to the study of complex circumstances prevalent in different parts of the world. The perception of pre-colonial and colonial India that he put forth in the *Tribune* is a classic product of such application.

It took a long time for Marx's articles in the *Tribune* to obtain the recognition and appreciation they deserved. Partly, the reason was that, being printed in a newspaper, they were for long not published in book form. The articles on Palmerston were, indeed, republished as a pamphlet titled *Palmerston and Russia* (London, 1853), but did not carry Marx's name as the author. Only in 1896 did Marx's daughter, Eleanor Marx–Aveling, publish the nineteen articles written by Engels during 1851–52 but ascribed to Marx in the *Tribune*, as *Revolution and Counter-Revolution [in Germany]* (London, 1896). This was followed the next year by another set of Marx's *Tribune* articles, jointly edited by Eleanor and her husband, Edward Aveling, under the title *The Eastern Question, A Reprint of Letters Written in 1853–56, Dealing with the Events of the Crimean War* (London, 1897). As the title indicates, this volume was concerned only with the relations of Britain, France and Turkey with Czarist Russia.

It is, therefore, not surprising that when the great debate took place around the theme of imperialism before and during World War I, neither Rosa Luxemburg in her *Accumulation of Capital* (1913)[4] nor Lenin in his *Imperialism – the Highest Stage of Capitalism* (1917)[5] showed any awareness of Marx's *Tribune* articles, and his explicit recognition of the link between Free Trade and colonial conquests. It is difficult to speculate how much they would have modified their divergent concepts of the genesis of imperialism, had the fact of Marx's extreme scepticism about the anti-colonialism of the Free Traders been known to them.

---

[3] The history of the relations between the *New York Daily Tribune* and Karl Marx as its correspondent is summarized in Boris Nicolaievsky and Otto Menchen-Helfen, *Karl Marx: Man and Fighter* (London, 1936), pp. 233–37 and 251.

[4] English translation by Agnes Schwarzschild, with an Introduction by Joan Robinson (London, 1951).

[5] Translation from Lenin's original version (Progress Publishers, Moscow, 18th printing, 1982).

One further reason for the delay in the republication of the *Tribune* articles, undoubtedly, was that much of the material that Marx and, at his request, Engels contributed, was printed in the *Tribune* without their names. The *Tribune* editors at first let Marx's articles appear in his name, but then began to print some of them as unsigned leading articles, allowing Marx's name to appear only on what Marx considered to be lightweight reports. When he protested at this practice, they banished his name altogether.[6] The *Tribune* archives being no longer extant, it is only the surviving papers (correspondence and notebooks) of Marx and Engels that can tell us which of the *Tribune*'s leading articles and reports from unnamed correspondents are from Marx's pen (or from Engels', in certain cases). The necessary research into these documents was carried out by the Marx–Engels–Lenin Institute (later designated 'Institute of Marxism–Leninism') in Moscow, USSR, during the 1920s and 1930s. One of the first results in English was the volume edited by Dona Torr, *Marx on China: Articles from the New York Daily Tribune, 1853–1860* (London, 1951; Bombay, 1952), which contained in a large part such newly detected material.

A selection of Marx's articles on India from the *Tribune*, confined presumably to the signed articles, was published from Allahabad 'between 1934 and 1938', as Socialist Book Club Publication No. 4, with Mulk Raj Anand as editor.[7] An edition of Marx's *Articles on India* was brought out from London in 1940; it was edited by R.P. Dutt, who provided an Introduction along with a considerable amount of annotation. Eight articles from the *Tribune* (all signed ones) were included in this slim volume; reprints were published from Bombay in 1943 and 1951. The volume *On Britain* by Marx and Engels, published from Moscow in 1953, included the article, 'The Indian Revolt', published in the *Tribune* on 16 September 1857, thus bringing to the notice of Indian readers for the first time the fact that Marx had also written on the 1857 Rebellion; the article concerned had been printed in the *Tribune* without Marx's name.

The major access to Marx's writings in the *Tribune* on colonial questions and India came with the publication in 1959 of two volumes from Moscow: Marx and Engels, *On Colonialism*, a fourth (enlarged) edition being issued in 1968; and Marx and Engels, *The First Indian War of Independence*, with its sixth printing in 1988. Both were based on the primary work done at the Institute of Marxism–Leninism, Moscow, in locating Marx's and Engels' unsigned pieces. The two volumes, between them, contained the bulk of articles (and portions of articles) relating to India contributed by Marx and Engels to the *Tribune*, the texts being reproduced from the newspaper directly. The articles exclusively relating to India were abstracted from these two volumes (text as well as notes) by Berch Berberoglu in *India: National Liberation and Class Struggle: A Collection of Classical Marxist Writings* (Meerut, 1985). For a more recent selection of

[6] See Marx's letters to Engels, 2 November 1853, 22 April and 29 September 1854 (*CW*, Vol. 39, pp. 395, 439, 483–84).

[7] For this edition, see D.D. Kosambi, *An Introduction to the Study of Indian History* (Bombay, 1956), pp. 15–16.

the articles on India (including some unsigned ones), see Karl Marx and Frederick Engels, *On the National and Colonial Questions*, edited by Aijaz Ahmad, (LeftWord Books, New Delhi, 2001), pp. 61–113.

An effort was made by Shlomo Avineri to incorporate the entire colonial and non-European and non-American material contributed by Marx to the *Tribune* in a single volume, *Karl Marx, On Colonialism and Modernization* (New York, 1968; paperback, 1969). In his Preface, Avineri censured the two Moscow volumes (*On Colonialism* and *The First Indian War of Independence*) for their 'not very scrupulous' editorial standards, and for 'abound[ing] in errors and omissions'. The criticism is excessively harsh: in fact, the Moscow editors were cautious in not including any material from the *Tribune* whenever there was no firm evidence that it had been contributed to the paper by Marx or Engels. Avineri himself included some pieces that cannot really be ascribed to Marx (and for this reason are relegated to the Appendices in the present volume). His own annotation is in fact poorer than that of the two Moscow volumes. There are also slips and misprints in Avineri's text (some of which are noted in this volume), and, in one or two cases, the omissions of the Moscow volumes are found in Avineri's collection as well.

When publication of the massive series of the *Collected Works* (in English) of Marx and Engels began, it included, within Volumes 11–17 and 19 (Moscow, 1979–81; 1984), the entire collection of *Tribune* articles by Marx and Engels. In our volume there are only two articles (*Tribune*, 5 and 26 April 1858) that we hold to be by Marx but which are not admitted in *Collected Works*. The editors of *Collected Works* also provided fairly adequate annotations about persons, events and works mentioned in the writings of Marx and Engels. The inconvenience in using the *Collected Works* lies only in this, that the *Tribune* articles are there scattered over eight thick volumes from which material has to be culled.

Given the importance of the *Tribune* material for an understanding of Marx's views on India, a plan began to take shape at Aligarh over fifteen years ago, to bring out an authentic and comprehensive collection of Marx's articles relating to India published originally in the *Tribune*. Professor Irfan Habib suggested that I might utilize my visit to the United States in 1990 under an Indo–US Educational Foundation fellowship to explore the *New York Daily Tribune* files directly. I was gratified to find that the Alderman Library, University of Virginia, to which I was assigned, had both the actual files and microfilm copies of the newspaper for the period concerned. (I later found that even the Library of Congress, Washington, had only microfilms, not the actual files of the newspaper.) I first checked the text of the articles included in the Avineri volume, noting the variations and thus establishing the actual text as printed in the *Tribune*. I then went through the rest of the files and obtained microfilms and photocopies of several unsigned articles which could possibly have come from Marx's pen. Further study made me realize that many of these could not have come from Marx; and of the rest, the likelihood was so slim that I had to put them in the Appendices to this volume, to let the readers judge for themselves. It should be borne in mind that the *Tribune* had two other sources for material on India. One was Bayard Taylor (1825–1878), a well-known American journalist and a regular correspondent of the *Tribune* throughout the period of Marx's association with the paper. Marx noted with some bitterness in a letter to Engels (22 April 1854) that the *Tribune* had spent £500 on Taylor's visit to India, though 'the chap's reports from there are worse and shorter' than Marx's own from London.[8] Taylor also published a volume of verses in 1854, called *Poems of the Orient*. The other source was a Polish-born Hungarian nationalist, Ference Aurelius Pulszky (1814–1897), who signed as 'APC', and became the *Tribune's* London correspondent. He was described by Marx as his 'rival', one who 'cribs unblushingly from the London newspapers'.[9] Either of these two men could have penned some of the articles placed by us in the Appendices.

On my return to India, I continued comparing the *Tribune* texts, as I had found them, with not only Avineri but also *On Colonialism* and *The First Indian War of Independence* and, finally, the *Collected Works*. The texts in the *Collected Works* were found to be the closest to the *Tribune* texts, and it is obvious that these have been quite carefully checked with the originals.

In this volume, the *Tribune* texts, as originally printed, have been faithfully followed. Misprints have been noted, not silently removed. Since the *Tribune* used the American system of spelling (e.g., 'labor' for 'labour'), that system has been retained. Only in two places, where Marx declared that words used by him had been replaced by others, have the original words used by him been restored, with the substitution duly recorded in footnotes. Since many of Marx's contributions were used as leading articles by the *Tribune* editors, they tended to insert certain sentences of their own, occasionally so framed as to imply American authorship of the material. Such obvious insertions have been retained, though the fact of insertion is usually indicated in footnotes. Where an article was contributed by Frederick Engels at Marx's request, his name is given by us above the heading of the article. All articles by him on India appeared as unsigned lead articles in the *Tribune*. Divergences from the *Tribune* text in previous editions, including Avineri's volume, have been noted, but completeness in this respect has not been attempted.

Any article which appeared in the *Tribune* over Karl Marx's name is identified as such in the initial footnote under it in this volume. But most of his articles included here are unsigned. For establishing whether an unsigned piece in the *Tribune* is by Marx, Marx's own notebooks, and the Marx–Engels correspondence for the period 1852–64, published (in English translation from the German original) in *Collected Works*, Volumes 39–41 (Moscow, 1983–85), through their references to individual articles, provide a firm means of identification which the editors of the *Collected Works* have fully used. It is only in the case of a small number of unsigned articles that we have to rely on our judgement as to

---

[8] CW, Vol. 39 (Moscow, 1983), p. 439. Bayard Taylor visited India in the winter of 1852–53 and his reports of his travels appeared in the *Tribune* under his signature.

[9] Letters to Engels, 11 March and 10 October 1854, ibid., pp. 418, 485.

whether these conform sufficiently to Marx's style of writing to be treated as his. Those which, in our opinion, do not meet this test are still included in this volume as Appendices. Titles of articles are retained as given by the *Tribune* editors, except in one case where Marx seems to have given another title. Where the *Tribune* editors fail to furnish a heading or title, a title appropriate to the subject has been framed and put within square brackets. In some cases the title is derived from the Marx MSS, in which case the brackets are dispensed with.

A Supplement in the present volume contains extracts from the letters of Marx and Engels of the period 1852–62, in which references are made to India or to British policies towards India, and to articles on India to be written for or actually published in the *Tribune*. These are all taken from the volumes of the *Collected Works*, reference to which is supplied under each extract.

All footnotes have been supplied by the editor, there being none in the original *Tribune* articles. In the notes the editor does not aim at giving particulars on such well-known events and personalities of Indian history as any Indian reader would be expected already to be familiar with. Notes are provided, however, for the British, European and American personalities mentioned, the main sources of information being *The Concise Dictionary of National Biography*, Part 1 (to 1900), edited by Sydney Lee (London, 1953), the *New Columbia Encyclopaedia* (1975) and the biographical notices furnished by editors of the *Collected Works* in each volume. All works mentioned by Marx have been traced and, in the case of quotations, these have been checked, wherever possible, with the original passages, the divergences, if any, being noted. In a number of cases, the researches of the editors of the *Collected Works* have been drawn upon, with due acknowledgement.

Despite or, perhaps, due to the richness of Marx's writing on India found in the *Tribune*, the ideas he expresses here need to be set alongside his theoretical writings and his other (mainly subsequent) comments on India. This task should have been attempted by the editor, but I abstain from doing so, since this has already been performed by Irfan Habib in his Marx's death-centenary essay, 'Marx's Perception of India', originally published in *The Marxist*, Vol. I, No. 1 (Delhi, July–September 1983). At my request, Professor Irfan Habib has furnished a revised, updated version, with considerable additions and modifications, and a thorough rechecking of the references, to serve as an Introduction to this volume. He has also compiled a list of References to India in the writings of Marx and Engels other than those included in the present volume. This list precedes the Bibliography, and should be helpful to readers who wish to see how India figures in the other writings of the founders of Marxism.

Professor Prabhat Patnaik, the noted economist, has placed us in great debt by contributing an Appreciation, which considers the significance of Marx's *Tribune* corpus in terms of constructing a further theoretical understanding of capitalism and its relationship with dependent economies. He aptly sees it as a window to 'the Other Marx'.

IQBAL HUSAIN

Introduction:
Marx's Perception of India

IRFAN HABIB

A hundred and fifty-two years ago, Karl Marx wrote two seminal essays on India as part of his assignment as the London correspondent of a leading New York newspaper. In these two articles, 'The British Rule in India' and 'The Future Results of the British Rule in India', published in *New York Daily Tribune* (25 June and 8 August 1853), Marx consciously set himself to interpret the basic mechanics of the pre-colonial civilization of India, the impact of British rule on India, and the future course of India's development and liberation. Brilliant as they are, these two articles do not yet constitute the complete statement of Marx's understanding of India. In part, this is because Marx wrote other pieces on India as well, and in part, because he continued to study and reflect after he had written these articles in 1853.

Through the 1850s, Marx wrote various articles for the same newspaper, in which he made important observations on India; some important supplementary statements also occur in the letters that Marx and Engels wrote to each other during the decade, and in articles that Engels wrote at the request of Marx.[1]

During 1857–58, Marx set down on paper the famous *Grundrisse*, his notes for self-clarification preparatory to *Capital*, and here he tried to set India in his scheme of pre-capitalist formations.[2] But it is in *Capital* itself, notably in

[1] The two popular collections used by me in which the articles of Marx and Engels have been published are Karl Marx and Frederick Engels, *On Colonialism* (fourth enlarged edition, Moscow, 1976), and Karl Marx and Frederick Engels, *The First Indian War of Independence, 1857–1859* (Moscow, 1959), cited respectively as *On Colonialism* and *FIWI*. For the few articles on India not included in either of the two collections, I have used *Karl Marx, On Colonialism and Modernization*, edited by Shlomo Avineri (New York, 1969), cited as 'Avineri'. An earlier publication, Karl Marx, *Articles on India*, introduction by R.P. Dutt (first Indian edition, Bombay, 1943), is now of historical interest only. For their letters, I have used Marx and Engels, *Selected Correspondence, 1846–1895*, edited by Dona Torr (Calcutta, 1945); other publications (especially Marx and Engels, *Collected Works*) are cited wherever the Dona Torr collection omits a letter or truncates its text. *Note*: In the present volume, the *Tribune* articles can be traced from the dates of issue of the newspaper given in the notes below; and the letters of the period 1852–62 by the dates of the letters cited.

[2] I have used Karl Marx, *Grundrisse*, translated with foreword by Martin Nicolaus (London, 1973). The historical portion of *Grundrisse* was translated by Jack Cohen, with an introduction by E.J. Hobsbawm, as *Pre-Capitalist Economic Formations* (London, 1964). Where the reference is to the portion of *Grundrisse* contained in the latter, its translation has been followed.

Volume I (1867), that Marx contributed a partial restatement (with important emendations, cautions and new elaborations) of his main theses on India, which obtains added significance by being placed within the classical presentation of his full-scale analysis of capitalism. Scattered statements of value also occur in the posthumous two volumes of *Capital* edited by Engels from Marx's notes.[3]

After 1867, references to India become relatively infrequent in Marx's published writings, but he did not cease to inform himself, as his extensive notes on Indian history taken some time after 1870 amply bear witness.[4] There was a renewed interest, too, in the village community, arising out of Marx's reading of Morgan and Kovalevsky.[5]

Any assessment of Marx's views on India must take into account all his writings spread over practically three decades. We cannot, moreover, simply fix all the pieces together, since, over time, Marx's views might well have undergone some change, this being especially true of his interpretation of pre-colonial India.

Pre-Colonial Society
The Inherited Generalizations
When Marx wrote in 1853 of Indian society before the British conquest, he seems to have taken as his starting point the descriptive elements in Hegel's interpretation of the Indian civilization.

'The Hindoos have no history,' Hegel had said, 'no growth expanding into a veritable political condition.'[6] The admitted diffusion of Indian culture had been 'a dumb, deedless expansion'. Thus, 'the people of India have achieved no foreign conquests, but have on every occasion been vanquished themselves.'[7] It is essentially this judgement that is repeated by Marx in the well-known passage: 'Indian society has no history, at least no known history. What we call its history is but the history of successive intruders who founded their empires on the passive basis of that unresisting and unchanging society.'[8]

---

[3] For *Capital*, Volume I, I have cited the standard page-to-page reprint of the Moore–Aveling translation (London, 1887), edited by Dona Torr (London, 1938). For Volumes II and III, I have used the translations published in Moscow: 1957 (Vol. II) and 1959 (Vol. III).

[4] Karl Marx, *Notes on Indian History (1664–1858)* (Moscow, n.d.). It is unluckily not made clear by the publishers when exactly Marx took down these notes. But it would be presumably after 1870, when Robert Sewell's book, *The Analytical History of India*, was published. The other work used, Elphinstone's *History of India*, had been published as early as 1841, though a new edition appeared in 1874.

[5] On those two fresh sources of interest for Marx, see Daniel Thorner, 'Marx on India and the Asiatic Mode of Production', *Contributions to Indian Sociology*, IX (December 1966), pp. 58–63.

[6] G.W. Friedrich Hegel, *The Philosophy of History*, translated by J. Sibree (New York, 1956), p. 163.

[7] Ibid., p. 142.

[8] *Tribune*, 8 August 1853; *On Colonialism*, p. 81. For a criticism of the historicity of this judgement, see D.D. Kosambi, *An Introduction to the Study of Indian History* (Bombay, 1956), p. 11.

Hegel saw in the ideology of the Indian ('Hindoo') culture a pantheism of 'Imagination', expressed in the 'universal deification of all finite existence and degradation of the Divine', a deprivation of man 'of personality and freedom';[9] 'the morality which is involved in respect for human life is not found among the Hindoos'.[10] Marx, too, similarly speaks of 'murder itself [being] a religious rite in Hindustan – a brutalizing worship of nature, exhibiting its degradation in the fact that man, the sovereign of nature, fell down on his knees in adoration of Hanuman, the monkey, and Sabbala, the cow'.[11]

In the actual organization of society, the multiplication of divine forms was paralleled by the multiplicity of castes. This was recognized by Hegel to be an advance over an undifferentiated society, but then was immediately condemned by him as establishing 'the most degrading spiritual serfdom'.[12] In the organization of the Indian village, he discerned a similar immutable rigidity:

> The whole income belonging to every village is, as already stated, divided into two parts, of which one belongs to the rajah, the other to the cultivators; but proportionate shares are also received by the provost of the place, the judge, the water-surveyor, the brahmin, who superintends religious worship, the astrologer (who is also a brahmin, and announces the days of good and ill omen), the smith, the carpenter, the potter, the washerman, the barber, the physician, the dancing girls, the musician, the poet. This arrangement is fixed and immutable, and subject to no one's will. All political revolutions, therefore, are matters of indifference to the common Hindoo, for his lot is unchanged.[13]

All this Marx repeats, giving an identical description of the village community for which he quotes *in extenso* from what was probably Hegel's authority as well, a passage in the celebrated *Fifth Report* of 1812.[14] Marx not only condemns these communities as being 'contaminated by distinctions of caste, and by slavery', but also stresses their isolation from political events. He writes indignantly of 'the barbarian egotism' of the Indian villages, which, 'concentrating on some miserable patch of land, had quietly witnessed the ruin of empires, the perpetration of unspeakable cruelties, the massacre of the population of large towns, with no other consideration bestowed upon them than on natural events'.[15]

The comparisons of Hegel in 1830 and Marx in 1853 are brought out not to show that Marx was simply repeating Hegel but merely to underline the fact that, in spite of his vastly different critical apparatus, Marx had to begin

---

[9] Hegel, *Philosophy of History*, p. 141.

[10] Ibid., p. 150.

[11] *Tribune*, 25 June 1853; *On Colonialism*, p. 41.

[12] Hegel, *Philosophy of History*, p. 144.

[13] Ibid., p. 154.

[14] *Fifth Report from the Select Committee on the Affairs of the East India Company*, 1812, photo-offset edition, Irish University Press Series of British Parliamentary Papers, Colonies: East India: 3, Shanon, 1969, p. 85. Marx reproduces the passage in *Tribune*, 25 June 1853; *On Colonialism*, pp. 39–40.

[15] *Tribune*, 25 June 1853; *On Colonialism*, p. 40.

from such an assessment of Indian culture as happened to be the accepted one among the best bourgeois thinkers of his day. What is of signal importance, of course, is how he revised it and set it in a totally different analytical framework.

For one thing, right from the beginning, Marx accepted only those factual pillars of the Hegelian generalizations that he believed to be sufficiently substantiated. Already, in 1853, he had consulted the *Fifth Report*, a voluminous document; also Mark Wilks' *Historical Sketches of South India* (1810), whose passage on the village communities he seems to have drawn on in a letter to Engels;[16] John Campbell's *Modern India* (1852) and James Mill's *History of British India* (1806–18);[17] and volumes of parliamentary debates and reports, especially those preceding the Charter Act of 1853. He refers to the *Manusmriti* ('Manu'), which he might well have read in the translation of Sir William Jones;[18] and he specifically alludes to his recent reading of François Bernier's *Travels*, which contained a striking description of the Mughal empire in Aurangzeb's time.[19]

This was reasonably large reading, enough to check Hegel's more exorbitant pronouncements. Yet, Marx's conception of India was by no means an edited restatement of Hegel. He did the same with the great philosopher's interpretation of India as he had done with his dialectics; that is, he 'inverted' it. He had already posed the question in a letter to Engels: 'Why does the history of the East *appear* as a history of religions?'[20] The religious peculiarities that Hegel saw at the foundations of the peculiarities of Indian culture were really themselves the consequences of Indian social organization, pre-eminently the village community.[21] This last, as Marx saw things in 1853, was the crucial institution and explained practically everything.

---

[16] Marx takes recourse to Wilks' passage – Lt. Col. Mark Wilks, *Historical Sketches of South India* (originally published in London, 1810), I, edited by Murray Hammick (Mysore, 1930), pp. 136–39 – to insert additions into the quotation from the *Fifth Report* that he gives in his letter to Engels, 14 June 1853; *On Colonialism*, pp. 313–14. Wilks is expressly cited as authority for the description of the village community in *Capital*, I, p. 352n.

[17] Quotations from Campbell occur more than once in the *Tribune* articles; *On Colonialism*, pp. 65, 67, 68, 73, 79, 85, 182, 208. See also *Capital*, I, p. 352n. Mill's *History* is also quoted by Marx in *Tribune*, 11 July 1853; *On Colonialism*, pp. 47–48.

[18] Marx's reference to Manu occurs in a letter of 14 June 1853, *Selected Correspondence*, p. 62; *On Colonialism*, p. 315.

[19] *Selected Correspondence*, pp. 57–58. Marx also quotes Bernier in *A Contribution to the Critique of Political Economy*, English translation (Moscow, 1970), p. 130. Bernier well deserved Marx's admiration, since he consciously attempts an analysis of the factors behind the decline of the Mughal empire. For Engels' remarks on Bernier, see his letter of 6 June 1853, *Selected Correspondence*, p. 60. Engels' interest in things Asian extended to learning Persian, and so securing access to Hafiz's poetry and Mir Khwand's history (*Rauzatu-s Safa*) in the original (letter to Marx, 6 June 1853, *Collected Works*, Vol. 39, pp. 339–42; see also extract from the letter in the present volume).

[20] Letter of 2 June 1853, *Selected Correspondence*, p. 57. Marx's emphasis.

[21] *Tribune*, 25 June 1853; *On Colonialism*, pp. 40–41.

The Village Community

Marx's excitement at his discovery of the Indian village community at this time is not surprising. Already, in *The German Ideology*, prepared by him and Engels, there was a groping towards an elucidation of the main pre-capitalist forms of property. They had distinguished, in order of sequence, (a) 'tribal' property corresponding to the 'undeveloped stage of production' – hunting and fishing and early agriculture; (b) 'ancient communal and state ownership', generating class differentiation between citizens and slaves; and (c) 'feudal or estate property with an enserfed small peasantry'.[22] These forms had largely been hypothetical, though form (b) derived from Marx's understanding of Roman society, and form (c) from that of medieval western Europe. Now India too seemed to illustrate, through actual survivals, a system of property, and economic and social relationships, which broadly accorded with form (b);[23] and the descriptions of English observers themselves could be shown to reinforce the basic point that pre-capitalist societies moved according to 'laws of motion' different from those of the capitalist society.

In *Capital*, I (1867), Marx gives as the first feature of the Indian village community, the prevalence of 'possession in common of the land'.[24] What exactly did this mean? Marx often spoke as if it implied that the villagers in some places at least 'cultivated' the land 'in common'. His source for this seems to have been Wilks, who had said: 'In some instances the lands of a village are cultivated in common, and the crop divided up in the proportion of the labour contributed, but generally each occupant tills his own field.'[25] This statement does not appear in the *Fifth Report*, which is quoted for the Indian village community in Marx's 1853 *Tribune* article; but he already shows knowledge of Wilks' description in a letter of 1853: 'In some of these communities the lands of the village are cultivated in common; in most cases each occupant tills his own field.'[26] In *Grundrisse* (1857–58), Marx refers to the 'common organization of labour' surviving in 'some tribes of India'.[27] In *Capital*, I, he follows Wilks closely, and indeed expressly cites him; he further assigns communal cultivation to village communities of the 'simplest form'.[28]

A formulation of the historical relationship between communal agriculture and communal ownership was already offered by Marx in *Grundrisse*: it was from communal agriculture that communal property originated; but once

---

[22] Karl Marx and Frederick Engels, *The German Ideology* (Moscow, 1964), pp. 32–36.
[23] This is presumed in Engels' question (letter of 6 June 1853): 'How does it come about that the orientals do not arrive at landed property even in its feudal form?'. *Selected Correspondence*, p. 59.
[24] *Capital*, I, p. 350. In E. and C. Paul's translation, Part I (London, 1930), p. 377, 'communal ownership of the land'. See also *Capital*, I, p. 325, where Marx ascribes to the Indian communities 'ownership in common of the means of production'.
[25] Wilks, *Historical Sketches of South India*, p. 137.
[26] Letter of 14 June 1853, *On Colonialism*, p. 280.
[27] *Pre-Capitalist Formations*, p. 70; *Grundrisse*, p. 473.
[28] *Capital*, I, p. 351.

established, communal property tended to survive the development of individual peasant agriculture.[29]

In an article that Marx contributed to the *Tribune* while he was composing *Grundrisse*, he appealed to 'a more thorough study of the institutions of Hindustan' to support 'the opinion that by the original Hindu institutions, the property of the land was in the village corporations, in which resided the power for allotting it out to individuals for cultivation'.[30] Here Marx has obviously in mind the common practice by village headmen of allotting wasteland for cultivation to outsiders or willing peasants. The right tended to establish, in Marx's eyes, corporate village ownership.

In *Grundrisse*, Marx argues that such ownership by the village community demarcated the 'Asiatic' form of the community from the two other developed forms of that institution, viz. the Roman (where land was owned by the urban community) and the Germanic (where the unit of ownership was the homestead).[31]

Besides common land ownership, Marx saw in the Indian village community two phenomena that were apparently contradictory but well integrated into it. On the one hand, there was a lack of development of division of labour, which resulted in 'the domestic union of agricultural and manufacturing pursuits'. This observation occurs in one of the *Tribune* articles of 1853, but it continued to occupy a central position in Marx's analysis and recurs in *Grundrisse* and in *Capital*, I, as well as elsewhere.[32] On the other hand, there was a development on the opposite extreme: the establishment of 'an unalterable division of labour'. This was realized through the caste system supplying, 'with the irresistible authority of the law of nature', the hereditary 'individual artificer, the smith, the carpenter, and so on'. The economic basis for this was the 'unchanging market' that the community provided to the artisan, prohibiting any alteration in the social division of labour once fixed.[33] Though the classic statement of this division is formulated in *Capital*, I, Marx had surely from the beginning been aware of the hereditary occupations and the system of caste within the community.[34]

---

[29] *Pre-Capitalist Formations*, pp. 68–69; *Grundrisse*, p. 472. It followed, then, that 'the Asiatic or Indian property forms everywhere mark the beginning [that is, the original forms] in Europe [as well]', a 'new proof' of which Marx found in the researches of Georg Ludwig van Maurer (d. 1872) in early Germanic village communities and the later evolution of individual property rights within it (Marx to Engels, 14 March 1868, *Collected Works*, Vol. 42, Moscow, 1987, p. 547). See also *Pre-Capitalist Formations*, p. 139.

[30] *Tribune*, 7 June 1858; *On Colonialism*, p. 192.

[31] *Pre-Capitalist Formations*, pp. 71–82; *Grundrisse*, pp. 474–86.

[32] *Tribune*, 25 June 1853, *On Colonialism*, p. 39; *Pre-Capitalist Formations*, pp. 70, 83, 91; *Grundrisse*, pp. 473, 486, 493; *Capital*, I, p. 350.

[33] *Capital*, I, pp. 351–52. On castes as arising out of the 'conversion of fractional work into the life-calling of one man', see *Capital*, I, p. 331.

[34] See, for example, the reference to 'hereditary means of subsistence' and 'the distinctions of caste' in *Tribune*, 25 June 1853; *On Colonialism*, pp. 39–40.

Marx, in 1853, spoke deprecatingly of the 'stagnatory, vegetative life' inherent in the Indian community.[35] In 1857–58, he went on to argue that the cause of this imperviousness to change lay within the community's structure, that is, within those elements of domestic industry and caste specialization that have been just described. He says:

> The Asiatic form [of the community, as against the Roman and Germanic] necessarily survives longest and most stubbornly. This is due to the fundamental principle on which it is based, that is, that the individual does not become independent of the community, that the circle of production is self-sustaining, unity of agriculture and craft manufacture, etc.[36]

Elsewhere, Marx argues that conquests of one tribe by another, given other internal structures of the conquered society, have helped to alter the form of property, leading to either slavery or serfdom. But, owing to the internal solidity of the Indian community, subjugation does not subvert its basic nature: 'Slavery and serfdom are simply further developments of property based on tribalism. They necessarily modify all its forms. This they are least able to do in the Asiatic form.'[37]

What one must remember here is that Marx is speaking of the internal conditions of the community, not of society as a whole; and even within the village community, he had noticed the existence of slavery as early as the *Tribune* article of 1853.[38] What he means is that 'conquerors' could obtain larger surplus by exploiting the community, economically solidified as it was, than by exploiting directly the individuals who composed it.[39] To the system of exploitation to which the Indian village communities came to be subjected, Marx gave the designation of despotism; and only with its description could his picture of pre-colonial Indian society be regarded as complete.

Despotism, Surplus and Commodities

Marx had already read Bernier in 1853, and, in a letter to Engels, he quotes him extensively. Now, Bernier's main thesis was that the Mughal empire and the other oriental states were decaying because there was no private property in the soil. Marx noted Bernier's statement that the king was 'the sole and only proprietor of the land', and added: 'Bernier rightly considers that the basic form of all phenomena in the East – he refers to Turkey, Persia, Hindustan – is to

---

[35] *Tribune*, 25 June 1853; *On Colonialism*, p. 41.
[36] *Pre-Capitalist Formations*, p. 83; *Grundrisse*, p. 486.
[37] *Pre-Capitalist Formations*, p. 91; *Grundrisse*, p. 493.
[38] *Tribune*, 25 June 1853; *On Colonialism*, p. 41.
[39] See *Capital*, III, pp. 771–72, where Marx says that individual bondage in the form of serfdom is not necessary where, 'as in Asia', the state is the 'landlord'. 'Under such circumstances there need exist no stronger political or economic pressure than that common to all subjection to that state.'

be found in the fact that *no private property in land existed*. This is the real key even to the oriental heaven.'[40]

But Bernier's description, while it showed that the Indian property system was quite different from that of Europe, could not be reconciled with the existence of communal property in India. Marx sought to resolve the problem in *Grundrisse*: whether the property resided in the community or the state, he argued, the individual 'is in fact propertyless'. Marx then introduces a distinction between 'property' and 'possession', so that 'the all-embracing unity which stands above all these small common bodies may appear as the higher or sole proprietor, the real communities only as hereditary possessors'.[41] Further:

> The despot here appears as the father of all the numerous lesser communities, thus realizing the common unity of all. . . . The surplus product . . . belongs to this highest unity. Oriental despotism therefore appears to lead to a legal absence of property. In fact, however, its foundation is tribal or common property.[42]

This rather mystical view of the property of the ruler was apparently abandoned by Marx within barely months of putting it down on paper. In a *Tribune* article of 1858, on Indian land tenures, he was willing to quote approvingly an opinion that the

> alleged property in the government [is] nothing more than the derivation of title from the sovereign, theoretically acknowledged in all countries the codes of which are based on the feudal law and substantially acknowledged in all countries whatever in the power of the Government to levy taxes on the land to the extent of the needs of the Government.[43]

In the last words of this quotation Marx seems to suggest that the sovereign's property in land was related to the size of the land tax. If it accounted for the bulk of the surplus, that is, if it was practically rent, then the king was, in fact, claiming what was the due of the land-owner.[44] It was this that was central to

---

[40] Letter of 2 June 1853, *Selected Correspondence*, p. 58. Emphasis in original. The statement in question occurs in François Bernier, *Travels in the Mughal Empire*, AD *1656–1668*, translated by A. Constable, edited by V.A. Smith (Oxford, 1916), pp. 5, 204, 226, 232, 238.

[41] *Pre-Capitalist Formations*, p. 69; *Grundrisse*, pp. 472–73.

[42] *Pre-Capitalist Formations*, pp. 69–70; *Grundrisse*, p. 473.

[43] *Tribune*, 25 May 1858; *On Colonialism*, p. 191. In another article published in *Tribune*, 3 April 1858, it is even asserted: 'The land, however, in India did not belong to the government, the greater proportion of it being as much private property as in England, many of the natives holding their estates by titles six or seven hundred years old' (Avineri, p. 278). This article does not, however, appear to have been written by Marx at all: it is not included in Marx and Engels, *Collected Works*. (For its text, see Appendices in the present volume.)

[44] The claim that the king was the owner of the soil is not made by any Indian authority before the eighteenth century, whereas it was the usual statement on the lips of European observers from the sixteenth century onwards. It was clearly the land-tax,

any recognition of the sovereign as the proprietor. The argument is made entirely explicit in *Capital*, III, the draft of which was composed by Marx in 1863–67:

> ... in Asia ... [where the state] stands over them [the direct producers] as their landlord and simultaneously as sovereign, then rent and taxes coincide, or rather, there exists no tax which differs from this form of ground-rent [labour rent converted into tributary relationship]. Sovereignty here consists in the ownership of land concentrated on a national scale. But on the other hand, no private ownership of land exists, although there is both private and common possession of the land.[45]

'Oriental despotism', in Marx's analysis, is therefore essentially rent-receiving sovereignty and stands practically divested of the other political features assigned to it in European liberal thought, such as arbitrary and absolute monarchy.[46]

The 1858 article in the *Tribune* which we have quoted shows that Marx was aware of the actual complexities of the pre-British Indian society, where there existed not a simple 'tributary relationship' between peasant and state but a triangular one, involving another class of claimants to the surplus, namely, the '*zamindars*'. Marx recognizes that the *zamindars* claimed to be land-owners (subject to certain assessments due to the government), treating the peasants as mere 'tenants-at-will'. He, however, invoked the contrary official British view that 'the zamindars and talukadars were nothing but officers of the government appointed to look after, to collect, and to pay over to the prince the assessment due from the village'.[47] In other words, their claimed rights were a usurpation of those of the state. Yet 'prescription [was] in their favour'; and 'in Oudh these feudal land-holders had gone very far in curtailing alike the claims of the government and the rights of the cultivators'.[48]

The crucial implication of these observations is that, to Marx, the Asiatic state did not represent simply a single person or even only a simple 'higher community'; it implied the existence of a definite social class, which appropriated the surplus through the mechanism of the tax-rent. Only out of such a class, in the process of a territorial dispersal of the claims to surplus, could develop local magnates as those of Oudh, with such exercise of the rights of lordship as to obtain from even so careful a writer as Marx the designation of 'feudal land-owners'.

If it is once recognized that individual land-ownership could be created

---

often termed by them 'rent', which suggested to them the existence of an all-embracing royal property in land. See Irfan Habib, *Agrarian System of Mughal India*, (second edition, New Delhi, 1999), pp. 123–25.

[45] *Capital*, III, pp. 771–72.

[46] Compare Macaulay who, in his obituary of Lord William Bentinck, contrasted 'British freedom' with 'oriental despotism'. The eulogy is quoted in V.A. Smith, *Oxford History of India* (second edition, London, 1922), p. 657.

[47] *Tribune*, 7 June 1858, *On Colonialism*, p. 192.

[48] *Tribune*, 7 June 1858; *On Colonialism*, pp. 192–93.

out of state landlordism by acts of usurpation, could not state landlordism itself have been created by acts of conquest, the supreme usurpation? In fact, in 1853, Marx thought that the institution of 'no property in land', i.e. of state property, might have been established by the Muslims 'throughout the whole of Asia'.[49] This piece of speculation had great potentiality, suggesting that in its fullest form the tax-rent was the particular characteristic of Islamic polities. This was never taken up by Marx later on; but it remains of singular value in suggesting that he was prepared to recognize even in 1853 that history could well have had a part to play, after all, in shaping the basic forms of structure of Indian or Asiatic societies.

In one major respect, Marx seems to have revised or refined his ideas during the ten years or so preceding the publication of *Capital*, I. This was the realm of exchange or commodity production within the pre-colonial Indian society, a fundamental issue for any understanding of its historical nature. In *Grundrisse*, Marx notes that in communities of all types (Indian, Roman, Germanic), 'the economic object is the production of use-values', so that the communities could have produced only little for exchange.[50] Indeed, the 'system of production founded on exchange' characterized the 'historic dissolution' of the communal form.[51] In *Capital*, III, the 'Indian community', like the society of European antiquity and the middle ages, is said to possess, through the union of agriculture and handicraft, a 'mode of production' able to sustain a 'natural economy' – or an economy without exchange.[52] In *Capital*, I, Marx shows that surplus could be exacted and consumed without any mediation of exchange. The case of the Indian magnate is cited as an illustration: he appropriates the agricultural 'surplus-product' as 'tribute or rent', and then sets out to partly consume the surplus in kind, partly have it used by 'non-agricultural labourers'. 'Production and reproduction on a progressively increasing scale go on their way here', not only without the intervention of capital, as Marx stresses, but in fact without any commodity circulation at all.[53]

Apparently, Richard Jones is Marx's authority for this illustration; and if we had nothing else from Marx, we may well have supposed that the old Indian society was marked by an absence of commodity exchange in all its sectors, inside the community as well as outside. But the classic passage on the Indian community in the same volume of *Capital* dispels all doubts on the matter, and shows that Richard Jones' Indian magnate was not, in Marx's view, characteristic of the Indian society as a whole: he merely illustrated a possibility, and no more.

This is because in the passage of *Capital* we are speaking of, Marx contrasts the internal conditions of production of the village with 'the division of labour brought about in Indian society as a whole, by means of the exchange of

---

[49] Letter of 14 June 1853, *Selected Correspondence*, p. 62.
[50] *Pre-Capitalist Formations*, pp. 80–81; *Grundrisse*, p. 485.
[51] *Grundrisse*, p. 882.
[52] *Capital*, III, p. 767.
[53] *Capital*, I, p. 610.

commodities'. Thus, outside the village, it was the commodity and not the 'natural economy' that reigned. This is made explicit by the very words that Marx uses to qualify the domain of exchange in the society containing the communities: 'It is the surplus alone that becomes a commodity, and a portion of even that, not until it has reached the hands of the state into whose hands from time immemorial a certain quantity of these products has found its way in the shape of rent in kind.'[54]

These statements are of crucial significance, though their implications have been seldom recognized. These may be summed up as follows:

(a) The peasant raised a part of his produce for his own subsistence, and this did not go on the market. The combination of agriculture with handicraft ensured that the peasant did not buy anything on the market. He himself lived in a 'natural economy'.

(b) Of the remainder of the produce – the surplus product – the peasant parted with a portion in payment of rent-in-kind. This, Marx thought, was the normal mode of surplus acquisition in Asia.[55] The part of the product taken in rent was put on the market after it had been obtained by the state, and thus was converted into commodities outside the village.

(c) Another portion of the surplus (presumably the smaller) became a commodity inside the village in that it was raised for sale on the market by the peasant who then paid money-rent; the market for the product, however, remained outside the village.

Natural economy was thus confined to the village; outside of it commodity circulation dominated, creating a division of labour based on its own operation. The contrast is striking between these conditions postulated for pre-colonial India and what Marx describes as the situation 'in many Roman latifundia, or upon the villages of Charlemagne, or more or less during the entire [European] Middle Ages', where not the whole or bulk of the surplus, but 'only a relatively small portion of that part of the product which represents the landlord's revenue' enters 'the process of circulation'.[56] Is it, then, possible that Marx was allowing a much higher level of monetization in pre-colonial India than in medieval Europe?

It is a pity that we have little means of knowing why Marx felt he had to introduce these general qualifications to allow for such a large realm of commodity circulation in Indian society. He may possibly have come across statements in the *Fifth Report* about Indian peasants paying the land-tax or rents in money.[57] Moreover, he had spoken in a *Tribune* article of the original *zamindars*

---

[54] Ibid., p. 351.

[55] *Capital*, III, p. 776.

[56] Ibid., p. 767.

[57] Sir John Shore, in his famous Minute of 18 June 1789, forming Appendix I to the *Fifth Report*, says: 'In general, throughout Bengal, the rents are paid by the ryots in money' (*Fifth Report*, p. 192, paragraph 226).

in Bengal being replaced wholesale by 'mercantile speculators', under the imp-
etus of the Permanent Settlement. These speculators must have been present in
the older society as possessors of large enough merchant capital if they could
later buy over 'all the land of Bengal'.[58]

Marx also knew that the urban structure sustained by the agrarian surplus contained within it an exchange economy. Richard Jones himself distinguishes, in a passage quoted by Marx, between the town artisan in India ('where
the admixture of Europeans has not changed the scene'), who was dependent on
the vagaries of the market, and the rural artisan directly maintained by the
village.[59] In *Capital*, I, Marx quotes another authority for the description of the
Indian weaver as 'merely a *detached* individual working a web when ordered by
a customer'.[60] Caste here operated not to weld the artisan permanently into the
community but essentially to enable 'special skill' to be 'accumulated from
generation to generation'.[61] Here, then, the Indian caste system could be quite
consistent with independent petty production in an environment of commodity
circulation.

In 1853, Marx had derived the information from Bernier that the seven-
teenth-century Indian cities had been 'properly speaking, nothing but military
camps'. Through a long quotation from Bernier he seems to emphasize the large
numbers of soldiers and camp-followers, and their ability to live at a bare subsistence level.[62] This tallied with Richard Jones' observation that the 'artisans of
the towns' in India drew their wages from 'surplus revenue from land' – a fund
the greater part of which was 'distributed by the state and its officers'; the urban
artisans thus had to migrate to whatever new seats their royal or aristocratic
customers shifted to. In the quotation that Marx gives from Jones, the latter
contrasted this migratory nature of the Indian artisan with the dependence of the
European worker on the locales of 'fixed capital'.[63] But one may, perhaps, see
the main difference between India and post-feudal Europe to lie in the nature of
the market for urban craft-products: in India, it was confined to the aristocracy
and its dependents, while in Europe it included the rural gentry as well as the
emerging middle classes.

A question that Marx sought to answer from 1853 onwards was, why the
state in India or Asia should have succeeded in converting its tax into rent, while
this did not happen in Europe. This could partly be explained by the 'unresisting'

[58] *Tribune*, 5 August 1853; *On Colonialism*, p. 78.

[59] *Theories of Surplus Value*, III (Moscow, 1971), pp. 434–35.

[60] *Capital*, I, pp. 331–32. The quotation (emphasis ours) is taken by Marx from Hugh
Murray and James Wilson, *Historical and Descriptive Account of British India*, Vol.
II (Edinburgh, 1832).

[61] *Capital*, I, pp. 331–32.

[62] Letter of 2 June 1853, *Selected Correspondence*, pp. 57–58. The quotations Marx
gives appear to be taken from the French passages corresponding to Bernier, *Travels*,
pp. 219–20, 251–52, 381–90. Marx makes a brief reference to Bernier in this context
also in *Theories of Surplus Value*, III, p. 435.

[63] *Theories of Surplus Value*, III, p. 435.

nature of the Indian community; but, working upon a suggestion originally made by Engels, he found an economic factor behind the state's direct control over the produce. This was artificial irrigation, which, on the scale needed in India, could only be undertaken by a centralized despotism.[64] The thesis, after being put forward in 1853, was repeated in *Grundrisse*, and then again – in a rather low key – in *Capital*, I.[65] Engels, in 1878, was to set it forth again in *Anti-Dühring*.[66] The substantiation offered always remained rather slender, though it provided fuel enough for large-scale theorization about 'hydraulic' societies in subsequent literature, crowned by Karl A. Wittfogel's *Oriental Despotism* (New Haven, 1957).[67]

The 'Asiatic Mode': Reconsiderations

Well before 1867, Marx had thus evolved a comprehensive notion of the fundamental elements of the economic and political system of India and (as he thought) of much of Asia before the colonial incursion. In 1859, he appeared confident that the 'Asiatic' merited a separate place in the classification of the major 'modes of production' in human history.[68]

This system of production, in Marx's conception, clearly consisted, as we have seen, of two elements: the village community and Oriental despotism. The first was perhaps more crucial in that it defined the form of the labour process: self-sustaining petty production without individual bondage but with fixed occupations. The 'despotism' lay in the identity of tax with rent, that is, the appropriation of the surplus through the agency of the state. While 'natural economy' prevailed in the village, commodity circulation could still develop outside of it on the basis of the disposal of the surplus.

This being so, the pre-colonial Indian society (as the classic 'Asiatic' type) was clearly a developed class society, with a ruling class of surplus appropriators and a division of labour based on exchange outside the village community. Hobsbawm can, therefore, hardly be right when he supposes that Marx's 'Asiatic system is not yet a class society, or, if it is a class society, then it is the most primitive form of it.'[69] This not only runs counter to Marx's whole concept

---

[64] In a letter to Marx, 6 June 1853, Engels spoke of 'artificial irrigation' as 'the first condition of agriculture' in the large zone extending from the Sahara to 'India and Tartary'. He went on to distinguish three departments of oriental governments: finance, war and public works. *Selected Correspondence*, p. 59. Marx bodily incorporated these ideas in *Tribune*, 25 June 1853; *On Colonialism*, pp. 37–38.

[65] *Pre-Capitalist Formations*, pp. 70–71; *Grundrisse*, pp. 473–74; and *Capital*, I, p. 523n.

[66] *Anti-Dühring*, Moscow, 1947, p. 269.

[67] I offered a critique of this work in *Enquiry*, No. 6, Delhi, pp. 54–73.

[68] 'In broad outlines, the Asiatic, the ancient, the feudal and the bourgeois modes of production may be designated as epochs marking the progress of the economic development of society.' Preface to *A Contribution to the Critique of Political Economy* (Moscow, 1978), p. 21.

[69] E.J. Hobsbawm, Introduction, *Pre-Capitalist Formations*, p. 34. If no classes then no class struggles. Thus Wittfogel: 'The history of hydraulic society suggests that class struggles, far from being a chronic disease of all mankind, is the luxury of multi-centered and open [western] societies.' *Oriental Despotism*, p. 71.

of the existence of surplus appropriation in the 'Asiatic system' but is also contradicted by what Engels says in *Anti-Dühring* (1878), a book whose text was checked
and approved by Marx. There Engels expressly describes the emergence of 'an
oriental despot or satrap' as part of the 'process of formation of classes' with 'the
separate individual rulers [uniting] into a ruling class'.[70] The Asiatic society
was, then, a full-fledged class society.

The first question related to the place of the Asiatic system in the order
Persuasive as Marx's analysis of the pre-colonial economy set in the
form of the 'Asiatic mode' may appear to us, there is good reason to believe that
Marx developed considerable reservations about the 'Asiatic' concept after 1867.
For one thing, there were too many questions that had been left unresolved.

The first question related to the place of the Asiatic system in the order
of stages of social progress. In his 1859 preface to the *Critique of Political
Economy*, Marx speaks as if the Asiatic system preceded classical antiquity. He
also says in the same work that the 'Indian communal property' contained the
'various prototypes of Roman and German property'.[71] In the 1867 German text
of *Capital*, I, Marx put the rise of the classical (Roman) community 'after the
primitive oriental communal ownership of the land had disappeared'.[72] He re-
iterated the same view in his letters in 1868 and 1870.[73] But the classic Indian
communities produced a surplus which was necessary to maintain Asiatic despotism, as we have seen, while the original primitive communities were unable
to produce a surplus at all, as is made clear by Engels in *Anti-Dühring*: slavery
originated as soon as the community began to produce a surplus.[74] The Asiatic
system (i.e. the surplus-producing community and the rent-receiving state) could
not therefore have preceded slavery; at best it could only have developed parallel
to the formation of slave and feudal societies. Such seems to be Engels' own view
(and since Marx gave his approval to his text, the view of Marx as well), since,
in *Anti-Dühring*, the emergence of the 'oriental despot or satrap' is treated as
part of the very process that also produced the division of society into master and
slave.[75]

While the Indian or Asiatic society thus lost its primitive antiquity, Marx
could not have been unaware of a process that he had so far assumed but to
whose implications he had previously paid little attention. If in the original form
the Indian community had practised communal cultivation, then the change to
individual petty production, which was now the dominant form,[76] must represent

[70] *Anti-Dühring*, pp. 268–69.
[71] *A Contribution to the Critique of Political Economy*, pp. 21, 33n.
[72] *Capital*, I, translated by E. and C. Paul, p. 351n. The word 'oriental' is omitted in the
Moore–Aveling translation, *Capital*, I, p. 325n.
[73] The letter of 14 March 1868 has already been quoted in footnote 29. In a letter of 17
February 1870, Marx says still more positively that 'communal property', whether
Slavic or other, is 'of Indian origin'. Marx, *Letters to Dr Kugelmann* (London, 1935?),
p. 99.
[74] *Anti-Dühring*, pp. 267–71.
[75] Ibid., pp. 268–69.
[76] This is acknowledged to be the case by Marx right from his 1853 writings (see above).

a fundamental alteration in the very essence of that 'unchanging' community. A contradiction must exist, too, between communal property and individual production. The matter was brought forcefully to Marx's notice in relation not to India but to Russia: yet the logic applies to both. In the combination of 'common ownership [and] divided petty cultivation', 'mobile property, an element which plays an increasing part even in agriculture, gradually leads to differentiation among the members of the community, and therefore makes it possible for a conflict of interests to arise, particularly under fiscal pressure of the state'.[77]

This may be considered alongside the fact that Marx, in his notes on Kovalevsky's work, *Communal Landholding* (1879), had already marked the emergence of private property within the Indian village community leading to the genesis of contradictions within it.[78] It was, therefore, no longer possible to hold that the Indian community had been internally a totally stagnant institution.

In these same notes on Kovalevsky, Marx restates his view that the Indian communities belonged to a system different from that of Germano–Roman feudalism. What is interesting here is that the main points of difference noted are the absence of serfdom in India, and the lack of inalienability of land to 'non-members of the noble class'.[79] These are hardly features that could put the Indian communities in a lower historical position, even from the point of view of development of commodity circulation and private property.

If the Indian community was subject to historical development, it was all the more the case with the economic and political superstructure above it, the apparatus of the so-called 'Oriental despotism'. In 1853, Marx had touched upon the question whether the Islamic polities had been responsible for the sovereign's claims to property in land.[80] It is possible that later on Marx became aware of the controversy regarding this matter. Kovalevsky, in the same work of 1879 read by Marx, criticized the ascription to the 'Mahometan theory and practice' of an alleged rejection of private property in land.[81] Thus, even the notion of the state as the landed proprietor in Asia and the absence of individual private

---

[77] Second draft of letter to Vera Zasulich, 8 March 1881, *Pre-Capitalist Formations*, p. 143. A slightly different translation, but with no substantive difference in meaning, will be found in Marx and Engels, *Collected Works*, Vol. 24 (Moscow, 1989), p. 363.

[78] See Daniel Thorner in *Contributions to Indian Sociology*, II (1966), pp. 60–62. One wonders what Marx would have said if he had come across the earliest known description of the functioning of the Indian village community in the *Milindapanho* (c. first century AD). When the village headman summons all the villagers to assemble, it is only the 'heads of houses' who are expected to respond: 'There are many who do not come: women and men, slave girls and slaves, hired workmen, servants, peasantry [lit., villagers], sick people, oxen, buffaloes, sheep and goats and dogs – but all these do not count.' *Questions of King Milinda*, I, translated by Rhys Davids, pp. 208–09.

[79] Quoted in Hobsbawm, Introduction, *Pre-Capitalist Formations*, p. 58.

[80] Letter of 14 June 1853, *On Colonialism*, p. 315.

[81] See Rosa Luxemburg, *The Accumulation of Capital*, translated by A. Schwarzchild (London, 1951), pp. 372–73n.

property in land seemed to dissolve, though this did not necessarily affect the practical identity of the tax with the surplus ('rent').

Marx's further reading on India included Mountstuart Elphinstone's *History of India*, from which, some time during the 1870s, he took copious notes. Most of the facts taken down related to straightforward dynastic history; in respect of Akbar, the great Mughal emperor (1556–1605), however, Marx wrote down (and underlined) a summary of his principal revenue measures. He noted that Akbar fixed one-third of the produce as the tax-standard, and, still more important, that he took the tax in cash by averaging past prices for purposes of commutation.[82] As we have seen, Marx, in *Capital*, I, had already allowed for part-payment of land revenue in cash. But this new information could also have modified the assumption, stated in *Capital*, III, that the rent-in-kind was the mainstay of 'the stationary social conditions' in Asia:[83] the introduction of the cash-nexus contradicted both elements in this assumption, one, of the dominance of rent-in-kind, and the other, of 'stationary conditions'.

Finally, even the institution of Asiatic 'despotism' began to lose its previous awesome individuality. A.L.H. Gunawardana points out that in his notes on Henry Sumner Maine's *Lectures on the Early History of Institutions* (1875), Marx expresses direct opposition to the idea of the state standing above society and insists that everywhere it arose out of social contradictions.[84]

There is thus enough evidence that Marx's continued reading on India after 1867 led him to reconsider the force of a number of his earlier ideas on pre-colonial India. Moreover, the new theoretical formulation of primitive communism, reinforced by L.H. Morgan's work (*Ancient Society*, 1877), suggested a universalization of some characteristics of the Indian community (notably the alleged original communal cultivation) and their relegation everywhere to an earlier epoch. Correspondingly, the basic mechanics of social evolution subsequent to that primitive stage also tended to be universalized. The stagnant Asiatic mode no longer fitted the theoretical framework as it was now refined, just as more detailed investigations had suggested a reformulation of some of the earlier theses on the Indian communities and fiscal system. It is certain that Engels alone is not to blame for the abandonment of the Asiatic mode.[85]

The reserve apparently entertained by Marx in his later years in respect

---

[82] Karl Marx, *Notes on Indian History*, p. 42.

[83] *Capital*, III, p. 776.

[84] *Indian Historical Review*, II (2), p. 387. Gunawardana, using Lawrence Krader's *The Ethnological Notebooks of Karl Marx* (Assen, 1972) (not available to me), infers that Marx's notes on Maine reflect 'Marx's dissatisfaction with his own formulation in the *Grundrisse* on the nature of the oriental state'.

[85] When Engels wrote his *Origin of the Family, Private Property and the State* (1884), he made not the slightest allusion to this system. See, especially, the passage where he speaks of 'the three great epochs of civilization' (English edition, Moscow, 1948, p. 240). Hobsbawm's explanation for this omission is rather strained; see Introduction, *Pre-Capitalist Formations*, p. 52n. See also Wittfogel, *Oriental Despotism*, p. 386.

of the Asiatic category did not imply that he was willing to overlook the specific features of Indian society and economy. This is clear from his objection to any designation of the Indian communities as 'feudal'. It is also best to remember that his thesis of the union of agriculture and craft, on the one hand, and an immutable division of labour, on the other, as the twin pillars of the Indian village economy, remains of lasting value. Furthermore, the economic historian today must ask the same questions as Marx did, about the precise implications of the extraction of 'rent' in the shape of land-tax. The contrast that Marx drew, between an exchange economy based on the disposal of the surplus and the 'natural economy' within the village serving for its basis, must still stand, though the intrusion of commodity production and differentiation within the village might yet have been more extensive than Marx had allowed for. In his view, the urban economy was largely parasitical; and here we have an important suggestion as to why the potentialities of capitalistic development in the Indian economy remained thwarted.[86] All these form an important legacy of ideas for Indian historians, who may thereby be inspired still more to explore the mechanics of change in a society that Marx himself had once thought, rather unjustly, to be unchanging.

Colonialism and India
The Tribute

The parliamentary debates preceding the Charter Act of 1853 provided Marx with considerable information on the English East India Company, and this he supplemented from other literature. He was able to trace the pre-colonial history of the Company from the beginning of the eighteenth century, when, in England, 'the old landed aristocracy [had] been defeated, and the bourgeoisie [was] not able to take its place except under the banner of moneyocracy, or the "haute finance"'.[87] The East India Company was a great corporate organization of the latter class, claiming a monopoly of the East India trade and invoking commercial freedom to export treasure: Marx comments wryly on 'the curiosity' that 'the Indian monopolists were the first preachers of free trade in England'.[88]

Marx saw the conquest of India as emanating from the financiers' desire to enlarge their capital by the revenues of conquered territories. They 'had even

---

[86] This, of course, is an important subject of debate among Indian historians. I have presented my own views in 'Potentialities of Capitalistic Development in the Economy of Mughal India', *Enquiry*, NS, III, 3, pp. 1–56. By designating the medieval Indian society as 'feudal', some Indian and Soviet historians assume that there were possibilities of a growth of capitalism but that these were still-born owing to the British conquest. V.I. Pavlov surveys the debate with much direct use of evidence in his *Historical Premises for India's Transition to Capitalism* (Moscow, 1978), pp. 4–159.

[87] *Tribune*, 11 July 1853; *On Colonialism*, p. 45.

[88] *Tribune*, 11 July 1853; *On Colonialism*, p. 50. Marx especially refers to the two great partisans of the Company in the mercantilist controversy: Thomas Mun, author of *A Discourse of Trade, from England unto the East Indies* (1621), and Sir Josiah Child, who wrote *A Treatise wherein is demonstrated 1. That East India Trade is the Most National of all Foreign Trade* (1668).

as early as 1689 conceived the establishment of a dominion in India, and making territorial revenues one of their sources of emolument'.[89] This direct plunder of India by taxation remained the key feature of the English regime in India: 'During the whole course of the eighteenth century the treasures transported from India to England were gained much less by comparatively insignificant commerce than by the direct exploitation of that country, and by the colossal fortunes there extorted and transmitted to England.'[90]

By the 'direct exploitation' of the country was meant, first of all, the appropriation of the income of the government. The Company took over the sovereign's right to tax-rent already established in India, and greatly enlarged it. In *Capital*, III, Marx spoke of the disastrous consequences for the direct producer when the rent-in-kind 'is met with and exploited by a conquering commercial nation, e.g., the English in India'.[91] This urge for 'fiscal exploitation' naturally reduced the expenditure on public works to the barest minimum. Out of gross revenues of £19.8 million in 1851–52, less than £0.17 million were spent on 'roads, canals, bridges and other works of public necessity'.[92] As for the main object of expenditure, Marx noted that 'nowhere [else] so extravagant is a provision made for the governing class itself' as in India.[93]

The plunder of India was carried out not only through taxation, but also through the creation of personal fortunes. These, in the eighteenth century, had been mainly created by extortion, bribery and monopoly.[94] In *Capital*, I, Marx cited the estimated figure of £6 million for the value of 'gifts' obtained from Indians during the ten years 1757–66; he also gave an illustration of how money was made by favoured Englishmen through inland commercial monopolies.[95] The large incomes continued into the nineteenth century, but now mainly as the principal burden on the revenues. Investigating these in 1857, Marx found that 'the profits and benefits which accrue to individual British subjects' were 'very considerable'; and 'their gain goes on to increase the sum of the national wealth' of England. He, however, noted that part of the costs of the possession of India had now begun to be placed on the British tax-payer.[96]

Marx was, of course, not the first to speak of the drain of wealth from

---

[89] *Tribune*, 11 July 1853; *On Colonialism*, p. 48.

[90] *Tribune*, 11 July 1853; *On Colonialism*, p. 51.

[91] *Capital*, III, p. 777.

[92] Marx is here referring to a speech by Bright, *Tribune*, 22 June 1853; *On Colonialism*, p. 34. See also *Tribune*, 5 August 1853; *On Colonialism*, p. 77, for the low percentage of revenue expended on public works in different provinces.

[93] *Tribune*, 23 July 1858; *On Colonialism*, p. 209.

[94] 'Did they [the English] not, in India, to borrow an expression of that great robber, Lord Clive himself, resort to atrocious extortion when simple corruption could not keep pace with their rapacity?' *Tribune*, 8 August 1853; *On Colonialism*, p. 86.

[95] *Capital*, I, p. 777.

[96] *Tribune*, 21 September 1857 (*On Colonialism*, pp. 168–72) and 30 April 1859 (Avineri, pp. 366–74).

India. It was recognized as the basis of the Indian connection with Britain as early as the eighteenth century by parliamentarians like Burke, and administrators like Sir John Shore and Lord Cornwallis.[97] The ruin of India through the levy of tribute continued to strain the consciences of English liberals such as James Mill and Montgomery Martin.[98] Marx himself made use of Bright's criticisms of the financial exploitation of India, though he observed that Bright's 'picture of India ruined by the fiscal exertions of the company and government did not, of course, receive the supplement of India ruined by Manchester and Free Trade'.[99]

Marx devoted an article in the *Tribune* to an analysis of Bright's view of India as a very heavily taxed country. He expressed some reserve about Bright's calculations, but made the important point that:

> In estimating the burden of taxation, its annual amount must not fall heavier in the balance than the method of raising it, and the manner of employing it. The former is detestable in India, and in the branch of land-tax, for instance, wastes perhaps more produce than it gets. As to the application of the taxes, it will suffice to say that no part of them is returned to the people in works of public utility.[100]

In order to maximize the revenue collections, the English carried out 'agrarian revolutions', subverting the existing property relationships. They created various 'forms of private property in land – the great desideratum of Asiatic society'.[101] But the real purpose was, by this means, to sustain or increase the tax-paying capacity of the country: 'The zamindari and ryotwari settlements were both of them agrarian revolutions, effected by British ukases – both made not for the people, who cultivate the soil, nor for the holder, who owns it, but for the government that taxes it.'[102] The *zamindari* (or the Permanent) settlement was merely 'a caricature of English landlordism', the *ryotwari* of 'French peasant-proprietorship':

> A curious sort of English landlord was the zamindar, receiving only one-tenth of the rent, while he had to make over nine-tenths of it to the Government. A

---

[97] Burke is quoted in R.C. Dutt, *Economic History of India in Early British Rule* (second edition, London, 1906), pp. 49–50. Sir John Shore's observations are in his Minute of 18 June 1789, paragraphs 131–42, *Fifth Report*, p. 183. Cornwallis, in his Minutes of 10 February 1790, spoke of India's value in 'furnishing a large annual investment to Europe', and of the baneful effect on Indian agriculture and commerce of 'the heavy drains of wealth' to England; *Fifth Report*, p. 493.

[98] See quotations in Dadabhai Naoroji, *Poverty and Un-British Rule in India* (originally published in London, 1901; Delhi, 1962), pp. iv, 35–36; also R.C. Dutt, *The Economic History of India in the Victorian Age* (eleventh edition, London, 1950), pp. 115–16.

[99] *Tribune*, 22 June 1853; *On Colonialism*, p. 33.

[100] *Tribune*, 23 July 1858; *On Colonialism*, pp. 208–09.

[101] *Tribune*, 8 August 1853; *On Colonialism*, p. 82.

[102] *Tribune*, 5 August 1853; *On Colonialism*, p. 78.

curious sort of French peasant was the ryot, without any permanent title in the soil, and the taxation changing every year in proportion to his harvest.[103]

There is undoubtedly an element of overstatement in these pronouncements. The standard of one-eleventh (not one-tenth) of rental for the share of the *zamindar* in the Permanent Settlement had little practical relevance since, with the rise in prices and expansion of cultivation, the *zamindar's* share in the rent increased considerably. Indeed, Marx himself elsewhere recognized that the Settlement created a 'landed gentry' in Bengal, adversely affecting the interests of the government as well as 'the actual cultivators'.[104] These landlords were 'mercantile speculators' who had replaced the old *zamindars* and had created 'a hierarchy of middle men' or *patnidars*, 'which presses with its entire weight on the unfortunate cultivator'.[105]

As for the *ryotwari* system, Marx's statement that the revenue varied every year according to harvests is only partly correct. If the *ryot* brought wasteland under cultivation, he had to pay more; and there was provision made for varying the tax according to changes in prices. Marx was right, however, in saying that the *ryotwari* system had often disregarded superior rights like 'mirassis, jagirs, etc.',[106] and the revenue assessed on the peasant was by no means light. Elsewhere, Marx presented evidence of how the peasants were tortured by the Company's officials in the process of revenue collection in these same *ryotwari* areas.[107]

Marx felt that, far from there being left any margin for saving or 'profit' for the 'direct producer', the rent burden imposed on him by the English made any 'expansion of production more or less impossible'; the peasant was reduced to 'the physical minimum of the means of subsistence'.[108] Moreover, though the *ryot* 'manages his farm as an independent producer', the usurer would 'not only rob him of his entire surplus by means of interest', but also eat into his 'wage'.[109]

As for the superior land-holding classes, it was not only that their claims suffered in the *ryotwari* settlements. As Marx shows in an article of 1858, these classes were under pressure in northern India as well, this being illustrated by the example of the Oudh *taluqdars*.[110]

Under the impulse of the same drive for revenue came the absorption of Indian princely states. The Company's policy towards them was that of the Romans: 'a system of fattening allies, as we fatten oxen, till they were worthy of being devoured'.[111] In a later article, Marx, discussing a speech by Disraeli,

---

[103] Ibid. See also *Capital*, III, p. 328n.
[104] *Tribune*, 7 June 1858; *On Colonialism*, p. 192.
[105] *Tribune*, 5 August 1853; *On Colonialism*, p. 78.
[106] Ibid.
[107] *Tribune*, 17 September 1857; *On Colonialism*, pp. 162–67.
[108] *Capital*, III, p. 777.
[109] Ibid., p. 211.
[110] *Tribune*, 7 June 1858; *On Colonialism*, pp. 191–94.
[111] *Tribune*, 25 July 1853; *On Colonialism*, p. 71.

showed how 'the forcible destruction of native princes' had accelerated owing to 'the financial difficulties' of the Company, which had reached a high point in 1848.[112]

Marx did not harbour any particular sympathy for the Indian princes: most of them did not even possess 'the prestige of antiquity', and were 'the most servile tools of English despotism' to boot.[113] And yet, he was aroused to indignation at the way British power dealt with its own creatures. Thus he wrote a scathing condemnation of the methods by which the annexation of Oudh (1856) was managed:

> This denying the validity of treaties which had formed the acknowledged base of intercourse for twenty years; this seizing violently upon independent territories in open infraction even of the acknowledged treaties; this final confiscation of every acre of land in the whole country;[114] all these treacherous and brutal modes of proceeding of the British toward the natives of India . . .[115]

Finally, the direct exploitation of India began to require for its continuance an intensified pressure upon China. The British government in India 'depends for full one-seventh of its revenue on the sale of opium to the Chinese' (1853).[116] Marx sketched an account of how opium, monopolized by the Company in India, was forced on China in increasingly larger quantities through organized smuggling and war.[117]

The opium monopoly was not only an indispensable pillar of the fiscal exploitation of India; the opium trade to China formed an important mode of realization of the Indian tribute by England. Marx gives figures to show that in 1858 Britain had a trade deficit of more than £6 million with China:

> Now this balance due to China by England, Australia and the United States is transferred from China to India, as a set-off against the amount due by China to India, on account of opium and cotton. . . . [The] imports from China to India have never yet reached the amount of £1,000,000 Sterling, while the exports to China from India realize the sum of nearly £10,000,000.[118]

---

[112] *Tribune*, 14 August 1857; *On Colonialism*, pp. 140–41.

[113] Nor was he unsympathetic to the argument that the princes were 'the stronghold of the present abominable English system and the greatest obstacles to Indian progress'; and he was plainly sceptical of the pleadings of Munro and Elphinstone on behalf of the 'native aristocracy'. *Tribune,* 25 July 1853; *On Colonialism*, pp. 71–72.

[114] This refers to Canning's proclamation confiscating the *taluqdars'* lands in Oudh, 1857.

[115] *Tribune*, 28 May 1858; *On Colonialism*, pp. 189–90.

[116] *Tribune*, 14 June 1853; *On Colonialism*, p. 25. In 1858 the ratio is given as one-sixth (see reference in the next note).

[117] *Tribune*, 25 September 1858; *On Colonialism*, pp. 220–21. Marx underlines one 'flagrant self-contradiction of the Christianity-canting and civilization-mongering British Government': 'While openly preaching free trade in poison [opium], it secretly defends the monopoly of its manufacture [in India].'

[118] *Tribune*, 10 October 1859; *On Colonialism*, pp. 243–44.

Thus the large quantities of tea and silk which England obtained from China gratis were mainly received in payment of the Indian tribute – but at what an enormous moral and social cost to the Chinese people![119]

In addition, there was the excess of Indian exports over imports in the direct trade to England. Marx gives the figures from parliamentary enquiries, which showed that the excess amounted to £2,250,000 in 1855: 'England simply consumes this tribute without exporting anything in return.'[120] Marx, while writing this, seems to overlook the principal means of realization of the tribute, which, in this period, was via China, and which would naturally give a far higher remuneration to England for the 'good government' that it furnished, opium and all.[121]

In *Capital*, I, published in 1867, Marx came to regard this drain of wealth from India and other colonies as an important source of 'primary [primitive] accumulation', which he now held to have been an essential pre-requisite for the genesis of industrial capitalism in Britain.[122] This effect of the tribute is by no means widely admitted, even by British historians writing under the influence of the Marxist interpretation. In Maurice Dobb's *Studies in the Development of Capitalism*, the exploitation of the colonies appears as an element of mercantilist policy rather than as a source of primary accumulation.[123] This is surprising, because the magnitude of the inflow of wealth from India and the West Indies is seldom denied.[124] It might have amounted to an apparently small part of British national income, say, 4.8 per cent in 1801, but at that size, it would still have

---

[119] It is worth mentioning that India's great spokesman, Dadabhai Naoroji, writing in 1880, saw the opium trade in the same light as Marx and was equally indignant: 'Because India cannot fill up the remorseless drain; so China must be dragged in to make it up, even though it be by being "poisoned". . . . This opium trade is a sin on England's head and a curse on India for her share in being the instrument.' *Poverty and Un-British Rule in India* (Delhi, 1962), p. 190.

[120] *Capital*, III, pp. 569–70.

[121] A question by Sir Charles Wood to a witness before a Parliamentary Committee (1857): 'Then, the export, which you state, is caused by the East India drafts, is an export of good government, and not of produce?' Quoted by Marx, *Capital*, III, p. 569.

[122] *Capital*, I, p. 777. The Moore–Aveling translation of *Capital*, I, has given currency to the term 'primitive', whereas a better rendering (as, for example, in E. and C. Paul's translation) would be 'primary'. For Marx's discovery of the significance of 'primary accumulation' and the role of force in it, see Irfan Habib, 'The Reading of History in the *Communist Manifesto*', in *A World to Win*, edited by Prakash Karat (New Delhi, 1999), pp. 60–64.

[123] See Dobb, *Studies in the Development of Capitalism* (London, 1946), pp. 208–09, for colonial plunder; primitive accumulation is discussed on pp. 177–86. See also E.J. Hobsbawm, *Industry and Empire*, Pelican Economic History, Vol. 3 (1969), p. 54, where not colonialism but 'commerce with the underdeveloped world' is said to be an important factor behind the growth of 'our industrial economy'.

[124] Phyllis Deane and W.A. Cole (in *British Economic Growth, 1688–1959*, Cambridge, 1962, p. 34) state that in 1797–98, the colonies accounted for 9 per cent of English exports but 24 per cent of imports (including re-exports).

equalled nearly 70 per cent of the British annual net domestic investment.[125] The major argument seems to be that the English 'nabobs', and others who made colonial gains, are not known to have directly invested in industry.[126]

One cannot, of course, be confident about how Marx would have answered such objections. In *Capital*, I, he seems to suggest that in so far as the colonial plunder enlarged commercial capital, it cleared the path for British industrial growth: 'In the period of manufacture properly so called it is . . . the commercial supremacy that gives industrial dominance [and not vice versa]. Hence the preponderant role that the colonial system plays at that time.'[127] The matter may, however, be looked at a little differently as well. At the level of money capital, whether the 'nabobs' bought estates or houses, their acts of purchase would have released other funds to flow into industry. Again, in terms of goods received through colonial exploitation, England was enabled to obtain large quantities of raw materials and wage goods gratis from other countries; this, in effect, added to industrial capital in the same proportion as that capital increased its sway over British economy.

Given the possibility that the Indian tribute swelled primary accumulation in the eighteenth century, one must ask if it continued to perform the same function in the nineteenth century as well. Taken literally, Marx's 'primary [or primitive] accumulation' was one that 'preced[ed] capitalist accumulation', being 'not the result of the capitalist mode of production, but its starting point'.[128] But it is not necessary to interpret Marx's definition in a purely chronological spirit.[129] Direct extraction of surplus from non-capitalist economies (the tax-rent and monopoly of sale of their products), 'the bleeding process' of which Marx spoke in a letter of 1881, must have gone on augmenting industrial capital within the metropolitan country:

---

[125] Sayera I. Habib, in *Proceedings of the Indian History Congress*, 36th Session (Aligarh, 1975), Section IV, pp. XXII–XXIV. The entire quantitative evidence has now been closely re-examined again by Utsa Patnaik in 'New Estimates of British Trade and their Relation to Transfers from Tropical Countries', in K.N. Panikkar, T.J. Byres and Utsa Patnaik (eds), *The Making of History* (New Delhi, 2000), pp. 359–402, and 'The Free Lunch: Transfers from the Tropical Colonies and Their Role in Capital Formation in Britain during the Industrial Revolution', in Jomo K.S. (ed.), *Globalization under Hegemony* (Delhi, forthcoming).

[126] See François Crouzet (ed.), *Capital Formation in the Industrial Revolution* (London, 1972), pp. 175–77.

[127] *Capital*, I, p. 779.

[128] Ibid., p. 739.

[129] As, for example, in Dobb, *Studies in the Development of Capitalism*, p. 178. That Marx himself was far from considering primary accumulation an obsolete process in his own day, is shown by his remarks in *Capital*, I, p. 790: 'In Western Europe, the home of political economy, the process of primitive [primary] accumulation is more or less accomplished. . . . It is otherwise in the colonies.' See also ibid., pp. 798–99, for a specific contemporary method of 'primitive accumulation' by the English government in the colonies.

What the English take from them [the people of India] annually in the form of rent, dividends for railways useless to the Hindus, pensions for military and civil servicemen, for Afghanistan and other wars, etc., – what they take from them *without any equivalent* and *quite apart* from what they appropriate to themselves annually within India – speaking only of the *value of the commodities* the Indians have gratuitously and annually to send over to England – it amounts to *more than the total sum of income of 60 million of agricultural and industrial labourers of India*! This is a bleeding process with a vengeance![130]

This was 'primary accumulation', pure and simple; and it was similar in many respects to the 'accumulation' obtained from the continuous political subjugation by capitalist countries of non-capitalist economies that Rosa Luxemburg described in 1913.[131] It was not just the Indian market but the Indian empire that helped to sustain the tempo of the British industrial revolution once it had begun.

There was thus an ultimate unity underlying the conflict that Marx saw between the interests of the British 'moneyocracy' and oligarchy, which sought direct tribute, and of the 'millocracy', which found its markets in India constricted by the burden of the tribute.[132] Could one say that this visible conflict essentially represented the contradiction between the urge for primary accumulation and the need simultaneously for an expanding market for British capitalism? And could the search for a resolution of this contradiction not lead inescapably to the 'Imperialism of Free Trade', spurring a new spurt of colonial expansion designed simultaneously to add new sources of tribute and to increase the area subject to Free Trade?[133]

Classical political economy had held that such colonial expansion was not really necessary, since the economics of comparative advantage would spontaneously create markets for the industrially more productive nation. Influenced

---

[130] Letter to F. Danielson, 19 February 1881 (emphasis by Marx), *Selected Correspondence*, pp. 340–41.

[131] Rosa Luxemburg, *The Accumulation of Capital*, translated by A. Schwarzchild (London, 1951), especially pp. 369–70. Luxemburg too believed that Marx had thought primary accumulation to belong exclusively to the period of the genesis of capitalism; see ibid., pp. 364–65. This may have been due to her unfamiliarity with Marx's writings on India and China, notably in the *Tribune*. She apparently did not know that her own indignant account of the subjugation of the east by the colonial powers was so much in the tradition of Marx himself.

[132] See, especially, *Tribune*, 11 July 1853; *On Colonialism*, pp. 52–53. The contradiction had an early history; Marx speaks in the same article of parliamentary intervention invoked by 'the industrial class' against the East India Company's imports of Indian textiles and refers to John Pollexfen's tract, *England and East-India Inconsistent in Their Manufactures* (1697) – a title, he says, 'strangely verified a century and a half later, but in a very different sense' (*Tribune*, 11 July 1853; *On Colonialism*, p. 50).

[133] For the phenomenon, not its causes, see the essay under this title by John Gallagher and Ronald Robinson, *Economic Review*, second series, IV, 1 (1953). See also R.J. Moore, 'Imperialism and Free Trade Policy in India', ibid., XVII (1946). Both essays are reprinted in A.G.L. Shaw, *Great Britain and the Colonies, 1815–1865* (London, 1970), pp. 142–63, 184–96.

by this notion, Marx and Engels wrote in the *Communist Manifesto* in 1848 that 'the prices of its commodities are the heavy artillery with which it [the bourgeoisie] batters down all Chinese walls' – as if naked violence need not be involved in the process.[134] But they were awakened soon enough to facts of life. They could not but see that the years 1843–56, the very period of the triumph of Free Trade doctrines in England, represented the most relentless phase of British expansion in India and other parts of the world. Already, in 1852, Engels noted how 'the conquest of Sind, the Punjab, etc., etc.', had led to an increase in the quantity of 'English industrial goods' exported to India – a point immediately taken up by Marx.[135] In 1853 he himself spoke of 'English canon forcing [opium] upon China' this being surely the grossest marriage of violence with Free Trade.[136]

Marx was now healthily sceptical about the anti-colonial professions of the Free Traders. When India was in the process of annexation, all of them had kept quiet. Now (1853), when its 'natural limits' had been reached, they had 'become the loudest with their hypocritical peace-cant'. But, then, 'firstly, of course they had to get it in order to subject it to their sharp philanthropy'.[137] Speaking six years later of the enormous costs at which the Rebellion of 1857 had been suppressed, Marx sarcastically referred to 'the "glorious" reconquest of India' as having been achieved essentially for 'securing the monopoly of the Indian market to the Manchester Free Traders'.[138] There could not be a better characterization of the Imperialism of Free Trade than this.

The Industrial 'Expropriation'

Engels once wrote of how 'the conquest of India' pursued in search of 'imports' – the material form of tribute, that is to say – helped to transform the metropolitan country, creating within it the need for 'exports' and the development of large-scale industry. He seems to set 1800 as the dividing line between the 'import' and 'export' phases of British colonialism.[139] This was clearly in line with Marx's own perceptions. Marx put the change after 1813:

> After the opening of the trade in 1813 [by the Charter Act] the commerce with India more than trebled in a very short time. But this was not all. The whole

---

[134] See the text of the *Manifesto* in *A World to Win*, edited by Prakash Karat, p. 93.

[135] Engels to Marx, 20 April and 29 November 1852 (*Collected Works*, Vol. 39, pp. 82, 253), and Marx to Adolph Cluss, 22 April 1852, and to J. Weydemeyer, 30 April 1852 (ibid., pp. 84, 96).

[136] *Tribune*, 14 June 1853; *On Colonialism*, p. 19.

[137] *Tribune*, 11 July 1853; *On Colonialism*, p. 49. Had Lenin known of these writings from Marx's pen, it is doubtful if he could have said the following without any qualification: 'In the most flourishing period of free competition, i.e. between 1840 and 1860, the leading bourgeois politicians were *opposed* to colonial policy' (*Imperialism, the Highest Stage of Capitalism*, Moscow, 1982, p. 74: emphasis as in the original).

[138] *Tribune*, 30 April 1859; Avineri, p. 374.

[139] Engels, letter to Conrad Schmidt (27 October 1890), *Selected Correspondence*, pp. 420–21.

character of the trade was changed. Till 1813 India had been chiefly an exporting country, while it now became an importing one.[140]

Marx, in defining exports and imports, was clearly giving consideration
to industrial goods alone: 'India, the great workshop of cotton manufacture for
the world, since immemorial times, became now inundated with English twists
and cotton stuffs.'[141] He gave precise quantitative data for the expansion of the
British exports of cotton manufactures to India: 'From 1818 to 1836 the export of
twist from Great Britain to India rose in the proportion of 1 to 5,200. In 1824 the
export of British muslins to India hardly amounted to 1,000,000 yards, while in
1837 it surpassed 64,000,000 yards.'[142]

The importance of the trade for Britain rose in proportion to the expansion of British exports to India: in 1850, Marx tells us, Great Britain's exports to
India amounted to one-eighth of its entire exports, and cotton exports to one-
fourth of 'the foreign cotton trade'. After reminding the reader that cotton manufactures employed one-eighth of the population of Great Britain, he continues:
'At the same rate at which the cotton manufactures became of vital interest for
the whole social frame of Great Britain, East India became of vital interest for
the British cotton manufacture.'[143]

If such was the importance for England of its textile exports to India,
what about their impact on India? Marx regarded these as the source of an immense transformation of its social and economic conditions:

> English interference having placed the spinner in Lancashire and the weaver in
> Bengal, or sweeping away both Hindu spinner and weaver, dissolved these
> small semi-barbarian, semi-civilized communities, by blowing up their economi-
> cal basis, and thus produced the greatest, and, to speak the truth, the only
> social revolution ever heard of in Asia.[144]

To understand the scale of economic disruption that Marx is speaking
about, it may be recalled that, according to Ellison, English cloth accounted for
3.9 per cent of Indian cloth consumption in 1813–35, but 35.3 per cent of it in
1856–60 and 58.4 per cent in 1880–81.[145] When one remembers that, in addition
to cloth, yarn also was imported, one may understand what Marx means by
saying that the traditional 'union between agriculture and manufacturing industry' in India was radically disrupted.[146] The peasant would buy cloth produced
in Lancashire, dispensing with the domestic spinner as well as with the village
weaver. And the weaver would attempt to continue with the cheaper Lancashire

---

[140] *Tribune*, 11 July 1853; *On Colonialism*, p. 51.
[141] *Tribune*, 11 July 1853; *On Colonialism*, p. 52.
[142] *Tribune*, 25 June 1853; *On Colonialism*, p. 38.
[143] *Tribune*, 11 July 1853; *On Colonialism*, p. 52.
[144] *Tribune*, 25 June 1853; *On Colonialism*, p. 40.
[145] Thomas Ellison, *The Cotton Trade of Great Britain* (first edition, 1886, London, 1968), pp. 62–63.
[146] *Tribune*, 25 June 1853; *On Colonialism*, pp. 38–39; *Capital*, III, p. 328.

yarn, dispensing in this case too with the home spinner. The earlier natural economy would collapse and, in order to buy the imported manufactures, the peasant would have to sell on the market much more than the surplus product, to which commodity circulation, according to Marx, had up till now been confined.[147]

Once agriculture was commercialized, peasants must raise raw materials for the world market instead of crops for domestic or direct village-level consumption: 'In this way East India was compelled to produce cotton, wool, hemp, jute and indigo for Great Britain.'[148] The transformation was naturally of deadly consequence for the weaver and spinner. First the loss of the European market, and then the influx of Lancashire cloth into India, brought about a 'decline of Indian towns celebrated for their fabrics'.[149] Marx quotes the Governor-General as reporting in 1833–34 that 'the bones of the cotton-weavers are bleaching the plains of India'.[150] And again: 'After 1833, the extension of the Asiatic markets is enforced by "destruction of the human race" (the wholesale extinction of Indian handloom weavers).'[151]

The ruin of Indian weavers was almost unanimously accepted for a fact until an American scholar initiated a debate by suggesting that the imported yarn reinforced the position of the Indian weaver, and that the total Indian demand expanded so as to absorb British imports without curtailing the consumption of Indian cloth.[152] By and large, there has been no factual substantiation of these arguments, while the objections to the thesis have been formidable.[153] It may be recalled that, according to Ellison's estimates, the Indian production of cloth per head fell from 2.4 lb in 1831–35 to 1.6 lb in 1856–60, and to just above 1.0 lb in 1880–81; and by 1880–81 it already included Indian factory-made cloth.[154]

Ellison's figures bear out Marx's description of the destruction of the Indian craft industry; but they also bear out his insistence that 'the work of [its]

[147] See *Capital*, II, p. 34, for the effects of 'capitalist world commerce on such nations as the Chinese, Indians, Arabs, etc.'. The translation reads 'excess' where Marx clearly intended 'surplus'.

[148] *Capital*, I, p. 453.

[149] *Tribune*, 25 June 1853; *On Colonialism*, p. 38. The population of Dacca fell, says Marx, from 150,000 to 20,000 inhabitants presumably between 1824 and 1837. These figures do not accord with those given in W.W. Hunter's official *Statistical Account of Bengal*, V (London, 1875), p. 68 – 1800: 200,000 inhabitants (Taylor's estimate); 1823: 300,000 (Hebert's estimate, probably inflated); 1830: 66,989 (town census); 1867: 51,656 (official estimate); 1872: 69,212 (census). The enormous decline in the town's population is quite as obvious from these figures as from Marx's.

[150] *Capital*, I, p. 432. I have not been able to trace the source from which Marx has taken this quotation.

[151] *Capital*, I, p. 461. Parentheses as in the original.

[152] Morris D. Morris, *Indian Economic and Social History Review* (*IESHR*), V, 1, pp. 8–9.

[153] Bipan Chandra, *IESHR*, V, 1, pp. 52–68; Meghnad Desai, *IESHR*, VII, 4, pp. 317–61. Marx, by the way, was aware of Lancashire yarn being used by the Indian weaver. See *Tribune*, 25 June 1853; *On Colonialism*, p. 40. Yet, he made fun of Thiers for saying that 'the inventor of the spinning machine has ruined India'; the real culprit, says Marx, was the power-loom; see *Capital*, I, p. 443n.

[154] Ellison, *The Cotton Trade of Great Britain*, p. 63 (table).

dissolution proceeds very gradually' because 'the substantial economy and saving in time afforded by the association of agriculture with manufacture put up a
stubborn resistance to the products of the big industries, whose prices include the
faux frais of the circulation process which pervades them'.[155]

It is implicit in Marx's analysis of the impact of industrial goods on
India that the unemployed artisans should have turned into landless labourers;
moreover, the expansion of commodity production that he so greatly stressed
must inevitably have led to the subsidence of a large strata of the poorer peasants
into the ranks of the rural proletariat. R.P. Dutt and Surendra J. Patel adduced
considerable evidence for the increase in the numbers of this class from the latter
half of the nineteenth century.[156] Even the figures given by Dharma Kumar, who
otherwise disputes the thesis, tend to confirm the phenomenal growth of landless-
ness in the nineteenth century.[157]

Impressed with all such forms of dissolution of the older relationships
and the suffering inherent in that dissolution, Marx always spoke very feelingly
of 'India ruined by Manchester and Free Trade'.[158] Already, in 1847, he drew the
balance-sheet in very human terms when he spoke of 'the millions of workers
who had to perish in the East Indies [India] so as to procure for the million and a
half workers employed in England in the same [textile] industry, three years'
prosperity out of ten'.[159] The sale of British goods thus accomplished in India
what had already taken place in Britain – the large-scale 'expropriation' of the
petty producer, summed up in that portentous chapter in *Capital*, I, on the 'Historical Tendency of Capitalist Accumulation'.[160]

But was there something much more fundamental still for metropolitan
capitalism in this relationship? Rosa Luxemburg, in 1913, published a critique of
Marx's concept of capitalist accumulation, in which surplus value seemed to be
generated by labour within the capitalist economy alone. She argued, on the
contrary, that surplus value in capitalist production could be 'realized' by the

---

[155] *Capital*, III, p. 328. The point had been made by Marx earlier in 1859 as well: 'this
combination of husbandry with manufacturing industry for a long time withstood,
and still checks, the export of British wares to East India'. *Tribune*, 3 December 1859;
Avineri, p. 398. If the resistance in India, unlike China, had at last weakened, it was
because, by the acquisition of political control and by becoming 'supreme landlords of
the country', the British had been able to 'forcibly convert part of the Hindoo self-
sustaining communities into mere farms, producing opium, cotton, indigo, hemp and
other raw materials, in exchange for British stuffs' (ibid.). We here encounter once
again the close connection between imperialism and Free Trade.

[156] R.P. Dutt, *India Today* (Bombay, 1947), pp. 198–200; Surendra J. Patel, *Agricultural
Labourers of India and Pakistan* (Bombay, 1952), pp. 1–20. Some of Patel's interpret-
ations need to be refined, but his is nevertheless a pioneer work.

[157] Dharma Kumar, *Land and Caste in South India* (Cambridge, 1965), pp. 166–82. She
concedes an increase in the number of agricultural labourers from 17 or 19 per cent to
27 or 29 per cent of the total agricultural population in south India; yet, she declines
to see in it 'a radical transformation of the agrarian economy'.

[158] The words are from *Tribune*, 22 June 1853; *On Colonialism*, p. 33.

[159] Marx, *The Poverty of Philosophy* (Moscow, n.d.), p. 113.

[160] *Capital*, I, pp. 786–89.

capitalists only through the enforced system of commodity exchange with pre-capitalist (colonial and peasant) economies.[161] (This is to be distinguished, of course, from the simple primary accumulation gained from India, which was certainly recognized and stressed by Marx down to 1881, as we have seen.) It is to the credit of Nikolai Bukharin that, while he criticized the basic premises of Luxemburg's theory, he drew attention to two passages in Marx where he had amply acknowledged that the 'advanced' country with higher labour productivity in selling manufactures to a backward country (and in buying raw materials from the latter) obtains an advantage, a 'surplus-profit', in that its products of smaller amounts of labour exchange as equivalents of those of larger amounts of labour: 'In this case,' Marx says, 'the richer country exploits the poorer one.'[162] Thus, even if the surplus value was not 'realized' through the colonies, it was certainly continually enlarged through unequal exchange with the colonies. Industrial expropriation in India was thus a process of 'exploitation' of the colony, as much to Marx as to Luxemburg.

Resistance

In 1853, in the first of the two well-known articles in the *Tribune*, Marx presented a particular dilemma. On the one hand, he realized how 'sickening to human feeling' must be the sight of 'the sea of woes' into which the Indian rural population had been plunged; the members of the village communities 'losing at the same time their ancient form of civilization and their hereditary means of subsistence'. On the other, it was impossible to demand that the old system should have continued when it 'restrained the mind within the smallest possible compass', cultivated a 'barbarian egotism' and supported vile superstition, in effect depriving society of 'all grandeur and historical energies', of all capacity for change.[163] The old production system and culture had to be destroyed, just as petty production had to be annihilated in Europe to bring about the onset of modern industry.[164] Marx had, therefore, quoted Goethe to justify his approval of the entire dreadful process of change let loose by British rule.[165]

[161] Rosa Luxemburg, *The Accumulation of Capital*. For a brief and hostile critique see Paul M. Sweezy, *The Theory of Capitalist Development* (London, 1946), pp. 202–07. See also Irfan Habib, 'Capital Accumulation and the Exploitation of the "Unequal" World: Insights from a Debate within Marxism', *Social Scientist*, Vol. 31, 3–4, March–April 2003, pp. 3–26.

[162] *Capital*, III, pp. 232–33, and *Theories of Surplus Value*, III, pp. 105–06. See also Nikolai Bukharin, *Imperialism and the Accumulation of Capital*, English translation, edited by K.J. Tarbuck (New York, 1972), pp. 244–45. It may be noted that Marx's thesis would apply to any act of exchange between two economies at different stages of development. It is not dependent upon any acceptance of David Ricardo's concept of specialization of production through the pressures of Comparative Advantage – a concept recently investigated by Utsa Patnaik: 'Ricardo's Fallacy', in Jomo K.S. (ed.), *The Pioneers of Development Economics* (New Delhi, 2005).

[163] *Tribune*, 25 June 1853; *On Colonialism*, pp. 40–41.

[164] 'To perpetuate it [petty production] would be, as Pecqueur rightly says, "to decree universal mediocrity".' *Capital*, I, p. 787.

[165] *Tribune*, 25 June 1853; *On Colonialism*, p. 41.

But when rebellion actually broke out in 1857, in total revulsion against British rule, Marx was unable to heed his own advice. His natural sympathies were on the side of the rebels; and, with his usual acuteness, he accurately analysed the unfolding of the events even when the material at his disposal was necessarily limited.

For one thing, Marx saw the rebellion as 'not a military mutiny, but a national revolt'.[166] 'As to the talk about the apathy of the Hindus [Indians], or even their sympathy with British rule, it is all nonsense.'[167] Indeed, the British forces were tending to become 'small posts planted on insulated rocks in a sea of revolution'.[168]

The real reason for British isolation was the absence towards them of 'the good feelings of the peasantry'.[169] The fact that the revolt did not originate with the peasants was explained by an analogy with the French Revolution:

> The first blow dealt to the French monarchy proceeded from the nobility, not from the peasants. The Indian revolt does not [similarly] commence with the ryots, tortured, dishonoured, stripped naked by the British, but with the sepoys, clad, fed, patted, fatted and pampered by them.[170]

The paragraph shows great insight, because the participation of the peasants, though hardly mentioned in the textbooks, excited great ire of the British administrators.[171]

The higher agrarian classes were also involved. Marx wrote a long despatch on a speech by Disraeli in which he had shown how, apart from the deposed princes, 'the jagirdar' and 'the enamdar' too had been aggrieved by the British invasion of their rights.[172] Subsequently, he wrote an article on Canning's

---

[166] *Tribune*, 14 August 1857 (approvingly citing Disraeli); *FIWI*, p. 53. Also Marx's despatch datelined 31 July 1857 published in *Tribune*, 14 August; *FIWI*, p. 56.

[167] *Tribune*, 29 August 1857; *FIWI*, p. 65. Marx's employment of the word 'Hindu' in the general sense of 'Indian' (apart from its specific sense) follows the English usage of his time.

[168] *Tribune*, editorial, 15 September 1857; *FIWI*, p. 85.

[169] *Tribune*, 29 August 1857; *FIWI*, p. 65.

[170] *Tribune*, 16 September 1857; *FIWI*, pp. 91–92; *On Colonialism*, p. 152. Here Marx could well claim to have been a true prophet, for in 1853 he had spoken of 'the native army organized and trained by the British drill-sergeant' as 'the sine qua non of the Indian self-emancipation'. *Tribune*, 8 August 1853; *On Colonialism*, p. 82.

[171] 'However paradoxical it may appear it is a matter of fact that the agricultural labouring class – the class who above all others have derived the most benefit from our rule – were the most hostile to its continuance, while the large proprietors who have suffered under our rule, almost to a man stood by us.' The recipe for the British government: 'throw itself on the large proprietors and repress the peasantry'. Mark Thornhill, 15 November 1858, quoted by Eric Stokes, *The Peasant and the Raj* (Cambridge, 1978), pp. 195–96. The large proprietors, however, were by no means as universally loyal as Thornhill pictures them to be.

[172] *Tribune*, 14 August 1857; *FIWI*, pp. 51–52; *On Colonialism*, pp. 141–42. Iqbal Husain suggests that the original term used by Disraeli was a corrupt form of *aimmadar*, rather than 'enamdar'.

Oudh proclamation, in which he spoke of the dispute about the *taluqdars'* rights after the annexation of Oudh. The resulting 'discontent on their [the *taluqdars'*] part led them to make common cause with the revolted sepoys'.[173] Marx at least had a more realistic view of the rebellion than some later interpreters, one of whom has characterized it as 'a peasant war against indigenous landlordism and foreign imperialism'.[174]

Marx's sympathy for the rebels shows itself in a number of ways: his scornful scepticism of the claims of an early British capture of Delhi from the mutineers;[175] his detection of exaggeration in the horror stories of atrocities committed by the rebels and his justifications of these as events inescapable in such revolts anywhere;[176] and, finally, his denunciation of the atrocities committed by British officers and troops.[177]

However sympathetic, by natural instinct, Marx was with the 1857 rebels, he was clear enough in his mind that the rebellion was a response of the old classes to the process of pauperization of a large mass of the Indian people and the dissolution of a whole old way of life; it was not the product of the Indian 'regeneration' that he himself looked forward to. He admitted in respect of the Mutiny that 'It is a curious quid pro quo to expect an Indian revolt to assume the features of a European revolution.'[178]

In 1853 Marx had criticized the English for tolerating religious superstition in India;[179] but it was precisely the apprehension concerning British intentions towards their religion that proved to be the immediate catalyst for the sepoy rebellion.[180] Moreover, except for the sepoys there was no modern element in the ranks of the rebels that Marx could identify; and, as Engels said, 'even they [the sepoys] entirely lacked the scientific element, without which an army is nowadays hopeless'.[181] The rebellion was therefore doomed, much as Marx and Engels would have liked it to continue even in the form of a guerrilla war.[182]

---

[173] *Tribune*, 7 June 1858; *FIWI*, p. 159.

[174] Talmiz Khaldun in *Rebellion 1857*, edited by P.C. Joshi (1957), p. 52.

[175] *Tribune*, 29 August and 15 September 1857; *FIWI*, pp. 63–65, 78–82.

[176] *Tribune*, 16 September 1857; *FIWI*, pp. 91, 93–94; *On Colonialism*, pp. 152, 154–55.

[177] *Tribune*, 16 September 1857; *FIWI*, pp. 92–93; *On Colonialism*, pp. 153–54. Marx returned to the subject of atrocities against the rebels in *Tribune*, 5 April 1858; Avineri, pp. 280–84. See also Engels, *Tribune*, 25 May and 26 June 1858; *FIWI*, pp. 145–48, 164–66; *On Colonialism*, pp. 179–81, 196–97.

[178] *Tribune*, 29 August 1857; *FIWI*, p. 65.

[179] *Tribune*, 8 August 1853; *On Colonialism*, pp. 86–87.

[180] *Tribune*, 15 July and 14 August 1857; *FIWI*, pp. 40, 50; *On Colonialism*, pp. 131, 140.

[181] Engels, *Tribune*, 5 December 1857; *FIWI*, p. 117. It is interesting, however, that Engels approved some of the plans for the defence of Delhi adopted by the sepoys, showing that 'some notions of scientific warfare had penetrated among the sepoys'. He even wondered if 'they originated with Indians, or with some of the Europeans that are with them'; there were, of course, no Europeans at all with the mutineers. *Tribune*, 5 December 1857; *FIWI*, p. 123.

[182] Engels, *Tribune* 25 May, 15 and 26 June, and 21 July 1858; *FIWI*, pp. 149, 163, 166–68, 175–80.

Regeneration

In 1853, Marx defined the dual historical character of British rule: 'England has to fulfil a double mission in India: one destructive, the other regenerating – the annihilation of old Asiatic society, and the laying of the material foundations of western society in Asia.'[183] The two roles were not performed in any distinct sequential stages; the creative was rooted in the destructive, and, therefore, apparently secondary and less visible: 'The work of regeneration hardly transpires through a heap of ruins. Nevertheless it has begun.'[184] The constructive 'mission' was in fact blind and unintended: Britain, like the bourgeoisie in general, created 'these material conditions of a new world in the same way as geological revolutions have created the surface of the earth'.[185]

The process of dissolution of the old Indian village economy laid the foundation for regeneration by loosening the strong grip of tradition and superstition over the Indian people.[186] The negative effect was supplemented by certain positive achievements: the political unification of the country reinforced by the electric telegraph; effective defence secured by a modern 'native army'; a new consciousness engendered by a 'free press'; the introduction of private landed property; the provision, on a limited scale, of western education; and railways and steam transport which brought the country closer still to the western world.[187] Here were thus the pre-requisites for the creation of an Indian bourgeoisie: 'From the Indian natives, reluctantly and sparingly educated at Calcutta, a fresh class is springing up, endowed with the requirements of government and imbued with European science.'[188]

Marx held that the laying of the network of railways inside the country was of crucial importance. At the time (1853), these were only just beginning to be laid out from the three great port towns of Calcutta, Bombay and Madras. But in a remarkable passage Marx thus foresaw the future:

> I know that the English millocracy intend to endow India with railways with the exclusive view of extracting at diminished expenses the cotton and other raw

---

[183] *Tribune*, 8 August 1853; *On Colonialism*, p. 82. The duality was recognized by early nationalist spokesmen. Thus Dadabhai Naoroji, writing in 1870–71: 'If India is to be regenerated by England, India must make up its mind to pay the price.' Quoted by Bipan Chandra, *The Rise and Growth of Economic Nationalism in India* (New Delhi, 1966), p. 638. Edward Said's denunciation of Marx's thesis of the regenerative consequences of colonial rule (*Orientalism*, second edition, London, 1995, p. 154) is characteristic of his own unhistorical attitude that ignores the impact of the transmission of western ideas, science and technology, which colonialism, for its own purposes, facilitated. See Aijaz Ahmad, *In Theory: Classes, Nations, Literatures* (Delhi, 1994), pp. 224–25; and Irfan Habib, 'In Defence of Orientalism: Critical Notes on Edward Said', *Social Scientist*, Vol. 33, 1–2, January–February 2005, pp. 40–46.

[184] *Tribune*, 8 August 1853; *On Colonialism*, p. 82.

[185] *Tribune*, 8 August 1853; *On Colonialism*, p. 87.

[186] This is implied in *Tribune*, 25 June 1853; *On Colonialism*, pp. 40–41.

[187] *Tribune*, 8 August 1853; *On Colonialism*, pp. 82–83.

[188] *Tribune*, 8 August 1853; *On Colonialism*, p. 82.

materials for their manufactures. But when you have once introduced machinery into the locomotion of a country, which possesses iron and coal, you are
unable to withhold it from its fabrication. You cannot maintain a net of railways over an immense country without introducing all those industrial processes necessary to meet the immediate and current wants of railway locomotion,
and out of which there must grow the application of machinery to those branches
of industry not immediately connected with railways. The railway system will
therefore become, in India, truly the forerunner of modern industry.[189]

And so it proved to be, at least in part. Indian railway mileage exceeded
5,000 miles in 1871 and 10,000 in 1882. And already by March 1877 there were
estimated to be 1,231,284 spindles employed in Indian factories, so that Manchester was up in arms for tariff measures to throttle the young industry.[190] Marx
naturally could not have foreseen how Britain would now use administrative
measures to throttle India's industrial development.[191]

In spite of his critical view of the past culture of India, Marx believed
firmly that the Indian people were endowed with sufficient capacities to create a
modern society. He reserved considerable sarcasm for Sir Charles Wood, President of the Board of Control (the British Minister for India), for saying that 'In
India you have a race of people, slow of change, bound up by religious prejudices and antiquated customs. There are, in fact, all obstacles to rapid progress.'[192]

Marx did not also agree with Munro and Elphinstone in their favourable
opinion of the Indian aristocracy. 'A fresh class', on the contrary, had to be
created to fill administrative offices in India; and Marx quoted Campbell to say

---

[189] *Tribune*, 8 August 1853; *On Colonialism*, p. 84.

[190] R.C. Dutt, *The Economic History of India in the Victorian Age* (London, 1950),
p. 411, for the number of spindles.

[191] This was recognized by Engels, who in two letters to N.F. Danielson, of 18 June and
22 September 1892, wrote that if Russia had not imposed protective tariffs and
otherwise safeguarded its own industries, it would have just become another India —
'a country economically subject to the great Central Workshop, England'. The 18
June letter where the last statement occurs is printed in Marx and Engels, *Selected
Correspondence*, Moscow, 1956, pp. 527–29, while the 22 September letter is included in *Selected Correspondence*, edited by Dona Torr, pp. 437–40. British measures to
suppress Indian industry in fact went much beyond Free Trade. Even the support that
railway purchases might have given to Indian industry was withheld by exclusively
seeking British sources of supply at the ultimate expense of the Indian tax-payer. The
leading authority on Indian railway construction notes: 'India's loss from the purchase policies of the railways was not limited to her lack of progress in developing
heavy industry. She also failed to reap the benefits of the spread effects of industry
which would have occurred. Instead the spread effects stimulated the British economy.'
(J.M. Hurd, sub-chapter on Railways in *Cambridge Economic History of India*,
Vol. II, edited by Dharma Kumar, with assistance of Meghnad Desai, Cambridge,
1982, p. 749.)

[192] Marx added in parentheses: 'Perhaps there is a Whig Coalition Party in India.' He also
remarked that Sir Charles Wood 'seems to have the particular gift of seeing everything bright on the part of England and everything black on the side of India'.
Tribune, 22 June 1853; *On Colonialism*, p. 31.

that 'from the acuteness and aptness to learn of the inferior classes, this can be done in India as it can be done in no other country'.[193] Marx drew upon Prince Soltykov who found that 'even in the most inferior classes', the Indians were 'more subtle and adroit than the Italians'.[194] And finally Campbell, again, but most relevant of all: 'the great mass of the Indian people possesses a great industrial energy, is well fitted to accumulate capital, and remarkable for a mathematical clearness of head and talent for figures and exact sciences. . . . Their intellects . . . are excellent.'[195] There should have been really no difficulty, Marx thought, in Indians 'accommodating themselves to entirely new labour and acquiring the requisite knowledge of machinery'.[196]

Indians were thus well suited to become capitalists as well as industrial workers. The Indian industrial proletariat, once it was created, would be caste-free: 'Modern industry, resulting from the railway system, will dissolve the hereditary divisions of labour upon which rest the Indian castes, those decisive impediments to Indian progress and Indian power.'[197] This was confident prophecy; and the Indian working class has largely fulfilled it, though not to the extent, perhaps, that Marx might have expected.

While the material conditions were being created for the implantation of a modern society in India under the impact of British rule, the process could not reach its fulfilment under that regime. This was because a basic conflict of interest existed between the English bourgeoisie and the Indian people: 'All the English bourgeoisie may be forced to do will neither emancipate nor materially mend the social condition of the mass of the people, depending not only on the development of their productive powers, but on their appropriation by the people.'[198]

In these circumstances, the genesis of the modern elements in India under the aegis of British dominance could not create any lasting groundwork for collaboration between the new classes and the British rulers; on the contrary, the process of regeneration produced new contradictions.

As early as 1858, Marx could note a divergence of outlook between the young Indian bourgeoisie and the East India Company. When the Company floated a loan in Calcutta, it obtained poor response. 'This proves that the Indian capitalists are far from considering the prospects of British supremacy in the same sanguine spirit which distinguishes the London press.'[199]

The suppression of the 1857 Rebellion shattered the sepoy army and the resistance under traditional auspices. But the conditions that generated disaffec-

---

[193] *Tribune*, 25 July 1853; *On Colonialism*, p. 73.
[194] *Tribune*, 8 August 1853; *On Colonialism*, pp. 85–86.
[195] Ibid.
[196] Ibid.
[197] Ibid.
[198] Ibid.
[199] *Tribune*, 9 February 1858; *On Colonialism*, p. 175. The Calcutta middle class was, however, generally hostile to the Mutiny.

tion continued. In 1871, the General Council of the International Workingmen's Association – of which Marx was the real moving spirit – received a letter from Calcutta drawing attention to the 'great discontent . . . among the people' and 'the wretched conditions of the workers' in India.[200] In a letter Marx wrote in 1881, he referred to the 'bleeding process' to which India was subjected and to the imminence of famine. He then went on to speak of 'an actual conspiracy going on where Hindus and Mussalmans cooperate', the true scale of which was not realized by the British government.[201] This was certainly a period of grave mass unrest, marked by the Deccan peasant riots of 1875 and the bourgeois-led agitation against removal of import duties on cotton goods in 1879. A.O. Hume derived a similar impression of conditions of widespread 'unrest' and 'danger to the government' during the very same years.[202] These conditions of unrest formed the prelude to the formation of the Indian National Congress in 1885, from which event the formal history of the Indian national movement begins.

Whether the moderate beginnings of 1885 would have satisfied Marx, one cannot say. But surely what followed till the finale of 1947 contained much that should have gratified him, for it was all according to the perspective he had outlined in 1853:

> The Indians will not reap the fruits of the new elements of society scattered among them by the British bourgeoisie, till in Great Britain itself the new ruling classes shall have been supplanted by the industrial proletariat, or till the Hindus themselves shall have grown strong enough to throw off the English yoke altogether.[203]

---

[200] Extracts from the minutes of the Council and newspaper report of the letter are given in P.C. Joshi and K. Damodaran, *Marx Comes to India* (Delhi, 1975), p. 2. The Council advised the correspondent in Calcutta (not identified) to start a branch of the Association with special attention to 'enrolling natives'.

[201] Letter to N.Y. Danielson, 19 February 1881, *Selected Correspondence*, pp. 340–41; *On Colonialism*, p. 340. It is possible that Marx was here relying on the memoranda submitted in 1880 by Dadabhai Naoroji to the Secretary of State for India. Naoroji drew attention to the growing unrest, and said: 'Those Englishmen who sleep such foolish sleep of security know very little of what is going on. . . . Hindus, Mahommedans and Parsees are alike asking whether the English rule is to be a blessing or a curse'; *Poverty and Un-British Rule in India*, pp. 182–83. In the same letter to Danielson, Marx gives details of the drain of wealth, and these may be based on a memorandum of Naoroji (13 September 1880), where he gave a computation of the annual loss to India (£30 million) (ibid., p. 176). Very possibly, the information reached Marx through H.M. Hyndman, who is mentioned by Naoroji as a friend of India (ibid., p. 184) and who was also a frequent visitor of Marx's house until the summer of 1881 (*Selected Correspondence*, pp. 344, 351).

[202] Sir William Wedderburn, *Allan Octavian Hume, Father of the Indian National Congress* (1913), pp. 50, 80–81; quoted in R.P. Dutt, *India Today* (Bombay, 1947), pp. 258–59.

[203] *Tribune*, 8 August 1853; *On Colonialism*, p. 85. (As noted earlier, Marx often uses the word 'Hindu' as a substitute for Indian.) It is interesting to compare Engels' reflections on the same theme in his letter to Karl Kautsky, 12 September 1882, *Selected Correspondence*, pp. 352–53; *On Colonialism*, p. 340: he too thought 'India will, perhaps, indeed very probably, make a revolution.'

If there is one man in modern history who does not stand in need of adjectives, that is Karl Marx; and what eulogy, in any case, can be adequate for this passage? In 1853, to set colonial emancipation, not just colonial reform, as an objective of the European socialist movement; and, still more, to look forward to a national liberation ('throw[ing] off the English yoke') attained through their struggle by the Indian people, as an event that might even precede the emancipation of the European working class – such insight and vision could belong to Marx alone.

Appreciation:
The Other Marx

PRABHAT PATNAIK

I

Karl Marx's *New York Daily Tribune* articles on India have certainly not received the international attention they deserve. They have been discussed among Indian Marxists, among some professional historians of India and among Marxist scholars working on the colonial question. But outside of this relatively small circle they have not attracted much attention, not even among Marxist writers in general, which is a great pity, since they open a window to a Marxist perspective that is much wider, and visualizes many more possibilities, than what emerges from Marx's own *magnum opus, Capital*.[1]

To be sure, the articles focus on India, and brilliantly so. Indeed, one can say that, in their totality, they constitute perhaps the finest body of essays ever written on India. The sheer boldness of his explanation of India's pre-colonial 'non-history'; the remarkable insight into the nature of colonial rule which made it so different from all previous conquests of the country; the lucidity of the exposition of the dialectics of the colonial impact; the passionate sympathy for the suffering of the Indians who suddenly became exposed both to intensified material exploitation and to a shattering of their 'old world', and, at the same time, the utterly dispassionate account of the *historical* course that opened up before the country as a result of this very same painful encounter, entirely independent of the will and consciousness of the colonial rulers themselves; all these combine to make the *Tribune* set of articles a real classic on Indian history.

But the articles are more than that. They throw valuable light on Marx's overall understanding, including his understanding of capitalism, and thereby complement *Capital*. They do so in the relatively obvious sense that any discussion of a pre-capitalist society, by providing a contrast to capitalism, highlights the latter's *sui generis* characteristics more clearly than a mere depiction of such characteristics does; likewise, any discussion of a pre-capitalist society that remains more or less frozen in time makes clear, through contrast, the conditions on the basis of which capitalist society with its immanent and relentless drive for

---

[1] One writer who is an exception in this regard is Jean-Paul Sartre, who highlights these articles as an example of 'the synthetic view which gives *life* to the objects of the analysis'. See his essay, *Search for a Method* (Vintage Books, New York, 1963), p. 26, fn. 6. Sartre, however, is concerned exclusively with methodological issues.

change comes into being. In short, the *Tribune* articles, by discussing a world 'other' to capitalism, reveal simultaneously the latter's true nature.

This is a point worth emphasizing. Professor Irfan Habib, in his Introduction to the present volume, has discussed, with great lucidity and depth, Marx's explanation for the stagnation of pre-colonial Indian society, the various elements of that society which, in Marx's view, contributed to its lack of any inner drive for change, and has examined whether these elements were actually a part of the Indian historical reality; he has also highlighted Marx's changing views on the subject as new material kept coming to his notice. Now, whether or not Marx's changing list of characteristics that in their totality contributed to India's historical stagnation has any *historical* validity, it is nonetheless *conceptually* valuable for showing what elements in his perception *can* hamper the emergence of capitalism. True, the questionable historical relevance of these elements leaves open, once again, the task of explaining *India*'s stagnation; but these elements are still useful for telling us what capitalism needs as a condition for its emergence, such as, for instance, the division of labour brought about by commodity production as distinct from the division of labour entailed in the *jajmani* system, and so on.

II

There is, however, a deeper sense in which the *Tribune* articles complement *Capital*: they give a hint of a broader perspective within which *Capital*, and the perspective surrounding *Capital*, has got to be located. This comes out most clearly in Marx's remark:

> The Indians will not reap the fruits of the new elements of society scattered among them by the British bourgeoisie, till in Great Britain itself the new ruling classes shall have been supplanted by the industrial proletariat, or till the Hindoos themselves shall have grown strong enough to throw off the English yoke altogether.[2]

Marx here is actually visualizing not just a successful national liberation struggle, but *one that may even precede the proletarian revolution in the metropolis*.

Now, in the analysis of *Capital* there is not much scope for a national liberation struggle. The attention is focused on the capitalist system proper, with its two main *dramatis personae*, the bourgeoisie and the proletariat, and the objective is to show how the working of the system itself creates the condition for its own supersession through a proletarian revolution. Capitalism, having come into being through a process of 'primary accumulation of capital', consisting in the expropriation of a vast mass of petty producers and the concentration of the means of production to which they had access in the hands of a small number of

---

[2] Marx, 'The Future Results of British Rule in India', *New York Daily Tribune*, 8 August 1853.

capitalists, carries forward this process through 'centralization', where 'one capitalist kills many' through the mechanism of competition.[3] The means of survival
in this Darwinian struggle *that goes on among capitalists* is capital accumulation, increase in the scale of production and technological progress. Capitalists
are driven to accumulate capital, increase the scale of production and introduce
new technology, not because they like doing so but owing to objective necessity.
But this still does not prevent centralization, and so the frenzied drive goes on,
amassing ever larger numbers of workers, who would eventually bring about a
system that is as much the ultimate consummation of the process of centralization as its fundamental negation.

    Capital points inexorably towards a socialist revolution. In its tight and
compelling logic there is no room for any national liberation struggle, since
there are no other modes of production to be considered (except through passing
references). The notion of the twin revolutions, accordingly, has been attributed
usually to Lenin, who showed how in the era of imperialism, the exploitation of
workers at home is combined with the domination of the world by a 'handful of
the richest or most powerful nations', rivalry among whom inevitably precipi-
tates wars, where the oppressed, both domestic workers and those recruited from
the colonies and semi-colonies, are made to kill one another across trenches for
determining which finance capital should get the larger 'economic territory'.[4] To
save mankind from this disastrous *denouement*, Lenin saw the necessity for link-
ing the two revolutions, so that once the imperialist chain is broken at its 'weak-
est link', a revolutionary process is unleashed all over the world, marking
mankind's progress, through a number of stages, from imperialism, the 'last
stage of capitalism', towards socialism.

    It is remarkable, therefore, that the notion of the twin revolutions had
already been in Marx's mind as early as in 1853, *even before the Indian Mutiny
could have possibly brought it to his consciousness*. And it is equally remarkable
that Marx had favoured the idea of advanced country workers supporting the
national liberation struggles even at that stage, when there was as yet no imperialism, nor any world wars unleashed by it, and hence no threat of destruction
of mankind.

    What had been of some concern to Marx was this: if capitalism was a
growing force outside of the metropolis, if it was on a historical upswing in the
rest of the world, then, could there be a successful proletarian revolution within
the metropolis? Might not such a revolution be swamped by the rising tide in
favour of the bourgeois mode in the rest of the world? From this, the obvious and
inevitable question must have arisen: if successful national liberation struggles
would accelerate the pace of development of capitalism in the colonies, then,

---

[3] This basic perception is outlined in *Capital*, Volume 1 (Progress Publishers, Moscow,
1974), Chapter XXXII, titled 'Historical Tendency of Capitalist Accumulation'.
[4] V.I. Lenin, *Imperialism the Highest Stage of Capitalism*, in *Selected Works* (3 volumes),
Vol. 1 (Progress Publishers, Moscow, 1977).

might not such successful struggles come in the way of the victory of the proletariat in the metropolis? Might not such struggles, in other words, give rise to
forces inimical to the revolutionary cause of the advanced country proletariat?[5]

While there is no record of Marx and Engels debating this question, the
fact of such a debate is evident from the phrasing of the very definite answer that
Engels provides to this question in a famous letter to Kautsky: 'India will perhaps, indeed very probably, produce a revolution. . . . The same thing might also
take place elsewhere, e.g., in Algiers and Egypt, and *would certainly be the best
thing for us*'[6] (emphasis added). Engels is very clear here that the proletarian
revolution in Europe would gain from, and not be hindered by, a successful anti-
colonial struggle for national liberation. But the fact that he has to say it suggests
that there must have been debates and misgivings on it.

Engels does not explain why he thinks that successful struggles for
national liberation 'would certainly be the best thing for us'. Two factors, one
can only surmise, might have gone into his (and Marx's) conclusion regarding
the favourable fall-out of successful national liberation struggles for the proletarian revolution in the metropolis. The first is the awareness, which had informed his letter to Kautsky on 12 September 1882, and which he had also shared
with Marx in a letter as early as on 7 October 1858, that the extraction of surplus
value from the colonies provided a degree of stability to metropolitan capitalism, which made the task of bringing about a European proletarian revolution
that much more difficult.[7] The second must have been the perception that even if
successful national liberation struggles were followed by attempts at capitalist
development in the colonies, the nascent bourgeoisie there would be too weak to
come in the way of the European proletariat.

The wider cognition of revolutionary possibilities in the *Tribune* articles,
therefore, is linked to the fact that these articles see capitalism, necessarily, within
a wider setting, not in isolation but as existing amidst and coupled to pre-capitalist formations, which are no longer pristine but which have been transformed by
capitalism in accordance with its own needs, through political domination in the
form of colonial rule.

III

Such a perception of capitalism, as existing not in isolation but in the
midst of pre-capitalist formations which it dominates and moulds to its own
requirements, immediately brings to the fore two questions. First, what is the
mode of functioning of capitalism as a system seen in this wider setting, as

---

[5] Marx's concern in this regard has been discussed at greater length in my article 'Karl
Marx as a Development Economist', in Jomo K.S. (ed.), *The Pioneers of Development
Economics* (Tulika Books, Delhi, 2005).

[6] Engels' letter to Karl Kautsky, 12 September 1882.

[7] Both these letters are referred to in Lenin, *Imperialism the Highest Stage of Capitalism*, pp. 714–15.

distinct from capitalism existing in isolation, which Marx had analysed so profoundly in *Capital*? How, for instance, does this latter analysis get modified by the fact of capitalism existing concretely within a subjugated pre-capitalist environment? And, second, does capitalism necessarily have to have such a subjugated environment for its functioning?

Within the Marxist tradition, Rosa Luxemburg was the first to have raised both these questions.[8] Her argument was that capitalization of the surplus value was not possible within a closed and isolated capitalist system. Capitalization required, first, the realization of surplus value, and, second, the conversion of the proceeds of realization into additional elements of constant and variable capital (Marx's terms, respectively, for the portion of capital not laid out in wages and the portion employed in payment of wages). The fact that capitalism requires, as elements of constant and variable capital, material products which are not available within its own boundaries, and has perforce to go in search of them in the pre-capitalist world existing outside, which therefore has to be 'opened up' for commerce, its natural economy forcibly torn asunder, was emphasized by her. But she did not consider this to be her central *theoretical* point, which concerned the question of realization of surplus value. To be sure, the surplus value is never *separately* realized, so that to talk of the realization of the surplus value *per se* appears erroneous, but what she has in mind is quite clear: while there is a demand corresponding to every other bit of the produced good, out of the proceeds of the produced good itself, there is no demand corresponding to the unconsumed part of the surplus value unless we postulate a prior desire on the part of capitalists to convert it into additional elements of constant and variable capital. This prior desire, or what a modern-day economist would call 'inducement to invest', must already exist if the entire surplus value, and hence, by implication, the entire value of the produced output, is to be realized.

It is not enough to say, as Bukharin did in his critique of Luxemburg, that the drive to accumulate being integral to capitalism, there would always be such an inducement to invest.[9] If capital is sought to be accumulated in the form of *money*, the problem of realization would still remain (which is the central point that Keynes made, with the wisdom gained from the experience of the Great Depression of 1929–32, twenty-two years after Luxemburg's book was published). Of course, since accumulation of constant and variable capital continuously goes on, this fact itself should provide the inducement for fresh accumulation *in this material form*, without there being any sudden desire on the part of capitalists to rush into holding money. But if such accumulation occurs entirely on its own steam, it may equally easily run out of steam and collapse

[8] See Rosa Luxemburg, *The Accumulation of Capital* (Routledge, London, 1963).
[9] N.I. Bukharin's critique of Luxemburg's argument, together with her *Anti-Kritik* (a reply to Otto Bauer's earlier criticism), has been brought out as K. Tarbuck (ed.), *Imperialism and the Accumulation of Capital* (Allen Lane, London, 1972).

altogether: *sustained* accumulation, in other words, is impossible to explain within a closed capitalist system.[10]

It is for this reason that Luxemburg saw accumulation under capitalism not as a consequence of exchange between the two departments of production (capital goods and consumer goods), as Marx had explained, but as an exchange between the capitalist and pre-capitalist sectors. In *Capital*, the pre-capitalist sector had figured only in the discussion of the 'primary accumulation of capital' (apart from passing references), as if, once the capitalist sector stood on its feet, it could become a self-sustaining entity, without needing the crutches provided by a surrounding pre-capitalist sector, and could work out its immanent tendencies in solitary splendour. Against this perception, Luxemburg argued that 'primary accumulation' in the sense of the capitalist sector making inroads into the surrounding pre-capitalist sector was a perennial feature of capitalism, which she saw, in the limit, as 'collapsing' when no more pre-capitalist environment remained available.

The *Tribune* articles, however, present Marx's position somewhat differently. As Professor Habib argues, they show Marx also visualizing 'primary accumulation' as a continuous process that accompanies 'normal' accumulation under capitalism. While, in working out the immanent tendencies of capitalism in *Capital*, Marx ignored its pre-capitalist surroundings, its concrete history is one of continuous interaction with these surroundings, an interaction that is nothing else but a continuation of the process of 'primary accumulation of capital'.

In this particular respect Marx's writings do anticipate Luxemburg's assertion, and Professor Habib is right in remarking that Luxemburg would not have made the claim that Marx had confined the scope of primary accumulation of capital only to the pre-history or early history of capitalism if she had had access to the *Tribune* articles (which she did not have), but the *Tribune* articles certainly do not vindicate Luxemburg's position on the second of the two questions mentioned above. This relates to the *theoretical necessity for capitalism to subjugate its surrounding pre-capitalist sector for a continuation of its accumulation process*. While recognizing the reality of the exploitation of colonies like India by British capitalism, while drawing attention to the 'drain of wealth' from India to Britain, while emphasizing the importance of the role of the Indian market for British textiles and the disastrous consequences that this had for the Indian producers, Marx nowhere takes any *theoretical* cognizance of it. And, in this respect, Luxemburg continues to be unique among Marxist writers. (Lenin's theory of imperialism relates to a later phase of capitalism and he never said anything explicitly on the theoretical necessity of imperialism for capitalism as such.) Even the remarkable statement of Marx about exploitation through

---

[10] This argument is elaborated in M. Kalecki, 'The Problem of Effective Demand with Rosa Luxemburg and Tugan-Baranovski', *Selected Essays on the Dynamics of the Capitalist Economy* (Cambridge University Press, Cambridge, 1971). See also P. Patnaik, *Accumulation and Stability under Capitalism* (Clarendon Press, Oxford, 1997), Chapter 2.

exchange, which Bukharin had drawn attention to and which Professor Habib highlights, while it is of great value, says nothing *per se* about any theoretical necessity of imperialism for the capitalist mode of production. One can, of course, argue that since such exploitative exchange between the metropolis and the colony is a means of offsetting the falling rate of profit, subjugation of the 'outlying regions' by capitalism becomes necessary for it to overcome this tendency. Indeed, several theories of imperialism have been built on this basis.

But the problem here is that, first, this is only one of the several possible offsetting tendencies; second, the status of the law of the tendency of the rate of profit to fall is itself not very clear; third, the logical basis of the law itself is not very firm, since technological progress in the capital goods sector could well have the effect of *lowering* the capital–output ratio (if one may use a more contemporary term), so that, the share of wages in output remaining unchanged, the rate of profit could rise instead of fall; and, finally, a theory of imperialism built on the argument that imperialism provides an offset to the falling rate of profit can at best be a theory of the *inevitability* of imperialism, rather than a theory of the *necessity* of imperialism.

The question, of course, may be legitimately raised: why do we need a theory of the necessity of imperialism? Why should a theory of the inevitability of imperialism not be enough? Just because Rosa Luxemburg argued the necessity of imperialism does not mean that it is actually necessary. Given the fact that capitalism is always concretely surrounded by pre-capitalist formations, and can derive great advantage for itself through access to otherwise unavailable raw materials and primary commodities, through extraction of surplus value by a 'drain' of unrequited exports, through finding markets for its commodities, through exploitative exchange that is always advantageous for capitalism, whether or not it provides an offset to a falling rate of profit, it would inevitably subjugate these pre-capitalist territories, as actually happened in history. Do we need to show the *theoretical incompleteness* of capitalism as a closed system in order to explain imperialism? Judging by the *Tribune* articles, not to mention *Capital*, Marx does not appear to have thought so. There is, however, an important sense in which capitalism is an incomplete system, to which Marx's own analysis points and to which we shall now turn.

IV

One exceedingly important issue on which Marx differed from Ricardo was the latter's acceptance of Say's Law that 'supply creates its own demand', which amounted to a denial of the possibility of generalized over-production. Marx, a trenchant critic of 'the trite Monsieur Say', took Ricardo to task for denying the possibility of generalized over-production, and showed that in any money economy, money would necessarily be a form of holding wealth, and that this fact was quite enough for the possibility of generalized over-production. If, in the C–M–C (Commodity–Money–Commodity) circuit, the second metamorphosis, of M into C, is delayed or postponed, which is the same as an increased desire to hold wealth in the form of money, then, there would be an excess demand for money and an excess supply (or a generalized over-production) of commodities.[11] While Ricardo recognized the role of money only as medium of circulation, Marx saw it as a store of value, a form in which wealth could be held.[12] Indeed, he made the profound observation that if money was not a store of value, it could not even serve as a medium of circulation. But money would not be able to fulfil this role, without which a monetary economy would become impossible to sustain, unless there was a degree of stability in its relative value vis-à-vis the world of commodities.

While the foregoing emerges clearly from Marx's own analysis, what Marx was not sensitive to is the fact that the spontaneous functioning of a capitalist economy would not necessarily achieve this relative stability in the value of money. If the rate of accumulation proceeds rapidly, for instance, giving rise to a shortage of raw materials, the prices of such raw materials would rise, providing a signal for capital to move into these shortage sectors and increasing their supplies. But there are several raw materials whose supply, as Marx himself notes, can be augmented only after a considerable time-lag, since *inter alia* their increase is subject to natural processes that take time. The shortage in their supplies meanwhile could cause considerable price increases, upsetting the role of money as a store of value. Likewise, when workers get together through their trade unions to increase their money wages, if capitalists combine (Adam Smith had already noted that capitalists are forever in implicit collusion) to raise their prices, a wage-price spiral would ensue, which the fact of money being commodity money may not be able to control. Again, in such a case, the store of value function of money would be undermined, causing great damage to a monetary economy.

But if materials could be diverted from *their existing uses*; if any wage-price spiral could be broken by having a significant segment of workers, catering to the needs of the capitalist sector through producing commodities for it even if not directly employed by it, who, by virtue of being placed in the midst of large labour reserves (or even because of coercion), cannot enforce money wage increases when faced with rising prices; then, the stability of the value of money, and thereby the stability of the system based on the use of money, could be ensured. All this *necessitates* the subjugation of the surrounding pre-capitalist sector.

The diversion of materials from their existing uses means diversion from uses within the pre-existing pre-capitalist sector. Likewise, having an ocean of labour reserves, within which workers remain unorganized and are willing to act as 'price-takers', is of course possible within the capitalist sector itself, which,

[11] Marx's criticism of Ricardo's denial of the possibility of generalized over-production is contained in his *Theories of Surplus Value*, Part II (Lawrence and Wishart, London, 1969).

[12] Marx made this point in his *A Contribution to the Critique of Political Economy* (Lawrence and Wishart, London, 1971).

after all, is what the concept of the reserve army of labour refers to; but precisely the fact that the workers in the capitalist sector are organized enough to raise money wages in the first place, presupposes a size of the reserve army of labour that is not large enough to break a wage-price spiral once started. It follows that, apart from the reserve army internal to capitalism, there must be substantial labour reserves at arm's length (to preserve the social stability of capitalism), within which a whole group of workers and petty producers catering to the needs of capital must be located.[13] And this can be only within a subjugated pre-capitalist sector. Thus the preservation of a subjugated and degraded pre-capitalist or semi-capitalist sector, constituting the environment within which the capitalist sector functions, appears to be a necessary condition for its functioning.

This is something that even Rosa Luxemburg appears to have missed. While she saw incursion into the pre-capitalist sector as a condition for the accumulation of capital under capitalism, such incursion had the effect of assimilating the pre-capitalist sector into the capitalist sector. This resulted, in her perception, in a continuous spread of the capitalist sector at the expense of the pre-capitalist sector, leading ultimately to the impossibility of any further accumulation, to the limit-point of 'collapse'. While there are stray signs that she visualizes an alternative possibility of a degraded pre-capitalist sector persisting, these are only stray signs. But it is really this persistence that capitalism requires; it alone is what makes it possible for capitalism to overcome its intrinsic *incompleteness* and acquire its much-vaunted stability.

V

An essential instrument for this degradation of the pre-capitalist sector to make it an adjunct of the capitalist sector, providing the latter with a cushion for achieving stability and flexibility which the market alone could not ensure, is the 'drain' of surplus that Marx drew attention to in his *Tribune* articles. So much misunderstanding exists on the implications of this drain that a few words on the subject are in order here.

The 'drain', or exports 'without any quid pro quo' (to use Marx's words), appeared in India's case as an export surplus, which however was not recognized as such, since it was offset by items like the 'Home Charges' on the invisible account. Now, it would appear that if a country is having an export surplus, then, *irrespective of whether it is getting credit for this surplus or not*, this should have a stimulating effect on the economy. Since in India's case, however, this 'drain' was financed from the budget, so that corresponding to the export surplus there was a fiscal surplus, the level of activity in the economy should get neither stimulated nor deflated (if all taxes came out of private consumption). *But the 'drain' was essentially a mechanism for deflation, and, indeed, its usefulness to metropolitan capitalism lay to a significant extent in this very fact.* The question

---

[13] This argument is elaborated in P. Patnaik, *Accumulation and Stability under Capitalism*.

arises: how can a 'drain' be deflationary, contrary to the obvious tenets of macro-economics?

The answer can be given with a simple example. Suppose in an economy there are 100 peasants who produce 100 units of output ('food') of which they themselves consume 50 and use the remaining 50 to sustain a group of 100 artisans. These artisans in turn produce 100 units of manufactured goods. Assuming that a peasant's and an artisan's incomes are identical, and that all income is consumed, the exchange ratio between food and the manufactured good would be 1:1, and each working person, whether peasant or artisan, would be consuming half a unit of food and half a unit of the manufactured good. Let us assume that the price of each good is Re. 1 per unit, and that each person must first buy the food before buying the manufactured good.

Now, if the government wants to raise taxes worth Rs 50 and use it for financing an export surplus of the manufactured good, then, it would tax the artisans, who would reduce their manufactured good consumption by Rs 50 and release an equivalent amount for export surplus. *In this case, no reduction in output or employment in the economy would have occurred, in conformity with what usual macroeconomics would claim.* But, suppose the government wishes to use the tax proceeds for exporting food, then, it would tax the peasants, who would reduce their manufactured good consumption by Rs 50. *In this case, however, artisan production would get wiped out altogether, reducing employment in the economy by 100, and output by Rs 100. But the government would have got Rs 50 of export surplus.* Thus, whether an export surplus, when matched by a fiscal surplus that squeezes consumption to an equivalent degree, has a deflationary or a neutral effect, depends upon the commodity composition of the export surplus, a fact that is not taken notice of in usual macroeconomics since the implicit assumption there is of one good (or, equivalently, similar sets of commodities).

It is for this reason that the 'drain' releases food and raw materials from their existing uses, thus keeping inflationary pressures in check, and also generates an ocean of labour reserve, which makes the producers 'price-takers' for the commodities they provide to the metropolitan market, even when there is a wage-price spiral in the metropolis, and thereby brings the spiral to an end. The stability of capitalism, therefore, is intimately bound up, throughout its history, with its ability to impose deflationary policies on pre-capitalist and underdeveloped economies via a 'drain' of surplus (made possible historically through political control), and to reduce them to the status of being its adjuncts.

VI

While Luxemburg saw the role of the pre-capitalist economies essentially in the context of the realization problem, and while her concern with this problem was theoretically perfectly legitimate, unlike what many of her contemporaries thought (and notwithstanding the several erroneous propositions she advanced in arguing her central thesis), the main exogenous stimulus for accumulation in pre-First World War capitalism actually came from an altogether different source, namely, the spread of metropolitan capitalism to the temperate regions of White settlement. Indeed, Keynes, in his classic work, *The Economic Consequences of the Peace* (which Lenin used so extensively in his speech to the Second Congress of the Communist International, to argue that a European Revolution was historically on the agenda[14]), had made not only this very point, but also the suggestion that, since the scope for expanding this frontier had got exhausted, capitalism would enter a period of crisis and stagnation unless new stimuli for investment were found for it;[15] and Keynes' suggestion about the 'exhaustion of the frontier' had been used by the well-known American Keynesian economist, Alvin Hansen, for explaining the Great Depression.[16]

No matter whether one agrees with Keynes and Hansen on this latter point,[17] it remains true nonetheless that pre-capitalist markets can scarcely be claimed to have been of great significance for the *particular purpose of providing the stimulus for accumulation*. Their main role during pre-First World War capitalism lay elsewhere, namely, in sustaining the balance of payments of the leading capitalist country of the time, Britain, and thereby sustaining the Gold Standard and, with it, the entire protracted boom from the mid-nineteenth century to the First World War.

Starting from the late nineteenth century, Britain had a persistent current account deficit vis-à-vis Continental Europe within which several of the newly industrializing countries of the time were located. Britain met this current account deficit, *and made substantial capital exports to the temperate regions of White settlement*, by using two mechanisms: first, the fact that the markets of her tropical colonies like India 'were on tap' (to use S.B. Saul's words), where her goods could make inroads at will; second, the enormous 'drain' from these countries.[18] A current account surplus vis-à-vis colonies like India could thus be 'manufactured', since their markets were kept 'wide open' (to use Saul's words again) for British goods, for which there was declining demand elsewhere, and also since Britain was exporting fictitious items like 'good administration', the payment for which constituted the 'drain'.

Thus India had a current account surplus vis-à-vis Continental Europe and the United States, which Britain used for settling her own current account

---

[14] V.I. Lenin, 'Report on the International Situation and the Fundamental Tasks of the Communist International', presented to the Second Congress on 19 July 1920; *Selected Works* (3 volumes), Vol. 3 (Progress Publishers, Moscow, 1975).

[15] Joseph Schumpeter, in his essay, 'John Maynard Keynes', in *Ten Great Economists* (London, 1966), emphasized this particular vision of Keynes.

[16] A.H. Hansen, *Fiscal Policy and Business Cycles* (London, 1941).

[17] Paul Baran and Paul Sweezy in their *Monopoly Capital* (Penguin, 1973), p. 234, find Hansen's explanation inadequate.

[18] S.B. Saul, *Studies in British Overseas Trade* (Liverpool University Press, Liverpool, 1970); see also A.K. Bagchi, 'Some International Foundations of Capitalist Growth and Underdevelopment', *Economic and Political Weekly*, Special Number (August 1972).

deficit vis-à-vis Continental Europe and for making capital exports to the temperate regions of White settlement, including the United States. And she paid for this to India partly with nothing (the 'drain'), and partly with cotton textiles which were facing declining demand everywhere and which were a cause of de-industrialization within India.

The role of colonies like India, therefore, was two-fold: first, the 'drain of surplus' from them provided the wherewithal for Britain's capital exports to the temperate regions of White settlement; and second, while they themselves did not provide the main stimulus for investment in the metropolis, they transformed 'unwanted goods' (British textiles which were in declining demand both in the US and in Continental Europe) into 'wanted goods' (raw materials produced by themselves which were in heavy demand in the US and Continental Europe). Thus, while they themselves may not have provided the main stimulus for investment, which came from elsewhere, they made possible the fulfilment of this stimulus for investment.

To be sure, in this totality that constitutes the state of pre-First World War capitalism, a separation of what the main stimulus for investment is from what makes possible the satisfaction of that stimulus, may sound arbitrary; nonetheless, the role of the different elements of this totality must be clearly delineated. And it is clear that, but for colonies like India, the diffusion of capitalism into Continental Europe (which benefited from access to the British market) and into the temperate regions of White settlement (which benefited from capital exports from Britain) would not have been possible. British balance of payments would have got into a crisis, resulting in protectionism, an abandonment of the Gold Standard, a truncation of the protracted pre-war boom and an acute crisis, as indeed happened in the inter-war period.[19]

Paradoxically, however, the role of the colonies in sustaining the pre-war boom has been missed by most economic historians, with the notable exception of Saul and Bagchi. A part of the reason for the lack of recognition of this role has been false aggregation. Thus, even Eric Hobsbawm, by taking 'the empire' as his unit of observation, and not separating the tropical colonies within the empire from those temperate regions of White settlement which were still a part of the empire, misses the point about the importance of the 'drain' and the 'wide open markets'.[20] Others, by looking at the aggregate British balance of payments data, have blandly concluded that British capital exports were made

---

[19] One of the reasons for dissatisfaction with the Alvin Hansen type of explanation of the Great Depression arises precisely from the fact that while focusing on the exhaustion of the pre-war investment stimulus, they do not appreciate the changed context in the inter-war period when colonies like India could not play the same role as they had done earlier, because of the growth of domestic industries and the Japanese onslaught on Britain's Asian markets. For a longer discussion, see P. Patnaik, *Accumulation and Stability under Capitalism*.

[20] Instead, he sees both British capital exports and British commodity exports as going into a single unit called the 'empire'; see his *Industry and Empire* (Penguin, 1969), p. 146.

possible by her strong invisible account owing to shipping, insurance and interest earnings. Where these earnings came from and how, are questions that have not exercised them. In short, phenomena that were visible to Karl Marx (even if not in their entirety, since he scarcely lived to see them in their entirety) have remained opaque to the large body of economists and economic historians to this day.

VII

For any reader of Marx's *Tribune* articles, however, an intriguing question still remains: why is there such a dichotomy between the perspective of *Capital* and that of the *Tribune* articles? The bulk of Marx's research work that was to be enshrined in his *magnum opus* was carried out roughly around the same time as he was writing the *Tribune* articles.[21] The plan of *Capital* must have crystallized around that time as well, even though the book was to come out much later. Why should two works roughly originating at the same time have such divergent perspectives?

Of course, Marx's project remained an unfinished one. The sequence of volumes he proposed to write after *Capital* remained unwritten. Perhaps, the wider perspective of which one gets a glimpse in the *Tribune* articles, of a capitalist mode located in the midst of a subjugated pre-capitalist hinterland, would have emerged in the subsequent volumes. But the non-cognition of this hinterland in *Capital* itself is nonetheless intriguing. A common answer to this puzzle would be to emphasize the need for a movement 'from the abstract to the concrete': the law of motion of capitalism, its immanent tendencies arising from the mode of appropriation of surplus that is specific to it, had to be unearthed first, before the manner of its interaction with its environment could be meaningfully analysed.

This answer, however, is not altogether satisfactory, for at least two reasons. First, the law of motion itself, if unearthed by focusing attention on a particular domain which is a sub-set of a larger domain, may well remain incomplete for this reason. After all, the determination of what is abstract and what is concrete is not itself independent of what is perceived as the law of motion of capitalism. To cordon off a particular domain *a priori* as abstract, and then to derive the law of motion on the basis of an analysis of this domain, is to run the risk of unearthing an incomplete picture of the law of motion. Second, in focusing attention on a closed capitalist system, we are also implicitly closing our eyes to a whole wealth of Marx's own insights that remain unutilized for the analysis at his particular level (a typical case is Marx's theory of money and his recognition of the possibility of generalized over-production). There can be little theoretical justification for such an under-utilization of Marx's insights.

---

[21] In fact, already in May 1851, Lassalle was writing to Marx: 'I have heard that your economics will at last see the light of day. . . . I am burning to contemplate on my desk the giant three volume work of the Ricardo-turned-socialist and the Hegel-turned-economist.' Quoted in David McLellan's *Karl Marx: A Biography* (Papermac, London, 1973), p. 254.

Perhaps, the answer to this puzzle lies not in the theoretical domain at all but in the fairly obvious fact that, notwithstanding his recognition of the possibility of successful national liberation struggles even pre-dating the proletarian revolution, it was the latter that he actually saw as imminent. Because of this, his theory naturally got pulled much more towards analysing metropolitan capitalism proper, without undue concern for its pre-capitalist environment. This might also explain why his *Tribune* articles receded into the background and constituted only a sub-theme, at best, around the main theme of a European proletarian revolution, overthrowing capitalism and ushering in a transition to socialism. This might also explain why even today in the metropolitan centres, where, naturally, the focus of attention in Marxist circles continues to be on the praxis of the proletariat, the *Tribune* articles continue to be deprived of the attention they so richly deserve; and since, even in the matter of Marxist intellectual activity, what happens in the metropolitan centres has an overwhelming influence all over the world, this relative neglect of the *Tribune* articles gets generalized.

It is a matter of extreme gratification for all who are interested in Marxism, therefore, that this definitive volume, *Karl Marx on India*, which brings together Marx's *Tribune* articles and the relevant Marx–Engels correspondence, is being brought out by the Aligarh Historians Society and Tulika Books. Every student of the subject owes a deep debt of gratitude to Dr Iqbal Husain, whose painstaking scholarship has brought this volume together. Professor Irfan Habib, who remains for all of us a teacher on this particular issue, namely, Karl Marx's views on India, as he is on most other issues, also deserves our deep gratitude for his illuminating Introduction.

New York Daily Tribune **1853**

India

(*New York Daily Tribune*, June 9, 1853)
London, Tuesday, May 24, 1853

The Charter of the East India Company expires in 1854.[1] Lord John Russell[2] has given notice in the House of Commons that the Government will be enabled to state, through Sir Charles Wood,[3] their views respecting the future Government of India, on the 3rd of June. A hint has been thrown out in some ministerial papers, in support of the already accredited public rumor, that the coalition have found a means of reducing even this colossal Indian question to Lilliputian dimensions. *The Observer*[4] prepares the mind of the English people to undergo a new disenchantment. 'Much less', we read in that confidential journal in Aberdeen, 'than is generally supposed will remain to be done in new organization for the Government of our Eastern Empire.'[5] Much less even than is supposed will have to be done by my Lords Russell and Aberdeen.[6]

The leading features of the proposed change appear in two very small items. Firstly, the Board of Directors[7] will be 'refreshed' by some additional

From 'Affairs in Holland, Denmark, conversion of the British Debt, India, Turkey and Russia'. This is the first long comment by Marx on India. See *CW*, Vol. 12, p. 649 n. 84. The report is signed: Karl Marx.

[1] It was to expire on 30 April 1854.

[2] Lord John Russell (1792–1878): Whig statesman; Premier, 1846–52; Foreign Secretary in Aberdeen's ministry, 1852; resigned as Foreign Secretary but remained in the Cabinet, 1853; retired in 1855.

[3] Sir Charles Wood, first Viscount Halifax (1800–1885): Liberal MP (Member of Parliament) for Grimsby in 1826, Halifax in 1832–65; President of Board of Control (for India) in 1852–55; Secretary of State for India, 1859–66; MP for Ripon, 1865.

[4] *The Observer*, a British weekly established in London in 1791, then of a Tory persuasion.

[5] *The Observer*, 22 May 1853. Cf. *CW*, Vol. 12, p. 103 n.

[6] George Hamilton–Gordon (1784–1860), fourth Earl of Aberdeen: Foreign Secretary, 1841–46, preserved peace with France through his friendship with Guizot; followed Peel out of office; brought about the defeat of Lord Derby by joining the Whigs in 1852; Premier 1852–55; forced into the Crimean War by Palmerston and Stratford Canning in 1854; resigned after the carrying of Roebuck's vote of censure of the ministry's conduct of war in 1855.

[7] The correct designation is 'Court of Directors', not 'Board'. It was the governing body of the East India Company, elected (a third by rotation annually) from amongst those holding shares in the Company worth not less than £2,000, the voters being shareholders each holding shares of not less than £1,000. The Court enjoyed extensive powers in India which were gradually curtailed. It was dissolved in 1858 with the abolition of the East India Company.

members, appointed directly by the Crown, and even this new blood will be infused 'sparingly at first.' The cure of the old directorial system is thus meant to be applied so that the portion of the blood now[8] infused with 'great caution' will have ample time to come to a standstill before a second infusion will be proceeded upon. Secondly, the union of Judge and Excisemen in one and the same person will be put an end to, and the Judges shall be educated men. Does it not seem, on hearing such propositions, as if one were transported back into that earliest period of the middle ages, when the feudal lords began to be replaced as Judges by lawyers who were required, at any rate, to have a knowledge of reading and writing?

The 'Sir Charles Wood', who, as President of the Board of Control,[9] will bring forward this sensible piece of reform, is the same timber,[10] who, under the late Whig administration, displayed such eminent capacities of mind that the Coalition[11] were at a dreadful loss what to do with him, till they hit upon the idea of making him over to India. Richard the Third offered a kingdom for a horse, the Coalition offers an ass for a kingdom. Indeed, if the present official idiocy of an Oligarchical Government be the expression of what England *can* do now, the time of England's ruling the world must have passed away.

On former occasions, we have seen that the Coalition has invariably some fitting reason for postponing every,[12] even the smaller[13] measure. Now, with respect to India, their postponing propensities *are* supported by the public opinion of two worlds. The people of England and the people of India simultaneously demand the postponement of all the legislation on Indian affairs, until the voice of the natives shall have been heard, the necessary materials collected, the pending enquiries completed. Petitions have already reached Downing Street from the three Presidencies,[14] deprecating precipitate legislation. The Manchester School have formed an 'Indian Society'[15] which they will put immediately

---

[8] 'now' omitted in Av.

[9] The Board of Control was set up under Pitt's India Act, 1784. This Act gave the British government control over certain aspects of the Company's affairs and administration in India. The President of the Board of Control was a member of the British Cabinet and, in effect, the Minister for India. The Board of Control had powers to send direct orders to India through a Secret Committee consisting of three Directors of the Company.

[10] 'member' in Av.

[11] The Coalition Cabinet was led by Aberdeen (1852–55), and comprised Whigs, Free Traders and Peelites.

[12] 'any' in Av.

[13] 'smallest' in Av.

[14] The petitions were sent by the Bengal British Association, Bombay Association and Madras Native Association, urging upon the British Government not to renew the Charter of the East India Company.

[15] A reference to the Indian Reform Association, founded by the Free Trader John Dickinson in March 1853. See CW, Vol. 12, p. 651 n. 89.

into motion, to get up public meetings in the Metropolis and throughout the country, for the purpose of opposing any legislation on the subject for this session. Besides, two Parliamentary Committees are now sitting with a view to report respecting the state of affairs in the Indian Government. But this time, the Coalition Ministry is inexorable. It will not wait for the publication of any Committee's advice. It wants to legislate instantly and directly for 150 millions of people, and to legislate for 20 years at once. Sir Charles Wood is anxious to establish his claim as the modern Menu.[16] Whence, of a sudden, this precipitate legislative rush of our 'cautious' political valetudinarians?

They want to renew the old Indian Charter for a period of 20 years. They avail themselves of the eternal pretext for Reform. Why? The English oligarchy have a presentiment of the approaching end of their days of glory, and they have a very justifiable desire to conclude such a treaty with English legislation, that even in the case of England's escaping soon[17] from their weak and rapacious hands, they shall still retain for themselves and their associates the privilege of plundering India for the space of 20 years.

[16] Manu, the traditional law-giver, to whom is attributed the *Manusmriti*. This text was first translated into English by Sir William Jones at Calcutta in 1794, reprinted in 1796 (London), and translated into German in 1797. Marx could have seen either the English or the German translation.

[17] 'soon' omitted in Av.

Revolution in China and in Europe

(*New York Daily Tribune*, June 14, 1853. Printed as a leading article.)
[Excerpt]

At the same time it is to be observed with regard to India, that the British Government of that country depends for full one seventh of its revenue on the sale of opium to the Chinese, while a considerable proportion of the Indian demand for British manufactures depends on the production of that opium in India. The Chinese, it is true, are no more likely to renounce the use of opium than are the Germans to forswear tobacco. But as the new Emperor is understood to be favourable to the culture of the poppy and the preparation of opium in China itself, it is evident that a death-blow is very likely to be struck at the business of opium-raising in India, the Indian revenue, and the commercial resources of Hindostan. Though this blow would not immediately be felt by the interests concerned, it would operate effectually in due time, and would come in to intensify and prolong the universal financial crisis whose horoscope we have cast above.[1]

Full article published in CW, Vol. 12, pp. 93–100, the passage excerpted occurring on p. 99.

[1] That is, in the same article.

Sir Charles Wood's East Indian Reforms

(*New York Daily Tribune*, June 22, 1853)
London, Saturday, May 7, 1853[1]

The last India Bill of 1783 proved fatal to the Coalition Cabinet of Mr Fox[2] and Lord North.[3] The new India Bill of 1853 is likely to prove fatal to the Coalition Cabinet of Mr Gladstone[4] and Lord John Russell. But if the former were thrown overboard because of their attempts to abolish the Courts of Directors and Proprietors, the latter are threatened with a similar fate for the opposite reason. On 3 June, Sir Charles Wood moved for leave to bring in a bill to provide for the Government of India. Sir Charles commenced by excusing the anomalous length of the speech he was about to deliver by the 'magnitude of the subject' and 'the 150,000,000 of souls he had to deal with'.[5] For every 30,000,000 of his fellow subjects, Sir Charles could do no less than sacrifice one hour's breath. But why this precipitate legislation on the 'great subject' while you postpone it 'for even the most trifling matters'? Because the charter of the East India Company expires on the 30th April, 1854. But why not pass a temporary continuance bill, reserving to future discussion more permanent legislation? Because it cannot be expected that we shall even find again 'such an opportunity of dealing quietly with this vast

From 'The Russian Humbug – Gladstone's Failure – Sir Charles Wood's East Indian Reforms'. This article was later republished in Marx and Engels, *The Eastern Question,* compiled by Eleanor Marx and Edward Aveling (London, 1887); see CW, Vol. 12, p. 652 n. 98. In *NYDT* the article is signed: Karl Marx.

[1] The date is an obvious mistake for 7 June 1853. Since Marx discusses Charles Wood's House of Commons address of 3 June 1853, he must have written this article between 3 and 8 June, as the steamer *Humboldt* which carried Marx's letter to New York left London on 8 June 1853. See CW, Vol. 12, p. 115 n. (a).

[2] Charles James Fox (1749–1806), statesman: formed a coalition with North in April 1783; introduced measures to reform Government of India by the creation of a Supreme Council of seven and a Commercial Board of assistant directors nominated by Parliament for four years; dismissed with colleagues in December 1783; enabled by the possession of a majority in the Commons to defeat younger Pitt's India Bill, passed next year; attacked Warren Hastings, 1786–87, and moved an impeachment on Benares in 1788.

[3] Frederick North, better known as Lord North (1732–1792): first Earl of Guilford, was the main figure in the ministry, named after him, 1767–82. He combined with Fox and overthrew Shelburne's ministry in 1783, but his own ministry fell over the passage of Fox's India Bill, 1783.

[4] William Eward Gladstone (1809–98): conservative MP for Newark in 1832, 1835, 1837, and again in 1841–44; opposed the first Opium War with China in 1840; resigned as Prime Minister in 1855.

[5] Hereafter Marx quotes Charles Wood's speech from the report in *The Times*, No. 21447, 6 June 1853. Cf. CW, Vol. 12, p. 120 n. (c).

and important question'– i.e.– of burking it in a Parliamentary way. Besides, we are fully informed on the matter, the Directors of the East India Company express the opinion that it is necessary to legislate in the course of the present session, and the Governor-General of India, Lord Dalhousie,[6] summons the Government by an express letter by all means to conclude our legislation all at once. But the most striking argument wherewith Sir Charles justifies his immediate legislation is that, prepared as he may appear to speak of a world of questions, 'not comprised in the bill he proposed to bring in', the '*measure* which he has to submit is, so far as legislation goes, *comprised in a very small compass.*' After this introduction, Sir Charles delivered himself of an apology for the administration of India for the last twenty years. 'We must look at India with somewhat of an Indian eye' – which Indian eye seems to have the particular gift of seeing everything bright on the part of England and everything black on the side of India. 'In India you have a race of people slow of change, bound up by religious prejudices, and antiquated customs. There are, in fact, all obstacles to rapid progress.' (Perhaps there is a Whig Coalition party in India.) 'The points', said Sir Charles Wood, 'upon which the greatest stress has been laid, and which are the heads of the complaints contained in the petitions presented to the Committee, relate to the administration of Justice, the want of public works, and the tenure of land.'

With regard to the public works, the Government *intends* to undertake some of the 'greatest magnitude and importance.' With regard to tenure of lands, Sir Charles proves very successfully that its three existing forms – the *Zemindari*,[7] the *Ryotwari*[8] and the *village*[9] systems are only so many forms of fiscal *exploitation* in the hands of the Company, none of which could well be made general, nor deserved to be made so. An idea of establishing another form, of an altogether opposite character, does not in the least preoccupy the mind of Sir Charles. 'With regard to the *administration of Justice*', continues he, 'the complaints relate principally to the inconvenience arising from the technicalities of English law, to the alleged incompetency of English Judges, and to the corruption of the native officers and judges.'

And now, in order to prove the hard labor of providing for the administration of Justice in India, Sir Charles relates that already, as early as 1833, a Law Commission was appointed in India. But in what manner did this Commission act, according to Sir Charles Wood's own testimony? The first and last result of the labors of that Commission was a *Penal Code*, prepared under the auspices of Mr Macaulay. This code was sent to the various local authorities in India, which sent it back to Calcutta, from which it was sent to England, to be again returned

---

[6] Governor General of India, 1848–56.

[7] By '*Zemindari*' Marx obviously means here the zamindari system under the Permanent Settlement established in Bengal in 1790.

[8] The settlement with revenue-payers (largely peasant owners, paying revenue by the field), imposed in the Madras and Bombay Presidencies.

[9] The *mahalwari* system, where there was a collective obligation on *pattidars*, is probably intended here.

from England to India. In India Mr Macaulay having been replaced in legislative counsel by Mr Bethune,[10] the code was totally altered, and on this plea the Governor-General not being then of opinion 'that delay is a source of weakness and danger', sent it back to England, and from England it was returned to the Governor-General, with authority to pass the code in whatever shape he thought best. But now, Mr Bethune having died, the Governor-General thought best to submit the code to a third English lawyer,[11] and to a lawyer who knew nothing about the habits and customs of the Hindoos,[12] reserving himself the rights of afterwards rejecting a code concocted by wholly incompetent authority. Such have been the adventures of the yet unborn code. As to the technical absurdities of the law in India, Sir Charles takes his stand on the no less absurd technicalities of the English law-procedure itself, but while affirming the perfect incorruptibility of the English judges in India, he nevertheless is ready to sacrifice them by an alteration in the manner of nominating them. The general progress of India is demonstrated by a comparison of the present state of Delhi with that under the invasion of Khuli Khan.[13] The salt-tax is justified by the arguments of the most renowned political economists, all of whom have advised taxation to be laid on some article of first necessity. But Sir Charles does not add what those same economists would have said on finding that, in the two years from 1849–50 and 1851–52, there had been a decrease in the consumption of salt, of 60,000 tons, a loss of revenue to the amount of £415,000, the total salt revenue amounting to £2,000,000. The measures proposed by Sir Charles and 'comprised in a very small compass' are:

1. The Court of Directors to consist of eighteen instead of twenty-four members, twelve to be elected by the Proprietors and six by the Crown.
2. The revenue of Directors to be raised from £300 to £500 a year; the Chairman to receive £1,000.
3. All the ordinary appointments in the civil service, and all the scientific in the military service of India, to be thrown open to public competition, leaving to the Directors the nomination of the Cadetships in the Cavalry-of-the-Line.
4. The Governor-Generalship to be separated from the Governorship of Bengal, and power to be given to the Supreme Government to constitute a new presidency in the districts on the Indus.
5. And lastly, the whole of this measure only to continue until the Parliament shall provide otherwise.

[10] John Elliot Drinkwater Bethune (1801–1851): legislative member of the Supreme Council of India in 1848.

[11] B. Peacock: see *CW*, Vol. 12, p. 122 n. (a).

[12] It seems that the word 'Indians' possibly originally used by Marx was replaced by the editor of *New York Daily Tribune* with 'Hindoos' here and elsewhere to avoid confusion with the 'Red Indians' for his American readers.

[13] Nadir Quli Beg, better known as Nadir Shah (1688–1747), whose sack of Delhi took place in 1739.

The speech and measure of Sir Charles was subjected to a very strong satirical criticism by Mr Bright,[14] whose picture of India ruined by the fiscal exertions of the Company and Government did not, of course, receive the supplement of India ruined by Manchester and Free Trade. As to the last night's speech of an old East-India man, Sir J. Hogg,[15] Director or ex-Director of the Company, I really suspect that I have met with it already in 1701, 1730, 1743, 1769, 1772, 1781, 1783, 1784, 1793, 1813, etc., and am induced, by way of answer to his directorial panegyric, to quote merely a few facts from the annual Indian accounts published, I believe, under his own superintendence.

Total Net Revenues of India

1849–50	£20,275,831	Loss of revenue within three
1850–51	£20,249,932	years: £348,792
1851–52	£19,927,039	

Total Charges

1849–50	£16,687,382	Increase of expenditure
1850–51	£17,170,707	within three years:
1851–52	£17,901,666	£1,213,284[16]

Land Tax

Bengal oscillated in last four years from £3,500,000 to £3,560,000.

North-West oscillated in last four years from £4,870,000 to £4,990,000.

Madras oscillated in last four years from £3,640,000 to £3,470,000.

Bombay oscillated in last four years from £2,240,000 to £2,300,000.

Gross Revenue in 1851–52

Bengal	£10,000,000
Madras	£5,000,000
Bombay	£4,300,000[17]

Expenditure on Public Works in 1851–52

Bengal	£87,800
Madras	£20,000
Bombay	£58,590

Out of £19,300,000, net £166,390 have been expended on roads, canals, bridges, and other works of public necessity.

---

[14] John Bright (1811–1889): famous Radical and Free Trader; chairman of Select Committee to enquire into obstacles to cultivation of cotton in India in 1848; recommended that the Government of India should be made a department of the British government in 1853; later advocated decentralization in India, 1858 and 1879.

[15] Sir James Weir Hogg (1790–1876): British politician, Peelite, MP, 1835–57; President of the Court of Directors of the East India Company, 1846–47, 1852–53; later Member of Indian Council, 1858–72.

[16] Rect. 1,214,284.

[17] £4,800,000 in *On Colonialism*, p. 34; and CW, Vol. 12, p. 124.

The British Rule in India

(*New York Daily Tribune*, June 25, 1853)
London, Friday, June 10, 1853

Telegraphic dispatches from Vienna announce that the pacific solution of the Turkish, Sardinian and Swiss questions, is regarded there as a certainty.

Last night the debate on India was continued in the House of Commons, in the usual dull manner. Mr Blackett[1] charged the statements of Sir Charles Wood and Sir J. Hogg with bearing the stamp of optimist falsehood. A lot of Ministerial and Directorial advocates[2] rebuked the charge as well as they could, and the inevitable Mr Hume[3] summed up by calling on ministers to withdraw their bill. Debate adjourned.

Hindostan is an Italy of Asiatic dimensions, the Himalayas for the Alps, the Plains of Bengal for the Plains of Lombardy, the Deccan for the Apennines, and the Isle of Ceylon for the Island of Sicily. The same rich variety in the products of the soil, and the same dismemberment in the political configuration. Just as Italy has, from time to time, been compressed by the conqueror's sword into different national masses, so do we find Hindostan, when not under the pressure of the Mohammedan, or the Mogul, or the Briton, dissolved into as many independent and conflicting States as it numbered towns, or even villages. Yet, in a social point of view, Hindostan is not the Italy, but the Ireland of the East. And this strange combination of Italy and of Ireland, of a world of voluptuousness and of a world of woes, is anticipated in the ancient traditions of the religion of Hindostan. That religion is at once a religion of sensualist exuberance, and a religion of self-torturing asceticism; a religion of the Lingam, and of the Juggernaut; the religion of the Monk, and of the Bayadere.[4]

I share not the opinion of those who believe in a golden age of Hindostan, without recurring, however, like Sir Charles Wood, for the confirmation of my

---

The article is signed: Karl Marx. Marx, in his letter of 14 June 1853 to Engels, speaks of this as 'my first [full-scale] article on India'; see *CW*, Vol. 39, p. 346. Marx draws upon some points suggested by Engels; see Engels's letter to Marx dated 6 June 1853, in *CW*, Vol. 39, p. 335.

[1] John Fenwick Burgoyne Blackett (1821–1856): British MP.
[2] That is, supporters of the Court of Directors of the East India Company.
[3] Joseph Hume (1777–1856): radical politician; entered medical service of the East India Company in 1797; MP from Montrose, 1842–55.
[4] Dancing girl, from Portuguese *bailadeira*.

view, to the authority of Khuli Khan.[5] But take, for example, the times of Aurungzeb; or the epoch, when the Mogul appeared in the North, and the Portuguese in the South; or the age of Mohammedan invasion, and of the Heptarchy[6] in Southern India; or, if you will, go still more back to antiquity, take the mythological chronology of the Brahman himself, who places the commencement of Indian misery in an epoch even more remote than the Christian creation of the world.

There cannot, however, remain any doubt but that the misery inflicted by the British on Hindostan is of an essentially different and infinitely more intensive kind than all Hindostan had to suffer before. I do not allude to European despotism, planted upon Asiatic despotism, by the British East India Company, forming a more monstrous combination than any of the divine monsters startling us in the Temple of Salsette.[7] This is no distinctive feature of British colonial rule, but only an imitation of the Dutch, and so much so that in order to characterize the working of the British East India Company it is sufficient to literally repeat what Sir Stamford Raffles, the *English* Governor of Java, said of the old Dutch East India Company:

> The Dutch Company, actuated solely by the spirit of gain, and viewing their subjects with less regard or consideration than a West India planter formerly viewed a gang upon his estate, because the latter had paid the purchase money of human property, which the other had not, employed all the existing machinery of despotism to squeeze from the people their utmost mite of contribution, the last dregs of their labor, and thus aggravated the evils of a capricious and semi-barbarous Government, by working it with all the practised ingenuity of politicians, and all the monopolizing selfishness of traders.[8]

All the civil wars, invasions, revolutions, conquests, famines, strangely complex, rapid and destructive as the successive action in Hindostan may appear, did not go deeper than its surface. England has broken down the entire framework of Indian society, without any symptoms of reconstitution yet appearing. This loss of his old world, with no gain of a new one, imparts a particular kind of melancholy to the present misery of the Hindoo[9] and separates Hindostan, ruled by Britain, from all its ancient traditions, and from the whole of its past history.

---

[5] Mistranscription apparently of Khafi Khan (author of *Muntakhabu'l Lubab*), whose statements about disturbed conditions in the early eighteenth century were well known.

[6] Heptarchy, the seven Anglo-Saxon kingdoms that were supposed to have divided England among themselves before the tenth century. Marx apparently uses this word by analogy to denote the political dismemberment of the Deccan before its conquest by the Mughals.

[7] Reference to cave sculptures in the island of Salsette, to the north of Mumbai.

[8] Raffles, *History of Java*, Vol. I (London, 1817), p. 151. The quotation is exact.

[9] Since 'Indian' in American usage referred to the American Indians ('Red Indians'), the editors of *NYDT* seem to have changed Marx's 'Indian' uniformly to 'Hindoo', unless Marx, in the knowledge of this usage, had already written 'Hindoo'.

There have been in Asia, generally, from immemorial times, but three departments of Government: that of Finance, or the plunder of the interior; that of War, or the plunder of the exterior; and, finally, the department of Public Works.[10] Climate and territorial conditions, especially the vast tracts of desert, extending from the Sahara, through Arabia, Persia, India and Tartary, to the most elevated Asiatic highlands, constituted artificial irrigation by canals and waterworks the basis of Oriental agriculture. As in Egypt and India, inundations are used for fertilizing the soil in Mesopotamia, Persia, etc.; advantage is taken of a high level for feeding irrigative canals. This prime necessity of an economical and common use of water, which, in the Occident, drove private enterprise to voluntary association, as in Flanders and Italy, necessitated, in the Orient where civilization was too low and the territorial extent too vast to call into life voluntary association, the interference of the centralizing power of Government. Hence an economical function devolved upon all Asiatic Governments, the function of providing public works. This artificial fertilization of the soil, dependent on a Central Government, and immediately decaying with the neglect of irrigation and drainage, explains the otherwise strange fact that we now find whole territories barren and desert that were once brilliantly cultivated, as Palmyra, Petra, the ruins in Yemen, and large provinces of Egypt, Persia and Hindostan; it also explains how a single war of devastation has been able to depopulate a country for centuries, and to strip it of all its civilization.[11]

Now, the British in East India accepted from their predecessors the department of finance and of war, but they have neglected entirely that of public works. Hence the deterioration of an agriculture which is not capable of being conducted on the British principle of free competition, of *laissez faire* and *laissez aller*.[12] But in Asiatic empires we are quite accustomed to see agriculture deteriorating under one government and reviving again under some other government. There the harvests correspond to good or bad governments, as they change in Europe with good or bad seasons. Thus the oppression and neglect of agriculture, bad as it is, could not be looked upon as the final blow dealt to Indian society by the British intruder, had it not been attended by a circumstance of quite different importance, a novelty in the annals of the whole Asiatic world. However changing the political aspect of India's past must appear, its social condition has remained unaltered since its remotest antiquity, until the first decennium of the 19th century. The hand-loom and the spinning-wheel, producing their regular myriads of spinners and weavers, were the pivots of the structure of that society. From immemorial times, Europe received the admirable textures of Indian labor sending in return for them her precious metals, and furnishing thereby his material to

---

[10] Borrowed from Engels's proposition in his letter to Marx, 6 June 1856, in *CW*, Vol. 39, p. 339.

[11] Marx here enlarges upon Engels's insistence on the necessity of irrigation for oriental agriculture in his letter. See ibid., pp. 339–40.

[12] *Laissez faire*, 'let everyone do as he pleases'; *laissez aller*, 'let go without constraint'.

the goldsmith, that indispensable member of Indian society, whose love of finery
is so great that even the lowest class, those who go about nearly naked, have
commonly a pair of golden earrings and a gold ornament of some kind hung
round their necks. Rings on the fingers and toes have also been common. Women
as well as children frequently wore massive bracelets and anklets of gold or
silver, and statuettes of divinities in gold and silver were met with in the house-
holds. It was the British intruder who broke up the Indian hand-loom and destroyed the spinning-wheel. England began with driving the Indian cottons from
the European market; it then introduced twist into Hindostan and in the end
inundated the very mother country of cotton with cottons. From 1818 to 1836 the
export of twist from Great Britain to India rose in the proportion of 1 to 5,200. In
1824 the export of British muslins to India hardly amounted to 1,000,000 yards,
while in 1837 it surpassed 64,000,000 yards. But at the same time the population
of Dacca decreased from 150,000 inhabitants to 20,000. This decline of Indian
towns celebrated for their fabrics was by no means the worst consequence. British steam and science uprooted, over the whole surface of Hindostan, the union
between agriculture and manufacturing industry.

These two circumstances – the Hindoo, on the one hand, leaving, like
all Oriental peoples, to the Central Government the care of the great public
works, the prime condition of his agriculture and commerce, dispersed, on the
other hand, over the surface of the country, and agglomerated in small centres by
the domestic union of agricultural and manufacturing pursuits – these two circumstances had brought about, since the remotest times, a social system of particular features – the so-called *village system*, which gave to each of these small
unions their independent organization and distinct life. The peculiar character of
this system may be judged from the following description, contained in an old
official report of the British House of Commons on Indian affairs:[13]

> A village, geographically considered, is a tract of country comprising some
> hundred or thousand acres[14] of arable and waste lands; politically viewed it
> resembles a corporation or township. Its proper establishment of officers and
> servants consists of the following descriptions: the *potail* or head inhabitant,
> who has the general superintendence of the affairs of the village, settles the
> disputes of the inhabitants, attends to the police, and performs the duty[15] of
> collecting the revenue[16] within the village, a duty which his personal influence
> and minute acquaintance with the situation and concerns of the people render
> him the best qualified for this charge.[17] The *kurnum*[18] keeps the accounts of

---

13 The following quotation is from the *Fifth Report* (hereafter *FR*) of the Select Committee on Affairs of the East India Company (London, 1812), p. 85. Variations from the
original text are noted by giving the words of the *Fifth Report* in footnotes hereafter.
14 *FR*: 'some hundred and thousands of acres'.
15 *FR* adds: 'already described'.
16 *FR*: 'revenues'.
17 *FR*: 'renders him best qualified to discharge'.
18 *FR*: 'Curnum who'.

cultivation, and registers everything connected with it. The *tallier* and the *totie*, the duty of the former of which consists[19] in gaining information of crimes and offences, and in escorting and protecting persons travelling from one village to another; the province of the latter appearing to be more immediately confined to the village, consisting, among other duties, in guarding the crops and assisting in measuring them. The *boundaryman*, who preserves the limits of the village, or gives evidence respecting them in cases of dispute. The superintendent of Tanks and Water-courses distributes the water[20] for the purposes of agriculture. The Brahmin,[21] who performs the village worship. The schoolmaster, who is seen teaching the children in a village to read and write in the sand. The calendar-Brahmin,[22] or astrologer, etc.[23] These officers and servants generally constitute the establishment of a village; but in some parts of the country it is of less extent; some of the duties and functions above described being united in the same person; in others it exceeds the above-named number of individuals.[24]

Under this simple form of municipal government, the inhabitants of the country have lived from time immemorial. The boundaries of the villages have been but seldom altered; and though the villages themselves have been sometimes injured, and even desolated by war, famine or[25] disease, the same name, the same limits, the same interests, and even the same families, have continued for ages. The inhabitants gave[26] themselves no trouble about the breaking up and divisions[27] of kingdoms; while the village remains entire, they care not to what power it is transferred, or to what sovereign it devolves; its internal economy remains unchanged. The potail is still the head inhabitant, and still acts as the petty judge or[28] magistrate, and collector or rentor of the village.[29]

---

[19] *FR:* 'appearing to consist in a wider and more enlarged sphere of action'.

[20] *FR* adds: 'therefrom'.

[21] *FR:* 'Bramin'.

[22] *FR:* 'calendar-Bramin'.

[23] A large omission from *FR* occurs here in lieu of 'etc.': 'who proclaims the lucky or unpropitious periods for sowing and threshing. The Smith and Carpenters who manufacture the implements of agriculture, and build for the dwelling of the ryot. The Potman, or potter, the Washerman, the Cow keeper, who looks after the cattles, the Dancing Girl, who attends the rejoicing, the Musicians and the poet'.

[24] *FR* adds: 'which have been described'.

[25] *FR:* 'and'.

[26] *FR:* 'give'.

[27] *FR:* 'division'.

[28] *FR:* 'and'.

[29] In a letter to Engels, dated 14 June 1853 (*CW*, Vol. 39, p. 347), Marx quotes this passage from the *Fifth Report,* but also incorporates within the quotation material from Wilks, *Historical Sketches* (originally published, London, 1810). The passage on which Marx drew occurs in Murray Hammick's edition of the work (Mysore, 1930), Vol. I, pp. 136–37. Wilks's passage was itself probably the main source for the account of the village community in the *Fifth Report.*

These small stereotype forms of social organism have been to the greater part dissolved, and are disappearing, not so much through the brutal interference of the British tax gatherer and the British soldier, as to the working of English steam and English free trade. Those family-communities were based on domestic industry, in that peculiar combination of hand-weaving, hand-spinning and hand-tilling agriculture which gave them self-supporting power. English interference having placed the spinner in Lancashire and the weaver in Bengal, or sweeping away both Hindoo spinner and weaver, dissolved these small semi-barbarian, semi-civilized communities, by blowing up their economical basis, and thus produced the greatest, and, to speak the truth, the only social revolution ever heard of in Asia.

Now, sickening as it must be to human feeling to witness these myriads of industrious patriarchal and inoffensive social organization disorganized and dissolved into their units, thrown into a sea of woes, and their individual members losing at the same time their ancient form of civilization, and their hereditary means of subsistence, we must not forget that these idyllic village communities, inoffensive though they may appear, had always been the solid foundation of Oriental despotism, that they restrained the human mind within the smallest possible compass, making it the unresisting tool of superstition, enslaving it beneath traditional rules, depriving it of all grandeur and historical energies. We must not forget the barbarian egotism which, concentrating on some miserable patch of land, had quietly witnessed the ruin of empires, the perpetration of unspeakable cruelties, the massacre of the population of large towns, with no other consideration bestowed upon them than on natural events, itself the helpless prey of any aggressor who deigned to notice it at all. We must not forget that this undignified, stagnatory, and vegetative life, that this passive sort of existence, evoked on the other part, in contradistinction, wild, aimless, unbounded forces of destruction, and rendered murder itself a religious rite in Hindostan. We must not forget that these little communities were contaminated by distinctions of caste and by slavery, that they subjugated man to external circumstances instead of elevating man to be the sovereign of circumstances, that they transformed a self-developing social state into never changing natural destiny, and thus brought about a brutalizing worship of nature, exhibiting its degradation in the fact that man, the sovereign of nature, fell down on his knees in adoration of Hanuman,[30] the monkey, and Sabbala,[31] the cow.

England, it is true, in causing a social revolution in Hindostan, was actuated only by the vilest interests, and was stupid in her manner of enforcing them. But that is not the question. The question is, can mankind fulfil its destiny without a fundamental revolution in the social state of Asia? If not, whatever

---

[30] The famous monkey-god, helper to Lord Rama. 'Kanuman' in the original, as in *CW*, Vol. 12, p. 132, is an obvious misprint.

[31] Śabala is one of the names of the divine cow Surabhi, who grants boons and who herself rose from the Milk Ocean.

may have been the crimes of England she was the unconscious tool of history in bringing about the revolution.

Then whatever bitterness the spectacle of the crumbling of an ancient world may have for our personal feelings, we have the right, in point of history, to exclaim with Goethe:

> Sollte diese Qual uns quälen,
> Da sie unsre Lust vermehrt,
> Hat nicht myriaden Seelen
> Timur's Herrschaft aufgezehrt?
>
> [Should his shrill complaint torment us
> Since it has increased our joy?
> Did not Timur's harsh dominion
> Myriads of souls destroy][32]

[32] The stanza is from Goethe's *Westöstlicher Divan*, '*An Suleika*'; the English rendering, not in the original, is that of Alexander Rogers. Goethe here tells us of the nightingale's complaint against the destruction of rosebuds to produce the rose-scent that Zuleikha uses. The first stanza of the poem thus reads:
> Thee with sweet scents to caress
> Still thy pleasure to increase,
> A thousand rose-buds none the less
> Must in flames their beings cease.

See Goethe, *Reineke Fox, West-Eastern Divan, and Achillied*, translated by Alexander Rogers (London, 1890), p. 268.

India

(*New York Daily Tribune*, July 1, 1853)
London, Friday, June 17, 1853

On the 13th instant Lord Stanley[1] gave notice to the House of Commons that on the second reading of the India Bill (23rd instant) he would bring in the following resolution:

> That in the opinion of this House further information is necessary to enable Parliament to legislate with advantage for the permanent Government of India, and that at this late period of the session, it is inexpedient to proceed into a measure which, while it disturbs existing arrangements, cannot be regarded as a final settlement.[2]

But in April 1854, the Charter of the East India Company will expire, and something must accordingly be done one way or the other. The Government wanted to legislate permanently; that is, to renew the Charter for twenty years more. The Manchester School wanted to postpone all legislation, by prolonging the Charter at the most for one year. The Government said that permanent legislation was necessary for the 'best' of India. The Manchester men replied that it was impossible for want of information. The 'best' of India, and the want of information, are alike false pretences. The governing oligarchy desired, before a Reformed House should meet, to secure at the cost of India, their own 'best' for twenty years to come. The Manchester men desired no legislation at all in the unreformed Parliament, where their views had no chance of success. Now, the Coalition Cabinet through Sir Charles Wood,[3] has, in contradiction to its former statements, but in conformity with its habitual system of shifting difficulties, brought in something that looked like legislation, but it dared not, on the other hand, to propose the renewal of the Charter for any definite period, but presented

From 'English Prosperity – Strikes – The Turkish Question – India'. Signed: Karl Marx. In Av. this article appears under the title 'The Government of India Bill'.

[1] Edward Henry Stanley (1826–1893), fifteenth Earl of Derby; statesman; MP, 1848–69; Under Secretary for Foreign Affairs in 1852; K.G. 1884.
[2] *The Times*, No. 21454, 14 June 1853. Reference in *CW*, Vol. 12, p. 139 n. (a).
[3] Marx here refers to Sir Charles Wood's speech in the Commons on 3 June 1853 – a large portion of which was taken from Dalhousie's paper, 'The Government of India' (13 October 1852). Wood, endorsing Dalhousie's opinion, pleaded against a change in the Charter.

a 'settlement', which it left to Parliament to unsettle whenever that body should determine to do so. If the Ministerial proposition were adopted, the East India Company would obtain no renewal but only a suspension of life. In all other respects, the Ministerial project but apparently alters the Constitution of the India Government, the only serious novelty to be introduced being the addition of some new Governors, although a long experience has proved that the parts of East India administered by simple Commissioners[4] go on much better than those blessed by the costly luxury of Governors and Councils. The Whig invention of alleviating exhausted countries by burdening them with new sinecures for the paupers of aristocracy, reminds one of the old Russell administration, when the Whigs were suddenly struck with the state of spiritual destitution, in which the Indians and the Mohammedans of the East were living, and determined upon relieving them by the importation of some new Bishops, the Tories, in the pleni-tude of their power, having never thought more than one to be necessary. That resolution having been agreed upon, Sir John Hobhouse,[5] the then Whig Presi-dent of the Board of Control, discovered immediately afterwards that he had a relative admirably suited for a Bishopric, who was forthwith appointed to one of the new sees. 'In cases of this kind', remarks an English writer, 'where the fit is so exact, it is really hardly possible to say whether the shoe [was made][6] for the foot, or the foot for the shoe.' Thus, with regard to the Charles Wood invention, it would be very difficult to say, whether the new Governors are made for Indian provinces, or Indian provinces for the new Governors.

But this as it may, the Coalition Cabinet believed it has met all clamors by leaving to Parliament the power of altering its proposed act at all times. Unfortunately, in steps Lord Stanley, the Tory, with his resolution which was loudly cheered by the 'Radical' Opposition, when it was announced. Lord Stanley's resolution is, nevertheless, self contradictory. On one hand, he rejects the Minis-terial proposition, because the House requires more information for permanent legislation. On the other hand, he rejects it because it is no permanent legisla-tion, but alters existing arrangements, without pretending to finality. The Con-servative view is, of course, opposed to the bill, because it involves no change at all. Lord Stanley, in these coalescent times, has found a formula in which the opposite views are combined together, against the Ministerial view of the sub-ject. The Coalition Ministry affects a virtuous indignation against such tactics, and *The Chronicle,* its organ, exclaims: 'Viewed as a party-move, the proposed motion for delay is in a high degree factious and discreditable. . . . This motion is brought forward solely, because some supporters of the Ministry are pledged to

---

[4] Here Marx is apparently referring to Dalhousie's paper (ibid.), where the latter sug-gested relieving the Governor General of the charge of local affairs of Bengal by placing it under a 'Lieutenant Governor'.

[5] John Cam Hobhouse (1786–1869): British Whig statesman; President of the Board of Control for India, 1835–41 and 1846–52.

[6] Insertion 'was made' (Av.) not in original.

separate in this particular question from those with whom they usually act.'[7]

The anxiety of the Ministers seems indeed to be serious. *The Chronicle* of to-day, again recurring to the subject, says: 'The division on Lord Stanley's motion will probably be decisive of the fate of the India Bill; it is therefore of the *utmost importance* that those who feel the *importance* of early legislation should use every exertion to strengthen the Government.'[8] On the other hand, we read in *The Times* of to-day: 'The fate of the Government of India Bill has been more respectively delineated. . . . The danger of the Government lies in the entire conforming of Lord Stanley's objections with the conclusion of public opinion. Every syllable of this amendment tells with deadly effect against the Ministry.'

I shall expose, in a subsequent letter,[9] the bearing of the Indian Question on different parties in Great Britain, and the benefit, the poor Hindoo may reap from the quarrelling of the aristocracy, the moneyocracy, and the millocracy about his amelioration.

---

[7] *The Morning Chronicle*, No. 26981, 15 June 1853. See *CW*, Vol. 12, p. 140 n. (a).
[8] *The Morning Chronicle*, No. 26983, 17 June 1853. See *CW*, Vol. 12, p. 140 n. (b).
[9] 'The East India Company – Its History and Results', published in *New York Daily Tribune (NYDT)* on 11 July 1853.

The East India Company – Its History and Results

(*New York Daily Tribune*, July 11, 1853)
London, Friday, June 24, 1853[1]

The debate on Lord Stanley's motion to postpone legislation for India, has been deferred until this evening. For the first time since 1783 the Indian Question has become a Ministerial one in England. Why is this?

The true commencement of the East India Company cannot be dated from a more remote epoch than the year 1702, when the different societies, claiming the monopoly of the East India trade, united together in one single Company. Till then the very existence of the original East India Company was repeatedly endangered, once suspended for years under the protectorate of Cromwell, and once threatened with utter dissolution by parliamentary interference under the reign of William III. It was under the ascendancy of that Dutch Prince when the Whigs became the farmers of the revenues of the British Empire, when the Bank of England[2] sprung into life, when the protective system was firmly established in England, and the balance of power in Europe was definitively settled, that the existence of an East India Company was recognized by Parliament. That era of apparent liberty was in reality the era of monopolies not created by Royal grants, as in the times of Elizabeth and Charles I, but authorized and nationalized by the sanction of Parliament. This epoch in the history of England bears, infact, an extreme likeness to the epoch of Louis Philippe in France, the old landed aristocracy having been defeated, and the bourgeoisie not being able to take its place except under the banner of moneyocracy, or the *haute finance*. The East India Company excluded the common people from the commerce with India, at the same time that the House of Commons excluded them from Parliamentary representation. In this as well as in other instances, we find the first decisive victory of the bourgeoisie over the feudal aristocracy coinciding with the most pronounced reaction against the people, a phenomenon which has driven more than one popular writer, like Cobbett,[3] to look for popular liberty rather in the past than in the future.

Signed article by Karl Marx.

[1] The *New York Daily Tribune* (*NYDT*) gave an incorrect date line: 'Saturday, June 21' (21 June was a Tuesday). It has been corrected according to Marx's notebook in which the mailing of the article is dated 24 June 1853. See CW, Vol. 12, p. 148 n.
[2] Founded in 1694.
[3] William Cobbett (1762–1835): English radical writer and politician.

The union between the Constitutional Monarchy and the monopolizing moneyed interest, between the Company of East India and the 'glorious' revolution of 1688[4] was fostered by the same force by which the liberal interests and a liberal dynasty have at all times and in all countries met and combined, by the force of corruption, that first and last moving power of Constitutional Monarchy, the guardian angel of William III and the fatal demon of Louis Philippe. So early as 1693, it appeared from Parliamentary inquiries, that the annual expenditure of the East India Company, under the head of 'gifts' to men in power, which had rarely amounted to above £1,200 before the revolution, reached the sum of £90,000. The Duke of Leeds was impeached for a bribe of £5,000, and the virtuous King himself convicted of having received £10,000. Besides these direct briberies, rival Companies were thrown out by tempting Government with loans of enormous sums at the lowest interest, and by buying off rival Directors.

The power the East India Company had obtained by bribing the Government, as did also the Bank of England, it was forced to maintain by bribing again, as did the Bank of England. At every epoch when its monopoly was expiring, it could only effect a renewal of its Charter by offering fresh loans and by fresh presents made to the Government.

The events of the Seven-Years War[5] transformed the East India Company from a commercial into a military and territorial power. It was then that the foundation was laid of the present British Empire in the East. Then East India stock rose to £263, and dividends were then paid at the rate of 12-½ percent. But then there appeared a new enemy to the Company, no longer in the shape of rival societies, but in the shape of rival ministers and of a rival people. It was alleged that the Company's territory had been conquered by the aid of British fleets and British armies, and that no British subjects could hold territorial sovereignties independent of the Crown. The Ministers of the day and the people of the day claimed their share in the 'wonderful treasures' imagined to have been won by the last conquests. The Company only saved its existence by an agreement made in 1767 that it should annually pay £400,000 into the National Exchequer.

But the East India Company, instead of fulfilling its agreement, got into financial difficulties, and, instead of paying a tribute to the English people, appealed to Parliament for pecuniary aid. Serious alterations in the Charter were the consequence of this step. The Company's affairs failing to improve, notwithstanding their new condition, and the English nation having simultaneously lost their colonies in North America, the necessity of elsewhere regaining some great Colonial Empire became more and more universally felt. The illustrious Fox[6]

---

[4] This refers to the events of 1688, which brought William III of Orange to power after overthrowing James II.
[5] It was during the period of the Seven Years War, 1756–63, that the East India Company acquired dominance in Bengal and the Carnatic.
[6] Charles James Fox (1749–1806), the famous Whig statesman, introduced the India Bill as Joint-Secretary of State in Lord North's ministry in 1783. The bill fell along with the ministry in December 1783.

thought the opportune moment had arrived, in 1783, for bringing forward his famous India bill, which proposed to abolish the Courts of Directors and Proprietors, and to vest the whole Indian government in the hands of seven Commissioners appointed by Parliament. By the personal influence of the imbecile King over the House of Lords, the bill of Mr Fox was defeated, and made the instrument of breaking down the then Coalition Government of Fox and Lord North, and of placing the famous Pitt at the head of the Government. Pitt carried in 1784 a bill through both Houses, which directed the establishment of the Board of Control, consisting of six members of the Privy Council, who were 'to check, superintend and control all acts, operations and concerns which in any wise related to the civil and military Government, or revenues of the territories and possessions of the East India Company.'

On this head, Mill, the historian, says:

> In passing that law two objects were pursued. To avoid the imputation of what was represented as the heinous object of Mr Fox's bill, it was necessary that the principal part of the power should appear to remain in the hand of the Directors. For ministerial advantage it was necessary that it should in reality be all taken away. Mr Pitt's bill professed to differ from that of his rival, chiefly in this very point, that while the one destroyed the power of the Directors, the other left it almost entire. Under the act of Mr Fox the powers of the ministers would have been avowedly held. Under the act of Mr Pitt, they were held in secret and by fraud. The bill of Fox transferred the power of the Company to Commissioners appointed by Parliament. The bill of Mr Pitt transferred them to Commissioners appointed by the King.[7]

The years of 1783 and 1784 were thus the first, and till now the only years, for the India question to become a ministerial one. The bill of Mr Pitt having been carried, the charter of the East India Company was renewed, and the Indian question set aside for twenty years. But in 1813 the Anti-Jacobin war,[8] and in 1833 the newly introduced Reform Bill[9] superseded all other political questions.

This, then, is the first reason of the India question's having failed to become a great political question, since and before 1784; that before that time the East India Company had first to conquer existence and importance; that after that time the Oligarchy absorbed all of its power which it could assume without incurring responsibility; and greatly that afterwards the English people in

---

[7] James Mill, *The History of British India*, Vol. V (London, 1840), pp. 88–92. Marx has put together different sentences from Mill's text.

[8] This term, which should have applied only to Britain's war against the Jacobin regime in France (1793–94), is obviously used here for both the Revolutionary and Napoleonic Wars that kept England and France as antagonists from 1792 to 1815.

[9] Allusion to the Reform Act, 1832, which greatly changed the mode of representation to the House of Commons, and greatly extended suffrage.

general were at the very epochs of the renewal of the Charter, in 1813 and 1833, absorbed by other questions of overbearing interest.

We will now take a different view. The East India Company commenced by attempting merely to establish factories for their agents, and places of deposit for their goods. In order to protect them they erected several forts. Although they had, even as early as 1689, conceived the establishment of a dominion in India, and of making territorial revenue one of their sources of emolument, yet, down to 1744, they had acquired but a few unimportant districts around Bombay, Madras, and Calcutta. The war which subsequently broke out in the Carnatic had the effect of rendering them after various struggles, virtual sovereigns of that part of India. Much more considerable results arose from the war in Bengal and the victories of Clive. These results were the real occupation of Bengal, Bihar, and Orissa. At the end of the Eighteenth Century and in the first years of the present one, there supervened the wars with Tippoo Saib [Sahib], and in consequence of them a great advance of power, and an immense extension of the subsidiary system.[10] In the second decennium of the Nineteenth Century the first convenient frontier, that of India within the desert, had at length been conquered. It was not till then that the British Empire in the East reached those parts of Asia, which had been, at all times, the seat of every great central power in India. But the most vulnerable point of the Empire, from which it had been overrun as often as old conquerors were expelled by new ones, the barriers of the Western frontier, were not in the hands of the British. During the period from 1838 to 1849, in the Sikh and Afghan wars, British rule subjected to definitive possession the ethnographical, political, and military frontiers of the East Indian Continent by the compulsory annexation of the Punjab and of Scinde.[11] These were possessions indispensable to repulse any invading force issuing from Central Asia, and indispensable against Russia advancing to the frontiers of Persia. During this last decennium there have been added to the British Indian territory 167,000 square miles, with a population of 8,572,630 souls. As to the interior, all the native States now became surrounded by British possessions, subjected to British *suzerainete* under various forms, and cut off from sea-coast, with the sole exception of Guzerat and Scinde. As to its exterior, India was now finished. It is only since 1849, that the one great Anglo-Indian Empire has existed.

Thus the British Government has been fighting, under the Company's

---

[10] The subsidiary system was established by Lord Wellesley in 1798, when its principles were incorporated in the treaty signed with the Nizam, which was essentially designed against Tipu Sultan, the ruler of Mysore, who was overthrown by the British the next year. Under the subsidiary system, the princely states were brought under the complete subjugation of the East India Company in their foreign affairs; the Indian ruler had to allow the stationing of a 'subsidiary' force of the Company, maintained and kept at the cost of the ruler himself through a 'subsidy' paid by him to the Company.

[11] Punjab was annexed after two wars, in 1845–46 and 1848–49; Sind was annexed in 1843.

name, for two centuries, till at last the natural limits of India were reached. We understand now, why during all this time all parties in England have connived in silence, even those which had resolved to become the loudest with their hypocritical peace-cant, after the *arrondissement*[12] of the one Indian Empire should have been completed. Firstly, of course, they had to get it, in order to subject it afterward to their sharp philanthropy. From this view we understand the altered position of the Indian question in the present year, 1853, compared with all former periods of Charter renewal.

Again, let us take a different view. We shall still better understand the peculiar crisis in Indian legislation, on reviewing the course of British commercial intercourse with India through its different phases.

At the commencement of the East India Company's operations, under the reign of Elizabeth, the Company was permitted for the purpose of profitably carrying on its trade with India, to export an annual value of £30,000 in silver, gold, and foreign coin. This was an infraction against all the prejudices of the age, and Thomas Mun was forced to lay down in *A Discourse of Trade, from England to the East Indies*,[13] the foundation of the 'mercantile system', admitting that the precious metals were the only real wealth a country could possess, but contending at the same time that their exportation might be safely allowed, provided the balance of payments was in favor of the exporting nation.[14] In this sense, he contended that the commodities imported from East India were chiefly re-exported to other countries, from which a much greater quantity of bullion was obtained than had been required to pay for them in India. In the same spirit, Sir Josiah Child[15] wrote *A Treatise Wherein It Is Demonstrated that the East-India Trade is the Most National Trade of All Trades*.[16] By and by the partisans of the East India Company grew more audacious, and it may be noticed as a curiosity, in this strange Indian history, that the Indian monopolists were the first preachers of free trade in England.

Parliamentary intervention, with regard to the East India Company, was again claimed, not by the commercial, but by the industrial class, at the latter end of the 17th century, and during the greater part of the 18th, when the importation of East Indian cotton and silk stuffs was declared to ruin the poor British manufacturers, an opinion put forward in John Pollexfen's *England and India*

---

[12] From the French *arrondir*, 'to make round'.

[13] Thomas Mun (1571–1641): well-known mercantilist; Director of the East India Company, 1615; published *A Discourse of Trade from England unto the East Indies* in 1621.

[14] Here Marx summarizes Mun's arguments based on the assertion that the trade with East Indies was about £480,000 and imports £120,000 per annum, turning the balance of trade in favour of England (that is, £360,000). See, for details, Mun, *Discourse of Trade*, pp. 22–23.

[15] Sir Josiah Child (1630–1699): author of *A New Discourse of Trade*, 1668 (fourth edition, 1693); despotic Chairman of East India Company; retained power by bribing the Court.

[16] 'Trades' omitted in Av.

Inconsistent in Their Manufactures; London, 1697,[17] a title strangely verified a century and a half later, but in a very different sense. Parliament did then interfere. By the Act 11 and 12 William III, cap. 10, it was enacted that the wearing of wrought silks and of printed or dyed calicoes from India, Persia and China should be prohibited, and a penalty of £200 imposed on all persons having or selling the same. Similar laws were enacted under George I, II and III, in consequence of the repeated lamentations of the afterward so 'enlightened' British manufacturers. And thus, during the greater part of the 18th century, Indian manufactures were generally imported into England in order to be sold on the Continent, and to remain excluded from the English market itself.

Besides this Parliamentary interference with East India, solicited by the greedy home manufacturer, efforts were made at every epoch of the renewal of the Charter, by the merchants of London, Liverpool and Bristol, to break down the commercial monopoly of the Company, and to participate in the commerce, estimated to be a true mine of gold. In consequence of these efforts, a provision was made in the Act of 1773 prolonging the Company's Charter till March 1, 1814, by which private British individuals were authorized to export from, and the Company's Indian servants permitted to import into, England almost all sorts of commodities. But this concession was surrounded with conditions annihilating its effects, in respect to the exports to British India by private merchants. In 1813 the Company was unable to further withstand the pressure of general commerce, and except the monopoly of the Chinese trade, the trade to India was opened, under certain conditions, to private competition. At the renewal of the Charter in 1833, these last restrictions were at length superseded, the Company forbidden to carry on any trade at all – their commercial character destroyed, and their privilege of excluding British subjects from the Indian territories withdrawn.

Meanwhile the East Indian trade had undergone very serious revolutions, altogether altering the position of the different class interests in England with regard to it. During the whole course of the 18th century the treasures transported from India to England were gained much less by comparatively insignificant commerce, than by the direct exploitation of that country, and by the colossal fortunes there extorted and transmitted to England. After the opening of the trade in 1813 the commerce with India more than trebled in a very short time. But this was not all. The whole character of the trade was changed. Till 1813 India had been chiefly an exporting country, while it now became an importing one; and in such a quick progression, that already in 1823 the rate of exchange, which had generally been 2/6 per rupee, sunk down to 2/ per rupee.[18]

---

[17] Marx's preparatory materials on India (Notebook XXI) include passages from MacCulloch's *Literature of Political Economy* (London, 1845). The book contains extracts from the works of English economists of an earlier period on British trade with India, among them being the treatises of J. Child, T. Mun and J. Pollexfen. See *CW*, Vol. 12, p. 656 n. 127.

[18] That is, a decline in the value of the rupee from 30d. to 24d. (1s = 12d.).

India, the great workshop of cotton manufacture for the world, since immemorial times, became now inundated with English twists and cotton stuffs. After its own produce had been excluded from England, or only admitted on the most cruel terms, British manufactures were poured into it at a small and merely nominal duty, to the ruin of the native cotton fabrics once so celebrated. In 1780 the value of British produce and manufactures amounted only to £386,152, the bullion exported during the same year to £15,041, the total value of exports during 1780 being £12,648,616, so that the Indian trade amounted to only 1/32[19] of the entire foreign trade. In 1850 the total exports to India from Great Britain and Ireland were £8,024,000 of which cotton goods alone amounted to £5,220,000, so that it reached more than 1/8 of whole export, and more than 1/4 of the foreign cotton trade. But, the cotton manufacture also employed now 1/8 of the population of Britain, and contributed 1/12[20] of the whole national revenue. After each commercial crisis the East Indian trade grew of more paramount importance for the British cotton manufacturers, and the East Indian continent became actually their best market. At the same rate at which the cotton manufactures became of vital interest for the whole social frame of Great Britain, East India became of vital interest for the British cotton manufacture.

Till then the interests of the moneyocracy which had converted India into its landed estates, of the oligarchy who had conquered it by their armies, and of the millocracy who had inundated it with their fabrics, had gone hand in hand. But the more the industrial interest became dependent on the Indian market, the more it felt the necessity of creating fresh productive powers in India, after having ruined her native industry. You cannot continue to inundate a country with your manufactures, unless you enable it to give you some produce in return. The industrial interest found that their trade declined instead of increasing. For the four years ending with 1846, the imports to India form Great Britain were to the amount of 261 million rupees; for the four years ending 1850 they were only 253 millions, while the exports for the former period, 274 millions of rupees, and for the latter period, 254 millions. They found out that the power of consuming their goods was contracted in India to the lowest possible point, that the consumption of their manufactures by the British West Indies, was of the value of about 14s. per head of the population per annum, by Chile, of 9s. 3d., by Brazil, of 6s. 5d., by Cuba, of 6s. 2d., by Peru, of 5s. 7d., by Central America, of 10d., while it amounted in India only to about 9d. Then came the short cotton crop in the United States, which caused them a loss of £11,000,000 in 1850, and they were exasperated at depending on America, instead of deriving a sufficiency of raw cotton from the East Indies. Besides, they found that in all attempts to apply capital to India they met with impediments and chicanery on the part of the Indian authorities. Thus India became the battle-field in the contest of the industrial interest on the one side, and of the moneyocracy and oligarchy on the

---

[19] In *NYDT* this is misprinted as '1.32'.
[20] Misprinted in the original as '1.12'.

other. The manufacturers, conscious of their ascendancy in England, ask now for the annihilation of these antagonistic powers in India, for the destruction of the whole ancient fabric of Indian government, and for the final eclipse of the East India Company.

And now to the fourth and last point of view, from which the Indian question must be judged. Since 1784 Indian finances have got more and more deeply into difficulty. There exists now a national debt of 50 million pounds, a continual decrease in the resources of the revenue, and a corresponding increase in the[21] expenditure, dubiously balanced by the gambling income of the opium tax, now threatened with extinction by the Chinese beginning themselves to cultivate the poppy, and aggravated by the expenses to be anticipated from the senseless Burmese war.[22] 'As the case stands,' says Mr Dickinson, 'as it would ruin England to lose her Empire in India, it is stretching our own finances with ruin, to be obliged to keep it.'[23]

I have shown thus, how the Indian question has become for the first time since 1783, an English question, and a ministerial question.

[21] The words 'resources of the revenue, and a corresponding increase in the' are omitted in Av.
[22] Reference to the Second Burma War (1852).
[23] Here Marx has summarized Dickinson's text (*India Reform*, London, 1853, p. 50), which reads in part as follows: '. . . for as the case stands, although it would ruin England to lose her empire in India, it is threatening our own finances with ruin to be obliged to keep it.'

The Indian Question

(*New York Daily Tribune*, July 11, 1853)
London, June 28, 1853

The debate on Lord Stanley's motion with respect to India commenced on the 23rd continued on the 24th, and adjourned to the 27th inst., has not been brought to a close. When that shall at length have arrived, I intend to resume my observations on the India question.

The Government of India

(*New York Daily Tribune*, July 20, 1853)
London, Tuesday, July 5, 1853

The House of Commons, in order to do justice to the colossal dimensions of the subject, has been spinning out its Indian debate to an unusual length and breadth, although that debate has failed altogether in depth and greatness of interest. The division leaving Ministers a majority of 322 against 142, is in inverse ratio to the discussion. During the discussion all was thistles for the Ministry, and Sir Charles Wood was the ass officially put to the task of feeding upon them. In the division all is roses, and Sir Charles Wood receives the crown of another Menu.[1] The same men who negatived the plan of the Ministry by their arguments, affirmed it by their votes. None of its supporters dared to apologize for the bill itself: on the contrary, all apologized for their supporting the bill, the one because it was an infinitesimal part of a measure in the right direction, the others because it was no measure at all. The former pretend that they will now mend it in Committee; the latter say that they will strip it of all the fancy Reform flowers it parades in. The Ministry maintained the field by more than one half of the Tory opposition running away, and a great portion of the remainder deserting with Herrico[2] and Inglis[3] into the Aberdeen camp,[4] while of the 142 opposite votes 100 belonged to the Disraeli fraction, and 42 to the Manchester School, backed by some Irish discontents and some inexpressibles. The opposition within the opposition has once more saved the Ministry.

Mr Halliday[5] one of the officials of the East India Company, when examined before a Committee of Inquiry, stated: 'That the Charter giving a twenty years' lease to the East India Company was considered by the natives of India as farming them out.'[6] This time, at least, the Charter has not been renewed for a

---

From 'The Turkish War Question – The *New York Tribune* in the House of Commons – The Government of India'. Signed: Karl Marx. The first paragraph is omitted in Av.

[1] Manu.
[2] Apparently a misprint for 'Herries'. John Charles Herries (1778–1855) was President of Board of Control in Derby's short-lived administration in 1852.
[3] Sir Robert Harry Inglis (1786–1855): British politician, Tory MP.
[4] George Hamilton Gordon, fourth Earl of Aberdeen (1784–1860), was Prime Minister, 1852–55, after having formed a coalition of Whigs and Peelites.
[5] Frederick James Halliday: in the service of the East India Company, 1825–52; Secretary to Government of India, 1848–52. See his own evidence before *Select Committee on Indian Territories*, 1853, pp. 106–07 (10 March 1853).
[6] *Parliamentary Papers*, 1852–53, Vol. 14, pp. 9, 17.

definite period, but is revokable at will by Parliament. The Company, therefore, will come down from the respectable situation of hereditary farmers, to the precarious conditions of tenants-at-will. This is so much gain for the natives. The Coalition Ministry has succeeded in transforming the Indian Government, like all other questions, into an open question. The House of Commons, on the other hand, has given itself a new testimonial of poverty, in confessing by the same division, its impotency for legislating, and its unwillingness to delay legislating.

Since the days of Aristotle the world has been inundated with a frightful quantity of dissertations, ingenious or absurd, as it might happen, on that question – Who shall be the governing power? But for the first time in the annals of history, the senate of a people ruling over another people numbering 156 millions of human beings and spreading over a surface of 1,368,113 sq. miles, have put their heads together in solemn and public congregations, in order to answer the irregular question – Who among us is the actual governing power over the foreign people of 150 millions of souls? There was no Oedipus[7] in the British senate capable of extricating this riddle. The whole debate exclusively twined[8] around it, as although a division took place, no definition of the Indian Government was arrived at.

That there is in India a permanent financial deficit, a regular over-supply of wars, and no supply at all of public works, an abominable system of taxation, and a no less abominable state of justice and law, that these five items constitute, as it were, the five points of the East India Charter, was settled beyond all doubt in the debates of 1853, as it had been[9] in the debates of 1833, and in the debates of 1813, as in all former debates of India. The only thing never found out was the party responsible for all this.

There exists, unquestionably, a Governor-General of India, holding the supreme power, but that Governor is governed in his turn by a home government. Who is that home government? Is it the Indian Minister, disguised under the modest title of President of the Board of Control, or is it the twenty-four Directors of the East India Company? On the threshold of the Indian religion, we find a divine trinity, and thus we find a profane trinity on the threshold of the Indian government.

Leaving, for the while, the Governor-General altogether on one side, the question at issue[10] resolves itself into that of the double Government, in which form it is familiar to the English mind. The Ministers in their bill and the House in its division, cling to this dualism.

When the Company of English merchant adventurers, who conquered India to make money out of it, began to enlarge their factories into an Empire, when their competition with the Dutch and French private merchants assumed

---

[7] The king of Thebes, who solved the riddle set by Sphinx, a monster who killed all who could not solve it.

[8] 'turned' in Av.

[9] 'as it had been' omitted in Av.

[10] 'at once' in Av.

the character of national rivalry, then, of course, the British Government commenced meddling with the affairs of the East India Company, and the double
Government of India sprang up, in fact if not in name. Pitt's Act of 1784, by
entering into a compromise with the company, by subjecting it to the superintendence of the Board of Control and by making the Board of Control an append-
age to the Ministry, accepted, regulated, and settled that double Government,
arisen from circumstances, in name as well as fact.

The Act of 1833 strengthened the Board of Control, changed the proprietors of the East India Company into mere mortgagees of the East India revenues,
ordered the Company to sell off its stock, dissolved its commercial existence,
transformed it as far as it existed politically, into a mere trustee of the Crown,
and did thus with the East India Company what the Company had been in the
habit of doing with the East India Princes. After having superseded them, it
continued for a while still to govern in their name. So far, the East India Company has, since 1833, no longer existed but in name and on sufferance. While,
thus, on the one hand, there seems to be no difficulty in getting rid of the Company altogether, it is on the other hand, very indifferent whether the English
nation rules over India under the personal name of Queen Victoria, or under the
traditional form of an anonymous society. The whole question, therefore,
appears to turn about a technicality of very questionable importance. Still, the
thing is not quite so plain.

It is to be remarked, in the first instance, that the Ministerial Board of
Control, residing in Cannon row [Row], is as much a fiction as the East India
Company, supposed to reside in Leadenhall Street. The members composing the
Board of Control are a mere cloak for the supreme rule[11] of the President of the
Board. The President is himself but a subordinate though independent member of
the Imperial Ministry. In India it seems to be assumed that if a man is fit for
nothing it is best to make him a judge, and get rid of him. In Great Britain, when
a party comes into office and finds itself encumbered with a tenth rate 'statesman', it is considered best to make him President of the Board of Control, successor of the Great Mogul, and in that way to get rid of him – *teste Carolo Wood*.[12]

The letter of the law entrusts the Board of Control, which is but another
name for its President, with 'full power and authority to superintend, direct, and
control all acts, operations, and concerns, of the East India Company which in
any wise relate to or concern the Government or revenues of the Indian[13] Territories'. Directors are prohibited 'from issuing any orders, instructions, dispatches,
official letters, or communications whatever relating to India, or to the Government thereof, until the same shall have been sanctioned by the Board'.[14] Directors are ordered to 'prepare instructions, or orders upon any subject whatever at

---

[11] 'role' in Av.
[12] 'witness Charles Wood'.
[13] 'East Indian' in Av.
[14] Dickinson, *India Reform*, p. 8.

fourteen days' notice from the Board, or else to transmit the orders of the Board on the subject of India'.[15] The Board is authorized to inspect all correspondence and dispatches to and from India, and the proceedings of the Courts of Proprietors and Directors. Lastly, the Court of Directors has to appoint a Secret Committee, consisting of their Chairman, their Deputy Chairman, and their senior member, who are sworn to secrecy, and through whom, in all political and military matters, the President of the Board may transmit his personal orders to India, while the Committee acts as a mere channel of his communications. The orders respecting the Afghan and Burmese Wars, and as to the occupation of Scinde were transmitted through this Secret Committee, without the Court of Directors being any more informed of them than the general public or Parliament. So far, therefore, the President of the Board of Control[16] would appear to be real Mogul, and, under all circumstances, he retains an unlimited power for doing mischief, as, for instance, for causing the most ruinous wars, all the while being hidden under the name of the irresponsible[17] Court of Directors. On the other hand, the Court of Directors is not without real power. As they generally exercise the initiative in administrative measures, as they form, when compared with the Board of Control, a more permanent and steady body, with traditional rules for action and a certain knowledge of details, the whole of the ordinary internal administration necessarily falls to their share. They appoint, too, under sanction of the Crown the Supreme Government of India, the Governor-General and his Councils; possessing, besides, the unrestricted power to recall the highest servants and even the Governor-General, as they did under Sir Robert Peel, with Lord Ellenborough.[18] But this is still not their most important privilege. Receiving only £300 per annum, they are really paid in patronage,[19] distributing all the writerships and cadetships, from whose number the Governor-General of India and the Provincial Governors are obliged to fill up all the higher places withheld from the natives. When the number of appointments for the year is ascertained, the whole are divided into 28 equal parts – of which two are allotted to the Chairman, and Deputy Chairman, two to the President of the Board of Control, and one to each of the Directors. The annual value of each share of patronage seldom falls short of 14,000.[20] 'All nominations', says Mr Campbell, 'are now, as it were, the private property of individuals being divided among the Directors, and each disposing of his share as he thinks fit.'[21] Now it is evident that the spirit of the Court of Directors must pervade the whole of Indian Upper Administration, trained as it is, at schools of Addiscombe and Haileybury and appointed, as it is, by their

[15] Ibid.

[16] 'Board of Trade' in Av., which is factually wrong as well.

[17] 'irresponsible' omitted in Av.

[18] Edward Law, first Earl of Ellenborough (1790–1871).

[19] Marx here seems to have in mind Dickinson, who says that the Directors' 'salaries are only 300 £ a year, because they are paid in patronage' (*India Reform*, pp. 17–18).

[20] Marx here paraphrases Dickinson, ibid., pp. 18–19.

[21] Campbell, *Modern India* (first published, London, 1852; London, 1892), pp. 263–64.

patronage. It is no less evident that this Court of Directors who have to distribute, year after year, appointments of the value of nearly £400,000 among the upper classes of Great Britain,[22] will find little or no check from the public opinion directed by those very classes. What the spirit of the Court of Directors is, I will show in a following letter on the actual state of India. For the present it may suffice to say that Mr Macaulay, in the course of the pending debates, defended the Court by the particular plea, that it was impotent to effect all the evils it might intend, so much so, that all improvements had been effected in opposition to it, and against it by individual Governors who acted on their own responsibility. Thus with regard to the suspension of Suttee, the abolition of the abominable transit duties, and the emancipation of the East India press.

The President of the Board of Control accordingly involves India in ruinous wars under the cover of the Court of Directors, while the Court of Directors corrupt the Indian administration under the cloak of the Board of Control.

On looking deeper into the framework of this anomalous government, we find at its bottom a third power, more supreme than either the Board or the Court, more irresponsible and more concealed from and guarded against the superintendence of public opinion. The transient President of the Board depends on the permanent clerks of his establishment in Cannon Row, and for those clerks, India exists not in India but in Leadenhall Street.[23] Now, who is the master at Leadenhall Street?

Two thousand persons, elderly ladies and valetudinarian gentlemen possessing Indian stock, having no other interest in India except to be paid their dividends out of Indian revenue, elect twenty-four Directors, whose only qualification is the holding of £1,000 stock. Merchants, bankers, and directors of companies incur great trouble in order to get into the Court for the interest of their private concerns. 'A banker', said Mr Bright, 'in the City of London commands 300 votes of the East India Company, whose word for the election of Directors is almost absolute law'. Hence the Court of Directors is nothing but a succursal[24] to the English moneyocracy. The so-called court forms in its turn, besides the above mentioned Secret Committee, three other Committees which are: (1) Political and Military; (2) Finance and Home; (3) Revenue, Judicial, and Legislative. These committees are every year appointed by rotation, so that a financier is one year on the Judicial and the next year of the Military Committee, and no one has any chance of a continued supervision over any particular department. The mode of election having brought in men utterly unfit for their duties, the system of rotation gives to whatever fitness they might perchance retain, the final blow. Who, then, govern in fact under the name of the Direction?[25] A large staff of irrespon-

---

[22] See Dickinson, *India Reform*, p. 19.
[23] A street in London where the East India Company had its seat, in a building known as the East India House or India House.
[24] 'Subsidiary establishment' (*OED*).
[25] So printed in the *NYDT*.

sible secretaries, examiners, and clerks at the India House, of whom, as Mr Campbell observes, in his *Scheme for the Government of India*, only one individual has ever been in India, and he only by accident. Apart from the trade in patronages, it is therefore a mere fiction to speak of the politics, the principles, and the system of the Court of Directors. The real Court of Directors, and the real Home Government & c., of India are really the permanent and irresponsible *bureaucracy*, 'the creatures of the desk and the creatures of favor' residing in Leadenhall Street. We have thus a Corporation ruling over an immense Empire, not formed, as in Venice, by eminent Patricians, but by old, obstinate clerks and the like odd fellows.

No wonder, then, that there exists no government by which so much is written and so little is done, as the Government of India. When the East India Company was only a commercial association, they, of course, requested a most detailed report on every item from the managers of their East India factories, as is done by every trading concern. When the factories grew into an Empire, the commercial items into shiploads of correspondence and documents, the Leadenhall clerks went on in their system, which made the Directors and the Board their dependents, and they succeeded in transforming the Indian Government into one[26] immense writing machine. Lord Broughton[27] stated in his evidence before the Official Salaries Committee, that with one single dispatch 45,000 pages of collection were sent.

In order to give you some idea of the time-killing manner in which business is transacted at the India House, I will quote from Mr Dickinson:[28]

> When a dispatch arrives from India, it is referred, in the first instance, to the Examiner's Department, to which it belongs, after which the chairs confer with the official in charge of that department, and settle with him the tenor of a reply, and transmit a draught of this reply to the Indian Minister,[29] in what is technically called 'P.C.' , i.e. 'previous communication'.[30] The chairs, in this preliminary state of P.C., depend mainly on the clerks.[31] Such is this dependence that even in a discussion in the Court of Proprietors, after previous notice, it is pitiable to see the Chairman referring to a Secretary who sits by his side, and keeps on whispering and prompting and chaffing[32] him as if he were a mere

---

[26] 'an' in Av.

[27] John Cam Hobhouse, Baron Broughton de Geyfford (1786–1869): statesman; President of the Board of Control, 1835–41 and 1846–52.

[28] The quoted passage occurs in Dickinson, *India Reform*, pp. 15–16.

[29] That is, the President of Board of Control, who was also a member of the British ministry.

[30] There is a gap in the quotation. The words omitted are: 'Now it is evident that, partly from the annual rotation in the function of the Directors, and every fourth-year in the men themselves, and principally from the mass of the business, the Chairs must, in the preliminary stage of P.C.'

[31] An omission occurs here: 'who are permanently in office, for information, advice, and assistance. Nay. . .'.

[32] In Dickinson's text: 'stopping'.

puppet; and the Minister at the other end of the system is in the same predicament. In this stage of P.C., if there is a difference of opinion on the draught it is discussed, and almost invariably settled in friendly communication between the Minister and the Chair; finally the draught is returned by the Minister, either adopted or altered; and then it is submitted to the Committee of Directors superintending the Department to which it belongs, with all papers bearing on the case, to be considered, and discussed and adopted or altered, and afterwards it is exposed to the same process in the aggregate Court, and then goes for the first time, as an official communication, to the Minister after which[33] it undergoes the same process in the opposite direction.

'When a measure is discussed in India', says Mr Campbell, 'the announcement that it has been referred to the Court of Directors, is regarded as an indefinite postponement.'[34]

The close and abject spirit of this bureaucracy deserves to be stigmatized in the celebrated words of Burke:[35]

This tribe of vulgar politicians are the lowest of our species. There is no trade so vile and mechanical as Government in their hands. Virtue is not their habit. They are out of themselves in any course of conduct recommended only by conscience and glory. A large, liberal and prospective view of the interests of States passes with them for romance, and the principles that recommend it, for the wanderings of a disordered imagination. The calculators compute them out of their senses. The jesters and buffoons shame them out of everything grand and elevated. Littleness is the object and in means to them appears soundness and sobriety.

The clerical establishments of Leadenhall Street and Cannon Row cost the Indian people the trifle of £160,000 annually.[36] The oligarchy involves India in wars, in order to find employment for their younger sons: the moneyocracy consigns it to the highest bidder; and a subordinate Bureaucracy paralyse its administration and perpetuate its abuses as the vital condition of their own perpetuation.

Sir Charles Wood's bill alters nothing in the existing system. It enlarges the power of the Ministry without adding to its responsibilities.

---

[33] The words 'after which' are not in Dickinson and are apparently added by Marx.
[34] Campbell, *Modern India*, p. 215.
[35] Edmund Burke (1729–1797), orator and statesman, critic of Warren Hastings, the first Governor-General.
[36] This figure is apparently taken from Dickinson, *India Reform*, p. 15.

The East India Question

(*New York Daily Tribune*, July 25, 1853)
London, Tuesday, July 12, 1853

The clauses of the India Bill are passing one by one, the debate scarcely offering any remarkable features,[1] except the inconsistency of the so-called India Reformers. There is, for instance, my Lord Jocelyn, MP,[2] who has made a kind of political livelihood by his periodical denunciation of Indian wrongs, and of the mal-administration of the East India Company. What do you think his amendment amounted to? To give the East India Company a lease for 10 years. Happily, it compromised no one but himself. There is another professional 'Reformer' Mr Jos. Hume,[3] who, during his long Parliamentary life, had succeeded in transforming opposition itself into a particular manner of supporting the ministry. He proposed not to reduce the number of East India Directors from 24 to 18. The only amendment of common sense, yet agreed to, was that of Mr Bright,[4] exempting Directors nominated by the Government from the qualification in East India Stock, imposed by the Directors elected by the Court of Proprietors. Go through the pamphlets published by the East Indian Reform Association,[5] and you will feel a similar sensation as when, hearing of one great act of accusation against Bonaparte, devised in common by Legitimists, Orleanists, Blue and Red Republicans, and even disappointed Bonapartists. Their only merit until now has been to draw public attention to Indian affairs in general, and further they cannot go in their present form of eclectic opposition. For instance, while they attack the

---

From 'The Russo-Turkish Difficulty – Ducking and Dodging of the British Cabinet – Nesselrode's last Note – The East India Question'. Signed: Karl Marx. This article appears under the title 'The Native States' in Av.

[1] The debate in the House of Commons took place on 8 July 1853. See CW, Vol. 12, p. 196 n.

[2] Robert Jocelyn (1788–1870), third Earl of Roden (an Irish earldom): MP from Dundalk, 1810–20; made British peer (Baron Clanbrassil) in 1821, and thereafter member of the House of Lords.

[3] Joseph Hume (1777–1855): radical politician; MP from Aberdeen, 1818–30, Middlesex, 1830–37, Kilkenny, 1837–41 and Montrose, 1842–55.

[4] John Bright (1811–1889): famous Radical and Free Trader; MP for Durham, 1843; Manchester, 1847, 1852; Chairman of the Select Committee to enquire into obstacles to cultivation of cotton in India; recommended that Government of India should be made a Department of the British government, 1853.

[5] The 'East India Reform Association' was founded by the Free Trader John Dickinson in March 1853.

doings of the English aristocracy in India, they protest against the destruction of the Indian aristocracy of native princes.

After the British intruders had once put their feet on India, and made up their mind to hold it, there remained no alternative but to break the power of the native princes by force or by intrigue. Placed with regard to them in similar circumstances as the ancient Romans with regard to their allies, they followed in the track of Roman politics. 'It was', says an English writer, 'a system of fattening allies as we fatten oxen, till they were worthy of being devoured'. After having won over their[6] allies in the way of ancient Rome, the East India Company executed them in the modern manner of Change-Alley.[7] In order to discharge the engagements they had entered into with the Company, the native princes were forced to borrow enormous sums from Englishmen at usurious interest.[8] When their embarrassment had reached the highest pitch, the creditor got inexorable, 'the screw was turned' and the princes were compelled either to concede their territories amicably to the Company, or to begin war; to become pensioners on their usurpers in one case, or to be deposed as traitors in the other. At this moment the native states occupy an area of 699,961 square miles – with a population of 52,941,263 souls, being, however, no longer the allies,[9] but only the dependents of the British Government upon multifarious conditions, and under the various forms of the subsidiary and of the protective systems. These systems have in common the relinquishment, by the native States of the right of self-defence, of maintaining diplomatic relations, and of settling the disputes among themselves without the interference of the Governor-General. All of them have to pay a tribute, either in hard cash, or in a contingent of armed forces commanded by British officers. The final absorption or annexation of these native States is at present eagerly controverted between the reformers who denounce it as a crime and the men of business who excuse it as a necessity.

In my opinion the question itself is altogether improperly put. As to the native *States*, they virtually ceased to exist from the moment they became subsidiary to or protected by the Company. If you divide the revenue of a country between two governments, you are sure to cripple the resources of the one and the administration of both. Under the present system the native States succumb under the double incubus of their native Administration and the tributes and inordinate military establishments imposed upon them by the Company. The conditions under which they are allowed to retain their apparent independence are at the same time, the conditions of a permanent decay, and of an utter inability of improvement. Organic weakness is the constitutional law of their existence, as of all existence living upon sufferance. It is, therefore, not the native

---

[6] 'their' omitted in Av.

[7] A narrow street in London, scene of the gambling in South Sea and other stocks (*OED*).

[8] Marx might have had in mind here the scandal of the Carnatic Debts, on which see R.C. Dutt, *Economic History of India*, Vol. I (London, 1906), pp. 64–72.

[9] 'the' omitted in Av.

States, but the native *Princes* and *Courts* about whose maintenance the question revolves. Now, is it not a strange thing that the same men who denounce 'the barbarous splendours of the Crown and Aristocracy of England' are shedding tears at the downfall of Indian Nabobs, Rajahs and Jagheerdars, the great majority of whom possess not even the prestige of antiquity, being generally usurpers of very recent date, set up by the English intrigue! There exists in the whole world no despotism more ridiculous, absurd and childish than that of those *Schazenans* and *Schariars* of the *Arabian Nights.* The Duke of Wellington, Sir J. Malcolm,[10] Sir Henry Russell, Lord Ellenborough, General Briggs,[11] and other authorities have pronounced in favor of the *status quo* but on what grounds? Because the native troops under English rule want employment in the petty warfares with their own countrymen, in order to prevent them from turning their strength against their own European masters. Because the existence of independent States gives occasional employment to the English troops. Because the hereditary princes are the most servile tools of English despotism, and check the rise of those bold military adventurers with whom India has and ever will abound. Because the independent territories afford a refuge to all discontented and enterprising native spirits. Leaving aside all these arguments, which state in so many words that the native princes are the strongholds of the present abominable English system and the greatest obstacles to Indian progress, I come to Sir Thomas Munro[12] and Lord Elphinstone,[13] who were at least men of superior genius and of real sympathy for the Indian people. They think that without a native aristocracy there can be no energy in any other class of the community, and that the subversion of that aristocracy will not raise but debase a whole people. They may be right as long as the natives, under direct English rule, are systematically excluded from all superior offices, military and civil. Where there can be no great men by their own exertion, there must be great men by birth, to leave to a conquered people some greatness of their own. That exclusion, however, of the native people from the English territory, has been effected only by the maintenance of the hereditary

[10] Sir John Malcolm (1769–1833): British administrator in India and diplomat; appointed Persian interpreter to the Nizam of Deccan in 1792; Private Secretary to Wellesley, 1801–02; published his political *History of India* in 1818; Governor of Bombay, 1826–30; published *Memoirs of Central India* in 1824, and *Administration of India* in 1833.

[11] General John Briggs (1785–1875): British officer in India; served in Maratha wars, became Agent of Satara; Senior Commissioner of Government of Mysore in 1831; left India in 1835; Major General in 1838; member of Court of Proprietors of East India Company; translated Farishta's *History of India.*

[12] Sir Thomas Munro (1761–1827): Governor of Madras, 1819–27; served against Hyder Ali, 1780–84; assisted in forming the civil administration of the Barahmahal, 1792–93; introduced *ryotwari* system of land tenure in the ceded districts south of Tungabhadra in 1800.

[13] Mountstuart Elphinstone (1779–1859): appointed to the Bengal Civil Services in 1796; escaped from Wazir Ali's massacre of Europeans in 1798; Resident of Poona, 1810–16; Governor of Bombay, 1819–27; prepared code of Bombay Presidency; author of *History of India* and *The Rise of British Power in the East.*

princes in the so-called independent territories. And one of these two concessions had to be made to the native army, on whose strength all British rule in India depends. I think we may trust the assertion of Mr Campbell,[14] that the native Indian Aristocracy are the least enabled to fill higher offices; that for all fresh requirements it is necessary to create a fresh class, and that 'from the acuteness and aptness to learn of the inferior classes, this can be done in India as it can be done in no other country'.[15]

The native princes themselves are fast disappearing by the extinction of their houses; but, since the commencement of this century, the British Government has observed the policy of allowing them to make *heirs by adoption*, or of filling up their vacant seats with puppets of English creation. The great Governor-General, Lord Dalhousie, was the first to protest against this system. Were not the natural course of things artificially resisted, there would be wanted neither wars nor expenses to do away with the native princes.

As to the *pensioned princes,* the £2,468,969 assigned to them by the British Government on the Indian revenue is a most heavy charge upon a people living on rice, and deprived of the first necessaries of life. If they are good for any thing, it is for exhibiting Royalty in its lowest stage of degradation and ridicule. Take, for instance, the Great Mogul, the descendant of Timour Tamerlane. He is allowed £120,000 a year. His authority does not extend beyond the walls of his palace, within which the royal idiotic race, left to itself, propagates as freely as rabbits. Even the police of Delhi is held by Englishmen above his control. There he sits on his throne, a little shriveled yellow old man, trimmed in a theatrical dress, embroidered with gold, much like that of the dancing girls of Hindostan. On certain State occasions, the tinsel-covered puppet issues forth to gladden the hearts of the loyal. On his days of reception strangers have to pay a fee, in the form of guineas, as to any other *saltimbanque*[16] exhibiting himself in public: while he, in his turn, presents them with turbans, diamonds, etc. On looking nearer at them, they find that the royal diamonds are like so many pieces of ordinary glass, grossly painted and imitating as roughly as possible the precious stones, and jointed so wretchedly, that they break in the hand like gingerbread.

The English money-lenders, combined with English Aristocracy, understand, we must own, the art of degrading Royalty, reducing it to the nullity of constitutionalism at home, and to the skeleton[17] of etiquette abroad. And now, here are the Radicals, exasperated at this spectacle.

---

[14] Sir George Campbell (1824–1892): Indian administrator; Collector at Badaun in 1843; Magistrate and Collector of Azamgarh in 1854; served in Indian Mutiny; wrote official account of the Mutiny of 1857 for the home authorities; headed Famine Commission in 1866; wrote several books including *Ethnology of India,* 1856.

[15] Campbell, *Modern India*, p. 64.

[16] Italian for mountebank, quack (*OED*).

[17] The *NYDT* has 'seclusion', while Marx had written 'skeleton'. See his letter to Adolf Cluss, 18 October 1853 (*CW*, Vol. 39, p. 390).

War in Burma

(*New York Daily Tribune*, July 30, 1853)
London, Friday, July 15, 1853

By the latest overland mail from India, intelligence has been received that the Burmese ambassadors have rejected the treaty proposed by General Godwin. The General afforded them 24 hours more for reflection, but the Burmese departed within 10 hours. A third edition of the interminable Burmese war appears to be inevitable.[1]

Of all the warlike expeditions of the British in the East, none have ever been undertaken on less warranted grounds than those against Burma. There was no possible danger of invasion from that side, as there was from the North-West, Bengal being separated from Burma by a range of mountains, across which troops cannot be marched. To go to war with Burma the Indian Government is obliged to go to sea. To speak of maritime aggressions on the part of the Burmese is as ridiculous, as the idea of their coast-junks fronting the Company's war steamers would be preposterous. The pretension that the Yankees had strong annexation propensities applied to Pegu, is borne out by no facts. No argument, therefore, remains behind, but the want of employment for a needy aristocracy, the necessity of creating, as an English writer says, 'a regular quality-workhouse, or Hampton Court in the East.'[2] The first Burmese war (1824–26), entered into under the Quixotic administration of Lord Amherst,[3] although it lasted little more than two years, added thirteen millions to the Indian debt. The maintenance of the Eastern settlements at Singapore, Penang and Malacca, exclusive of the pay of troops, causes an annual excess of expenditure over income amounting to £100,000. The territory taken from the Burmese in 1826 costs as much more. The territory of Pegu is still more ruinous. Now, why is it that England shrinks from the most necessary war in Europe, as now against Russia, while she tumbles, year after year, into the most reckless wars in Asia? The national debt has made her a trembler in Europe – the charges of the Asiatic wars are thrown

From 'War in Burma – The Russian Question – Curious Diplomatic Correspondence'.
Signed: Karl Marx.

[1] There had previously been the Burmese War of 1824–26, while the present one began in 1852. The English, satisfied with the acquisition of Pegu, did not push further into the country and so the third war expected by Marx did not take place until 1885–86, when the remaining part of Burma was finally annexed.

[2] 'Workhouse': where needy or unemployed persons were put to work. 'Hampton Court': royal palace many of whose rooms came to be occupied by royal pensioners.

[3] Governor-General of India, 1823–28.

on the shoulders of the Hindoos. But we may expect from the now impending extinction of the Opium revenue of Bengal, combined with the expenses of another Burmese war, that they will produce such a crisis in the Indian exchequer, as will cause a more thorough reform of the Indian Empire than all the speeches and tracts of the Parliamentary Reformers in England.

. . .[4]

In the subsequent Indian debate [yesterday] Mr Bright moved, that from the ninth clause which provides, 'that six of the directors not elected by the Crown, shall be persons who have been ten years in India in the service of the Crown or the Company', the words, 'in the service of the Crown or the Company', should be expunged. The amendment was agreed to. It is significant, that during the whole Indian debate no amendments are agreed to by the Ministry, and consequently carried by the House, except those of Mr Bright. The Peace Ministry, at this moment does everything to secure its *entente cordiale* with the Peace party, Manchester School,[5] who are opposed to any kind of warfare, except by cotton bales and price currents.

---

[4] A paragraph relating to Anglo-Russian relations occurs here.
[5] The school of 'radical' economists and politicians, headed by Richard Cobden and John Bright, who had their major supporters among the manufacturers of Manchester, and pursued the cause of Free Trade.

India

(*New York Daily Tribune*, August 5, 1853)
London, Tuesday, July 19, 1853

The progress of the India bill through the Committee has little interest. It is significant, that all amendments are thrown out now by the Coalition coalescing with the Tories against their own allies of the Manchester School.

The actual state of India may be illustrated by a few facts. The Home Establishment absorbs 3 per cent of the net revenue, and the annual interest for Home Debt and Dividends 14 per cent – together 17 per cent. If we deduct these actual remittances from India to England, the *military charges* amount to about two-thirds of the whole expenditure available for India, or to 66 per cent,[1] while the charges for *Public Works* do not amount to more than 2-¾ per cent[2] of the general revenue, or for Bengal 1 per cent, Agra 7-¾, Punjab ¹/₈, Madras ½, and Bombay 1 per cent of their respective revenues. These figures are the official ones of the Company itself.[3]

On the other hand nearly three-fifths of the whole net revenue are derived from the land, about one–seventh from *opium,* and upward of one–ninth from *salt.* These resources together yield 85 per cent of the whole receipts.

As to minor items of expenditure and charges, it may suffice to state that the *Moturpha*[4] revenue maintained in the Presidency of Madras, and levied on shops, looms, sheep, cattle, sundry profession, & c., yields somewhat about £50,000 while the yearly dinners of the East India House[5] cost about the same sum.

The great bulk of the revenue is derived from the land. As the various kinds of Indian land–tenure have recently been described in so many places, and in popular style, too, I propose to limit my observations on the subject to a few general remarks on the Zamindaree and Ryotwar systems.

The Zamindaree and the Ryotwar were both of them agrarian revolutions, effected by British ukases; and opposed to each other, the one aristocratic,

From 'The War Question – (with Russia), Doings of Parliament – India'. Signed: Karl Marx.

[1] So printed in the *New York Daily Tribune* (*NYDT*); in Av. misprinted as 60 per cent; Campbell, *Modern India,* p. 422, has 56 per cent.

[2] In Campbell, *Modern India,* 2-¼ per cent.

[3] Marx seems to have derived his information mainly from ibid., pp. 420–25, 427, but, as we have noted, some figures vary.

[4] From Persian *muhtarifa.* See Wilson, *Glossary,* pp. 350–51. Also see Campbell, *Modern India,* p. 396.

[5] Headquarters of the Court of Directors of the East India Company in Leadenhall Street, London.

the other democratic; the one a caricature of English landlordism, the other of French peasant proprietorship; but pernicious, both combining the most contradictory character – both made not for the people, who cultivate the soil, nor for the holder, who owns it, but for the Government that taxes it.

By the Zemindaree system, the people of the Presidency of Bengal were depossessed at once of their hereditary claims to the soil in favor of the native tax gatherers called *Zemindars*. By the Ryotwar system introduced into the Presidencies of Madras and Bombay, the native nobility, with their territorial claims, merassees,[6] jagheers, & c., were reduced with the common people to the holding of minute fields, cultivated by themselves in favor of the Collector of the East India Company. But a curious sort of English landlord was the Zemindar, receiving only one–tenth of the rent, while he had to make over nine–tenths of it to the Government. A curious sort of French peasant was the ryot, without any permanent title in the soil, and with the taxation changing every year in proportion to his harvest. The original class of Zemindars, notwithstanding their unmitigated and uncontrolled rapacity against the depossessed mass of the ex-hereditary landholders, soon melted away under the pressure of the Company, in order to be replaced by mercantile speculators who now hold all the land of Bengal, with exception of the estates returned under the direct management of the Government. These speculators have introduced a variety of the Zemindaree tenure called *patree*.[7] Not content to be placed with regard to the British Government in the situation of middlemen, they have created in their turn a class of 'hereditary' middlemen called *patnetas*,[8] who created again their sub-*patnetas*,[9] & c; so that a perfect scale of hierarchy of middlemen has sprung up, which presses with its entire weight on the unfortunate cultivator.[10] As to the ryots in Madras and Bombay, the system soon degenerated into one of forced cultivation, and the land lost all its value. 'The land', says Mr Campbell, 'would be sold for balances by the Collector, as in Bengal, but generally is not, for a very good reason, viz: that nobody would buy it.'[11]

Thus in Bengal, we have a combination of English landlordism, of the Irish middleman system, of the Austrian system, transforming the landlord into the tax-gatherer, and of the Asiatic system making the State the real landlord. In Madras and Bombay we have a French peasant proprietor who is at the same

---

[6] *Mirasi* from Arabic *miras*, inheritance, and therefore meaning hereditary tenures.

[7] So printed in the *NYDT*, an obvious mistake. It should be *Patnee*. Campbell (*Modern India*, p. 314) states that the '*Patnee*' was a tenure established by the great *zamindars* with the help of Government enactments.

[8] In Campbell (ibid., p. 314) the word is *Patnidars*. H.H. Wilson (*Glossary of Judicial and Revenue Terms . . . of British India*, London, 1875, p. 410) defines *Patnidars* as holders of an under–revenue tenure.

[9] In Campbell (ibid., p. 314), sub-*Patnidar*s.

[10] See ibid.: 'The patnees are like the middlemen, and the last screws the tenant to the uttermost.'

[11] The editors of *CW*, Vol. 12, p. 214 n., have traced this quotation on p. 359 of the 1852 edition of Campbell's *Modern India*. He expresses the same views on p. 315 of the 1892 edition.

time a serf, and a *metayer* of the State. The drawbacks of all these various systems accumulate upon him without his enjoying any of their redeeming features. The ryot is subject, like the French peasant, to the extortion of the private usurer; but he has no hereditary, no permanent title in his land like the French peasant. Like the serf he is forced to cultivation, but he is not secured against want like the serf. Like the *metayer* he has to divide his produce with the state but the state is not obliged, with regard to him, to advance the funds and the stock, as it is obliged to do with regard to the *metayer.* In Bengal, as in Madras and Bombay, under the *Zemindaree* as under the *Ryotwar,* the ryots – and they form $^{11}/_{12}$ths of the whole Indian population have – been wretchedly pauperized; and if they are, morally speaking, not sunk as low as the Irish cottiers, they owe it to their climate, the men of the South being possessed of less wants, and of more imagination than the men of the North.

Conjointly with the land–tax we have to consider the salt tax. Notoriously, the Company retain the monopoly of the article which they sell at three times its mercantile value – and this in a country where it is furnished by the sea, by the lakes, by the mountains and the earth itself. The practical working of this monopoly was described by the Earl of Albemarle in the following words:

> A great proportion of the salt for inland consumption throughout the country is purchased from the Company by large wholesale merchants at less than 4 rupees per measure; these mix a fixed proportion of sand, chiefly got a few miles to the southwest of Dacca, and send the mixture to a second, or, counting the Government as the first, to a third monopolist at about 5 or 6 rupees. This dealer adds more earth or ashes, and thus passing through more hands, from the large towns to villages, the price is still raised from 8 to 10 rupees and the proportion of adulteration from 25 to 40 percent. It appears then that the people pay from £21 £17s 2d. to 27 6s 2d for their salt, or in other words from 30 to 36 times as much as the wealthy people of Great Britain.[12]

As an instance of English bourgeois morals, I may allege, that Mr Campbell defends the Opium monopoly because it prevents the Chinese from consuming too much of the drug, and that he defends the Brandy monopoly (licenses for spirit selling in India) because it has wonderfully increased the consumption of Brandy in India.

The Zemindar tenure, the ryotwar, and the salt tax, combined with the Indian climate, were the hotbeds of the cholera – India's revenge[13] upon the Western World – a striking and severe example of the solidarity of human woes and wrongs.

---

[12] From Albemarle's speech in the House of Lords, published in *The Times,* No. 21470, 2 July 1853; see *CW,* Vol. 12, p. 215 n. George Thomas Keppel (1799–1891), who became the sixth Earl of Albemarle in 1851, and so became a member of the House of Lords, had served in India in his early career and was private secretary to Lord John Russell.

[13] 'ravages' in *NYDT.* But Marx, in his letter to Adolf Cluss dated 18 October 1853, complains that Dana, one of the editors of *NYDT,* changed his word 'revenge' to 'ravages'; see *CW,* Vol. 39, p. 390.

The Future Results of British Rule in India

(*New York Daily Tribune*, August 8, 1853)
London, Friday, July 22, 1853

I propose in this letter to conclude my observations on India.

How came it that English supremacy was established in India? The paramount power of the Great Mogul was broken by the Mogul Viceroys. The power of the Viceroys was broken by the Mahrattas. The power of the Maharattas was broken by the Affghans and while all were struggling against all, the Briton rushed in and was enabled to subdue them all. A country not only divided between Mohammedan and Hindoo, but between tribe and tribe, between caste and caste; a society whose framework was based on a sort of equilibrium, resulting from a general repulsion and constitutional exclusiveness between all its members. Such a country and such a society, were they not the predestined prey of conquest? If we knew nothing of the past history of Hindostan, would there not be the one great and incontestable fact, that even at this moment India is held in English thraldom by an Indian army maintained at the cost of India? India, then, could not escape the fate of being conquered, and the whole of her past history, if it be anything, is the history of the successive conquests she has undergone.

Indian society has no history at all, at least no known history. What we call its history, is but the history of the successive intruders who founded their empires on the passive basis of that unresisting and unchanging society.[1] The question, therefore, is not whether the English had a right to conquer India, but whether we are to prefer India conquered by the Turk, by the Persian, by the Russian, to India conquered by the Briton.

England has to fulfil a double mission in India: one destructive, the other regenerating – the annihilation of old Asiatic society, and the laying of the material foundation of Western society in Asia.

Arabs, Turks, Tartars, Moguls, who had successively overrun India, soon became *Hindooized*, the barbarian conquerors being, by an eternal law of history, conquered themselves by the superior civilization of their subjects. The British were the first conquerors superior, and therefore, inaccessible to Hindoo civilization. They destroyed it by breaking up the native communities, by uprooting

Article signed: Karl Marx.

[1] Marx here seems to be greatly influenced by Hegel, who said: '. . . the Hindoos have no history in the form of annals (*historia*), that they have no history in the form of transactions (*resgeslae*): that is, no growth expanding into a veritable political condition.' See *Philosophy of History*, translated by J. Sibree (New York, 1956), p. 163.

the native industry, and by levelling all that was great and elevated in the native society. The historic pages of their rule in India report hardly anything beyond that destruction. The work of regeneration hardly transpires through a heap of ruins. Nevertheless it has begun.

The political unity of India, more consolidated, and extending farther than it ever did under the Great Moguls, was the first condition of its regeneration. That unity, imposed by the British sword, will now be strengthened and perpetuated by the electric telegraph. The native army, organized and trained by the British drill-sergeant, was the *sine qua non* of Indian self-emancipation, and of India ceasing to be the prey of the first foreign intruder. The free press, introduced for the first time into Asiatic society, and managed principally by the common offspring of Hindoos and Europeans, is a new and powerful agent of reconstruction. The Zamindaree and Ryotwar themselves, abominable as they are, involve two distinct forms of private property in land – the great desideratum of Asiatic society. From the Indian natives, reluctantly and sparingly educated at Calcutta, under English superintendence, a fresh class is springing up, endowed with the requirements for government and imbued with European science. Steam has brought India into regular and rapid communication with Europe, has connected its chief ports with those of the whole south-eastern ocean, and has revindicated[2] it from the isolated position which was the prime law of its stagnation. The day is not far distant when, by a combination of railways and steam vessels, the distance between England and India, measured by time, will be shortened to eight days, and when that once fabulous country will thus be actually annexed to the Western World.

The ruling classes of Great Britain have had, till now, but an accidental, transitory and exceptional interest in the progress of India. The aristocracy wanted to conquer it, the moneyocracy to plunder it, and the millocracy to undersell it. But now the tables are turned. The millocracy have discovered that the transformation of India into a reproductive country has become of vital importance to them, and that, to that end, it is necessary, above all, to gift her with means of irrigation and of internal communication. They intend now drawing a net of railroads over India. And they will do it. The results must be inappreciable.

It is notorious that the productive powers of India are paralyzed by the utter want of means for conveying and exchanging its various produce. Nowhere, more than in India, do we meet with social destitution in the midst of natural plenty, for want of the means of exchange. It was proved before a Committee of the British House of Commons, which sat in 1848, that 'when grain was selling from 6s. to 8s. a quarter at Khandesh, it was sold 64s. to 70s. at Poonah, where the people were dying in the streets of famine, without the possibility of gaining supplies from Khandesh, because the clay roads were impracticable.'[3]

---

[2] 'Revindicate' means 'reclaim, recover, restore as a rightful possession' (*OED*).

[3] This quotation occurs in Dickinson, *India Reform*, pp. 81–82, where the words 'in the rains' occur additionally at the end.

The introduction of railroads may be easily made to subserve agricultural purposes by the formation of tanks, where ground is required for embankment, and by the conveyance of water along the different lines. Thus irrigation, the *sine qua non* of farming in the East, might be greatly extended, and the frequently recurring local famines, arising from the want of water, would be averted. The general importance of railways, viewed under this head, must become evident, when we remember that irrigated lands, even in the districts near Ghauts, pay three times as much in taxes, afford ten or twelve times as much employment, and yield twelve or fifteen times as much profit, as the same area without irrigation.

Railways will afford the means of diminishing the amount and the cost of the military establishment. Col. Warren, Town Major of the Fort St. William, stated before a Select Committee of the House of Commons:

> The practicability of receiving intelligence from distant parts of the country in as many hours as at present it requires days and even weeks, and of sending instructions with troops and stores, in the more brief period, are considerations which cannot be too highly estimated. Troops could be kept at more distant and healthier stations than at present, and much loss of life from sickness would by this means be spared. Stores could not to the same extent be required at the various depots, and the loss by decay, and the destructions incidental to the climate, would also be avoided. The number of troops might be diminished in direct proportion to their effectiveness.

We know that the municipal organization and the economical basis of the village communities has been broken up, but their worst feature, the dissolution of society into stereotype and disconnected atoms, has survived their vitality. The village isolation produced the absence of roads in India, and the absence of roads perpetuated the village isolation. On this plan a community existed with a given scale of low conveniences, almost without intercourse with other villages, without the desires and efforts indispensable to social advance. The British having broken up this self-sufficient *inertia* of the villages, railways will provide the new want of communication and intercourse. Besides,

> one of the effects of the railway system will be to bring into every village affected by it such a knowledge of the contrivances and appliances of other countries, and such means of obtaining them, as will first put the hereditary and stipendiary village artisanship of India to full proof of its capabilities, and then if needful[4] supply its defects. (Chapman, *The Cotton and Commerce of India*)[5]

I know that the English millocracy intend to endow India with railways with the exclusive view of extracting at diminished expenses, the cotton and

---

[4] The words 'if needful' are omitted in *On Colonialism*, *FIWI* and Av., as well as *CW*, Vol. 12.

[5] John Chapman, *The Cotton and Commerce of India*, London, 1851, p. 95. (Reference traced by Avineri and by editors of *CW*, Vol. 12.)

other raw materials for their manufactures. But when you have once introduced machinery into the locomotion of a country, which possesses iron and coals, you are unable to withhold it from its *fabrication*. You cannot maintain a net of railways over an immense country without introducing all those industrial processes necessary to meet the immediate and current wants of railway locomotion, and out of which there must grow the application of machinery to those branches of industry not immediately connected with railways. The railway system will therefore become, in India, truly the forerunner of modern industry. This is the more certain as the Hindoos are allowed by British authorities themselves to possess particular aptitude for accommodating themselves to entirely new labor, and acquiring the requisite knowledge of machinery. Ample proof of this fact is afforded by the capacities and expertness of the native engineers in the Calcutta mint, where they have been for years employed in working the steam machinery, by the natives attached to the several steam engines in the Hurdwar[6] coal districts, and by other instances. Mr Campbell himself, greatly influenced as he is by the prejudices of the East India Company, is obliged to avow, 'that the great mass of the Indian people possesses a great *industrial energy*, is well fitted to accumulate capital, and remarkable for a mathematical clearness of head, and talent for figures and exact sciences. Their intellects', he says, 'are excellent.'[7] Modern industry, resulting from the railway system, will dissolve the hereditary divisions of labor upon which rest the Indian castes, those decisive impediments to Indian progress and Indian power.

All the English bourgeoisie may be forced to do will neither emancipate nor materially mend the social condition of the mass of the people, depending not only on the development of the productive powers, but of their appropriation by the people. But what they will not fail to do is lay down the material premises for both. Has the bourgeoisie ever done more? Has it ever effected a progress without dragging individuals and people through blood and dirt, through misery and degradation?

The Indians will not reap the fruits of the new elements of society scattered among them by the British bourgeoisie, till in Great Britain itself the now ruling classes shall have been supplanted by the industrial proletariat, or till the Hindoos themselves shall have grown strong enough to throw off the English yoke altogether. At all events, we may safely expect to see, at a more or less remote period, the regeneration of that great and interesting country, whose gentle natives are, to use the expression of Prince Soltykov,[8] even in the most inferior

---

[6] Obvious printing error for 'Burdwan'.

[7] Marx here has paraphrased Campbell, who writes: 'In talents the Natives are by no means inferior to Europeans. Their intellects are excellent. They are remarkable for mathematical clearness of head and talent for figures and exact sciences, which is not general with us, and it is worthy of note that this talent is found most remarkable in the purer Hindu races . . .'. See Campbell, *Modern India*, pp. 59–60.

[8] Prince Alexei Dimitrievich Soltykoff (Soltykov) (1806–1859): Russian traveller, writer and painter, who travelled in India, 1841–43 and 1845–46. Information from *CW*, Vol. 12, pp. 725–26.

classes, '*plus fins et plus adroits que les Italiens*',[9] whose submission even coun-
terbalanced by a certain calm nobility, who, notwithstanding their natural langor[10]
have astonished the British officers by their bravery, whose country has been the
source of our languages, our religions, and who represent the type of the ancient
German in the Jat, and the type of the ancient Greek in the Brahmin.

I cannot part with the subject of India without some concluding remarks.

The profound hypocrisy and inherent barbarism of bourgeois civilization lies unveiled before our eyes, turning from its home, where it assumes respectable forms, to the colonies, where it goes naked. They are the defenders of
property, but did any revolutionary party ever originate agrarian revolutions
like those in Bengal, in Madras, and in Bombay? Did they not, in India, to
borrow an expression of that great robber, Lord Clive himself, resort to atrocious
extortion, when simple corruption could not keep pace with their rapacity?[11]
While they prated in Europe about the inviolable sanctity of the national debt,
did they not confiscate in India the dividends of the rayahs[12] [rajahs], who had
invested their private savings in the Company's own funds? While they combatted
the French revolution under the pretext of defending 'our holy religion', did they
not forbid, at the same time, Christianity to be propagated in India, and did they
not, in order to make money out of the pilgrims streaming to the temples of
Orissa and Bengal, take up the trade in the murder and prostitution perpetrated
in the temple of Juggernaut? These are the men of 'Property, Order, Family, and
Religion'.

The devastating effects of English industry, when contemplated with regard to India, a country as vast as Europe, and containing 150 millions of acres,
are palpable and confounding. But we must not forget that they are only the
organic results of the whole system of production as it is now constituted. That
production rests on the supreme rule of capital. The centralization of capital[13] is
essential to the existence of capital as an independent power. The destructive
influence of that centralization upon the markets of the world does but[14] reveal,
in the most gigantic dimensions, the inherent organic laws of political economy
now at work in every civilized town. The bourgeois period of history has to
create the material basis of the new world – on the one hand, the universal
intercourse founded upon the mutual dependency of mankind, and the means of
that intercourse; on the other hand, the development of the productive powers of
man and the transformation of material production into a scientific domination

[9] 'More subtle and adroit than the Italians'. Marx quotes from A.D. Soltykov's *Lettres
sur l'Inde* (Paris, 1861), p. 61. (Reference traced by Moscow editors.)
[10] Spelt 'langer' in *NYDT*.
[11] Clive is said to have amassed huge wealth from plundering Bengal.
[12] So spelt in *NYDT*.
[13] By centralization of capital, Marx means what in the parlance of modern economists is called 'concentration of capital'. By 'concentration of capital', on the other
hand, he meant the increase in the relative size of constant capital, that is capital
other than wage-fund. See Marx, *Capital*, edited by Dona Torr, Vol. I, pp. 587–89.
[14] Omitted in Av.

of natural agencies. Bourgeois industry and commerce create these material conditions of a new world in the same way as geological revolutions have created the surface of the earth. When a great social revolution shall have mastered the results of the bourgeois epoch, the market of the world and the modern powers of production, and subjected them to the common control of the most advanced peoples, then only will human progress cease to resemble that hideous pagan idol, who would not drink the nectar but from the skulls of the slain.

Railway Construction in India

(*New York Daily Tribune,* October 4, 1853)
London, Tuesday, September 20, 1853

Having dwelt in a former letter on the vital importance of railways for India,[1] I think fit to give now the latest news which has been published with regard to the progress and prospects of the intended network. The first Indian railways was the line now in operation between Bombay and Thane. Another line is now to be carried from Calcutta to Russnehael on the Ganges, a distance of 180 miles, Benares and Allahabad. From Allahabad it will be conducted across the Doab to Agra and thence to Delhi, traversing in this manner a space of 1,100 miles. It is contemplated to establish steam ferry-boats across the Soane and Tunona,[2] and that the Calcutta line will finally proceed from Delhi to Lahore. In Madras a railway is to be commenced forthwith, which, running 70 miles due west, will branch off into two arms – one pursuing the Ghats and terminating at Calicut, the other being carried on by Bellary and Poona to Bombay. This skeleton of the chain of railways will be completed by the Bombay, Baroda and Central India Railway, the preliminary surveys for which are now proceeding under the sanction of the Court of Directors. This line will pass from Bombay by Baroda to Agra, where it will meet the great trunk railway from Calcutta to Delhi, and by its means Bombay, the Capital of Western India and the best port of communication with Europe, for all Hindostan, will be put in communication with Calcutta on the one hand, and with the Punjab and the north-western provinces[3] on the other. The promoters of this scheme intend also to throw out branches into the great cotton district of the interior. In the meantime, measures are in progress for extending the electric telegraph throughout the whole of the peninsula of India.

From 'The Western Powers and Turkey – Imminent Economic Crisis – Railway Construction in India'. Signed: Karl Marx.

[1] Marx is referring to his article, 'The Future Results of British Rule in India', *NYDT*, 8 August 1853.
[2] So spelt. Slip for Jumuna?
[3] The 'North-Western Provinces' comprised the territory now covered by the state of Uttar Pradesh, excluding the area of 'Oude' which was annexed in 1856.

New York Daily Tribune **1855**

FREDERICK ENGELS

The Late British Government

(*New York Daily Tribune*, February 23, 1855. Printed as a leading article.)
[Excerpt]

The main feature of this session was the East India bill, by which the Ministry proposed, without any material improvement of Indian government, to renew the East India Company's charter for twenty years. This was too bad, even for such a Parliament, and had to be abandoned. The charter was to be revocable by Parliament at a year's notice. Sir Charles Wood, the late bungling Chancellor of the Exchequer of the Russell Cabinet, now proved his capabilities in the Board of Control, or Indian Board. The whole of the reforms proposed were confined to a few petty alterations of doubtful effect in the judicial system, and the throwing open of civil employments and the scientific military service to public competition. But these reforms were merely pretexts; the real gist of the bill was this: Charles Wood got his salary as President of the Board of Control raised from £1,200 to £5,000; instead of 24 India Directors elected by the Company, there were to be only 18, six of whom were in the gift of Government, an accession of patronage which was the less despicable as the Directors' salaries were raised from £300 to £500, while the Chairman and Deputy-Chairman received £1,000. Not satisfied with this waste of public money, the Governor-General of India, formerly at the same time Governor of Bengal, was now to have a separate Governor of that Presidency under him, while a new Presidency, with a new Governor, was to be created on the Indus. Every one of these Governors must, of course, have his Council, and overpaid and luxurious sinecures the seats in these Councils are. How happy India should be, governed as it is, at last, according to unsophisticated Whig principles!

Not included in *On Colonialism*, or in Avineri. But see CW, Vol. 13, pp. 622–23, for text corresponding to the excerpt. The CW editors tell us (p. 721 n. 440) that this article was written by Engels on the basis of Marx's letter of 31 January 1855 (see Letter No. 12 in this volume) and Marx's earlier articles on Gladstone.

New York Daily Tribune 1857

[Whose Atrocities?]

(*New York Daily Tribune*, April 10, 1857. Printed as a leading article.)
[Excerpt]

A few years since, when the frightful system of torture in India was exposed in Parliament Sir James Hogg,[1] one of the Directors of the most Honourable East India Company, boldly asserted that the statements made were unfounded. Subsequent investigation, however, proved them to be based upon facts which should have been well known to the Directors and Sir James had left him[2] to admit either 'wilful ignorance' or 'criminal knowledge of the horrible charge laid at the Company's doors'. Lord Palmerston, the present Premier of England, and the Earl of Clarendon, the Minister of Foreign Affairs, seem just now to be placed in a similar unenviable position [with regard to British atrocities in China] . . .

Title not given in *NYDT*. We have followed the title assigned by Dona Torr in *Marx on China* (Bombay, 1952), p. 38.

[1] Sir James Weir Hogg (1790–1876) was, in fact, President of the Court of Directors (1846–47, 1852–53); he later served as member of the Council of India, 1858–72.
[2] So printed, for 'had no choice left him but'?

The Revolt in the Indian Army

(*New York Daily Tribune*, July 15, 1857. Printed as a leading article.)

The Roman *divide et impera* was the great rule by which Great Britain, for about one hundred and fifty years, contrived to retain the tenure of her Indian Empire. The antagonism of the various races, tribes, castes, creeds and sovereignties, the aggregate of which forms the geographical unity of what is called India, continued to be the vital principle of British supremacy. In later times, however, the conditions of that supremacy have undergone a change. With the conquest of Scinde and the Punjaub, the Anglo-Indian Empire had not only reached its natural limits, but it had trampled out the last vestiges of independent Indian States. All warlike native tribes were subdued, all serious internal conflicts were at an end, and the late incorporation of Oude[1] proved satisfactorily that the remnants of the so-called independent Indian principalities exist on sufferance only. Hence a great change in the position of the East India Company. It no longer attacked one part of India by the help of another part, but found itself placed at the head, and the whole of India at its feet. No longer conquering, it had become the conqueror. The armies at its disposition no longer had to extend its dominion, but only to maintain it. From soldiers they were converted into policemen; 200,000,000 natives being curbed by a native army of 200,000 men, officered by Englishmen, and that native army, in its turn, being kept in check by an English army numbering 40,000 only.[2] On first view, it is evident that the allegiance of the Indian people rests on the fidelity of the native army, in creating which the British rule simultaneously organized the first general center of resistance which the Indian people was ever possessed of. How far that native army may be relied upon is clearly shown by its recent mutinies, breaking out as soon as the war with Persia[3] had almost denuded the Presidency of Bengal of its European soldiers. Before this there had been mutinies in the Indian army, but the

The title of the article accords with the entry in Marx's notebook for 1857–58. See CW, Vol. 15, p. 673 n. 347. Being an editorial, the *New York Daily Tribune* (NYDT) editors put no heading on the article.

[1] Marx alludes here to the British annexation of Awadh and deposition of Wajid Ali Shah in 1856.

[2] According to John William Kaye, the Indian army immediately before the Mutiny consisted of 45,137 Europeans and 2,77,746 Indians (Kaye, *History of the Sepoy War*, Vol. I, p. 626).

[3] Here Marx refers to the Anglo–Persian War of 1856–57. Herat had been the cause of dispute between Persia (Russian-supported) and Afghanistan (supported by the British). Herat fell to Persia in 1856. The British declared war against Persia and sent troops to Persia. The Indian rebellion compelled Britain to conclude peace with Persia.

present revolt is distinguished by characteristic and fatal features. It is the first time that Sepoy regiments have murdered their European officers; that Mussulmans and Hindoos, renouncing their mutual antipathies, have combined against their common masters; that 'disturbances beginning with the Hindoos, have actually ended in placing on the throne of Delhi a Mohammedan Emperor';[4] that the mutiny has not been confined to a few localities; and lastly, that the revolt in the Anglo-Indian army has coincided with a general disaffection exhibited against English supremacy on the part of the great Asiatic nations, the revolt of the Bengal army being, beyond doubt, intimately connected with the Persian and Chinese wars.

The alleged cause of the dissatisfaction which began to spread four months ago in the Bengal army was the apprehension on the part of the natives lest the Government should interfere with their religion. The serving out of cartridges, the paper of which was said to have been greased with the fat of bullocks and pigs, and the compulsory biting of which was, therefore, considered by the natives as an infringement of their religious prescriptions, gave the signal for local disturbances. On the 22nd of January an incendiary fire broke out in cantonments a short distance from Calcutta. On the 25th of February the 19th Native Regiment mutinied at Burrampoor, the men objecting to the cartridges served out to them. On the 31st of March that regiment was disbanded; at the end of March the 38th[5] Sepoy Regiment, stationed at Barrackpoor, allowed one of its men[6] to advance with a loaded musket upon the parade-ground in front of the line, and, after having called his comrades to mutiny, he was permitted to attack and wound the Adjutant and Sergeant-Major of his regiment.[7] During the hand-to-hand conflict, that ensued, hundreds of sepoys looked passively on, while others participated in the struggle, and attacked the officers with the butt ends of their muskets. Subsequently that regiment was also disbanded.

The month of April was signalized by incendiary fires in several cantonments of the Bengal army at Allahabad, Agra, Umballah, by a mutiny of the 3rd Regiment of Light Cavalry at Meerut, and by similar appearances of disaffection in the Madras and Bombay armies. At the beginning of May, an *emeute*[8] was preparing at Lucknow, the capital of Oude, which was, however, prevented by the promptitude of Sir H. Lawrence. On the 10th of May[9] the mutineers of the 3rd Light Cavalry of Meerut were marched off to jail, to undergo the various terms of imprisonment to which they were sentenced. On the evening of the following day the troopers of the 3rd Cavalry, together with the two native regiments, the 11th and 20th, assembled upon the parade-ground, killed the officers

---

[4] *The Times*, No. 22719, 29 June 1857, leading article. Reference taken from *CW*, Vol. 15, p. 298 n.
[5] So printed in *NYDT*. It should be 34th Sepoy Regiment.
[6] Mangal Pandey. See Campbell, *Narrative*, p. 8.
[7] Lieutenant Baugh, Adjutant of the 34th NI. See ibid.
[8] French, for popular uprising.
[9] It should be 9 May. See Kaye, *History of the Sepoy War*, Vol. II, pp. 51–54.

endeavouring to pacify them, set fire to the cantonments, and slew all the Englishmen they were able to lay hands on. Although the British part of the brigade
mustered a regiment of infantry, another of cavalry, and an overwhelming force
of horse and foot artillery, they were not able to move until nightfall. Having
inflicted but little harm on the mutineers, they allowed them to betake themselves to the open field and to throw themselves into Delhi, some forty miles
distant from Meerut. There they were joined by the native garrison, consisting of
the 38th, 54th and 74th regiments of infantry, and a company of native artillery.
The British officers were attacked, all Englishmen within reach of the rebels were
murdered, and the heir of the late Mogul of Delhi proclaimed King of India. Of
the troops sent to the rescue of Meerut, where order had been re-established, six
companies of native sappers and miners, who arrived on the 15th of May, murdered their commanding officer, Major Frazer, and made at once for the open
country, pursued by troops of horse artillery and several of the 6th Dragoon
Guards. Fifty or sixty of the mutineers were shot, but the rest contrived to escape
to Delhi. At Ferozepoor, in the Punjaub, the 57th and 45th Native Infantry regiments mutinied, but were put down by force. Private letters from Lahore state the
whole of the native troops to be in an undisguised state of mutiny. On the 19th of
May, unsuccessful efforts were made by the sepoys stationed at Calcutta to get
possession of Fort St. William. Three regiments arrived from Bushire at Bombay
were at once dispatched to Calcutta.

In reviewing these events, one is startled by the conduct of the British
commander at Meerut – his late appearance on the field of battle being still less
incomprehensible than the weak manner in which he pursued the mutineers.[10] As
Delhi is situated on the right and Meerut on the left bank of the Jumna – the two
banks being joined at Delhi by one bridge only – nothing could have been easier
than to cut off the retreat of the fugitives.

Meanwhile, martial law has been proclaimed in all the disaffected districts; forces, consisting of natives mainly, are concentrating against Delhi from
the north, the east and the south; the neighbouring princes are said to have pronounced for the English; letters have been sent to Ceylon to stop Lord Elgin[11] and
Gen. Ashburnham's forces, on their way to China; and finally, 14,000 British
troops were to be dispatched from England to India in about a fortnight. Whatever obstacles the climate of India at the present season, and the total want of
means of transportation may oppose to the movements of the British forces, the
rebels at Delhi are very likely to succumb without any prolonged resistance. Yet,
even then, it is only the prologue of a most terrible tragedy that will have to be
enacted.

[10] Hewitt, British general, commanded the garrison in Meerut in 1857. A reputedly
    kind-hearted, hospitable man, he lamented that Colonel Smyth had made that crucial
    experiment upon the fidelity of his regiment which had resulted in open mutiny. Ibid.,
    pp. 44–45.
[11] James Bruce, eighth Earl of Elgin (1811–1863): envoy to China in 1857; negotiated
    the Treaty of Tientsin in 1858. He was later to serve as Viceroy of India.

The Revolt in India

(*New York Daily Tribune*, August 4, 1857. Correspondence.)
London, July 17, 1857

On the 8th of June, just a month had passed since Delhi fell into the hands of the revolted Sepoys and the proclamation by them of a Mogul Emperor. Any notion, however, of the mutineers being able to keep the ancient capital of India against the British forces would be preposterous. Delhi is fortified only by a wall and a simple ditch, while the heights[1] surrounding and commanding it are already in the possession of the English, who, even without battering the walls, might enforce its surrender in a very short period by the easy process of cutting off its supply of water. Moreover, a motley crew of mutineering soldiers who have murdered their own officers, torn asunder the ties of discipline, and not succeeded in discovering a man upon whom to bestow the supreme command, are certainly the body least likely to organize a serious and protracted resistance. To make confusion more confused, the checkered Delhi ranks are daily swelling from the fresh arrivals of new contingents of mutineers from all parts of the Bengal Presidency, who, as if on a preconcerted plan, are throwing themselves into the doomed city. The two sallies which, on the 30th and 31st of May, the mutineers risked without the walls, and in both of which they were repulsed with heavy losses, seem to have proceeded from despair rather than from any feeling of self-reliance or strength. The only thing to be wondered at is the slowness of the British operations, which, to some degree, however, may be accounted for by the horrors of the season and the want of means of transport. Apart from Gen. Anson,[2] the commander-in-chief, French letters state that about 4,000 European troops have already fallen victims of the deathly heat, and even the English papers confess that in the engagements before Delhi the men suffered more from the sun than from the shot of the enemy. In consequence of its scanty means of conveyance, the main British force stationed at Umballah consumed about twenty-seven days in its march upon Delhi, so that it moved at the rate of about one and a half hours per day. A further delay was caused by the absence of heavy artillery

This article is presumably the one Marx referred to in his letter to Engels on 14 July 1857: 'The Indian revolt has placed me in some thing of a quandary. . . . I have already got together [the stuff] to make a readable article.' See *CW*, Vol. 40, p. 146 and n. (b).

[1] The Ridge, an outcrop of the Aravallis encircling Delhi on the west, is obviously meant.
[2] George Anson (1797–1857), Commander-in-Chief at Simla, came to Ambala and marched toward Delhi, but died of cholera before reaching Delhi.

at Umballah, and the consequent necessity of bringing over a siege-train from the nearest arsenal, which was as far off as Phillaur, on the further side of the Sutlej.

With all that, the news of the fall of Delhi may be daily expected; but what next? If the uncontested possession by the rebels during a month on the traditionary center of the Indian Empire acted perhaps as the most powerful ferment in completely breaking up the Bengal army, in spreading mutiny and desertion from Calcutta to the Punjaub in the north, and to Rajpootana in the east[3] and in shaking the British authority from one end of India to the other, no greater mistake could be committed than to suppose that the fall of Delhi, though it may throw consternation among the ranks of the sepoys, should suffice either to quench the rebellion, to stop its progress, or to restore the British rule. Of the whole native Bengal army, mustering about 80,000 men[4] – composed of about 28,000 Rajpoots, 23,000 Brahmins, 13,000 Mohammedans, 5,000 Hindoos of inferior castes, and the rest Europeans – 30,000 have disappeared in consequence of mutiny, desertion, or dismission from the ranks. As to the rest of that army, several of the regiments have openly declared that they will remain faithful and support the British authority, excepting in the matter in which the native troops are now engaged: they will not aid the authorities against the mutineers of the native regiments, and will, on the contrary, assist their 'bhaies' (brothers). The truth of this has been exemplified in almost every station from Calcutta. The native regiments remained passive for a time; but, as soon as they fancied themselves strong enough, they mutinied. An Indian correspondent of the *London Times* leaves no doubt as to the 'loyalty' of the regiments which have not yet pronounced, and the native inhabitants who have not yet made common cause with the rebels.

> If you read, he says, *that all is quiet*, understand it to mean that the native troops have not yet risen in open mutiny; that the discontented part of the inhabitants are not yet in open rebellion; that they are either too weak, or fancy themselves to be so, or that they are waiting for a more fitting time. Where you read of the 'manifestation of loyalty' in any of the Bengal native regiments, cavalry or infantry, understand it to mean that one–half of the regiments thus favourably mentioned only are really faithful; the other half are but acting a part, the better to find the Europeans off their guard, when the proper time arrives, or, by warding off suspicion, have it the more in their power to aid their mutinous companions.[5]

In the Punjaub, open rebellion has only been prevented by disbanding the native troops. In Oude, the English can only be said to keep Lucknow, the Residency, while everywhere else the native regiments have revolted, escaped

---

[3] So printed in the *New York Daily Tribune* (*NYDT*). It should be 'west'.

[4] According to an estimate the total strength of the Bengal Army in 1857 was 24,366 Europeans and 1,35,767 Indians. See H. Chattopadhyaya, *The Sepoy Mutiny* (Calcutta, 1957), pp. 65–66.

[5] Agra, 3 June, *The Times*, No. 22733, 15 July 1857. See *CW*, Vol. 15, p. 307 n.

with their ammunition, burned all the bungalows to the ground, and joined with the inhabitants who have taken up arms. Now, the real position of the English army is best demonstrated by the fact that it was thought necessary, in the Punjaub as well as the Rajpootana, to establish flying corps. This means that the English cannot depend either on their sepoy troops or on the natives to keep the communication open between their scattered forces. Like the French during the Peninsular war, they command only the spot of ground held by their own troops, and the next neighbourhood domineered by that spot; while for communication between the disjoined members of their army they depend on flying corps, the action of which, most precarious in itself, loses naturally in intensity in the same measure that it spreads over a greater extent of space. The actual insufficiency of the British forces is further proved by the fact that, for removing treasures from disaffected stations, they were constrained to have them conveyed by sepoys themselves, who, without any exception, broke out in rebellion on the march, and absconded with the treasures confided to them. As the troops sent from England will, in the best case, not arrive before November, and as it would be still more dangerous to draw off European troops from the Presidencies of Madras and Bombay – the 10th Regiment of Madras sepoys, having already shown symptoms of disaffection – any idea of collecting the regular taxes throughout the Bengal Presidency must be abandoned, and the process of decomposition be allowed to go on. Even if we suppose that the Burmese will not improve the occasion, that the Maharajah of Gwalior will continue supporting the English, and the Ruler of Nepaul, commanding the finest Indian army, remain quiet; that disaffected Peshawur will not combine with the restless hill tribes, and that the Shah of Persia will not be silly enough to evacuate Herat[6] – still, the whole Bengal Presidency must be reconquered, and the whole Anglo-Indian army remade. The cost of this enormous enterprise will altogether fall upon the British people. As to the notion put forward by Lord Granville in the House of Lords,[7] of the East India Company being able to raise, by Indian loans, the necessary means, its soundness may be judged from the effects produced by the disturbed state of the north-western provinces on the Bombay money market. An immediate panic seized the native capitalists, very large sums were withdrawn from the banks, government securities proved almost unsaleable, and hoarding to a great extent commenced not only in Bombay but in its environs also.

---

[6] The Persian forces occupied Herat in October 1856, which brought in British intervention; an expeditionary force left from India in November/ December 1856, and by landing at Bushire and advancing into Persia, forced the Persians to agree to vacate Herat by the Treaty of Paris (1857).

[7] Lord Granville's speech in the House of Lords on 16 July 1857, *The Times*, No. 22735, 17 July 1857. See *CW*, Vol. 15, p. 308 n.

The Indian Question

(*New York Daily Tribune*, August 14, 1857. Correspondence.)
London, July 28, 1857

The three hours' speech[1] delivered last night in 'the Dead House', by Mr Disraeli,[2] will gain rather than lose by being read instead of being listened to. For some time, Mr Disraeli affects an awful solemnity of speech, an elaborate slowness of utterance and a passionless method of formality, which, however consistent they may be with his peculiar notions of the dignity becoming a Minister in expectance, are really distressing to his tortured audience. Once he succeeded in giving even commonplaces the pointed appearance of epigrams. Now he contrives to bury even epigrams in the conventional dullness of respectability. An orator who, like Mr Disraeli, excels in handling the dagger rather than wielding the sword, should have been the last to forget Voltaire's warning that '*Tous les genres sont bons excepte le genre ennuyeux.*'[3]

Besides these technical peculiarities which characterize Mr Disraeli's present manner of eloquence, he, since Palmerston's accession to power, has taken good care to deprive his parliamentary exhibitions of every possible interest of actuality. His speeches are not intended to carry his motions, but his motions are intended to prepare for his speeches. They might be called self-denying motions, since they are so constructed as neither to harm the adversary, if carried, nor to damage the proposer, if lost. They mean, in fact, to be neither carried nor lost, but simply to be dropped. They belong neither to the acids nor to the alkalis; but are born neutrals. The speech is not the vehicle of action, but the hypocrisy of action affords the opportunity for a speech. Such, indeed, may be the classical and final form of parliamentary eloquence; but then, at all events, the final form of parliamentary eloquence must not demur to sharing the fate of all final forms of parliamentarism – that of being ranged under the category of nuisances. Action, as Aristotle said, is the ruling law of the drama. So it is of political oratory. Mr Disraeli's speech on the Indian revolt might be published in the tracts of the Society for the Propagation of Useful Knowledge, or it might be delivered to a mechanics' institution, or tendered as a prize essay to the Academy

---

[1] For the full text of the speech, see Hansard, *Parliamentary Debates*, Vol. CXLVII (20 July 1857–28 August 1857), pp. 420–33. Also *The Times*, No. 22744, 28 July 1857 (see *CW*, Vol. 15, p. 309 n.).

[2] Benjamin Disraeli (1804–1881), the famous English statesman, was then not in Government.

[3] 'All styles are good except the boring one.'

of Berlin. This curious impartiality of his speech as to the place where, and the time when, and the occasion on which it was delivered, goes far to prove that it fitted neither place, time, nor occasion. A chapter on the decline of the Roman Empire which might read exceedingly well in Montesquieu or Gibbon would prove an enormous blunder if put in the mouth of a Roman senator, whose peculiar business it was to stop that very decline. It is true that in our modern parliaments, a part lacking neither dignity nor interest might be imagined of an independent orator who, while despairing of influencing the actual course of events, should content himself to assume a position of ironical neutrality. Such a part was more or less successfully played by the late M. Garnier-Pagès[4] – not the Garnier-Pagès of Provisional Government memory in Louis Philippe's Chamber of Deputies;[5] but Mr Disraeli, the avowed leader of an obsolete faction would consider even success in this line as a supreme failure. The revolt of the Indian army afforded certainly a magnificent opportunity for oratorical display. But, apart from his dreary manner of treating the subject, what was the gist of the motion which he made the pretext for his speech? It was no motion at all. He feigned to be anxious for becoming acquainted with two official papers, the one of which he was not quite sure to exist, and the other of which he was sure not immediately to bear on the subject in question. Consequently his speech and his motion lacked any point of contact save this, that the motion heralded a speech without an object, and that the object confessed itself not worth a speech. Still, as the highly elaborated opinion of the most distinguished out-of-office statesman of England, Mr Disraeli's speech ought to attract the attention of foreign countries. I shall content myself with giving in his ipsissima verba[6] a short analysis of his 'considerations on the decline of the Anglo-Indian Empire'. 'Does the disturbance in India indicate a military mutiny,[7] or is it a National revolt? Is the conduct of the troops the consequence of a sudden impulse, or is it the result of an organised conspiracy?'

Upon these points Mr Disraeli asserts the whole question to hinge. Until the last ten years, he affirmed, the British Empire in India was founded on the old principle of *divide et impera* – but that principle was put into action by respecting the different nationalities of[8] which India consisted, by avoiding to tamper with their religion, and by protecting their landed property. The sepoy army served as a safety-valve to absorb the turbulent spirits of the country. But of late years a new principle has been adopted in the government of India the principle

[4] Etienne Joseph Louis Garnier-Pagès (1801–1841): French politician, headed the republican opposition after the revolution of 1830; member of the Chamber of Deputies (1831–34 and 1835–41). See *CW*, Vol. 15, p. 711.
[5] Louis Antoine Garnier–Pagès (1803–1878), member of Provisional Government, 1848. See ibid.
[6] Latin for 'precise words.'
[7] In Av. 'meetings', an obvious misreading.
[8] Misread 'on' in Av.

of destroying nationality. The principle has been realized by the forcible destruction of native princes, the disturbance of the settlement of property, and the
tampering with the religion of the people.[9] In 1848 the financial difficulties of the
East India Company had reached that point that it became necessary to augment
its revenues one way or the other. Then a minute in Council was published, in
which was laid down the principle, almost without disguise, that the only mode
by which an increased revenue could be obtained was by enlarging the British
territories at the expense of the native princes. Accordingly, on the death of the
Rajah of Sattara, his adoptive heir was not acknowledged by the East India
Company, but the Raj absorbed in its own dominions. From that moment the
system of annexation was acted upon whenever a native prince died without
natural heirs. The principle of adoption – the very cornerstone of Indian society
– was systematically set aside by the Government.[10] Thus were forcibly annexed
to the British Empire the Rajs of more than a dozen independent princes from
1848–54. In 1854 the Raj of Berar, which comprised 80,000 square miles of land,
a population from 4,000,000 to 5,000,000 and enormous treasures, was seized.
Mr Disraeli ends the list of forcible annexations with Oude, which brought the
East Indian Government in collision not only with the Hindoos, but also with the
Mohammedans. Mr Disraeli then goes on showing how the settlement of property in India was disturbed by the new system of government during the last ten
years. 'The principle of the law of adoption', he says, 'is not the prerogative of
princes and principalities in India, it applies to every man in Hindostan who has
landed property, and who professes the Hindo religion.'

I quote a passage:

> The great feudatory, or *jaghedar*[11] who holds his lands by public service to his
> lord; and the *emiadar*[12] who holds his land free of all land-tax, who corres-
> ponds, if not precisely, in a popular sense, at least, with our freeholder – both of
> these classes most numerous in India – always, on the failure of their natural
> heirs, find in this principle the means of obtaining successors to their estates.
> Those classes were all touched by the annexation of Sattara, they were touched
> by the annexation of the territories of the ten inferior but independent princes

---

[9] Compare this passage with the anonymous article published in *NYDT* on 11 August
1857, reprinted in the Appendices to this volume.

[10] Marx is probably referring here to Lord Dalhousie's Minute as Governor-General-in-
Council, dated 30 August 1848, in which it was stated that 'the British Government
is bound not to put aside or to neglect such rightful opportunities of acquiring territory or revenue as may from time to time present themselves.' A.C. Banerjee, *Indian
Constitutional Documents* (Calcutta, 1948), Vol. I, p. 343.

[11] So in the original for *jagirdar*. Misread 'jagirdar' in *On Colonialism*; 'jagheerdar' in
Av.; and 'jaguedar' in *CW*, Vol. 15.

[12] For *a'immadar*, holder of tax-free (*a'imma*) grant, see Irfan Habib, *Agrarian System
of Mughal India* (New Delhi, 1999), pp. 342–43 n., 346 n. The restoration to 'enamdar'
in *On Colonialism*; Av.; *CW*, Vol. 15; and other editions of this article seems to be an
error.

to whom I have already alluded, and they were more than touched, they were terrified to the last degree, when the annexation of the Raj of Berar took place. What man was safe? What feudatory, what freeholder who had not a child of his own loins was safe throughout India? [Hear, hear.] These were not idle fears; they were extensively acted upon and reduced to practice. The resumption of jagheers of inams commenced for the first time in India. There have been, no doubt, impolitic moments when attempts have been made to inquire into titles, but no one had ever dreamt of abolishing the law of adoption; therefore, no authority, no Government had ever been in a position to resume jagheers and inams the holders of which had left no natural heirs. Here was a new source of revenue; but while all these things were acting upon the minds of these classes of Hindoos the Government took another step to disturb the settlement of property, to which I must now call the attention of the House. The House is aware, no doubt, from reading the evidence taken before the Committee of 1853, that there are great portions of the land of India which are exempt from the land tax. Being free from land-tax in India is far more than equivalent to freedom from the land-tax in this country, for, speaking generally and popularly, the land-tax in India is the whole taxation of the state.

The origin of these grants is difficult to penetrate, but they are undoubtedly of great antiquity. They are of different kinds. Besides the private freeholds, which are very extensive, there are large grants of land free from the land-tax with which mosques and temples have been endowed.

On the pretext of fraudulent claims of exemption, the British Governor-General took upon himself to examine the titles of the Indian landed estates. Under the new system, established in 1848,

That plan of investigating titles was at once embraced, as a proof of a powerful Government, a vigorous Executive, and most fruitful source of public revenue. Therefore commissions were issued to inquire into titles to landed estates in the Presidency of Bengal and adjoining country. They were also issued in the Presidency of Bombay, and surveys were ordered to be made in the newly-settled provinces, in order that these commissions might be conducted, when the surveys were completed, with due efficiency. Now there is no doubt that, during the last nine years, the action of these commissions of Inquiry into the freehold property of landed estates in India has been going on at an enormous rate, and immense results have been obtained.

Mr Disraeli computes that the resumption of estates from their proprietors is not less than £500,000 a year in the Presidency of Bengal; £370,000 in the Presidency of Bombay; £200,000 in the Punjaub, etc. Not content with this one method of seizing upon the property of the natives, the British Government discontinued the pensions to the native grandees, to pay which it was bound by treaty. 'This', says Mr Disraeli, 'is confiscation by a new means, but upon a most extensive, startling and shocking scale.'

Mr Disraeli then treats the tampering with the religion of the natives, a point upon which we need not dwell. From all his premises he arrives at the conclusion that the present Indian disturbance is not a military mutiny, but a national revolt, of which the sepoys are the acting instruments only. He ends his harangue by advising the Government to turn their attention to the internal improvement of India, instead of pursuing its present course of aggression.

Indian News

(*New York Daily Tribune*, August 14, 1857. Correspondence.)
London, July 31, 1857

The last Indian mail, conveying news from Delhi up to the 17th June, and from Bombay up to the 1st July, realizes the most gloomy anticipations. When Mr Vernon Smith, the President of the Board of Control, first informed the House of Commons of the Indian revolt, he confidently stated that the next mail would bring the news that Delhi has been razed to the ground.[1] The mail arrived, but Delhi was not yet 'wiped out of the pages of history'. It was then said that the battery train could not be brought up before the 9th of June, and that the attack on the doomed city must consequently be delayed to that date. The 9th of June passed away without being distinguished by any remarkable incident. On the 12th and 15th June some events occurred, but rather in the opposite direction, Delhi being not stormed by the English, but the English being attacked by the insurgents, the repeated sorties of whom were, however, repulsed. The fall of Delhi is thus again postponed, the alleged cause being now no longer the sole want of siege-artillery, but General Barnard's[2] resolution to wait upon reinforcements, as his forces – about 3,000 men were totally inadequate to the capture of the ancient capital defended by 30,000 sepoys, and possessed of all the military stores. The rebels had even established a camp outside the Aymeer gate.[3] Until now, all military writers were unanimous in considering an English force of 3,000 men quite sufficient for crushing a sepoy army of 30,000 or 40,000 men; and if such was not the case, how could England – to use an expression of the London *Times* – ever be able to 'reconquer' India?

The British army in India amounts actually to 30,000 men. The utmost number they can dispatch from England within the next half year cannot exceed 20,000 or 25,000 men, of whom 6,000 men are to fill up vacancies among the European ranks in India, and of whom the additional force of 18,000 or 19,000

No heading in the *New York Daily Tribune* (*NYDT*). The title given here is according to the entry in Marx's notebook for 1857; see *CW*, Vol. 15, p. 676 n. 370.

[1] Robert Vernon Smith (1800–1873): MP; President of the Board of Control (1855–1858) under Lord Palmerston. His speech in the House of Commons on 29 June 1857 was published in *The Times*, 30 June 1857.

[2] Sir Henry William Barnard (1799–1857): Major-General, veteran of the Crimean War (1854–55); was posted in the Bengal Army; died of pestilence at Delhi.

[3] Misprint for Ajmeri Gate, the southwestern gate of the walled city of Delhi.

men will be reduced by loss from the voyage, by loss from the climate, and by other casualties to about 14,000 troops able to appear on the theatre of war. The British army must resolve upon meeting the mutineers in very disproportionate number, or it must renounce meeting them at all. Still we are at a loss to understand the slowness of the concentration of their forces around Delhi. If at this season of the year, the heat proves an invincible obstacle which it did not in the days of Sir Charles Napier[4] some months later, on the arrival of the European troops, the rains will afford a still more conclusive pretext for a standstill. It should never be forgotten that the present mutiny had, in fact, already begun in the month of January, and that the British Government had thus received ample warning for keeping its powder dry and its forces ready.

The prolonged hold of Delhi by the sepoys in face of an English besieging army has, of course, produced its natural result. The mutiny was spreading to the very gates of Calcutta, fifty Bengal regiments had ceased to exist, the Bengal army itself had become a myth of the past, and the Europeans, dispersed over an immense extent of land, and blocked up in insulated spots, were either butchered by the rebels, or had taken up a position of desperate defense. At Calcutta itself the Christian inhabitants formed a volunteer guard, after a plot, said to have been most complete in its details, for surprising the seat of the Government, had been discovered, and the native troops there stationed had been disbanded. At Benares, an attempt at disarming a native regiment was resisted by a body of Sikhs and the 13th Irregular Cavalry. This fact is very important, as it shows that the Sikhs, like the Mohammedans, were making common cause with the Brahmins, and that thus a general union against the British rule, of all the different tribes, was rapidly progressing. It had been an article of faith with the English people, that the Sepoy army constituted their whole strength in India. Now, all at once, they feel quite satisfied that very army constitutes their sole danger. During the last Indian debates, Mr Vernon Smith, the President of the Board of Control, still declared that 'the fact cannot be too much insisted upon that there is no connection whatever between the native princes and the revolt'.[5] Two days later the same Vernon Smith had to publish a dispatch containing this ominous paragraph: 'On the 14th of June the ex-King of Oude,[6] implicated in the conspiracy by intercepted papers, was lodged in Fort William, and his followers disarmed.' By and by there will ooze out other facts able to convince even John Bull himself that what he considers a military mutiny is in truth a national revolt.

The English press feigns to derive great comfort from the conviction that the revolt had not yet spread beyond the boundaries of the Bengal Presidency, and that not the least doubt was entertained of the loyalty of the Bombay and Madras armies. However, this pleasant view of the case seems singularly to

[4] Charles James Napier (1782–1853): he conquered Sind in 1843.
[5] See Ball, *History of the Indian Mutiny*, Vol. I, p. 626.
[6] Wajid Ali Shah, deposed in 1856 on the annexation of Oudh.

clash with the fact conveyed by the last mail of a mutiny of the Nizam's cavalry having broken out at Aurungabad. Aurungabad being the capital of the district of the same name which belongs to the Bombay Presidency, the truth is that the last mail announced a commencement of revolt of the Bombay army. The Aurungabad mutiny is, indeed, said to have been at once put down by General Woodburn. But was not the Meerut mutiny said to have been put down at once? Did not the Lucknow mutiny, after having been quenched by Sir H. Lawrence, make a more formidable reappearance a fortnight later? Will it not be recollected that the very first announcement of mutiny in the Indian army was accompanied with the announcement of restored order? Although the bulk of the Bombay and Madras armies is composed of low caste men, there are still mixed to every regiment some hundred Rajpoots, a number quite sufficient to form the connecting links with the high-caste rebels of the Bengal army. The Punjaub is declared to be quiet, but at the same time we are informed that 'at Ferozepore, on the 13th of June, military executions had taken place'; while Vaughan's corps[7] – 5th Punjaub Infantry – is praised for 'having behaved admirably in pursuit of the 55th Native Infantry'.[8] This, it must be confessed, is very queer sort of 'quiet'.

---

[7] Major John Luther Vaughan (1820–1911): leading the Punjab infantry on 25 May, pursued the deserters of 55 Native Infantry towards Swat. See Kaye, *History of the Sepoy War*, Vol. II, pp. 484–85.

[8] Quoted from the *Morning Post* of 30 July 1857 and *The Times*, No. 22747, 31 July 1857. See *CW*, Vol. 15, p. 317 n.

State of the Indian Insurrection

(*New York Daily Tribune*, August 18, 1857. Correspondence.)
London, August 4, 1857

On the arrival at London of the voluminous reports conveyed by the last Indian mail, the meagre outlines of which had been anticipated by the electric telegraph, the rumor of the capture of Delhi was rapidly spreading and winning so much consistency as to influence the transactions of the Stock Exchange. It was another edition of the capture of Sevastopol hoax, on a reduced scale.[1] The slightest examination of the dates and contents of the Madras papers, from which the favorable news was avowedly derived, would have sufficed to dispel the delusion. The Madras information professed to rest upon private letters from Agra dated June 17, but an official notification, issued at Lahore, on the 17th of June, announces that up to 4 o'clock in the afternoon of the 16th, all was quiet before Delhi, while *The Bombay Times*, dated July 1, states that 'General Barnard was waiting for reinforcements on the morning of the 17th, after having repelled several sorties.' This much, as to the date of the Madras information. As to its contents, these are evidently made up of General Barnard's bulletin, dated June 8, on his forcible occupation of the heights of Delhi, and of some private reports relating to the sallies of the besieged on the 12th and 14th June.

A military plan of Delhi and its cantonments has at last been compiled by Captain Lawrence, from the unpublished plans of the East India Company. Hence we see that Delhi is not quite so weakly fortified as was at first asserted, nor quite so strongly as is now pretended. It possesses a citadel, to be taken by escalade or by regular approaches. The walls, being more than seven miles in extent, are built of solid masonry, but of no great height. The ditch is narrow and not very deep, and the flanking works do not properly enfilade the curtain. Martello towers exist at intervals. They are semicircular in form, and loopholed for musketry. Spiral staircases lead from the top of the walls down through the towers to chambers, on a level with the ditch, and those are loopholed for infantry fire, which may prove very annoying to an escalading party crossing the ditch. The

---

See Marx's letter to Engels dated 15 August 1857, where he says that he was 'hold[ing] the fort for *you* as the *Tribune's* Military Correspondent'; *CW*, Vol. 40, p. 152 and n. (b)).

[1] The allusion here is to the deliberate spreading of a rumour in October 1854 in Paris, regarding the capture of Sevastopol by the allies. This rumour was circulated by the official press in France, Britain, Belgium and Germany. Later on the French Government had to deny the report. See *CW*, Vol. 15, p. 676.

bastions defending the curtains are also furnished with banquettes for riflemen, but these may be kept down by shelling. When the insurrection broke out, the arsenal in the interior of the city contained 900,000 cartridges, two complete siege-trains, a large number of field guns and 10,000 muskets. The powder magazine had been long since removed, at the desire of the inhabitants, from the city to the cantonments outside Delhi, and contained not less than 10,000 barrels. The commanding heights occupied by Gen. Barnard on the 8th of June are situated in a north-westerly direction from Delhi, where the cantonments outside the walls were also established.

From the description, resting on authentic plans, it will be understood that the stronghold of the revolt must have succumbed before a single *coup de main*,[2] if the British force now before Delhi had been there on the 26th of May, and they could have been there if supplied with sufficient carriage. A review of the list published in *The Bombay Times*, and republished in the London papers, of the number of regiments that had revolted, to the end of June, and of the dates on which they revolted, proves conclusively that, on the 26th of May, Delhi was yet occupied by 4,000 to 5,000 men only; a force which could not one moment have thought of defending a wall seven miles in extent. Meerut being only forty miles distant from Delhi, and having, since the commencement of 1853, always served as the headquarters of the Bengal artillery, possessed the principal laboratory for military scientific purposes, and afforded the parade-ground for exercise in the use of field and siege ordnance; it becomes the more incomprehensible that the British commander was in want of the means necessary for the execution of one of those *coups de main* by which the British forces in India always know how to secure their supremacy over the natives. First we were informed that the siege-train was waited for; then that reinforcements were wanted; and now *The Press*,[3] one of the best informed London papers, tells us, 'It is known by our Government for a fact that General Barnard is deficient in stores and ammunition, and that his supply of the latter is limited to 24 rounds a man.'

From General Barnard's own bulletin on the occupation of the heights of Delhi, which is dated the 8th of June, we see that he originally intended assailing Delhi on the following day. Instead of being able to follow up his plan, he was, by one accident or the other, confined to taking up the defensive against the besieged.

At this very moment it is extremely difficult to compute forces on either part. The statements of the Indian press are altogether self-contradictory; but we think some reliance may be put upon an Indian correspondence of the Bonapartist *Pays*, which seems to emanate from the French Consul at Calcutta. According to his statement, the army of Gen. Barnard was, on the 14th of June, composed of about 5,700 men, which was expected to be doubled (?) by the reinforcements expected on the 20th of the same month. His train was composed of 30 heavy

[2] French for 'sudden surprise attack'.
[3] *The Press*, a Tory weekly published in London from 1853 to 1866. See *FIWI*, p. 220 n. 40.

siege guns, while the forces of the insurgents were estimated at 40,000 men, badly organized, but richly furnished with all the means of attack and defence.

We remark *en passant*, that the 3,000 insurgents encamped without the Ajmere[4] gate, probably in the Ghazee Khan's tombs,[5] are not, as some London papers imagine, fronting the English force, but, on the contrary, separated from them by the whole breadth of Delhi; the Ajmere gate being situated on one extremity of the north western part of modern Delhi to the south of the ruins of ancient Delhi. On that side of the town nothing can prevent the insurgents from establishing some more such camps. On the south-eastern, or river side of the city, they command the ship bridge, and remain in continued connection with their countrymen, able to receive uninterrupted supplies of men and stores. On a smaller scale Delhi offers the image of a fortress, keeping (like Sevastopol) open its lines of communication with the interior of its own country.

The delay in the British operations has not only allowed the besieged to concentrate large numbers for the defence, but the sentiment of having held Delhi during many weeks, harassed the European forces through repeated sallies, together with the news daily pouring in of fresh revolts of the entire army, has, of course, strengthened the *morale* of the Sepoys. The English, with their small forces, can, of course, not think of investing the town, but must storm it. However, if the next regular mail bring not the news of the capture of Delhi, we may almost be sure that, for some months, all serious operations on the part of the British will have to be suspended. The rainy season will have set in real earnest, and protect the south-eastern face of the city by filling the ditch with 'the deep and rapid current of the Jumna' while a thermometer ranging from 75° to 102°, combined with an average fall of nine inches of rain, would scourge the Europeans with the genuine Asiatic cholera. Then would be verified the words of Lord Ellenborough,

> I am of opinion that Sir H. Barnard cannot remain where he is – the climate forbids it. When the heavy rains set in he will be cut off from Meerut, from Umballah and from the Punjaub; he will be imprisoned in a very narrow strip of land, and he will be in a situation, I will not say of peril, but in a situation which can only end in ruin and destruction. I trust that he will retire in time.

Everything, then, as far as Delhi is concerned, depends on the question whether or not Gen. Barnard found himself sufficiently provided with men and ammunition to undertake the assault of Delhi during the last weeks of June. On the other hand, a retreat on his part would immensely strengthen the moral force of the insurrection, and perhaps decide the Bombay and Madras armies upon openly joining it.

---

[4] So printed in the *NYDT*. In Av. 'Aymeer', an obvious mistake.
[5] A reference to the tomb of Mir Shihabuddin entitled Ghaziuddin Khan Bahadur Firuz Jang. The tomb stands about one hundred yards southwest of Ajmeri Gate.

The Indian Insurrection

(*New York Daily Tribune*, August 29, 1857. Correspondence.)
London, August 14, 1857[1]

When the Indian news, conveyed by the Trieste telegraph on the 30th of July, and by the Indian mail on the 1st of August, first arrived, we showed at once, from their contents and their dates, that the capture of Delhi was a miserable hoax, and a very inferior imitation of the never-to-be-forgotten fall of Sevastopol. Yet such is the unfathomable depth of John Bull's gullibility, that his minister, his stock-jobbers and his press had, in fact, contrived to persuade him that the very news which laid bare General Barnard's merely defensive position, contained evidence of the complete extermination of his enemies. From day to day this hallucination grew stronger, till it assumed at last such consistency as to induce even a veteran hand at similar matters, General Sir De Lacy Evans,[2] to proclaim on the night of the 12th of August, amid the cheering echoes of the House of Commons, his belief in the truth of the rumor of the capture of Delhi. After this ridiculous exhibition, however, the bubble was ripe for bursting, and the following day, the 13th of August, brought successive telegraphic dispatches from Trieste and Marseilles, anticipating the Indian mails, and leaving no doubt as to the fact that on the 27th of July[3] Delhi still stood where it had stood before, and that General Barnard, still confined to the defensive, but harassed by frequent furious sorties of the besieged, was very glad to have been able to hold his ground to that time.[4]

In our opinion the next mail is likely to impart the news of the retreat of the English army, or at least facts foreshadowing such a retrograde movement. It is certain that the extent of the walls of Delhi forbids the belief that the whole of them can be effectively manned, and, on the contrary, invites the *coups de main* to be executed by concentration and surprise. But Gen. Barnard seems imbued with European notions of fortified towns and sieges and bombardments, rather than prone to those bold eccentricities by which Sir Charles Napier knew how to thunderstrike Asiatic minds. His forces are, indeed, said to have increased to about 12,000 men, 7,000 Europeans and 5,000 'faithful natives'; but on the other

---

[1] See Marx's letter to Engels dated 15 August 1857, in *CW*, Vol. 40, p. 152 and n. (b).

[2] Sir De Lacy Evans (1787–1870): served in a campaign in Central India in 1807; MP in 1831, 1846, 1852, 1857 and 1859–65; General in 1861.

[3] So printed in the original. But the correct date should be 27 June, as in *CW*, Vol. 15, p. 327; *FIWI*, p. 63; and Av., p. 213.

[4] Barnard died on 5 July of cholera, while the siege was still in progress.

hand, it is not denied that the rebels were daily receiving new reinforcements, so that we may fairly assume that the numerical disproportion between besiegers and besieged has remained the same. Moreover, the only point by the surprise of which General Barnard might insure certain success is the Mogul's Palace, which occupies a commanding position, but the access to which from the riverside must become impracticable from the effect of the rainy season, which will have set in, while an attack on the palace between the Cashmere gate and the river would inflict on the assailants the greatest risk in case of failure. Finally, the setting in of the rains is sure to make the securing of his line of communication and retreat the principal object of the General's operations. In one word, we see no reason to believe that he, with his still inadequate forces, should venture upon risking, at the most impracticable period of the year, what he shrunk from undertaking at a more seasonable time. That in spite of the judicial blindness by which the London press contrives to fool itself, there are entertained serious misgivings in the highest quarters, may be seen from Lord Palmerston's organ, *The Morning Post*. The venal gentlemen of that paper inform us:

> We doubt whether even by the next mail after this, we shall hear of the capture of Delhi; but we do expect that, as *soon* as the troops now on their march to join their besiegers shall have arrived, with a *sufficiency of large guns*, which it seems are still missing, we shall receive intelligence of the fall of the stronghold of the rebels.

It is evident that, by dint of weakness, vacillation, and direct blunders, the British generals have contrived to raise Delhi to the dignity of the political and military center of the Indian revolt. A retreat of the English army, after a prolonged siege, or a mere staying on the defensive, will be regarded as a positive defeat, and give the signal to a general outbreak. It would moreover expose the British troops to a fearful mortality, from which till now they have been protected by the great excitement inherent to a siege full of sorties, encounters, and a hope of soon wreaking a bloody vengeance on their enemies. As to the talk about the apathy of the Hindoos, or even their sympathy with British rule, it is all nonsense. The princes, like true Asiatics, are watching their opportunity. The people in the whole Presidency of Bengal, where not kept in check by a handful of Europeans, are enjoying a blessed anarchy; but there is nobody there against whom they could rise. It is curious *quid pro quo* to expect an Indian revolt to assume the features of a European revolution.

In the Presidencies of Madras and Bombay, the army having not yet pronounced, the people of course do not stir. The Punjaub, at last, is to this moment the principal central station of the European forces, while its native army is disarmed. To rouse it, the neighboring semi-independent princes must throw their weight into the scale. But that such a ramification of conspiracy as exhibited by the Bengal army could not have been carried on such an immense scale without the secret connivance and support of the natives, seems as certain as that the great difficulties the English meet with in obtaining supplies and transports – the principal cause of the slow concentration of their troops – do not witness to the good feelings of the peasantry.

The other news conveyed by the telegraphic dispatches are so far important as they show us the revolt rising on the extreme confines of the Punjaub, in Peshawar, and on the other hand, striding in a southern direction from Delhi to the Presidency of Bombay, through the stations of Jhansi, Saugor, Indore, Mhow, till we arrive at last at Aurungabad, only 180 miles north-east of Bombay. With respect to Jhansi in Bundelcund, we may remark that it is fortified and may thus become another center of armed rebellion. On the other hand, it is stated that Gen. Van Cortlandt[5] has defeated the mutineers at Sirsah, on his road from the north-west to join Gen. Barnard's force before Delhi, from which he was still 170 miles distant. He had to pass by Jhansi,[6] where he would again encounter the rebels. As to the preparations made by the Home Government, Lord Palmerston seems to think that the most circuitous line is the shortest, and consequently sends his troops round the Cape, instead of through Egypt. The fact that some thousand men destined for China have been intercepted at Ceylon and directed to Calcutta, where the 5th Fusileers actually arrived on the 2nd of July, has afforded him the occasion for breaking a bad joke on those of his obedient Commons who still dared doubt that his Chinese war was quite a 'windfall'.

[5] Henry Charles Van Cortlandt (1815–1888) had taken part in the Punjab Wars (1845–46 and 1848–49) and was now marching from the Punjab.

[6] A slip: Jhansi was not on the route between Sirsa and Delhi.

[Despatch of Troops to India]

(*New York Daily Tribune*, September 5, 1857. Printed as a leading article.)

The last sitting but one of the Commons before their prorogation was seized upon by Lord Palmerston to allow them to take some faint glimpses at the entertainments he keeps in store for the English public during the interregnum between the session that has passed away and the session that is to come.[1] The first item of his programme is the announcement of the revival of the Persian war, which as he had stated some months ago, was definitely terminated by a peace concluded on the 4th of March. General Sir de Lacy Evans having expressed the hope that Col. Jacob was ordered back to India with his forces now stationed on the Persian Gulf,[2] Lord Palmerston stated plainly that until Persia had executed the engagements contracted by the treaty, Col. Jacob's troops could not be withdrawn. Herat, however, had not yet been evacuated. There were, on the contrary, rumours afloat affirming that additional forces had been sent by Persia to Herat. This, indeed, had been denied by the Persian Embassador at Paris; but great doubts were justly entertained of the good faith of Persia, and consequently the British forces under Col. Jacob would continue to occupy Bushire. On the day following Lord Palmerston's statement, the news was conveyed by telegraphic dispatch of the categorical demand pressed upon the Persian Government by Mr Murray for the evacuation of Heart – a demand which may be fairly considered the forerunner of a new declaration of war. Such is the first international effect of the Indian revolt.

The second item of Lord Palmerston's programme makes good for its want of details by the wide perspective it unrolls. When he first announced the withdrawal of large military forces from England to be dispatched to India, he answered his opponents, accusing him of denuding Great Britain of her defensive power, and thus affording foreign countries an opportunity to take advantage of her weakened position, that

---

The extract reproduced here comprises the first part of the article; the remaining article deals with European affairs. No heading given in *NYDT*.

[1] Palmerston's speech in the House of Commons on August 20, 1857, *The Times*, No. 22765, August 21, 1857 (*CW*, Vol. 15, p. 331 n.).

[2] Sir de Lacy Evans' speech in the House of Commons on August 20, 1857, *The Times*, No. 22765, August 21, 1857 (*CW*, Vol. 15, p. 331 n.).

the people of great Britain would never tolerate any such proceeding, and that men would be raised suddenly and rapidly, sufficient for any contingency that would arrive.[3]

Now, on the eve of the prorogation of Parliament, he speaks in quite a different strain. To the advice of Gen. De Lacy Evans to send out to India the troops in screw line-of-battle ships, he did not reply, as he had done before, by asserting the superiority of the sail to the screw-propeller, but on the contrary, admitted that the General's plan appeared in the first instance highly advantageous. Yet, the House ought to bear in mind, that

> there were other considerations to be kept in view, in regard to the propriety of keeping up sufficient military and naval forces at home. . . Certain circumstances pointed out the inexpediency of sending out of the country a greater naval force than was absolutely necessary. The steam line-of-battle ships were, no doubt, lying in ordinary, and were of no great use at present; but if any such events as had been alluded to took place, and they wanted their naval forces to put to sea, how could they meet *the danger which threatened*, if they allowed their line-of-battle ships to do the duty of transports to India? They should be falling into a grave error if they sent to India the fleet which *circumstances occurring in Europe* might render it necessary to arm *for their own defense at a very short notice*.[4]

Lord Palmerston, it will not be denied, plants John Bull on the horns of a very fine dilemma. If he uses the adequate means for a decisive suppression of the Indian revolt, he will be attacked at home; and if he allows the Indian revolt to consolidate, he will, as Mr Disraeli said,

> find other characters on the stage, with whom to contend, beside the princes of India.[5]

Before casting a glance at the 'European circumstances' so mysteriously alluded to, it may not be amiss to gather up the confessions made during the same sitting of the Commons in regard to the actual position of the British forces in India. First, then, all sanguine hopes of a sudden capture of Delhi were dropped as if by mutual agreement, and the highflying expectations of former days came

---

[3] Palmerston's speech in the House of Commons on August 11, 1857, *The Times*, No. 22757, August 12, 1857 (CW, Vol. 15, p. 332 n.).

[4] Palmerston's speech in the House of Commons on August 20, 1857, is printed in *The Times*, No. 22765, August 21, 1857 (CW, Vol. 15, p. 332 n.); but Marx has apparently drawn on some other report, since the words, though not the substance, are different from those of the *Times*.

[5] Disraeli's speech in the House of Commons on August 11, 1857, *The Times*, No. 22757, August 12, 1857 (CW, Vol. 15, p. 332 n.).

down to the more rational view that they ought to congratulate themselves, if the English were able to maintain their posts until November, when the advance of the re-enforcements sent from home was to take place. In the second instance, misgivings oozed out as to the probability of their losing the most important of those posts, Cawnpore, on the fate of which, as Mr Disraeli said, everything must depend, and the relief of which he considered of even greater import than the capture of Delhi.[6] From its central position on the Ganges, its bearing on Oude, Rohilcund, Gwalior, and Bundelcund, and its serving as an advanced for to Delhi, Cawnpore is, in fact, in the present circumstances, a place of prime importance. Lastly, Sir F. Smith, one of the military members of the House, called its attention to the fact that, actually, there were no engineers and sappers with their India army, as all of them had deserted, and were likely 'to make Delhi a second Saragossa.'[7] On the other hand, Lord Palmerston had neglected to forward from England either any officers or men of the engineer corps.

[6] Disraeli's speech in the House of Commons on August 20, 1857, *The Times*, No. 22765, August 21, 1857 (*CW*, Vol. 15, p. 333 n.).
[7] J.M.F. Smith's speech in the House of Commons on August 20, 1857, *The Times*, August 21, 1857 (*CW*, Vol. 15, p. 333 n.). Saragossa was a Spanish fortress which fell to Napoleon only after two sieges in 1808–09.

[The Revolt in India]

(*New York Daily Tribune*, September 15, 1857. Printed as a leading article. Written, September 1, 1857.)

The mail of the *Baltic* reports no new events in India, but has a mass of highly interesting details, which we proceed to condense for the instruction of our readers. The first point to be noticed is that so late as the 15th of July the English had not got into Delhi. At the same time, the cholera had made its appearance in their camp, the heavy rains were setting in, and the raising of the siege and the withdrawal of the besiegers appeared to be a question of time only. The British press would fain make us believe that the pest, while carrying off Gen. Sir H. Barnard, had spared his worse-fed and harder worked men. It is, therefore, not from explicit statements, communicated to the public, but only by way of inference from avowed facts, that we can arrive at some idea of the ravages of this terrible disease in the ranks of the besieging army. An officer in the camp before Delhi, writes, July 14:

> We are doing nothing toward taking Delhi, and are merely defending ourselves against sorties of the enemy. We have parts of five European regiments, but can muster only 2,000 Europeans for any effective attack; large detachments from each regiment having been left to protect Jullindur, Loodhiana, Subathoo, Dugshale, Kussowlie, Umballah, Meerut and Philaor.[1] In fact, small detachments only of each regiment have joined us. The enemy are far superior to us in artillery.

Now this proves that the forces arriving from the Punjaub found the great northern line of communication from Jullindur down to Meerut in a state of rebellion, and were consequently obliged to diminish their numbers by leaving detachments at the main posts. This accounts for the arrivals from the Punjaub not mustering their anticipated strength, but it does not explain the reduction of the European force to 2,000 men. The Bombay correspondent of *The London Times*, writing on July 30, attempts to explain in another way the passive attitude of the besiegers. He says:

> The reinforcements, indeed, have reached our camp – one wing of the 8th (King's), one of the 61st, a company of foot artillery, and two guns of a native

---

[1] Now spelt as Jalandhar, Ludhiana, Sabathu, Dagshai, Kasauli, Ambala, Meerut and Phillaur.

troops, the 14th[2] Irregular Cavalry Regiment (escorting a large ammunition train), the 2nd Punjaub Cavalry, the 1st Punjaub Infantry and the 4th Sikh Infantry; but the native portion of the troops thus added to the besieging force are not entirely and uniformly trustworthy, brigaded though they are with Europeans. The cavalry regiments of the Punjaub force contain many Mussulmans and high caste Hindoos, from Hindostan proper, and Rohilcund, while the Bengal Irregular Cavalry are mainly composed of such elements. These men are, as a class, utterly disloyal, and their presence with the force in any numbers must be embarrassing – and so it has proved. In the 2nd Punjaub Cavalry, it has been found necessary to disarm some 70 Hindostan men and to hang three, one a superior native officer. Of the 9th Irregulars, which have been some time with the force, several troopers have deserted, and the 4th Irregulars have, I believe, murdered their adjutant, while on detachment duty.[3]

Here another secret is revealed. The camp before Delhi, it seems, bears some likeness to the camp of Agramante,[4] and the English have to struggle not only with the enemy in their front, but also with the ally in their lines. Still, this fact affords no sufficient cause for there being only 2,000 Europeans to be spared for offensive operations. A third writer, the Bombay correspondent of *The Daily News*, gives an explicit enumeration of the forces assembled under Gen. Read,[5] Barnard's successor, which seems trustworthy, as he reckons up singly the different elements of which they are composed. According to his statement, about 1,200 Europeans and 1,600 Sikhs, irregular horse, etc., say altogether about 3,000 men, headed by Brigadier Gen. Chamberlain,[6] reached the camp before Delhi from the Punjaub between June 23 and July 3. On the other hand, he estimates the whole of the forces now assembled under Gen. Read at 7,000 men, artillery and siege-train included, so that the army of Delhi, before the arrival of the Punjaub reinforcements, could not have exceeded 4,000 men. The London *Times* of August 13, stated that Sir H. Barnard had collected an army of 7,000

[2] So in the original. In *CW*, Vol. 15, p. 343, it is 17th Irregular Cavalry; but Av. and editors of *FIWI* correctly read 14th.

[3] The letter of the Bombay correspondent, dated 30 July 1857, *The Times*, No. 22773, 31 August 1857. Reference from *CW*, Vol. 15, p. 343.

[4] This is explained in ibid., p. 678 n. 393. Agramante is the Moorish king in Lodovico Ariosto's poem *L'Orlando Furioso*. At war with Charlemagne, Agramante besieged Paris concentrating the bulk of his forces by the walls of that city. But soon dissensions began in the camp. When Marx compared the English camp near Delhi with that of Agramante he alluded to a line in Ariosto's poem, 'There is dissent in Agramante's Camp', which became a common dictum.

[5] So printed in the *NYDT*. Thomas Reed (1796–1883): entered the army in 1813, participated in the Anglo-Sikh War in December 1845; upon the death of Major-General Barnard, he acted temporarily as the commander-in-chief of the army in Bengal; joined the British army of Delhi at Alipur on 8 June. See C. Ball, *History of the Indian Mutiny*, Vol. I, pp. 476–77.

[6] Sir Neville Bowles Chamberlain (1820–1902): British General, commanded the irregular forces in the Punjab, 1854–58. See *CW*, Vol. 15, p. 706.

British and 5,000 natives. Although this was a flagrant exaggeration, there is every reason to believe that the European forces then amounted to about 4,000 men, backed by a somewhat smaller number of natives. The original force, then, under Gen. Barnard, was as strong as the force now collected under Gen. Read. Consequently, the Punjaub reinforcements have only made up for the wear and tear which have reduced the strength of the besiegers almost one-half, an enormous loss, proceeding partly from the incessant sorties of the rebels, partly from the ravages of the cholera. Thus we understand why the British can muster only 2,000 Europeans for any effective attack.

So much for the strength of the British forces before Delhi. Now for their operations. That they were not of a very brilliant character may be fairly inferred from the simple fact that, since June 8, when Gen. Barnard made his report on the capture of the heights opposite Delhi,[7] no bulletin whatever has been issued from headquarters. The operations, with a single exception, consist of sallies made by the besieged and repulsed by the besiegers. The besiegers were attacked now in front and then in the flanks, but mostly in the right rear. The sorties took place on the 27th and 30th of June, on the 3rd, 4th, 9th and 14th of July. On the 27th of June, fighting was confined to outpost skirmishes, lasting some hours, but toward the afternoon was interrupted by a heavy fall of rain, the first of the season. On the 30th of June, the insurgents showed themselves in force among the inclosures on the right of the besiegers, harassing their pickets and supports. On the 3rd of July, the besieged made early in the morning a feint attack on the right rear of the English position, then advanced several miles to that rear along the Kurnaul road as far as Alipore, in order to intercept a train of supplies and treasure under convoy to the camp. On their way, they encountered an outpost of the 2nd Punjaub. Irregular Horse, which gave way at once. On their return to the city, on the 4th, the rebels were attacked by a body of 1,000 infantry and two squadrons of cavalry dispatched from the English camp to intercept them. They contrived, however, to effect their retreat with little or no loss and saving all their guns. On the 8th of July, a party was sent from the British camp to destroy a canal bridge at the village of Bussy, some six miles from Delhi, which in the former sallies had afforded the insurgents facilities for attacking the extreme British rear, and interfering with the British communications with Kurnaul and Meerut. The bridge was destroyed. On the 9th of July, the insurgents came out again in force and attacked the right rear of the British position. In the official accounts telegraphed to Lahore on the same day, the loss of the assailants is estimated at about one thousand killed; but this account seems much exaggerated, since we read in a letter of July 13 from the camp: 'Our men buried and burnt two hundred and fifty of the enemy's dead, and large numbers were removed by themselves into the city.'[8]

---

[7] See Marx's article, 'State of Indian Insurrection', *NYDT*, 18 August 1857.
[8] Campbell (*Narrative*, p. 86, col. b) seems to quote from the same report.

The same letter, published in *The Daily News*, does not pretend that the British forced back the Sepoys, but, on the contrary, that 'the sepoys forced back all our working parties and then retired'. The loss of the besiegers was considerable, amounting, as it did, to two hundred and twelve, killed and wounded. On the 14th of July, in consequence of another sortie, another fierce fight took place, the details of which have not yet arrived.

The besieged had, meanwhile, received strong reinforcements. On the 1st of July, the Rohilcund mutineers from Bareilly, Muradabat[9] and Shahjehanpore, consisting of four regiments of infantry, one of irregular cavalry, and one battery of artillery, had contrived to effect their junction with their comrades at Delhi.

> It had been hoped, says the Bombay correspondent of the London *Times*, that they would find the Ganges impassable, but the anticipated rise of the river not taking place, it was crossed at Gurmukheser,[10] the Doab was traversed and Delhi was attained. For two days, our troops had the mortification of watching the long train of men, guns, horses and beasts of burden of all kinds (for there was a treasure with the rebels, say £50,000) streaming across the bridge of boats into the city, without a possibility of preventing or in any way annoying them.[11]

This successful march of the insurgents through the whole breadth of Rohilcund proves all the country east of the Jumna up to the hills of Rohilcund to be closed against the English forces, while the untroubled march of the insurgents from Neemuch to Agra, if connected with the revolts at Indore and Mhow, proves the same fact for all the country south-west of the Jumna and up to the Vindhya Mountains. The only successful – in fact, the only – operation of the English in regard to Delhi is, the pacification of the country to its north and its north-west by Gen. Van Cortlandt's Punjaub Sikh forces. Throughout the district between Loodianah and Sirsah, he had mainly to encounter the robber tribes inhabiting villages sparsely scattered over a wild and sandy desert. On the 11th of July, he is said to have left Sirsah for Futtehabad, thence to march on Hissar, thus opening up the country in the rear of the besieging force.

Besides Delhi, three other points in the North-Western Provinces – Agra, Cawnpore and Lucknow – had become centers of the struggle between the natives and the English. The affair of Agra bears this peculiar aspect, that it shows for the first time the mutineers setting out on a deliberate expedition over about 300 miles of ground with the intention of attacking a distant English military station. According to *The Mofussilite*,[12] a journal printed at Agra, the Sepoy regiments of Nusserabad and Neemuch, about 10,000 strong (say 7,000 infantry, 1,500 cavalry and 8 guns), approached Agra at the end of June, encamped in the

---

[9] So printed in *NYDT*, correct spelling: 'Moradabad'.
[10] So printed in *NYDT*, correct spelling: 'Garhmuktesar'.
[11] *The Times*, No. 22773, 31 August 1857. See *CW*, Vol. 15, p. 345.
[12] An English weekly published from Agra, from 1845. See S. Natarajan, *History of the Press in India* (Bombay, 1962), p. 85.

beginning of July on a plain in the rear of the village of Sussia, about 20 miles from Agra, and on the 4th of July seemed preparing an attack on the city. On this news, the European residents in the cantonments before Agra took refuge in the fort. The commander at Agra dispatched at first the Kotah contingent of horse, foot and artillery to serve as an advanced post against the enemy, but, having reached their place of destination, one and all bolted to join the ranks of the rebels. On July 5, the Agra garrison, consisting of the 3rd Bengal Europeans, a battery of artillery and a corps of European volunteers, marched out to attack the mutineers, and are said to have driven them out of the village into the plain behind it, but were evidently themselves in their turn forced back, and, after a loss of 49 killed and 92 wounded, of a total force of 500 men engaged, had to retire, being harassed and threatened by the cavalry of the enemy with such activity as to prevent their 'getting a shot at them', as *The Mofussilite* says. In other words, the English took to downright flight and shut themselves up in their fort, while the sepoys, advancing to Agra, destroyed nearly all the houses in the cantonment. On the following day, July 6, they proceeded to Bhurtpore, on the way to Delhi. The important result of this affair is the interruption by the muti-neers of the English line of communication between Agra and Delhi, and their probable appearance before the old city of the Moguls.

At Cawnpore, as was known from the last mail, a force of about 200 Europeans, under the command of Gen. Wheeler,[13] having with them the wives and children of the 32nd foot, was shut up in a fortified work and surrounded by an overwhelming mass of rebels, headed by Nena Sahib of Bithoor. Different assaults on the fort took place on the 17th and between the 24th and 28th of June, in the last of which, Gen, Wheeler was shot through the leg and died of his wounds. On June 28 Nena[14] Sahib invited the English to surrender on the condi-tion of being allowed to depart on boats down the Ganges to Allahabad. These terms were accepted, but the British had hardly put out into the middle of the stream when guns opened upon them from the right bank of the Ganges. The people in the boats that tried to escape to the opposite bank were caught and cut down by a body of cavalry. The women and children were made captives. Mes-sengers having been dispatched several times from Cawnpore to Allahabad with pressing demands for relief, on July 1 a column of Madras fusiliers and Sikhs started, under Major Renaud, on the way to Cawnpore. Within four miles of Futteypore it was joined, on July 13 at daybreak, by Brig-Gen. Havelock[15] who, at the head of about 1,300 Europeans of the 84th and 64th, the 13th Irregular

---

[13] General Hugh Massy Wheeler (1789–1857): Major General in 1854; served in the Afghan War, 1838–39 and Sikh Wars, 1845–49; in command at Kanpur in 1856; killed during the Rebellion in 1857.

[14] So printed in *NYDT*, correct spelling: Nana.

[15] Sir Henry Havelock (1795–1857) commanded a column which captured Kanpur on 17 July 1857; defeated the Sepoys at Unnao and Basiratganj; carried the Alambagh (Lucknow); cooperated with Sir Colin Campbell in November 1857; died of diar-rhoea in November 1857.

Horse, and the remnant of Oude Irregulars, reached Allahabad from Benares, July 3, and then followed up Major Renaud by forced marches. On the very day of his junction with Renaud, he was forced to accept battle before Futteypore, whither Nena Sahib had led his native forces. After an obstinate engagement, Gen. Havelock, by a move in the flank of the enemy, succeeded in driving him out of Futteypore in the direction of Cawnpore, where twice he had to encounter him again on the 15th and 16th of July. At the latter date, Cawnpore was recaptured by the English, Nena Sahib retreating to Bittoor, situated on the Ganges, twelve miles distant from Cawnpore, and said to be strongly fortified. Before undertaking his expedition to Futteypore, Nena Sahib had murdered all the captive English women and children. The recapture of Cawnpore was of the highest importance to the English, as it secured their Ganges line of communication.

At Lucknow, the capital of Oude, the British garrison found themselves nearly in the same plight which had proved fatal to their comrades at Cawnpore – shut up in a fort, surrounded by overwhelming forces, straitened for provisions, and deprived of their leader. The latter, Sir H. Lawrence, died July 4, of tetanus, from a wound in the leg, received on the 2nd, during a sortie. On the 18th and 19th of July, Lucknow was still holding out. Its only hope of relief rested on Gen. Havelock's pushing forward his forces from Cawnpore. The question is whether he would dare to do so with Nena Sahib in his rear. Any delay, however, must prove fatal to Lucknow, since the periodical rains would soon render field operations impossible.

The examination of these events forces the conclusion upon us that, in the north-west provinces of Bengal, the British forces were gradually drifting into the position of small posts planted on insulated rocks amid a sea of revolution. In Lower Bengal, there had occurred only partial acts of insubordination at Mirzapore, Dinapore and Patna, besides an unsuccessful attempt made by the roving Brahmins of the neighbourhood to recapture the holy city of Benares. In the Punjaub, the spirit of rebellion was forcibly kept down, a mutiny being suppressed at Sealkote, another at Jhylum, and the disaffection of Peshawur successfully checked. Emeutes[16] had already been attempted in Gujerat, at Punderpoor in Sattarah, at Nagpoor and Sagor in the Nagpoor territory, at Hyderabad in the Nizam's territory, and, lastly, as far south as Mysore, so that the calm of the Bombay and Madras Presidencies must be understood as by no means perfectly secure.

[16] French for 'popular rising'.

The Indian Revolt

(*New York Daily Tribune*, September 16, 1857. Correspondence.)
London, September 4, 1857

The outrages committed by the revolted Sepoys in India are indeed appalling, hideous, ineffable – such as one is prepared to meet only in wars of insurrections, of nationalities, of races, and above all of religion; in one word, such as respectable England used to applaud when perpetrated by the Vendeans on the 'Blues', by the Spanish guerrillas on the infidel Frenchmen, by Servians[1] on their German and Hungarian neighbors, by Croats on Viennese rebels, by Caviagnac's Garde Mobile or Bonaparte's Decembrists on the sons and daughters of proletarian France. However infamous the conduct of the Sepoys, it is only the reflex, in a concentrated form, of England's own conduct in India, not only during the epoch of the foundation of her Eastern Empire, but even during the last ten years of a long-settled rule. To characterize that rule, it suffices to say that torture formed an organic institution of its financial policy. There is something in human history like retribution; and it is a rule of historical retribution that its instrument be forged not by the offended, but by the offender himself.

The first blow dealt to the French monarchy proceeded from the nobility, not from the peasants. The Indian revolt does not commence with the Ryots, tortured, dishonoured and stripped naked by the British, but with the Sepoys, clad, fed, petted,[2] fatted and pampered by them. To find parallels to the Sepoy atrocities, we need not, as some London papers pretend, fall back on the middle ages, nor even wander beyond the history of contemporary England. All we want is to study the first Chinese war, an event, so to say, of yesterday. The English soldiery then committed abominations for the mere fun of it; their passions being neither sanctified by religious fanaticism nor exacerbated by hatred against an overbearing and conquering race, nor provoked by the stern resistance of a heroic enemy. The violations of women, the spittings of children, the roasting of whole villages, were then mere wanton sports, not recorded by Mandarins, but by British officers themselves.

Even at the present catastrophe it would be an unmitigated mistake to suppose that all the cruelty is on the side of the Sepoys, and all the milk of human kindness flows on the side of the English. The letters of the British officers are redolent of malignity. An officer writing from Peshawur gives a description of the disarming of the 10th Irregular Cavalry for not charging the 55th Infantry when

---

[1] Serbians.
[2] 'and' is inserted here in Av.

ordered to do so. He exults in the fact that they were not only disarmed, but stripped of their coats and boots, and after having received 12d. per man, were marched down to the riverside, and there embarked in boats and sent down the Indus, where the writer is delighted to expect every mother's son will have a chance of being drowned in the rapids. Another writer informs us that some inhabitants of Peshawur having caused a night alarm by exploding little mines of gunpowder in honor of a wedding (a national custom), the persons concerned were tied up next morning, and 'received such a flogging as they will not easily forget'. News arrived from Pindee[3] that three native chiefs were plotting. Sir John Lawrence replied to a message ordering a spy to attend to the meeting. On the spy's report, Sir John sent a second message, 'Hang them.' The chiefs were hanged.[4] An officer in the civil service, from Allahabad, writes: 'We have power of life and death in our hands, and we assure you we spare not.'[5] Another from the same place: 'Not a day passes but we string up from ten to fifteen of them (non-combatants).' One exulting officer writes: 'Holmes is hanging them by the score, like a "brick".'[6] Another, in allusion to the summary hanging of a large body of the natives: 'Then our fun commenced.' A third: 'We hold court-martials on horse back, and every nigger we meet with we either string up or shoot.'

From Benares we are informed that thirty zemindars were hanged on the mere suspicion of sympathizing with their own countrymen,[7] and whole villages were burned down on the same plea. An officer from Benares, whose letter is printed in the London *Times*, says: 'The European troops have become fiends when opposed to natives.'[8]

And then it should not be forgotten that, while the cruelties of the English are related as acts of martial vigour, told simply, rapidly, without dwelling on disgusting details, the outrages of the natives, shocking as they are, are still deliberately exaggerated. For instance, the circumstantial account first appearing in *The Times*, and then going the round of the London press, of the atrocities perpetrated at Delhi and Meerut, from whom did it proceed? From a cowardly parson residing at Bangalore, Mysore, more than a thousand miles, as the bird flies, distant from the scene of action. Actual accounts of Delhi evince the imagination of an English parson to be capable of breeding greater horrors than even the wild fancy of a Hindoo mutineer. The cutting of noses, breasts, & c., in one

---

[3] Rawalpindi.

[4] Letter from an artillery officer, dated Peshawur, 21 June 1857, *The Times*, No. 22766 22 August 1857. See CW, Vol. 15, p. 354 n.

[5] Allahabad, 28 June, *The Times*, No. 22768, 25 August 1857. Ibid.

[6] Letter from Tirhoot, dated 26 June, *The Times*, No. 22763, 19 August 1857. Ibid., p. 355 n.

[7] Bhola Nath Chundra, Company's employee, giving details of atrocities by the British forces in Banaras, says that nearly six thousand people were executed there. *Travels of a Hindoo*, edited by Talboy Wheeler, cited in Kaye, *History of the Sepoy War*, Vol. II (London, 1881), pp. 668–69.

[8] R.H. Bartrum, Benares, 13 July, *The Times*, No. 22775, 2 September 1857. See CW, Vol. 15, p. 355 n.

word, the horrid mutilations committed by the Sepoys, are of course more revolting to European feeling than the throwing of red-hot shell on Canton dwellings by a Secretary of the Manchester Peace Society,[9] or the roasting of Arabs pent up in a cave by a French Marshal, or the flaying alive of British soldiers by the cat-o'-nine-tails under drum-head court-martial, or any other of the philanthropical appliances used in British penitentiary colonies. Cruelty, like every other thing, has its fashion, changing according to time and place. Caesar, the accomplished scholar, candidly narrates how he ordered many thousand Gallic warriors to have their right hands cut off. Napoleon would have been ashamed to do this. He preferred dispatching his own French regiments, suspected of republicanism, to St. Domingo, there to die of the blacks and the plague.

The infamous mutilations committed by the Sepoys remind one of the practices of the Christian Byzantine Empire, or the prescriptions of Emperor Charles V's criminal law, or the English punishments for high treason, as still recorded by Judge Blackstone.[10] With Hindoos, whom their religion has made virtuosi in the art of self-torturing, these tortures inflicted on the enemies of their race and creed appear quite natural, and must appear still more so to the English, who, only some years since, still used to draw revenues from the Juggernaut festivals, protecting and assisting the bloody rites of a religion of cruelty.[11]

The frantic roars of the 'bloody old *Times*', as Cobbet[12] used to call it – its playing the part of a furious character in one of Mozart's operas, who indulges in most melodious strains in the idea of first hanging his enemy, then roasting him, then quartering him, then spitting him, and then flaying him alive – its tearing the passion of revenge to tatters and to rags – all this would appear but silly if under the pathos of tragedy there were not distinctly perceptible the tricks of comedy. The London *Times* overdoes its part, not only from panic. It supplies comedy with a subject even missed by Moliere, the Tartuffe[13] of Revenge. What it simply wants is to write up the funds and to screen the Government. As Delhi has not, like the walls of Jericho, fallen before mere puffs of wind,[14] John Bull is to be steeped in cries for revenge up to his very ears, to make him forget that his Government is responsible for the mischief hatched and the colossal dimensions it had been allowed to assume.

[9] Sir John Bowring (1792–1872): a Free-Trader; Consul at Canton in 1847 and Governor of Hong Kong in 1854. The Peace Society was an organization founded by the Quakers in London in 1816. The Society was supported by the Free Traders. See *CW*, Vol. 15, pp. 666, 703.

[10] Sir William Blackstone (1723–1780): English judge and famous constitutional lawyer. His *Commentaries on the Laws of England*, in 4 volumes, appeared in 1765–69.

[11] Here Marx alludes to the practice of suicide by devotees by throwing themselves under the wheels of the chariots carrying the idol of Jagannath during the *rathyatra* festival at Puri. Also see W.W. Hunter, *History of Orissa*, Vol. I, p. 5, and *Statistical Account of Bengal*, Vol. XIX, p. 6.

[12] William Cobbett (1762–1835): the famous English radical journalist and politician.

[13] A character, representing religious hypocrite, in Moliere's play with the same title.

[14] According to the Bible, the walls of Jericho fell at the blast of the conquerors' trumpets.

[Investigation of Tortures in India]

(*New York Daily Tribune*, September 17, 1857. Printed as a leading article.)

Our London correspondent, whose letter with regard to the Indian revolt we published yesterday, very properly referred to some of the antecedents which prepared the way for this violent outbreak.[1] We propose to-day to devote a moment to continuing that line of reflections, and to showing that the British rulers of India are by no means such mild and spotless benefactors of the Indian people as they would have the world believe. For this purpose, we shall resort to the official Blue Books on the subject of East Indian torture, which were laid before the House of Commons during the sessions of 1856 and 1857. The evidence, it will be seen, is of a sort which cannot be gainsaid.

We have first the report of the Torture Commission at Madras,[2] which states its 'belief in the general existence of torture for revenue purposes'. It doubts whether 'anything like an equal number of persons is annually subjected to violence on criminal charges, as for the fault of non-payment of revenue.' It declares that there was 'one thing which had impressed the Commission even more painfully than the conviction that torture exists; it is the difficulty of obtaining redress which confronts the injured parties.'

The reasons for this difficulty given by the Commissioners are: 1. The distances which those who wish to make complaints personally to the Collector have to travel involving expense and loss of time in attending upon his office; 2. The fear that applications by letter 'will be returned with the ordinary indorsement of a reference to the Tahsildar,' the district police and revenue officer – that is, to the very man who, either in his person or through his petty police subordinates, has wronged him; 3. The inefficient means of procedure and punishment provided by law for officers of Government, even when formally accused or convicted of these practices. It seems that if a charge of this nature were proved before a magistrate, he could only punish by a fine of fifty rupees, or a month's imprisonment. The alternative consisted of handing over the accused 'to the criminal Judge to be punished by him, or committed for trial before the Court of the

According to the entry 'India (Torture)' in Marx's notebook, this article was written by him on 28 August 1857. See *CW,* Vol. 15, p. 336.

[1] A reference to Marx's article, 'The Indian Revolt', *New York Daily Tribune* (*NYDT*), 16 September 1857. This sentence is obviously added by the *NYDT* editors.

[2] Report of the Commission for the Investigation of Alleged Cases of Tortures at Madras (London, 1855). See *CW,* Vol. 15, p. 336.

Circuit.' The report adds that 'these seem to be tedious proceedings, applicable only to one class of offenses, abuse of authority – namely, in police charges, and totally inadequate to the necessities of the case.'

A police or revenue officer, who is the same person, as the revenue is collected by the police, when charged with extorting money, is first tried by the Assistant Collector: he then can appeal to the Collector; then to the Revenue Board. This Board may refer him to the Government or to the civil courts: 'In such a state of the law, no poverty-stricken ryot could contend against any wealthy revenue officer; and we are not aware of any complaints having been brought forward under these two regulations (of 1822 and 1828) by the people.'

Further, this extorting of money applies only to taking the public money, or forcing a further contribution from the ryot for the officer to put into his own pocket. There is, therefore, no legal means of punishment[3] whatever for the employment of force in collecting the public revenue.

The report from which these quotations are made applies only to the Presidency of Madras; but Lord Dalhousie himself, writing in September, 1855, to the Directors,[4] says that 'he has long ceased to doubt that torture in one shape or other is practised by the lower subordinates in every British province.'

The universal existence of torture as a financial institution of British India is thus officially admitted, but the admission is made in such a manner as to shield the British Government itself. In fact, the conclusion arrived at by the Madras Commission is that the practice of torture is entirely the fault of the lower Hindoo officials, while the European servants of the Government had always, however unsuccessfully, done their best to prevent it. In answer to this assertion, the Madras Native Association presented, in January, 1856, a petition to Parliament, complaining of the torture investigation on the following grounds: 1. That there was scarcely any investigation at all, the Commission sitting only in the city of Madras, and for but three months, while it was impossible, except in very few cases, for the natives who had complaints to make to leave their homes; 2. That the Commissioners did not endeavor to trace the evil to its source; had they done so, it would have been discovered to be in the very system of collecting the revenue; 3. That no inquiry was made of the accused native officials as to what extent their superiors were acquainted with the practice. 'The origin of this coercion', says the petitioners, 'is not with the physical perpetrators of it, but descends to them from the officials immediately their superiors, which latter again are answerable for the estimated amount of the collection to their European superiors, these also being responsible on the same head to the highest authority of the Government.'

Indeed, a few extracts from the evidence on which the Madras Report professes to be founded, will suffice to refute its assertion that 'no blame is due to Englishmen'. Thus, Mr W.D. Kohlhoff, a merchant says: 'The modes of torture

---

[3] 'punishing' in Av.
[4] Directors of the East India Company.

practised are various, and suitable to the fancy of the tahsildar or his subordinates, but whether any redress is received from higher authorities, it is difficult for me to tell, as *all complaints are generally referred to the tahsildars* for investigation and information.'

Among the cases of complaint from natives, we find the following:

Last year, as our *peasanum* (principal paddy or rice crops) failed for want of rain, we were unable to pay as usual. When the Jamabundy was made we claimed a remission on account of the losses, according to the terms of the agreement entered into in 1837 by us, when Mr Eden was our collector. As this remission was not allowed, we refused to take our puttahs. The Tahsildar then commenced to compel us to pay with great severity, from the month of June to August. I and others were placed in charge of persons who used to take us in the sun. There we were made to stoop and stones were put on our backs, and we were kept in the burning sand. After 8 o'clock, we were let to go to our rice. Such like ill treatment was continued during three months, during which we sometimes went to give our petitions to the collector, who refused to take them. We took these petitions and appealed to the Sessions Court, who transmitted them to the collector. Still we got no justice. In the month of September, a notice was served upon us, and twenty-five days after, our property was distrained, and afterward sold. Beside what I have mentioned, our women were also ill treated; the kittee was put upon their breasts.

A native Christian states in reply to questions put by the Commissioners: 'When a European or native regiment passes through, all the ryots are pressed to bring in provisions, & c., *for nothing*, and should any of them ask for the price of the articles, they are severely tortured.' There follows the case of a Brahmin, in which he, with others of his own village and of the neighboring villages, was called on by the Tahsildars to furnish planks, charcoal, firewood, & c., gratis, that he might carry on the Coleroon bridge work; on refusing, he is seized by twelve men and maltreated in various ways. He adds:

I presented a complaint to the Sub-Collector, Mr W. Cadell, but he made no inquiry, and tore my complaint. As he is desirous of completing cheaply the Coleroon bridge-work at the expense of the poor and of acquiring a good name from the Government, whatever may be the nature of the murder committed by the Tahsildar, he takes no cognizance of it.

The light in which illegal practices, carried to the last degree of extortion and violence, were looked upon by the highest authority, is best shown by the case of Mr Brereton, the Commissioner in charge of the Loodhiana District in the Punjaub in 1855. According to the report of the Chief Commissioner for the Punjaub,[5] it was proved that

[5] (Lord) John Laird Mair Lawrence (1811–1879): later Viceroy of India, 1863–69.

in matters under the immediate cognizance or direction of the Deputy Commissioners, Mr Brereton himself, the houses of wealthy citizens had been causelessly searched; that property seized on such occasions was detained for lengthened periods; that many parties were thrown into prison, and lay there for weeks, without charges being exhibited against them; and that the laws relating to security for bad character had been applied with sweeping and indiscriminating severity. That the Deputy Commissioner had been followed about from district to district by certain police officers and informers, whom he employed wherever he went, and that these men had been the main authors of mischief.

In his minute on the case, Lord Dalhousie says:

We have irrefragable proof – proof, indeed, undisputed by Mr Brereton himself – that that officer has been guilty of each item in the heavy catalogue of irregularities and illegalities with which the Chief Commissioner has charged him, and which have brought disgrace on one portion of the British administration, and have subjected a large number of British subjects to gross injustice, to arbitrary imprisonment and cruel torture.

Lord Dalhousie proposes 'to make a great public example', and, consequently, is of opinion that: 'Mr Brereton cannot, *for the present*, be fitly intrusted with the authority of a Deputy Commissioner, but ought to be removed from that grade to the grade of a first class Assistant.'

These extracts from the Blue Books may be concluded with the petition from the inhabitants of Talook in Canara, on the Malabar coast, who, after stating that they had presented several petitions to the Government to no purpose, thus contrast their former and present conditions:

While we were cultivating wet and dry lands, hill tracts, low tracts and forests, paying the light assessments fixed upon us, and thereby enjoying tranquility and happiness under the administration of 'Ranee', Bahadur and Tippoo,[6] the then Circar servants, levied an additional assessment, but we never paid it. We were not subjected to privations, oppressions or ill-usages in collecting the revenue. On the surrender of this country to the Honorable Company, they devised all sorts of plans to squeeze out money from us. With this pernicious object in view, they invented rules and framed regulations, and directed their collectors and civil judges to put them in execution. But the then collectors and their subordinate native officials paid for some time due attention to our grievances, and acted in consonance with our wishes. On the contrary, the present collectors and their subordinate officials, *desirous of obtaining promotion on any account whatever*, neglect the welfare and interests of the people in general, turn a deaf ear to our grievances, and subject us to all sorts of oppressions.

---

[6] Rani Lakhsammanni (d. 1810), Hyder Ali (1761–83) and Tipu Sultan (1783–99).

We have here given but a brief and mildly-colored chapter from the real history of British rule in India. In view of such facts, dispassionate and thoughtful men may perhaps be led to ask whether a people are not justified in attempting to expel the foreign conquerors who have so abused their subjects. And if the English could do these things in cold blood, is it surprising that the insurgent Hindoos should be guilty, in the fury of revolt and conflict, of the crimes and cruelties alleged against them?

[British Incomes in India]

(*New York Daily Tribune*, September 21, 1857. Printed as a leading article.)

The present state of affairs in Asia suggests the inquiry, What is the real value of their Indian dominion to the British nation and people? Directly, that is in the shape of tribute, or surplus of Indian receipts over Indian expenditures, nothing whatever reaches the British Treasury. On the contrary, the annual outgo is very large. From the moment that the East India Company entered extensively on the career of conquest – now just about a century ago – their finances fell into an embarrassed condition, and they were repeatedly compelled to apply to Parliament, not only for military aid to assist them in holding the conquered territories, but for financial aid to save them from bankruptcy.[1] And so things have continued down to the present moment, at which so large a call is made for troops on the British nation, to be followed, no doubt, by corresponding calls for money. In prosecuting its conquests hitherto, and building up its establishments, the East India Company has contracted a debt of upward of £50,000,000 sterling,[2] while the British Government has been at the expense, for years past, of transporting to and from and keeping up in India, in addition to the forces, native and European, of the East India Company, a standing army of thirty thousand men. Such being the case, it is evident that the advantage to Great Britain from her Indian Empire must be limited to the profits and benefits which accrue to individual British subjects. These profits and benefits, it must be confessed, are very considerable.

First, we have the stockholders in the East India Company, to the number of about 3,000 persons, to whom under the recent charter[3] there is guaranteed, upon a paid-up capital of six millions of pounds sterling, an annual dividend of ten and a half percent, amounting to £630,000 annually.[4] As the East India stock is held in transferable shares, anybody may become a stockholder who has money enough to buy the stock, which under the existing charter, commands a premium

---

[1] This is with reference to the financial relief sought by the East India Company from the British Treasury, which led to the passage of the Regulating Act of 1773.

[2] Dickinson (in *The Government of India under a Bureaucracy*, No. VI of *India Reform*, p. 147), puts the debt in 1851 at £51,777,234, a figure very close to that of Marx.

[3] The Charter Act of 1853.

[4] In Campbell (*Modern India*, p. 410), the dividend referred to as 'interest' is put at £650,000 per annum.

of from 125 to 150 per cent. Stock to the amount of £500, costing say $6,000,[5] entitles the holder to speak at the Proprietors' meetings, but to vote he must have £1,000 of stock. Holders of £3,000 have two votes, of £6,000 three votes, and of £10,000 or upward four votes. The proprietors, however, have but little voice, except in the election of the Board of Directors,[6] of whom they choose twelve, while the Crown appoints six; but these appointees of the Crown must be quali-fied by having resided for ten years or more in India. One-third of the Directors go out of office each year, but may be re-elected or reappointed. To be a Director, one must be a proprietor of £2,000 of stock. The Directors have a salary of £500 each, and their Chairman and Deputy Chairman twice as much; but the chief in-ducement to accept the office is the great patronage attached to it in the appoint-ment of all Indian officers, civil, and military – a patronage, however, largely shared, and, as to the most important offices, engrossed substantially, by the Board of Control. This Board consists of six members, all Privy Councilors, and in general two or three of them Cabinet Ministers – the President of the Board being always so, in fact a Secretary of State for India.

Next come the recipients of this patronage, divided into five classes – civil, clerical, medical, military and naval. For service in India, at least in the civil line, some knowledge of the languages spoken there is necessary, and to prepare young men to enter their civil service, the East India Company has a college at Haileybury.[7] A corresponding college for the military service, in which, however, the rudiments of military science are the principal branches taught, has been established at Addiscombe, near London. Admission to these colleges was formerly a matter of favor on the part of the Directors of the Company, but under the latest modifications of the charter it has been opened to competition in the way of a public examination of candidates. On first reaching India, a civilian is allowed about $150 a month, till having passed a necessary examination in one or more of the native languages (which must be within twelve months after his arrival), he is attached to the service with emoluments which vary from $2,500 to near $50,000 per annum.[8] The latter is the pay of the members of the Bengal Council; the members of the Bombay and Madras Councils receive about $30,000 per annum. No person not a member of Council can receive more than about $25,000 per annum, and to obtain an appointment worth $20,000 or over, he must have been a resident in India for twelve years. Nine years' residence quali-fies for salaries of from $15,000 to $20,000; and three years' residence qualifies for salaries of from $7,000 to $15,000. Appointments in the civil service go nominally by seniority and merit, but really to a great extent by favor. As they

[5] At the premium mentioned by Marx, the stock of £500 would cost £1125 to 1250. In converting this cost to an approximate figure in dollars, Marx (or the *NYDT* editor) is obviously equating a pound to $5.

[6] A slip for 'Court of Directors'.

[7] See Campbell, *Modern India*, pp. 264–67, for details about the College.

[8] See ibid., p. 283, for the salary slabs of various Company officers, including the Governor General.

are the best paid, there is great competition to get them, the military officers leaving their regiments for this purpose whenever they can get a chance. The average of all the salaries in the civil service is stated at about $8,000, but this does not include perquisites and extra allowances, which are often very considerable. These civil servants are employed as Governors, Councilors, Judges, Embassadors,[9] Secretaries, Collectors of the Revenue etc. – the number in the whole being generally about 800. The salary of the Governor General of India is $125,000,[10] but the extra allowances often amount to a still larger sum. The Church service includes three bishops and about one hundred and sixty chaplains. The Bishop of Calcutta has $25,000 a year; those of Madras and Bombay half as much; the chaplains from $2,500 to $7,000, beside fees. The medical service includes some 800 physicians and surgeons, with salaries of from $1,500 to $10,000.

The European military officers employed in India, including those of the contingents which the dependent princes are obliged to furnish, number about 8,000. The fixed pay in the infantry is, for ensigns, $1,080; lieutenants, $1,344; captains, $2,226; majors, $3,810; lieutenant-colonels, $5,520; colonels, $7,680. This is the pay in cantonment. In active service, it is more. The pay in the cavalry, artillery and engineers, is somewhat higher. By obtaining staff situations or employments in the civil service, many officers double their pay.

Here are about ten thousand British subjects holding lucrative situations in India, and drawing their pay from the Indian service. To these must be added a considerable number living in England, whither they have retired upon pensions, which in all the services are payable after serving a certain number of years. These pensions, with the dividends and interest on debts due in England, consume some fifteen to twenty millions of dollars drawn annually from India, and which may in fact be regarded as so much tribute paid to the English Government indirectly through its subjects. Those who annually retire from the several services carry with them very considerable amounts of savings from their salaries, which is so much more added to the annual drain on India.

Beside those Europeans actually employed in the service of the Government, there are other European residents in India, to the number of 6,000 or more, employed in trade or private speculation. Except a few indigo, sugar and coffee planters in the rural districts, they are principally merchants, agents and manufacturers, who reside in the cities of Calcutta, Bombay and Madras, or their immediate vicinity. The foreign trade of India, including imports and exports to the amount of about fifty millions of dollars of each, is almost entirely in their hands, and their profits are no doubt very considerable.

It is thus evident that individuals gain largely by the English connection with India, and of course their gain goes to increase the sum of the national

---

[9] So spelt.

[10] According to Campbell (*Modern India*, p. 283), the Governor General received £25,000 per annum, which at $5 to the pound, would have been equal to $125,000.

wealth. But against all this a very large effect is to be made. The military and naval expenses paid out of the pockets of the people of England on Indian account have been constantly increasing with the extent of the Indian dominion. To this must be added the expense of Burmese, Affghan,[11] Chinese and Persian wars.[12] In fact, the whole cost of the late Russian war[13] may fairly be charged to the Indian account, since the fear and dread of Russia, which led to that war, grew entirely out of jealousy as to her designs on India. Add to this the career of endless conquest and perpetual aggression in which the English are involved by the possession of India, and it may well be doubted whether, on the whole, this dominion does not threaten to cost quite as much as it can ever be expected to come to.

[11] So printed in *NYDT*.
[12] Marx means the second Burmese War (1852), the first Anglo-Afghan War (1838–42), the first and second Opium Wars (1839–42 and 1856–60), and the Persian War (1856–57).
[13] The Crimean War, 1853–56.

[The Revolt in India]

(*New York Daily Tribune*, October 3, 1857. Printed as a leading article.)

The news from India, which reached us yesterday, wears a very disastrous and threatening aspect for the English, though, as may be seen in another column, our intelligent London correspondent regards it differently.[1] From Delhi we have details to July 29, and a later report, to the effect that, in consequence of the ravages of the cholera, the besieging forces were compelled to retire from before Delhi and take up their quarters at Agra. It is true, this report is admitted by none of the London journals, but we can, at the very utmost, only regard it as somewhat premature. As we know from all the Indian correspondence, the besieging army had suffered severely in sorties made on the 14th, 18th and 23rd of July.[2] On those occasions the rebels fought with more reckless vehemence than ever, and with a great advantage from the superiority of their cannon. 'We are firing', writes a British officer, '18 pounders and 8-inch howitzers, and the rebels are replying with twenty-fours and thirty-twos.' 'In the eighteen sallies', says another letter, 'which we have had to stand, we have lost one-third of our number in killed and wounded.'[3]

Of reinforcements all that could be expected was a body of Sikhs under Gen. Van Cortlandt. Gen. Havelock, after fighting several successful battles, was forced to fall back on Cawnpore, abandoning, for the time, the relief of Lucknow. At the same time, 'the rains had set in heavily before Delhi', necessarily adding to the virulence of the cholera. The dispatch which announces the retreat to Agra and the abandonment, for the moment, at least, of the attempt to reduce the capital of the Great Mogul, must, then, soon prove true, if it is not so already.

On the line of the Ganges the main interest rests on the operations of Gen. Havelock, whose exploits at Futteypoor, Cawnpore and Bittor have naturally been rather extravagantly praised by our London contemporaries. As we have stated above, after having advanced twenty-five miles from Cawnpore, he

---

This editorial, not in the name of Marx and carrying no heading, seems to have been touched up by the *New York Daily Tribune* (*NYDT*) editors here and there.

[1] The editors of *CW*, Vol. 15 (p. 679 n.) treat this as a reference by the *NYDT* editors to Ferenez Pulszki, a Hungarian writer and journalist who too sent his reports from London.
[2] See Fred Roberts's letter of 23 July 1857 to his mother from the camp near Delhi. Roberts, *Letters*, pp. 21–25.
[3] Letters from officers employed on the staff at Delhi, quoted in *The Times*, 4 September 1857. See *CW*, Vol. 15, p. 361.

found himself obliged to fall back upon that place in order not only to deposit his sick, but to wait for reinforcements. This is a cause for deep regret, for it indicates that the attempt at a rescue of Lucknow has been baffled. The only hope for the British garrison of the place is now in the force of 3,000 Goorkas sent from Nepaul to their relief by Jung Bahadoor. Should they fail to raise the siege, then the Cawnpore butchery will be re-enacted at Lucknow. This will not be all. The capture by the rebels of the fortress of Lucknow, and the consequent consolidation of their power in Oude, would threaten in the flank all British operations against Delhi, and decide the balance of the contending forces at Benares, and the whole district of Bahar.[4] Cawnpore would be stripped of half its importance and menaced in its communications with Delhi on the one side, and with Benares on the other, by the rebels holding the fortress of Lucknow. This contingency adds to the painful interest with which news from that locality must be looked for. On the 16th of June the garrison estimated their powers of endurance at[5] six weeks, on famine allowance. Up to the last date of the dispatches, five of these weeks had already elapsed. Everything there now depends on the reported, but not yet certain reinforcements from Nepaul.

If we pass lower down the Ganges, from Cawnpore to Benares and the district of Bahar the British prospect is still darker. A letter in the Bengal Gazette,[6] dated Benares, August 3, states –

> the mutineers from Dinapore, having crossed the Soane [Sone], marched upon Arrah. The European inhabitants, justly alarmed for their safety, wrote to Dinapore for reinforcements. Two steamers were accordingly dispatched with detachments of her Majesty's 5th, 10th and 37th. In the middle of the night one of the steamers grounded in the mud and stuck fast. The men were hastily landed, and pushed forward on foot, but without taking due precautions. Suddenly they were assailed on both sides by a close and heavy fire, and 150 of their small force, including several officers, put *hors de combat*. It is supposed that all the Europeans at the stations, about 47 in number, have been massacred.[7]

Arrah, in the British district of Shahabad, Presidency of Bengal, is a town on the road from Dinapore to Ghazepore,[8] twenty-five miles west of the former, seventy-five east of the latter. Benares itself was threatened. This place has a fort constructed upon European principles, and would become another Delhi if it fell into the hands of the rebels. At Mirzapore, situated to the south of

---

[4] Bihar.

[5] 'of' in Av.

[6] The reference evidently is to *The Calcutta Gazette*, an English newspaper published in Bengal from 1784.

[7] For eyewitness accounts of the events on the same lines, see, Campbell, *Narrative*, pp. 134–37. The French phrase *hors de combat* means 'disabled for fighting'.

[8] In Av. 'Shazepore', and in *FIWI*, 'Ghasipur'. The town of Ghazipur is meant.

Benares, and on the opposite bank of the Ganges, a Mussulman conspiracy has been detected: while at Bechampore[9] on the Ganges, some eighteen miles distant from Calcutta, the 63rd Native Infantry had been disarmed. In one word, disaffection on the one side and panic on the other were spreading throughout the whole Presidency of Bengal, even to the gates of Calcutta, where painful apprehensions prevailed of the great fast of the Mohurran,[10] when the followers of Islam, wrought up into a fanatical frenzy, go about with swords ready to fight on the smallest provocation, being likely to result in a general attack upon the English, and where the Governor-General has felt himself compelled to disarm his own bodyguard. The reader, will, then, understand at once that the principal British line of communications, the Ganges line, is in danger of being interrupted, intersected and cut off. This would bear on the progress of the reinforcements to arrive in November, and would isolate the British line of operations on the Jumna.

In the Bombay Presidency, also, affairs are assuming a very serious aspect. The mutiny at Kolapore[11] of the 27th Bombay Native Infantry is a fact, but their defeat by the British troops is a rumor only. The Bombay native army has broken out into successive mutinies at Nagpore, Aurangabad, Hyderabad, and finally, at Kolapore. The actual strength of the Bombay native army is 43,048 men, while there are, in fact, only two European regiments in that Presidency. The native army was relied upon not only to preserve order within the limits of the Bombay Presidency, but to send reinforcements up to Scinde in the Punjaub, and to form the columns moved on Mhow and Indore, to recover and hold these places, to establish communications with Agra, and relieve the garrison at that place. The column of Brigadier Stuart,[12] charged with this operation, was composed of 300 men of the 3rd Bombay European Regiment, 250 men of the 5th Bombay Native Infantry, 1,000 of the 25th Bombay Native Infantry, 200 of the 19th Bombay Native Infantry, 800 of the 3rd Cavalry Regiment of the Hyderabad contingent. There are with this force, amounting to 2,250 native soldiers, about 700 Europeans, composed chiefly of the Queen's 86th Foot and the 14th Queen's Light Dragoons. The English had, moreover, assembled a column of the native army at Aurangabad to intimidate the disaffected territories of Khandesh and Nagpore, and at the same time form a support for the flying columns acting in Central India.

In that part of India we are told that 'tranquility is restored', but on this result we cannot altogether rely. In fact it is not the occupation of Mhow which

---

[9] So printed in *NYDT,* for Berhampore.

[10] So printed in *NYDT,* for 'Muharram', the first month of the Hijri calander. The tragedy at *Karbala* took place in this month and there is much public mourning among Muslims, especially Shi'as. The month Muharram of the Hijri year 1274 began on 22 August 1857 and the tenth day of the month (being the day of Husain's martyrdom) coincided with 31 August.

[11] Kolhapur.

[12] 'Steward' in Av.

decides that question, but the course pursued by the Holkar and Scindiah, the two Mahratta princes. The same dispatch which informs us of Stuart's[13] arrival at Mhow adds that, although the Holkar still remained staunch, his troops had become unmanageable. As to the Scindiah's policy, not a word is dropped. He is young, popular, full of fire, and would be regarded as the natural head and rallying point for the whole Mahratta nation. He has 10,000 well-disciplined troops of his own. His defection from the British would not only cost them Central India, but give immense strength and consistency to the revolutionary league. The retreat of the forces before Delhi, the menaces and solicitations of the malcontents may at length induce him to side with his countrymen. The main influence, however, on the Holkar as well as the Scindiah, will be exercised by the Maharattas of the Deccan, where, as we have already stated, the rebellion has at last decidedly raised its head. It is here, too, that the festival of the Mohurran is particularly dangerous. There is, then, some reason to anticipate a general revolt of the Bombay army. The Madras army, too, amounting to 60,555 native troops, and recruited from Hyderabad, Nagpore, Malwa, the most bigoted Mohammedan districts, would not be long in following the example. Thus, then, if it be considered that the rainy season during August and September will paralyze the movements of the British troops and interrupt their communications, the supposition seems rational that in spite of their apparent strength, the reinforcements sent from Europe, arriving too late, and in driblets only, will prove inadequate to the task imposed upon them. We may almost expect, during the following campaign, a rehearsal of the Affghanistan[14] disasters.

---

[13] 'Stewart's' in Av.
[14] So spelt in *NYDT*.

[The Revolt in India]

(*New York Daily Tribune*, October 13, 1857. Printed as a leading article.)

The news received from India by the *Atlantic* yesterday has two prominent points, namely, the failure of Gen. Havelock to advance to the relief of Lucknow, and the persistence of the English at Delhi. This latter fact finds a parallel only in British annals, and in the Walcheren expedition.[1] The failure of that expedition having become certain toward the middle of August, 1809, they delayed re-embarking until November. Napoleon, when he learned that an English army had landed at that place, recommended that it should not be attacked, and that the French should leave its destruction to the disease sure to do them more injury than the cannon, without its costing one centime[2] to France. The present Great Mogul, even more favored than Napoleon, finds himself able to back the disease by his sallies and his sallies by the disease.

A British Government dispatch, dated Cagliari,[3] Sept. 27, tells us that 'latest dates from Delhi are to the 12th of August, when that city was still in possession of the rebels; but that an attack was expected to be made shortly, as Gen. Nicholson[4] was within a day's march with considerable reinforcements.'[5] If Delhi is not taken till Wilson[6] and Nicholson attack it with their present strength, its walls will stand till they fall of themselves. Nicholson's considerable forces amount to about 4,000 Sikhs – a reinforcement absurdly disproportionate for an

---

For this article, Marx has made obvious use of points made in Engels's letter of 24 September 1857 (Letter No. 16 in this volume).

[1] Walcheren, the westernmost island of the province of Zeeland in Holland. The English attempt to take it in 1809 from Napoleon ended in a fiasco and much loss of men.

[2] A French coin, one-hundredth of a franc.

[3] Port and capital of Sardinia, Italy. Apparently, the British government obtained the information from packets of reports arriving by sea at that port.

[4] General John Nicholson (1821–1857): Bengal infantry, 1839; served in Afghanistan in 1842 and was promoted Brigadier-General at the outbreak of the 1857 Rebellion; arrived at Delhi on 14 August 1857; shot while commanding the main assault party in the attack of Delhi on 14 September 1857, dying a few days later.

[5] *The Times*, No. 22798, 29 September 1857. Reference from *CW*, Vol. 15, p. 365 n.

[6] Sir Archdale Wilson (1803–1874): Colonel and Commandant of artillery at Meerut in 1856; promoted Major-General during the 1857 Rebellion. He led the assault on Delhi and was made K.C.B. in 1857 after its success.

attack upon Delhi, but just large enough to afford a new suicidal pretext for not breaking up the camp before the city.

After Gen. Hewitt had committed the fault, and one may even in a military point of view say the crime, of permitting the Meerut rebels to make their way to Delhi, and after the two first weeks had been wasted, allowing an irregular surprise of that city, the planning of the siege of Delhi appears an almost incomprehensible blunder. An authority which we shall take the liberty of placing even above the military oracles of *The London Times*, Napoleon, lays down two rules of warfare looking almost like commonplaces: 1st. That 'only what can be supported ought to be undertaken, and only what presents the greater number of chances of success'; and 2ndly. That 'the main forces should be employed only where the main object of war, the destruction of the enemy, lies'. In planning the siege of Delhi these rudimentary rules have been violated. The authorities in England must have been aware that the Indian Government itself had recently repaired the fortifications of Delhi so far that that city could be captured by a regular siege only, requiring a besieging force of at least 15,000 to 20,000 men, and much more, if the defense was conducted in an average style. Now, 15,000 to 20,000 men being requisite for this enterprise, it was downright folly to undertake it with 6,000 or 7,000. The English were further aware that a prolonged siege, a matter of course in consequence of their numerical weakness, would expose their forces in that locality, in that climate, and at that season, to the attacks of an invulnerable and invisible enemy, spreading the seeds of destruction among their ranks. The chances of success, therefore, were all against a siege of Delhi.

As to the object of the war, it was beyond doubt the maintenance of English rule in India. To attain that object, Delhi was a point of no strategical significance at all. Historical tradition, in truth, endowed it in the eyes of the natives with a superstitious importance, clashing[7] with its real influence, and this was sufficient reason for the mutinous sepoys to single it out as their general place of rendezvous. But if, instead of forming their military plans according to the native prejudices, the English had left Delhi alone and isolated it, they would have divested it of its fancied influence; while, by pitching their tents before it, running their heads against it, and concentrating upon it their main force and the attention of the world, they cut themselves off from even the chances of retreat, or rather gave to a retreat all the effects of a signal defeat. They have thus simply played into the hands of the mutineers who wanted to make Delhi the object of the campaign. But this is not all. No great ingenuity was required to convince the English that for them it was of prime importance to create an active field army, whose operations might stifle the sparks of disaffection, keep open the communications between their own military stations, throw the enemy upon some few points and isolate Delhi. Instead of acting upon this simple and self-evident plan,

---

[7] 'slashing' in Av.

they immobilize the only active army at their disposal by concentrating it before Delhi, leave the open field to the mutineers, while their *own* garrisons hold scattered spots, disconnected, far distant from each other, and blocked up by overwhelming hostile forces allowed to take their own time.

By fixing their main mobile column before Delhi, the English have not choked up the rebels, but petrified their own garrisons. But, apart from this fundamental blunder at Delhi, there is hardly anything in the annals of war to equal the stupidity which directed the operations of these garrisons, acting independently, irrespectively of each other, lacking all supreme leadership, and acting not like members of one army, but like bodies belonging to different and even hostile nations. Take, for instance, the case of Cawnpore and Lucknow. There were two adjacent places, and two separate bodies of troops, both very small and disproportionate to the occasion, placed under separate commands, though they were only forty miles apart,[8] and with as little unity of action between them as if situated at the opposite poles. The simplest rules of strategy would have required that Sir Hugh Wheeler, the military commander at Cawnpore, should be empowered to call Sir H. Lawrence, the Chief Commissioner of Oude, with his troops, back to Cawnpore, thus to strengthen his own position while momentarily evacuating Lucknow. By this operation, *both* garrisons would have been saved, and by the subsequent junction of Hevelock's troops with them, a little army been created able to check Oude and to relieve Agra. Instead of this, by the independent action of the two places, the garrison of Cawnpore is butchered, the garrison of Lucknow is sure to fall with its fortress,[9] and even the wonderful exertions of Havelock, marching his troops 126 miles in eight days, sustaining as many fights as his march numbered days, and performing all this in an Indian climate at the height of the summer season – even his heroic exertions are baffled. Having still more exhausted his overworked troops in vain attempts at the rescue of Lucknow, and being sure to be forced to fresh useless sacrifices by repeated expeditions from Cawnpore, executed on a constantly decreasing radius, he will, in all probability, have at last to retire upon Allahabad, with hardly any men at his back. The operations of his troops, better than anything else, show what even the small English army before Delhi would have been able to do if concentrated for action in the field, instead of being caught alive in the pestilential camp. Concentration is the secret of strategy. Decentralization is the plan adopted by the English in India. What they had to do was to reduce their garrisons to the smallest possible number, disencumber them at once of women and children, evacuate all stations not of strategical importance, and thus collect the greatest possible army in the field. Now, even the driblets of reinforcements, sent up the Ganges from Calcutta, have been so completely absorbed by the numerous isolated garrisons that not one detachment has reached Allahabad.

[8] The railway distance between Kanpur and Lucknow is 72 kilometres or 45 miles.
[9] Lucknow Residency.

As for Lucknow, the most gloomy previsions inspired by the recent previous[10] mails are now confirmed. Havelock has again been forced to fall back on Cawnpore; there is no possibility of relief from the allied Nepaulese force; and we must now expect to hear of the capture of the place by starvation, and the massacre of its brave defenders with their wives and children.

[10] 'previous' omitted in Av.

[The Revolt in India]

(*New York Daily Tribune*, October 23, 1857. Printed as a leading article.)

We yesterday received files of London journals up to the 7th inst.[1] In discussing the State of the Indian revolt they are full of the same optimism which they have cultivated from the beginning. We are not only told that a successful attack upon Delhi was to take place, but that it was to take place on the 20th of August. The first thing to ascertain is, of course, the present strength of the besieging force. An artillery officer, writing from the camp before Delhi on the 13th of August, gives the following detailed statement of the effective British forces on the 10th of that month:[2]

	British officers	British troops	Native officers	Native troops	Horses
Staff	30	–	–	–	–
Artillery	39	598	–	–	[823]
Engineers	26	39	–	–	–
Cavalry Ist Brigade	18	570	–	–	520
Her Majesty's 75th Regt.	16	502	–	–	–
Hon. Co.'s 2nd [*rect.* 1st] Fusiliers	17	487	–	–	–
Kumaon Battalion 2nd Brigade	4	–	13	435	–
Her Majesty's 60th Rifles	15	251	–	–	–
Hon. Co.'s 2nd Fusiliers	20	493	–	–	–
Timoor [*rect.* Sirmoor] Battalion 3rd Brigade	4	–	9	319	–
Her Majesty's 8th Regt.	15	153	–	–	–
Her Majesty's 61st Regt.	12	249	–	–	–
4th Sikhs	4	–	4	365	–
Guide Corps	4	–	4	196	–
Coke's Corps	5	–	16	709	–
Total	229	3,342	46	2,024	520[*rect.*1343]

---

[1] The first sentence must be presumed to be an interpolation by the *New York Daily Tribune (NYDT)* editors.

[2] The figures given here are almost certainly those supplied by Fred Roberts, Lieutenant, Bengal Horse (later Field Marshal Earl Roberts), who gave these in his letter of 13 August 1857 written from the Delhi camp, later published in his *Letters*. The figures relate to the period 8 June to 1 July 1857. The original table containing them is reproduced in the appendix to this letter. Marx drew his table apparently from the *Times*, and certain omissions or slips may have therefore come from that source. The omissions and slips are supplied or corrected in the table within square brackets.

The total effective British force in the camp before Delhi amounted, therefore, on the 10th of August to exactly 5,641 men. From these we must deduct 120 men (112 soldiers and 8 officers), who, according to the English reports, fell on the 12th of August during the attack upon a new battery which the rebels had opened outside the walls, in front of the English left. There remained, then, the number of 5,529[3] fighting men when Brigadier Nicholson joined the besieging army with the following forces from Ferozepore, escorting a second-class siege-train: the 52nd Light Infantry (say 900 men), a wing of the 61st (say 4 companies, 360 men), Bourchier's[4] field battery, a wing of the 6th Punjaub Regiment (say 540 men), and some Mooltan horse and foot; altogether a force of about 2,000 men, of whom somewhat more than 1,200 were Europeans. Now, if we add this force to the 5,529 fighting men who were in the camp on the junction of Nicholson's forces, we obtain a total of 7,529[5] men. Further reinforcements are said to have been dispatched by Sir John Lawrence, the Governor of the Punjaub, consisting of the remaining wing of the 8th foot, three companies of the 24th, with three horse-artillery guns of Captain Paton's[6] troops from Peshawer, the 2nd Punjaub Infantry, the 4th Punjaub Infantry, and the other wing of the 6th Punjaub. This force, however, which we may estimate at 3,000 men, at the utmost, and the bulk of which consists altogether of Sikhs, had not yet arrived. If the reader can recall the arrival of the Punjaub reinforcements under Chamberlayne[7] about a month earlier, he will understand that, as the latter were only sufficient to bring Gen. Reed's[8] army up to the original number of Sir H. Barnard's forces, so the new reinforcements are only sufficient to bring Brigadier Wilson's army up to the original strength of Gen. Reed; the only real fact in favor of the English being the arrival, at last, of a siege train. But suppose even the expected 3,000 men to have joined the camp, and the total English force to have reached the number of 10,000, the loyalty of one-third of which is more than doubtful, what are they to do? They will invest Delhi, we are told. But leaving aside the ludicrous idea of investing with 10,000 men a strongly – fortified city, more than seven miles in extent, the English must first turn the Jumna from its regular course before they can think of investing Delhi. If the English entered Delhi in the

<hr />

[3] Here and further below this figure is given in CW, Vol. 15, p. 370, and Av., as 5,521.

[4] George Bourchier (1821–1898): British army officer, took part in suppressing the uprising of 1857–58. Cf. ibid., p. 703.

[5] 7,521 in Av., and in CW, Vol. 15, p. 370.

[6] John Stafford Paton (1821–1898): British officer, later General; participated in the Anglo-Sikh Wars (1845–46 and 1848–49) and in suppressing the uprising of 1857–58.

[7] So printed in NYDT; the correct spelling is Chamberlain.

[8] Spelt as both 'Gen. Reid' and 'Gen. Reed' in NYDT. Major Reed commanded the Sirmoor battalion and was greatly praised by Major General Barnard 'for his usual cool courage and judgement'. He later took part in the seige of Delhi. See Forrest, Selections from the Letters, Despatches and other State Papers, Vol. I (Calcutta, 1893), pp. 298, 442. He is to be distinguished from Major General Reed, who was the Provincial Commander-in-Chief; he came from Peshawar, but could not take part in the action due to illness. See ibid., p. 438.

morning, the rebels might leave it in the evening, either by crossing the Jumna and making for Rohilcund and Oude, or by marching down the Jumna in the direction of Muttra and Agra. At all events, the investment of a square, one of whose sides is inaccessible to the besieging forces, while affording a line of communication and retreat to the besieged, is a problem not yet solved.

'All agree', says the officer from whom we have borrowed the above table, 'that taking Delhi by assault is out of the question.'[9] He informs us, at the same time, what is really expected in the camp, viz.: 'to shell the town for several days and to make a decent breach'. Now, this officer himself adds that, 'at a moderate calculation, the enemy must muster now nearly forty thousand men beside guns unlimited and well worked; their infantry also fighting well'.[10]

If the desperate obstinacy with which Mussulmans are accustomed to fight behind walls be considered, it becomes a great question indeed whether the small British army, having rushed in through a 'decent breach', would be allowed to rush out again.

In fact, there remains only one chance for a successful attack upon Delhi by the present British forces – that of internal dissensions breaking among the rebels, their ammunition being spent, their forces being demoralized, and their spirit of self-reliance giving way. But we must confess that their uninterrupted fighting from the 31st of July to the 12th of August seems hardly to warrant such a supposition. At the same time, a Calcutta letter gives us a broad hint why the English generals had resolved, in the teeth of all military rules, upon keeping their ground before Delhi. 'When,' it says, 'a few weeks ago it became a question whether our force should retreat from before Delhi, because it was too much harassed by daily fighting to support overwhelming fatigues much longer, that intention was strenuously resisted by Sir John Lawrence, who plainly informed the Generals that their retreat would be the signal for the rising of the populations around them, by which they must be placed in imminent danger. This counsel prevailed, and Sir John Lawrence promised to send them all the reinforcements he could muster.'[11]

Denuded as it has been by Sir John Lawrence, the Punjaub itself may now rise in rebellion, while the troops in the cantonments before Delhi are likely to be laid on their backs and decimated by the pestilential effluvia rising from the soil at the close of the rainy season. Of Gen. Van Cortlandt's forces, reported four weeks ago to have reached Hissar, and to be pushing forward to Delhi, no more is heard. They must, then, have encountered serious obstacles, or have been disbanded on their route.

---

[9] Here Marx slightly modifies Fred Roberts's statement (*Letters*, pp. 36–37): 'All agree taking it by assault is out of the question and our Batteries, on account of the great height of the glacis will have to be advanced.'

[10] See ibid., p. 34.

[11] For the generals' proposal to abandon Delhi and Lawrence's opposition thereto, see George Dangerfield, *Bengal Mutiny* (London, 1933), pp. 229–30.

The position of the English on the Upper Ganges is, in fact, desperate. Gen. Havelock is threatened by the operation of the Oude rebels, moving from Lucknow via Bittoor and trying at Futteypore, to the south of Cawnpore, to cut off his retreat; while simultaneously the Gwalior contingent is marching on Cawnpore from Calpee, a town situated on the right bank of the Jumna. This concentric movement, perhaps directed by Nena Sahib, who is said to wield the supreme command at Lucknow, betrays for the first time some notion of strategy on the part of the rebels, while the English seem anxious only to exaggerate their own foolish method of centrifugal warfare. Then we are told that the 90th Foot and the 5th fusiliers dispatched from Calcutta to reinforce Gen. Havelock have been intercepted at Dinapore by Sir James Outram, who has taken it into his head to lead them via Fyrzabad[12] to Lucknow. This plan of operation is hailed by *The Morning Advertiser* of London as the stroke of a master mind, because, it says, Lucknow will thus have been placed between two fires, being threatened on its right from Cawnpore and on its left from Fyrzabad. According to the ordinary rules of war, the immensely weaker army, which, instead of trying to concentrate its scattered members, cuts itself up into two portions, separated by the whole breadth of the hostile army, has spared the enemy the pains of annihilating it. For Gen. Havelock, the question, in fact, is no longer to save Lucknow, but to save the remainder of his own and Gen. Neill's[13] little corps. He will very likely have to fall back upon Allahabad. Allahabad is indeed a position of decisive importance, forming as it does, the point of junction between the Ganges and the Jumna, and the key to the Doab, situated between the two rivers.

On the first glance at the map, it will be seen that the main line of operations for an English army attempting the reconquest of the North-Western provinces runs along the valley of the Lower Ganges. The positions of Dinapore, Benares, Mirzapore, and, above all, of Allahabad, from which the real operations must commence, will therefore have to be strengthened by the withdrawal to them of the garrisons of all the smaller and strategically indifferent stations in the Province of Bengal Proper. That this main line of operations itself is seriously threatened at this moment may be seen from the following extract from a Bombay letter addressed to *The London Daily News*:

> The late mutiny of three regiments at Dinapore has cut off communications (except by steamers on the river) between Allahabad and Calcutta. The mutiny at Dinapore is the most serious affair that has happened lately, inasmuch as the whole of the Berar [Bihar] within 200 miles of Calcutta, is now in a blaze. Today a report has arrived that the Santhals have again risen, and the State of Bengal, overrun with 150,000 savages, who delight in blood, plunder and rapine, would be truly terrible.

---

[12] 'Fyzabad', now spelt Faizabad.
[13] James George Smith Neill (1810–1857): fought in the Crimean War; is remembered for his ruthless and savage killings in suppressing the uprising of 1857–58 in Allahabad and Kanpur.

The minor lines of operations, as long as Agra holds out, are those for the Bombay army, via Indore and Gwalior to Agra, and for the Madras army, via Saugor and Gwalior to Agra, with which latter place the Punjaub army, as well as the corps holding Allahabad, require to have their lines of communication restored. If, however, the wavering princes of Central India should openly declare against the English, and the mutiny among the Bombay army assume a serious aspect, all military calculation is at an end for the present, and nothing will remain certain but an immense butchery from Cashmere[14] to Cape Comorin. In the best case, all that can be done is to delay decisive events until the arrival in November of the European forces. Whether even this be effected will depend upon the brains of Sir Colin Campbell, of whom, till now, nothing is known but his personal bravery. If he is the man for his place, he will, at any expense, whether Delhi fall or not, create a disposable force, however small, with which to take the field. Yet, the ultimate decision, we must repeat, lies with the Bombay army.

[14] Kashmir.

[The Revolt in India]

(*New York Daily Tribune*, November 14, 1857. Printed as a leading article.)

The mail of the *Arabia* brings us the important intelligence of the fall of Delhi. This event, so far as we can judge from the meagre details at hand, appears to have resulted from the simultaneous occurrence of bitter dissensions among the rebels, a change in the numerical proportions of the contending parties, and the arrival on Sept. 5 of the siege-train which was expected as long ago as June 8.

After the arrival of Nicholson's reinforcements, we had estimated the army before Delhi at a total of 7,529[1] men, an estimate fully confirmed since. After the subsequent accession of 3,000 Cashmere troops, lent to the English by the Rajah Ranbeer Singh,[2] the British forces are stated by *The Friend of India*[3] to have amounted in all about 11,000 men. On the other hand, *The Military Spectator* of London affirms that the rebel forces had diminished in numbers to about 17,000 men, of whom 5,000 were cavalry; while *The Friend of India* computes their forces at about 13,000 including 1,000 irregular cavalry. As the horse became quite useless after the breach was once effected and the struggle within the town had begun, and, consequently, on the very entrance of the English they made their escape, the total forces of the Sepoys, whether we accept the computation of *The Military Spectator* or of *The Friend of India*, could not be estimated beyond 11,000 or 12,000 men. The English forces, less from increase on their side than from a decrease on the opposite one, had, therefore, become almost equal to those of the mutineers;[4] their slight numerical inferiority being more than made up by the moral effect of a successful bombardment and the advantages of the offensive enabling them to choose the points on which to throw their

---

See Marx's letter to Engels dated 20 October 1857, in *CW*, Vol. 40, pp. 191–94. In Av. this article is printed under the title 'The Fall of Delhi'.

[1] See the preceding dispatch, 'The Revolt in India', published in the *New York Daily Tribune* (*NYDT*) on 23 October 1857 as a leading article.
[2] Ranbir Singh (1829–1885): son of Gulab Singh, the Dogra ruler of Kashmir, who ascended the throne in February 1856.
[3] Newspaper first issued from Serampur in 1818; in 1850 it appeared once a week. See *FIWI*, p. 225.
[4] Forrest gives the following details of British forces in Delhi (effectives) on 11 September 1857: artillery, 1,270; cavalry, 1897; infantry, 5,305; total, 8,472. (See *History of the Indian Mutiny*, London, 1904, Vol. I, pp. 152–53.) But in a footnote he says that the effective strength of troops at Delhi on 11 September 1857 was 7,799.

main strength, while the defenders were obliged to disperse their inadequate forces over all the points of the menaced circumference.

The decrease on the part of the rebel forces was caused still more by the withdrawal of whole contingents in consequence of internal dissensions than by the heavy losses they suffered in their incessant sorties for a period of about ten days. While the Mogul spectre himself like the merchants of Delhi, had become averse to the rule of the Sepoys, who plundered them of every rupee they had amassed, the religious dissensions between the Hindoo and Mohammedan Sepoys, and the quarrels between the old garrison and the new reinforcement, sufficed to break up their superficial organization and to insure their downfall. Still, as the English had to cope with a force but slightly superior to their own, without unity of command, enfeebled and dispirited by dissensions in their own ranks, but who yet, after 84 hours' bombardment, stood a six days' cannonade and street fight within the walls, and then quietly crossed the Jumna on the bridge of boats, it must be confessed that the rebels at last, with their main forces, made the best of a bad position.[5]

The facts of the capture appear to be, that on Sept. 8 the English batteries were opened much in advance of the original position of their forces and within 700 yards of the walls. Between the 8th and the 11th British heavy ordnance guns and mortars were pushed forward still nearer to the works, a lodgment being effected and batteries established with little loss, considering that the Delhi garrison made two sorties on the 10th and 11th, and made repeated attempts to open fresh batteries, and kept up an annoying fire from rifle-pits. On the 12th the English sustained a loss of about 56 killed and wounded. On the morning of the 13th the enemy's expense[6] magazine, on one bastion, was blown up, as also the wagon of a light gun, which enfiladed the British batteries from the Talvara suburbs; and the British batteries effected a practicable breach near the Cashmere gate. On the 14th the assault was made on the city. The troops entered at the breach near the Cashmere gate without serious opposition, gained possession of the large buildings in its neighborhood and advanced along the ramparts to the Moree bastion[7] and Cabul gate, when the resistance grew very obstinate, and the loss was consequently severe.[8] Preparations were being made to turn the guns from the captured bastions on the city, and to bring up other guns and mortars to commanding points. On the 15th the Burn bastions and Lahore bastions were played upon by the captured guns on the Moree and Cabul bastions, while a breach was made in the magazine and the palace began to be

---

[5] A reference presumably to the retreat of Bakht Khan's contingent from Delhi. See P. Spear, *Twilight of the Mughals* (Delhi, 1969), pp. 216–17.

[6] Omitted in *CW*, Vol. 15, p. 375.

[7] The Mori Gate stands in the northern part of Delhi.

[8] Fred Roberts (in *Letters*, p. 65) says that the British lost 300 officers between 10th and 14th September 1857, and 1,174 men on 14 September, of which last, 64 were officers.

shelled. The magazine was stormed at daylight, Sept. 16, while on the 17th the mortars continued to play upon the palace from the magazine inclosure.

At this date, owing, it is said by *The Bombay Courier*, to the plunder of the Punjaub and Lahore mails on the Scinde frontier, the official accounts of the storm break off. In a private communication addressed to the Governor of Bombay, it is stated that the entire city of Delhi was occupied on Sunday, the 20th, the main forces of the mutineers leaving the city at 3 am, on the same day, and escaping over the bridges of boats in the direction of Rohilcund. Since a pursuit on the part of the English was impracticable until after the occupation of Selimgurh, situated on the river front, it is evident that the rebels, slowly fighting their way from the extreme north end of the city to its south eastern[9] extremity, kept, until the 20th, the position necessary for covering their retreat.

As to the probable effect of the capture of Delhi, a competent authority, *The Friend of India*, remarks that

> It is the condition of Bengal, and not the state of Delhi, that ought at this time to engage the attention of Englishmen. The long delay that has taken place in the capture of the town has actually destroyed any prestige that we might have derived from an early success; and the strength of the rebels and their numbers are diminished as effectually by maintaining the siege as they would be by the capture of the city.

Meanwhile, the insurrection is said to be spreading north-east from Calcutta, through Central India up to the north-west; while on the Assam frontier, two strong regiments of Poorbeahs, openly proposing the restoration of the ex-Rajah Parandur Singh,[10] had revolted; the Dinapore and Ranghur[11] mutineers, led by Kooer Singh,[12] were marching by Banda and Nagode in the direction of Subbulpore,[13] and had forced through his own troops, the Rajah of Rewah to join them.[14] At Subbulpore itself the 52nd Bengal Native Regiment had left their

[9] 'south-easterly' in Av.

[10] Ahom prince: accession in 1818; escaped in 1819 due to the internal conflict supported by the Burmese king; restored to power by the British East India Company in 1833; deposed in 1838 for not fulfilling the Company's demands; died in 1846 and was succeeded by his son. Kunwar Singh's revolt in Arrah (Bihar) led to restlessness among the sepoys of the Assam Light Infantry coming from Arrah. Here Marx seems to have confused Parandhur Singh's son with Parandhur Singh himself. See H.K. Barpujari, *Assam in the Days of the Company* (Calcutta, 1980), pp. 182–90.

[11] 'Ranghur' in *NYDT*, whence 'Bangpur' in *FIWI*, p. 114. 'Ranghur' is, however, a misprint for 'Ramghur'. For the incident see Campbell, *Narrative*, pp. 137–41.

[12] The *Zamindar* of Jagdishpur, he played an important role at Kanpur where Windham was defeated; he died of a wound which he received in an encounter with the British forces on 23 April 1858.

[13] The editors of *FIWI*, p. 114, have corrected this to Jubbalpore (now spelt Jabalpur). The editors of *CW*, Vol. 15, retain 'Subbulpore'.

[14] In fact, the Raja of Rewa soon changed his mind and fled. See Campbell, *Narrative*, p. 141.

cantonments, taking with them a British officer as a hostage for their comrades left behind. The Gwalior mutineers are reported to have crossed the Chumbul, and are encamped somewhere between the river and Dhalapore.[15] The Todhpore[16] Legion has, it appears, taken service with the rebel Rajah of Arwah, a place 90 miles south-west to Beawar. They have defeated a considerable force which the Rajah of Todhpore had sent against them, killing the General and Captain Monck Mason,[17] and capturing three guns. Gen. G. St. P. Lawrence[18] made an advance against them with some of the Nusserabad force, and compelled them to retreat into a town, against which, however, his further attempts proved unavailing.[19] The denuding of Scinde of its European troops had resulted in a widely extended conspiracy, attempts at insurrection being made at no less than five different places, among which figure Hyderabad, Kurrachee and Sikarpore. There is also an untoward symptom in the Punjaub, the communication between Moultan and Lahore having been cut off for eight days.[20]

In another place our readers will find a tabular statement of the forces dispatched from England since June 18; the days of arrival of the respective vessels being calculated by us on official statements, and therefore in favor of the British Government. From that list it will be seen that, apart from the small detachments of artillery and engineers sent by the over-land route, the whole of the army embarked amounts to 30,899 men, of whom 24,739 belong to the infantry, 3,826 to the cavalry, and 2,334 to the artillery. It will also be seen that before the end of October no considerable reinforcements were to be expected.[21]

Troops for India
The following is a list of the troops which have been sent to India from England since June 18, 1857

Date of arrival	Total	Calcutta	Ceylon	Bombay	Kurrachee	Madras
September 20	214	214	...	...	...	...
October 1[22]	300	300	...	...	...	...
October 15	1,906	124	1,782	...	...	...
October 17	288	288	...	...	...	...
October 20	4,235	3,845	390	...	...	...
October 30	2,028	479	1,549	...	...	...
Total for Oct.	8,757	5,036	3,721			

---

[15] That is, Dholpur on the bank of Chambal river.
[16] Misprint for Jodhpur (Rajasthan), here as well as on line 6 of this page.
[17] George Henry Monck Mason (1825–1857): English army officer and Resident in Jodhpur (see *CW*, Vol. 15, p. 719).
[18] Sir George Saint Patrick Lawrence (1804–1894): held command of the British forces in 1857–58 as Resident for the Rajputana States.
[19] *The Times*, Nos 22823, 22824, 28 and 29 October 1857. Reference in *CW*, Vol. 15, p. 377 n.
[20] *The Times*, No. 22822, 27 October 1857. *CW*, Vol. 15, p. 377.
[21] The statement showing the arrival of troops in India is omitted in Av.
[22] 2 October in *CW*, Vol. 40, p. 192.

Contd/-

Date of arrival	Total	Calcutta	Ceylon	Bombay	Kurrachee	Madras
November 1	3,495	1,234	1,629	...	632	...
November 5	879	879	...	...	...	...
November 10	2,700	904	340	400	1,056	...
November 12	1,633	1,633	...	...	...	...
November 15	2,610	2,132	478	...	...	...
November 19	234	...	...	...	234	...
November 20	1,216	...	278	938	...	...
November 24	406	...	406	...	...	...
November 25	1,276	...	...	...	...	1,276
November 30	666	...	462	204	...	...
Total for Nov.	15,115	6,782	3,593	1,542	1,922	1,276
December 1	354	...	...	354	...	...
December 5	459	...	...	201	...	258
December 10	1,758	...	607	...	1,151	...
December 14	1,057	...	...	1,057	...	...
December 15	948	...	...	647	301	...
December 20	693	185	...	300	208	...
December 25	624	...	...	...	624	...
Total for Dec.	5,893	1,851[23]	607	2,559	2,284	258
January 1	340	...	...	340	...	...
January 5	220	...	...	...	...	220
January 15	140	...	...	...	...	140
January 20	220	...	...	...	...	220
Total for Jan.	920	...	...	340	...	580
Sept.till Jan. 20	30,899	12,217	7,921	4,441	4,206	2,114

Troops dispatched by the overland route:

October 2	235 R.E.	117	...	...	118	...
October 12	221 Art.	221	...	...	...	...
October 14	244 R.E.[24]	122	...	...	122	...
Total for Oct.	700	460	...	...	240	...
Total						31,599
Men en route from Cape, partly arrived						4,000
Grand total						35,599

---

[23] Misprint for 185; corrected in *CW*, Vol. 40, p. 192.
[24] *CW*, Vol. 15, p. 378, reads 224 R.E., a slip.

FREDERICK ENGELS

[The Capture of Delhi]

(*New York Daily Tribune*, December 5, 1857. Written by Engels at Marx's request. Printed as a leading article.)

We will not join the noisy chorus which, in Great Britain, is now extolling to the skies the bravery of the troops that took Delhi by storm. No people, not even the French, can equal the English in self-laudation, especially when bravery is the point in question. The analysis of the facts, however, very soon reduces, in ninety-nine cases out of a hundred, the grandeur of this heroism to very commonplace proportions; and every man of common sense must be disgusted at this overtrading in other people's courage, by which the English pater familias who lives quietly at home, and is uncommonly averse to anything that threatens him with the remotest chance of obtaining military glory, attempts to pass himself off as a participator in the undoubted, but certainly not so very extraordinary, bravery shown in the assault on Delhi.

If we compare Delhi with Sevastopol, we of course agree that the Sepoys were no Russians; that none of their sallies against the British cantonment was anything like Inkermann;[1] that there was no Todtleben[2] in Delhi, and that the Sepoys, bravely as every individual man and company fought in most instances, were utterly without leadership, not only for brigades and divisions, but almost for battalions; that their cohesion did not therefore extend beyond the companies; that they entirely lacked the scientific element without which an army is nowadays helpless, and the defense of a town utterly hopeless. Still, the disproportion of numbers and means of action, the superiority of the Sepoys over the Europeans in withstanding the climate, the extreme weakness to which the force before Delhi was at times reduced, make up for many of these differences, and render a fair parallel between the two sieges (to call these operations sieges) possible.

This article reflects some of Engels's ideas about the siege of Delhi, as expressed in his letter to Marx on 24 September 1857 (Letter No. 16 in this volume). Engels refers to his preparation of this article for Marx in the letters to Marx dated 16 and 17 November 1857; see *CW*, Vol. 15, pp. 427 and 681 n. Also see Marx's letter to Engels dated 31 October 1857 for an article on Delhi, in *CW*, Vol. 40, p. 198 (Letter No. 19 in this volume).

[1] The battle of Inkermann took place in November 1854 during the Crimean War (1853–1856) when the Anglo-French forces beat back an attack of the Russian army.
[2] Eduard Ivanovich Todtleben (1818–1884): prominent Russian military engineer, general, one of the organizers of the Russian defence of Sevastopol, 1854–55. See *FIWI*, p. 240.

Again we do not consider the storming of Delhi as an act of uncommon or extra-heroic bravery, although as in every battle individual acts of high spirit no doubt occurred on either side, but we maintain that the Anglo-Indian army before Delhi has shown more perseverance, force of character, judgment and skill, than the English army when on its trial between Sevastopol and Balaklava.[3] The latter, after Inkermann, was ready and willing to re-embark, and no doubt would have done so if it had not been for the French. The former, when the season of the year, the deadly maladies consequent upon it, the interruption of the communications, the absence of all chance of speedy reinforcements, the condition of all Upper India, invited a withdrawal, did indeed consider the advisability of this step, but for all that, held out at its post.

When the insurrection was at its highest point, a movable column in Upper India was the first thing required. There were only two forces that could be thus employed – the small force of Havelock, which soon proved inadequate, and the force before Delhi. That it was, under these circumstances, a military mistake to stay before Delhi, consuming the available strength in useless fights with an unassailable enemy; that the army in motion would have been worth four times its value when at rest; that the clearing of Upper India, with the exception of Delhi, the re-establishing of the communications, the crushing of every attempt of the insurgents to concentrate a force, would have been obtained, and with it the fall of Delhi, as a natural and easy consequence, are indisputable facts. But political reasons commanded that the camp before Delhi should not be raised.[4] It is the wiseacres at headquarters who sent the army to Delhi that should be blamed – not the perseverance of the army in holding out when once there. At the same time we must not omit to state that the effect of the rainy season on this army was far milder than was to be anticipated, and that with anything like an average amount of the sickness consequent upon active operations at such a period, the withdrawal or the dissolution of the army would have been unavoid-able. The dangerous position of the army lasted till the end of August. The reinforcement began to come in, while dissensions continued to weaken the rebel camp.[5] In the beginning of September the siege-train arrived, and the defensive position was changed into an offensive one. On the 7th of September the first battery opened its fire,[6] and on the evening of the 13th two practicable breaches were opened. Let us now examine what took place during this interval.

If we were to rely, for this purpose, on the official dispatch of Gen. Wilson,[7] we should be very badly off indeed. This report is quite as confused as

[3] The battle of Balaklava took place on 25 October 1854. The Russian army inflicted serious losses on their adversaries specially on the British cavalry, but failed to achieve their main objective (CW, Vol. 15, p. 382.)

[4] Sir John Lawrance strongly disagreed with the proposal for a retreat from Delhi. See Marx's report, New York Daily Tribune (NYDT), 23 October 1875.

[5] See Campbell, Narrative, p. 158.

[6] See Roberts, Letters, p. 53.

[7] Despatch from General Wilson, The Times, No. 22839, 16 November 1857; see CW, Vol. 15, p. 394 n (a).

the documents issued from the English headquarters in the Crimea ever were.[8] No man living could make out from that report the position of the two breaches, or the relative position and order in which the storming columns were arranged. As to the private reports, they are, of course, still more hopelessly confused. Fortunately one of those skilful scientific officers who deserve nearly the whole credit of the success, a member of the Bengal Engineers and Artillery, has given a report of what occurred, in *The Bombay Gazette*, as clear and business-like as it is simple and unpretending.[9] During the whole of the Crimean war not one English officer was found able to write a report as sensible as this. Unfortunately he got wounded on the first day of the assault, and then his letter stops. As to later transactions, we are, therefore, still quite in the dark.

The English had strengthened the defences of Delhi so far that they could resist a siege by an Asiatic army. According to our modern notions, Delhi was scarcely to be called a fortress, but merely a place secured against the forcible assault by a field force. Its masonry wall, 16 feet high and 12 feet thick, crowned by a parapet of 3 feet thickness and 8 feet height, offered 6 feet of masonry beside the parapet, uncovered by the glacis and exposed to the direct fire of the attack. The narrowness of this masonry rampart put it out of the question to place cannon anywhere, except in the bastions and martello towers.[10] These latter flanked the curtain but very imperfectly, and a masonry parapet of three feet thickness being easily battered down by siege guns (field pieces could do it), to silence the fire of the defense, and particularly the guns flanking the ditch, was very easy. Between wall and ditch there was a wide berm[11] or level road, facilitating the formation of a practicable breach, and the ditch, under these circumstances, instead of being a *coupe-gorge*[12] for any force that got entangled in it, became a resting place to re-form those columns that had got into disorder while advancing on the glacis.

To advance against such a place, with regular trenches, according to the rules of sieges, would have been insane, even if the first condition had not been wanting, viz., a force sufficient to invest the place on all sides. The state of the defenses, the disorganization and sinking spirit of the defenders, would have rendered every other mode of attack than the one pursued an absolute fault. This mode is very well known to military men under the name of the forcible attack (*attaque de vive force*). The defenses, being such only as to render an open attack impossible without heavy guns, are dealt with summarily by artillery; the interior of the place is all the while shelled, and as soon as the breaches are practicable the troops advance to the assault.

The front under attack was the northern one, directly opposite to the English camp. This front is composed of two curtains and three bastions, forming

[8] See Roberts, *Letters*, pp. 53–55.
[9] *The Times*, 'India', same issue as containing Wilson's dispatch.
[10] Circular forts to prevent hostile landing or advance.
[11] Berm means ledge.
[12] Blocked passage.

a slightly re-entering angle at the central (the Cashmere) bastion. The eastern position, from the Cashmere to the Water bastion, is the shorter one, and projects a little in front of the Western position, between the Cashmere and the Moree bastions. The ground in front of the Cashmere and Water bastions was covered with low jungle, gardens, houses, & c., which had not been levelled down by the Sepoys, and afforded shelter to the attack. (This circumstance explains how it was possible that the English could so often follow the Sepoys under the very guns of the place, which was at that time considered extremely heroic, but was in fact a matter of little danger so long as they had this cover.) Besides, at about 400 or 500 yards from this front, a deep ravine ran in the same direction as the wall, so as to form a natural parallel for the attack. The river, besides, giving a capital basis to the English left, the slight salient formed by the Cashmere and water bastions was selected very properly as the main point of attack. The western curtain and bastions were simultaneously subjected to a simulated attack, and this maneuver succeeded so well that the main force of the Sepoys was directed against it. They assembled a strong body in the suburbs outside the Cabool gate, so as to menace the English right. This maneuver would have been perfectly correct and very effective, if the western curtain between the Moree and Cashmere bastions had been the most in danger. The flanking position of the Sepoys would have been capital as a means of active defence, every column of assault being at once taken in flank by a movement of this force in advance. But the effect of this position could not reach as far eastward as the curtain between the Cashmere and Water bastions; and thus its occupation drew away the best part of the defending force from the decisive point.

The selection of the places for the batteries, their construction and arming, and the way in which they were served, deserve the greatest praise. The English had about 50 guns and mortars, concentrated in powerful batteries, behind good solid parapets. The Sepoys had, according to official statements, 55 guns on the attacked front, but scattered over small bastions and Martello towers, incapable of concentrated action, and scarcely sheltered by the miserable three feet parapet. No doubt a couple of hours must have sufficed to silence the fire of the defence, and then there remained little to be done.

On the 8th, No. 1 battery, 10 guns, opened fire at 700 yards from the wall. During the following night the ravine aforesaid was worked out into a sort of trench. On the 9th, the broken ground and houses in front of this ravine were seized without resistance; and on the 10th, No. 2 battery, 8 guns, was unmasked. This latter was 500 or 600 yards from the wall. On the 11th, No. 3 battery, built very boldly and cleverly at 200 yards from the water bastion in some broken ground, opened fire with six guns, while ten heavy mortars shelled the town. On the evening of the 13th the breaches – one in the curtain adjoining the right flank of the Cashmere bastion, and the other in the left face and flank of the water bastion – were reported practicable for escalade, and the assault was ordered. The Sepoys on the 11th had made a counter approach on the glacis between the two menaced bastions, and threw out a trench for skirmishers about three hundred and fifty yards in front of the English batteries. They also advanced from this position outside the Cabool gate to flank attacks. But these attempts at active defense were carried out without unity, connection or spirit, and led to no result.

At daylight on the 14th five British columns advanced to the attack. One, on the right, to occupy the force outside the Cabool gate and attack, in case of success, the Lahore gate. One against each breach, one against the Cashmere gate, which was to be blown up, and one to act as a reserve. With the exception of the first, all these columns were successful. The breaches were but slightly defended, but the resistance in the houses near the wall was very obstinate. The heroism of an officer and three sergeants of the Engineers (for here there *was* heroism) succeeded in blowing open the Cashmere gate, and thus this column entered also. By evening the whole northern front was in the possession of the English. Here Gen. Wilson, however, stopped. The indiscriminate assault was arrested, guns brought up and directed against every strong position in the town. With the exception of the storming of the magazine, there seems to have been very little actual fighting. The insurgents were dispirited and left the town in masses. Wilson advanced cautiously into the town, found scarcely any resistance after the 17th, and occupied it completely on the 20th.

Our opinion on the conduct of the attack has been stated. As to the defense – the attempt at offensive counter-movements, the flanking position at the Cabool gate, the counter-approaches, the rifle-pits, all show that some notions of scientific warfare had penetrated among the Sepoys; but either they were not clear enough, or not powerful enough, to be carried out with any effect. Whether they originated with Indians, or with some of the Europeans that are with them, is of course difficult to decide; but one thing is certain: that these attempts, though imperfect in execution, bear a close resemblance in their groundwork to the active defense of Sevastopol, and that their execution looks as if a correct plan had been made for the Sepoys by some European officer, but that they had not been able to understand the idea fully, or that disorganization and want of command turned practical projects into weak and powerless attempts.

New York Daily Tribune **1858**

FREDERICK ENGELS

[The Siege and Storming of Lucknow]

(*New York Daily Tribune*, January 30, 1858. Printed as a leading article.)

The last mails from Calcutta brought some details, which have made their way to this country through the London journals, from which it is possible to form a judgement as to Sir Colin Campbell's performance at Lucknow. As the British press assert that this feat of arms stands forth in unrivalled glory in the history of warfare, the subject may as well be a little more closely examined.

The town of Lucknow is situated on the right bank of the River Goomtee, which at that locality runs in a south-easterly direction. At a distance of from two to three miles from the river a canal runs nearly parallel to it, intersects the town, and below it approaches the river, which it then joins about a mile further down. The banks of the river are not occupied by crowded streets, but by a succession of palaces, with gardens and insulated public buildings. At the junction of the canal and river, but on the right or southern bank of both, are situated, close together, a school, called La Martiniere,[1] and a hunting-palace and park, called Dilkhoosha.[2] Crossing the canal, but remaining on the southern side of the river, and close to its bank, the first palace and garden is that of Secunderbagh;[3] further west come barracks and Mess-house, and then the Motee Mahal (Pearl Palace),[4] which is but a few hundred yards from the Residency. This latter building is erected on the only high ground in the neighborhood; it commands the

See, for this article, Marx's letters to Engels dated 30 December 1857 and 1 January 1858, and Engels's reply to Marx dated 6 January 1858. *CW*, Vol. 40, pp. 233 and n., 239 and n. Article not included in *FIWI* and Avineri, but see *CW*, Vol. 15, pp. 419–25.

[1] The school was founded by General Claude Martine during the reign of Asaf-ud Daulah and completed by Joseph Quiros. According to Martine's will, it started functioning as a college in 1840, being entirely supported out of the funds bequeathed by the founder. The La Martiniere grounds served as a strong point of defence for the British during 1857–58. See E.H. Hilton, *The Mutiny Records* (Lahore, 1975), pp. 178–79.

[2] Palace built by Sa'adat Ali Khan (1798–1814) around which he laid an extensive park and stocked it with deer and other game. See ibid., p. 178.

[3] Sikandarbagh, which Wajid Ali Shah built for his Begam, Sikandar Mahal. It had a high walled enclosure of 120 square yards , carefully loopholed all round, with turrets at the angles, and a garden prettily laid with a summer house in the centre. A large portion of it was destroyed by Colin Campbell in 1857. See ibid., pp. 122, 205.

[4] The Moti Mahal or Pearl Palace was built by Sa'adat Ali Khan (1798–1814) on the right bank of the Gomti. It was one of the most beautiful buildings of old Lucknow. See ibid., p. 202.

town, and consists of a considerable inclosure with several palaces and out-houses within it. To the south of this line of buildings is the compact portion of the town, and two miles south of this is the park and palace of Alumbagh.[5]

The natural strength of the Residency at once explains how it was possi-ble for the English to hold out in it against far superior numbers; but this very fact at once shows also what class of fighters the Oudians are. In fact, men who, partly drilled under European officers and provided plentifully with artillery, have never yet been able to overcome a single miserable inclosure defended by Europeans – such men are, militarily speaking, no better than savages, and a victory over them cannot add much to the glory of any army, however great the odds may be in favor of the natives. Another fact which classes the Oudians with the most contemptible opponents to be met with, is the manner in which Havelock forced his way through the very thickest portion of the town, in spite of barri-cades, loopholed houses, and the like. His loss, indeed, was great; but compare such an engagement with even the worst-fought street-battle of 1848! Not one man of his weak column could have made good his way had there been any real fighting. The houses cannot have been defended at all; it would have required weeks to take as many of them as would have secured a clear passage. As to the judgment displayed by Havelock in thus taking the bull by the horns, we cannot form an opinion; it is said he was compelled to do so from the great strait to which the Residency was reduced, and other motives are mentioned; however, nothing authentic is known.

When Sir Colin Campbell arrived he had about 2,000 European and 1,000 Sikh infantry; 350 European and 600 Sikh cavalry; 18 horse-artillery guns, 4 siege guns, and 300 sailors with their heavy shipguns; in all 5,000 men, among which were 3,000 Europeans.[6] This force was about as strong in numbers as a very fair average of most Anglo-Indian armies that have accomplished great exploits; indeed, the field-force with which Sir C. Napier conquered Sinde was scarcely half as large, and often less. On the other hand, its large admixture of the European element and the circumstance that all its native portion consisted of the best fighting nation of India, the Sikhs, give it a character of intrinsic strength and cohesion far superior to the generality of Anglo-Indian armies. Its opponents, as we have seen, were contemptible, for the most part rough militia instead of trained soldiers. True, the Oudians pass for the most warlike race of Lower Hindostan, but this is the case merely in comparison with the cowardly Bengalees,

[5] The building in the centre of the garden of Alambagh was built by one of the Begams of Wajid Ali Shah. It was captured by General Havelock on 23 September 1857 while advancing to the relief of the Residency. General Havelock is buried here. See ibid., p. 206.
[6] Gubbins and Innes, who participated in this campaign, give the following details: 2,388 European Infantry, 109 European Voluntary Cavalry, 282 European Artillery, 341 Sikh Infantry and 59 Native Irregular Cavalry. Total, 3,179. See Gubbins, *An Account of the Mutinies* (Delhi, 1978), p. 313, and Innes, *Lucknow and Oudh in the Mutiny* (London, 1896), p. 215.

whose *morale* is utterly broken down by the most relaxing climate of the world and by centuries of oppression. The way in which they submitted to the 'filibustering' annexation of their country to the Company's dominions, and the whole of their behavior during the insurrection, certainly places them below the level of the Sepoys, as far as courage and intelligence are concerned. We are, indeed, informed that quantity made up for quality. Some letter-writers say there were as many as 100,000 in the town. They were, no doubt, superior to the British in the proportion of four or six to one, perhaps more; but with such enemies that makes little difference. A position can only be defended by a certain number, and if these are determined to run away it matters little whether four or five times that number of similar heroes are within half a mile. There is no doubt that many instances of individual bravery have been seen, even among these Oudians. Some among them may have fought like lions; but of what avail were these in a place which they were too weak to defend after the mere rabble among the garrison had run away? There appears to have never been among them any attempt at bringing the whole under a single command; their local chiefs had no authority except over their own men, and would not submit to anybody else.

Sir Colin Campbell advanced first on Alumbagh; then, instead of forcing his way through the town as Havelock had done, he profited by the experience gained by that General and turned toward Dilkhoosha and La Martiniere.[7] The ground in front of these inclosures was cleared of the Oudian skirmishers on Nov. 13. On the 15th the attack commenced. So neglectful had the enemy been that the preparations for intrenching the Dilkhoosha were not yet completed even then; it was taken at once, and without much resistance, and so was the Martiniere. These two positions secured to the English the line of the canal. The enemy advanced once more across this obstacle to retake the two posts, lost in the morning, but they were soon routed, with heavy loss. On the 16th the British crossed the canal and attacked the Secunderbagh Palace. The intrenchments here were in a little better order, consequently Gen. Campbell wisely attacked the place with artillery. After the defenses had been destroyed, the infantry charged and took the place. The Samuck, another fortified position, was next cannonaded for three hours and then taken, 'after one of the severest fights ever witnessed', says Sir C. Campbell[8] – and, adds a wise correspondent from the seat of war, 'few men have seen more of hard fighting than he'. We should like to know where he saw it. Surely not in the Crimea, where, after the battle of the Alma,[9] he had a very quiet life of it at Balaklava, only one of his regiments being engaged at the battle of Balaklava and none at Inkermann.

On the 17th the artillery was pointed on the barracks and Mess-house

---

[7] Here and below Engels draws on the 'Relief of Lucknow', *The Times*, 29 December 1857. See *CW*, Vol. 15, p. 423 n.

[8] C. Campbell's words were quoted by G.F. Edmonstone in the telegram published in *The Times*, 29 December 1857. Ibid.

[9] The battle took place on 20 September 1854, during the Crimean War (1853–56).

which formed the next position toward the Residency. This cannonade lasted till 3 o'clock, after which the infantry took the place by storm. The flying enemy was hotly pursued. One more position remained between the advancing army and the Residency – the Motee Mahal. Before dusk this, too, was carried, and the communication with the garrison was fully established.

Campbell should be praised for the judgment with which he took the easier route and with which he used his heavy artillery to reduce the intrenched position before he launched his columns. But the British fought with all the advantages of skilled soldiers obeying one chief over half savages commanded by nobody; and, as we see, they fully availed themselves of these advantages. They did not expose their men more than was absolutely necessary. They used artillery as long as there was anything to be battered down. No doubt they fought with valor; but what they deserve credit for is discretion. The best proof of this is in the number of the killed and wounded. It has not yet been published as far as the men are concerned; but there were five officers killed and thirty-two wounded. The army must have had, with 5,000 men, at least 250 to 300 officers. The English officers are certainly never sparing of their lives. To show an example of bravery to their men is in too many cases the part of their duty which they only know. And when in three day's consecutive fighting, under circumstances and in positions which are known to cost more lives than any other to conquer, the loss is only one in eight or nine, it is out of the question to call it hard fighting. To take an example from British history alone, what is all this Indian fighting put together against the single defense of Hougoumont and La Haye Sainte at Waterloo?[10] What would these writers who now turn every little skirmish into a pitched battle say of a contest like Borodino, where one army lost one-half and the other one-third of its combatants?[11]

[10] The castle of Hougoumont and the farm La Haye Sainte on the approaches to Waterloo were used by the English and Prussian troops as strong natural fortifications. The defenders of these camps offered stout resistance to the French despite their small numbers.

[11] A full-scale battle was fought by the French and Russian troops at Borodino, near Moscow, on 7 September 1812.

FREDERICK ENGELS

The Relief of Lucknow

(*New York Daily Tribune*, February 1, 1858)

We have at last before us the official dispatch of Sir Colin Campbell on the relief of Lucknow. It confirms in every respect the conclusions we drew from the first non-official reports on this engagement.[1] The contemptible character of the resistance offered by the Oudians is even more apparent from this document, while on the other hand Campbell himself appears to take more pride in his skillful generalship than in any uncommon bravery displayed either by him or his troops. The dispatch states the strength of the British troops at about 5,000, of whom some 3,200 were infantry, and 700 cavalry, the rest artillery, naval brigade, engineers, &c. The operations commenced, as stated, with the attack on Dilkhoosha. This garden was taken after a running fight. 'The loss was very trifling; the enemy's loss, too, was trifling, owing to the suddenness of retreat.'[2] There was, indeed, no chance of displaying heroism on this occasion. The Oudians retreated in such a hurry that they crossed at once through the grounds of La Martiniere without availing themselves of the new line of defense offered by this post. The first symptom of a more obstinate resistance was shown at the Secunderbagh, a high-walled, loop-holed inclosure 120 yards square, flanked by a loop-holed village about 100 yards distant. There Campbell at once displayed his less dashing but more sensible mode of warfare. The heavy and field artillery concentrated their efforts on the main inclosure, while one brigade attacked the barricaded village, and another drove back whatever bands of the enemy attempted the open field. The defense was lamentable. Two intrenched positions like those described flanking each other by their fire, in the hands of indifferent soldiers, or even of plucky undisciplined insurgents, would require a deal of fighting to take. But here there appears to have been neither pluck, nor concert, nor even a shadow of sense. We do not hear of any artillery used in the defense. The village (evidently a small cluster of houses) was taken at the first onset. The troops in the field were scattered without an effort. Thus in a few moments the Secunderbagh was quite isolated, and when, after an hour's cannonading, the

See Engels's letter to Marx, 14 January and Marx's letter to Engels, 16 January 1858, in *CW*, Vol. 40, pp. 247, 249 (Letters Nos. 26 and 27 in this volume). Article not included in *FIWI* and Avineri. See text in *CW*, Vol. 15, pp. 435–47.

[1] A reference to Engels's article, 'The Siege and Storming of Lucknow', published in the *New York Daily Tribune* (*NYDT*) on 30 January 1858.

[2] Here and below the quotations are drawn from *The Times*, 13 January 1858. *CW*, Vol. 15, p. 435 n.

walls gave way in one point, the Highlanders stormed the breach and killed every soul in the place; 2,000[3] natives are said by Sir C. Campbell to have been found dead in it.

The Shah Nujjeef[4] was the next post – a walled inclosure prepared for defense, with a mosque for a reduit; again one of those positions which a commander of brave but half-disciplined troops would exactly wish for. This place was stormed after a three hours' cannonade had opened the walls. On the next day, Nov. 17, the Mess-house was attacked. This was a group of buildings inclosed by a mud rampart and a scarped ditch twelve feet wide – in other words, a common field redoubt with a slight ditch and a parapet of problematical thickness and height. For some cause or other, this place appeared rather formidable to Gen. Campbell, for he at once resolved to give his artillery full time to batter it down before he stormed it. The cannonade accordingly lasted the whole morning, till 3 o'clock p.m., when the infantry advanced and took the position with a rash.[5] No sharp fighting here, at all events. The Motee Mahal, the last post of the Oudians on the line toward the Residency, was cannonaded for an hour; several breaches were made and then taken without difficulty, and this ended the fighting for the relief of the garrison.

The character of the whole engagement is that of an attack by well-disciplined, well-officered European troops, inured to war and of average courage, upon an Asiatic rabble, possessing neither discipline for officers, nor the habits of war, nor even adequate arms, and whose courage was broken by the consciousness of the double superiority possessed by their opponents, as soldiers over civilians and as Europeans over Asiatics. We have seen that Sir Colin Campbell nowhere appears to have been opposed by artillery. We shall see, further on, that Brigadier Inglis's[6] report leads to the conclusion that the great bulk of the insurgents must have been without fire-arms;[7] and if it is true that 2,000 natives were massacred in the Secunderbagh, it is evident they must have been very imperfectly armed, otherwise the greatest cowards would have defended the place against one assaulting column.

On the other hand, the conduct of the fight by Gen. Campbell deserves the highest praise for tactical skill. From the want of artillery in his opponents, he must have known that his progress could not be resisted; accordingly he used this arm to its full extent, clearing first the way for his columns before he launched

---

[3] See Hilton, *Mutiny Records*, p. 123.

[4] 'Shah Najaf' was built by Ghaziuddin Haidar, the first king of Awadh, and stands on the right bank of the Gomti. Ghaziuddin is buried here. It is said to be maintained out of the interest on the rupees one crore lent by the Ruler of Awadh to the British government in perpetuity in 1825. Ibid., p. 204.

[5] *NYDT* misprint for 'rush'?

[6] John Eardley Wilmot Inglis (1814–1862) was commander at the Lucknow Residency after Henry Lawrence's death.

[7] Here and below Engels has used the report from Brigadier Inglis, Commander of the Garrison of Lucknow, to the Secretary to Government, Military Department, Calcutta, published in *The Times*, 13 January 1858. See *CW*, Vol. 15, p. 437 n.

them. The attack upon Secunderbagh and its flanking defenses is a very excellent specimen of the mode of conducting such an affair. At the same time, having once ascertained the despicable nature of the defense, he did not treat such opponents with any unnecessary formality; as soon as there was a gap in the walls, the infantry advanced. Altogether, Sir C. Campbell ranks from the day of Lucknow as a general; hitherto he was known as a soldier only.

By the relief of Lucknow we are at last put in possession of a document describing the occurrences which took place during the siege of the Residency. Brigadier Inglis, the successor in command of Sir H. Lawrence, has made his report to the Governor-General;[8] and, according to Gen. Outram and the *unisono* of the British press, here is a conspicuous case of heroism, indeed[9] – for such bravery, such perseverance, such endurance of fatigue and hardships, have never been seen at any time, and the defense of Lucknow stands unparalleled in the history of sieges. The report of Brigadier Inglis informs us that on the 30th of June the British made a sortie against the natives, who were then just concentrating, but were repulsed with such heavy loss that they had at once to confine themselves to the defense of the Residency, and even to abandon and blow up another group of buildings in the vicinity, containing 240 barrels of powder and 6,000,000 musket cartridges.[10] The enemy at once invested the Residency, taking possession of and fortifying the buildings in its immediate vicinity, some within 50 yards of the defenses, and which, against the advice of the engineers, Sir H. Lawrence had refused to raze. The British parapets were still partly unfinished, and only two batteries were in working order, but, in spite of the terrific and incessant fire 'kept up by' 8,000 men firing 'at one time into the position', they were enabled to complete them very soon, and have 30 guns in battery. This terrific fire must have been a very wild and random kind of firing, not at all deserving the name of sharp-shooting with which Gen. Inglis adorns it; how otherwise could a man have lived in the place, defended as it was by perhaps 1,200 men? The instances related to show the terrific nature of this fire, that it killed women and children, and wounded men in places considered well sheltered, are very poor examples, as they occur never oftener than when the enemy's fire, instead of being aimed at different objects, is directed toward the fortification at large, and consequently never hits the actual defenders. On the 1st of July Lawrence was mortally wounded, and Inglis took the command. The enemy had by this time 20 or 25 guns in position, 'planted all round our post'. Very lucky for the defense, for if they had concentrated their fire on one or two places of the ramparts, the position would in all likelihood have been taken. Some of these guns were posted in places 'where our own heavy guns could not reply to them'.

---

[8] Charles John Canning.

[9] *The Times,* 13 January 1858, leading article. Cf. *CW,* Vol. 15, p. 437 n.

[10] Eventually, it was destroyed on 1 July 1857. See Campbell, *Narrative,* p. 220, and Forrest, *Selections,* Vol. II, p. 39.

Now, as the Residency is on commanding ground, these places can only have been so situated that the guns of the attack could not fire at the rampart, but merely at the tops of the buildings inside; which was very fortunate for the defense, as that did no great harm, and the same guns might have been far more usefully employed in firing at the parapet or barricades. Upon the whole, the artillery on both sides must have been miserably served, as otherwise a cannonade at such short range must have been very shortly put a stop to by the batteries mutually dismounting each other; and that this did not take place, is still a mystery.

On July 20, the Oudians exploded a mine under the parapet, which, however, did no damage. Two main columns immediately advanced to an assault, while sham attacks were attempted at other places; but the mere effect of the garrison's fire drove them back. On the 10th of August another mine exploded, and opened a breach, 'through which a regiment could have advanced in perfect order. A column charged this breach, flanked by the subordinate attacks; but at the breach only a few of the enemy advanced with the utmost determination.'[11]

These few were soon disposed of by the flank fire of the garrison, while at the flank attacks hand-grenades and a little firing drove the undisciplined masses back. The third mine was sprung on the 18th August; a new breach was formed,[12] but the assault was even more spiritless than before, and was easily repelled. The last explosion and assault took place on the 5th September, but again hand-grenades and musketry drove them back. From that time to the arrival of relief, the siege appears to have been converted into a mere blockade, with a more or less sustained fire of muskets and artillery.

This is, indeed, an extraordinary transaction. A mob of 50,000 men or more, composed of the inhabitants of Lucknow and the surrounding country, with perhaps 5,000 or 6,000 drilled soldiers among them, blockade a body of some 1,200 or 1,550 Europeans in the Residency of Lucknow and attempt to reduce them. So little order reigned among the blockading body, that the supplies of the garrison appear never to have been completely cut off, though their communications with Cawnpore were. The proceedings of what is called 'the siege' are distinguished by a mixture of Asiatic ignorance and wildness, with here and there a glimpse of some military knowledge introduced by European example and rule. There were evidently some artillerymen and sappers among the Oudians who knew how to construct batteries; but their action appears to have been confined to the construction of shelter from the enemy's fire. They even appear to have brought this art of sheltering themselves to great perfection, so much so that their batteries must have been very safe, not only for the gunners but also for the besieged; no guns could have been worked in them with any effect. Nor were they; or how is this unparalleled fact to be explained, that 30 guns inside and 25

---

[11] See Brigadier Inglis's letter to the Government of India, 26 September 1857, reproduced in Forrest, *Indian Mutiny*, Vol. I, pp. 37–52.

[12] Ibid., p. 42; Campbell, *Narrative*, p. 221.

outside worked against each other at exceedingly short ranges, some not more than 50 yards, and yet we hear nothing of dismounted guns or one party silencing the artillery of the other? As to the musketry fire, we first have to ask how it is possible that eight thousand natives could take position within musket range from the British batteries without being sent to the right about by the artillery? And if they did, how is it possible that they did not kill and wound every soul on the place? Still we are told that they did hold their own, and did fire day and night, and that in spite of all this the 32nd Regiment, which could at the very outside count 500 men after June 30, and had to bear the brunt of the whole siege, still was 300 strong at its end? If this is not an exact counterpart of the 'last surviving ten of the Fourth (Polish) Regiment', which marched into Prussia 88 officers and 1,815 rank and file strong, what then is it? The British are perfectly right that such fighting was never seen as there was at Lucknow – indeed it was not. In spite of the unassuming, apparently simple tone of Inglis's report, yet his queer observation about guns placed so that they could not be fired at, about 8,000 men firing day and night, without effect, about 50,000 insurgents blockading him, about the hardships of bullets going into places where they had no business to go, and about assaults carried out with the utmost determination, yet repulsed, without any effort – all these observations compel us to acknowledge the whole of this report is full of the most glaring exaggerations, and will not stand cool criticism for a moment.

But then surely the besieged underwent uncommon hardships? Listen: 'The want of native servants has also been a source of *much privation*. Several ladies have had to tend their children, and even, to wash their own clothes as well as to cook their scanty meals entirely unaided.' Pity the sorrows of a poor Lucknow lady! True, in these times of ups and downs, when dynasties are made and unmade in a day, and revolutions and commercial crashes combine to render the permanency of all creature comforts most splendidly insecure, we are not called upon to show any great sympathy if we hear of some ex-queen having to darn her own stockings, and even to wash them, not to speak of her cooking her own mutton-chop. But an Anglo-Indian lady, one of that vast number of sisters, cousins, or nieces to half-pay officers, Indian Government writers, merchants, clerks, or adventurers, who are, or rather were, before the mutiny, sent out every year, fresh from the boarding-school, to the large marriage-market in India, neither more nor less ceremoniously, and often far less willingly, than the fair Circassians that go to the Constantinople market – the very idea of one of these ladies having to wash her own clothes and cook her scanty meals entirely unaided – entirely! One's blood boils at it. Completely without 'native servants' – ay, having actually to tend their own children! It is revolting – Cawnpore would have been preferable!

The rabble investing the Residency may have counted 50,000 men; but then the large majority cannot have had any firearms. The 8,000 'sharp-shooters' may have had firearms; but of what description both arms and men were, the effect of their fire is there to tell. The twenty-five guns in the battery have been proved to have been most despicably served. The mining was as much at random as the firing. The assaults do not deserve the name even of reconnaissances. So much for the besiegers.

The besieged deserve full credit for the great strength of character with which they have held out for nearly five months, the greater portion of which time they were without any news whatever from the British forces. They fought, and hoped against hope, as it behoves men to do when they have their lives to sell as dearly as they can, and women and children to defend against Asiatic cruelty. Again, full credit do we give them for their watchfulness and perseverance. But, after the experiences of Wheeler's surrender at Cawnpore, who would not have done the same?

As to the attempt to turn the defense of Lucknow into a piece of unparalleled heroism,[13] it is ridiculous, especially after the clumsy report of Gen. Inglis. The privations of the garrison were confined to scanty shelter and exposure to the weather (which, however, did not produce any serious disease), and as to provisions, the very worst they had consisted in 'coarse beef and still coarser flour!'[14] far more comfortable fare than besieged soldiers are accustomed to in Europe! Compare the defense of Lucknow against a stupid and ignorant barbarian rabble with that of Antwerp, 1832, and the Fort of Malghera near Venice, in 1848 and '49, not to speak of Todtleben at Sevastopol, who had far greater difficulties to contend with than Gen. Inglis. Malghera was attacked by the best engineers and artillerymen of Austria, and defended by a weak garrison of raw levies; four-fifths of them had no bomb-proof shelter; the low soil created malaria more dangerous than an Indian climate; a hundred guns played upon them, and during the last three days of the bombardment, forty rounds were fired every minute; still the fort held out a month, and would have held out longer, if the Austrians had not taken hold of a position necessitating their retreat. Or take Dantzig,[15] where Rapp,[16] with the sick remnants of the French regiments returned from Russia, held out eleven months.[17] Take in fact any respectable siege of modern days, and you will find that more skill, more spirit, and quite as much pluck and endurance were shown against quite as great odds as in this Lucknow affair.

The Oude insurgents, however, though contemptible in the field, proved, immediately after the arrival of Campbell, the strength of a national insurrection. Campbell saw at once that he could neither attack the City of Lucknow with

---

[13] Campbell, *Narrative*, p. 221; Forrest, *Indian Mutiny*, p. 42.

[14] Engels's letter to Marx, 14 January 1858, on 'the Lucknow garrison's heroism', in that they lived on 'coarse beef' cooked by the ladies. *CW*, Vol. 40, p. 247.

[15] Danzig, then in Prussia, now in Poland.

[16] Jean Comte Rapp (1772–1821): French General, participated in Napoleon I's campaigns from January 1813 to January 1814. See *CW*, Vol. 15, p. 727.

[17] Rapp occupied it after the defeat of Napoleon's army in Russia in 1812. It was besieged by the Russian and Prussian troops in early 1813. On 2 January 1814, they occupied the fortress. See *CW*, Vol. 15, p. 684, n. 453.

his forces, nor hold his own. This is quite natural, and will appear so to any one who has attentively read the French invasion of Spain under Napoleon. The strength of a national insurrection does not lie in pitched battles, but in petty warfare, in the defense of towns, and in the interruption of the enemy's communications. Campbell accordingly prepared for the retreat with the same skill with which he had arranged the attack. A few more positions about the Residency were carried. They served to deceive the enemy as to Campbell's intentions, and to cover the arrangements for the retreat. With a daring perfectly justified in front of such an opponent, the whole army, a small reserve excepted, was employed to occupy an extensive line of outposts and pickets, behind which the women, the sick and wounded, and the baggage were evacuated. As soon as this preliminary operation was performed the outlying pickets fell back, concentrating gradually into more solid masses, the foremost of which then retreated through the next line, again to form as a reserve to the rear. Without being attacked, the whole of this maneuver was carried out with perfect order; with the exception of Outram and a small garrison left at Alumbagh (for what purposes we do not at present see), the whole army marched to Cawnpore, thus evacuating the Kingdom of Oude.

In the mean time unpleasant events had taken place at Cawnpore. Windham, the 'hero of the Redan',[18] another of those officers of whose skill we are told that they have proved it by being very brave, had on the 26th defeated the advanced guard of the Gwalior contingent, but on the 27th he had been severely beaten by them, his camp taken and burned, and he himself compelled to retreat into Wheeler's old intrenchment at Cawnpore. On the 28th they attacked this post, but were repulsed, and on the 6th Campbell defeated them with scarcely any loss, taking all their guns and train, and pursuing them for fourteen miles. The details of all these affairs are so far but scanty; but this much is certain, that the Indian Rebellion is as yet far from being quelled, and that, although most or all British re-enforcements have now landed, yet they disappear in an almost unaccountable manner. Some 20,000 men have landed in Bengal, and still the active army is no larger than when Delhi was taken. There is something wrong here. The climate must make terrible havoc among the newcomers.

---

[18] Here Engels alludes to General Windham's role in the Crimean War (1853–54).

The Approaching Indian Loan

(*New York Daily Tribune*, February 9, 1858)
London, January 22, 1858

The buoyancy in the London money market, resulting from the withdrawal of an enormous mass of capital from the ordinary productive investments, and its consequent transfer to the security markets, has, in the last fortnight, been somewhat lessened by the prospects of an impending *Indian loan* to the amount of eight or ten million pounds sterling. This loan, to be raised in England, and to be authorized by Parliament immediately on its assembling in February, is required to meet the claims upon the East India Company by its home creditors, as well as the extra expenditure for war materials, stores, transport of troops, & c., necessitated by the Indian revolt. In August, 1857, the British Government had, before the prorogation of Parliament, solemnly declared in the House of Commons that no such loan was intended, the financial resources of the Company being more than sufficient to meet the crisis. The agreeable delusion thus palmed on John Bull was, however, soon dispelled when it oozed out that by a proceeding of a very questionable character, the East India Company had laid hold on a sum of about £3,500,000 sterling, intrusted to them by different companies, for the construction of Indian railways; and had, moreover, secretly borrowed £1,000,000[1] from the Bank of England, and another million from the London Joint-Stock banks. The public being thus prepared for the worst, the Government did no longer hesitate to drop the mask, and by semi-official articles in *The Times*, *Globe*,[2] and other governmental organs, avow the necessity of the loan.

It may be asked why a special act on the part of the legislative power is required for launching such a loan, and then, why such an event does create the least apprehension, since, on the contrary, every vent for British capital, seeking now in vain for profitable investment, should, under present circumstances, be considered a windfall, and a most salutary check upon the rapid depreciation of capital.

It is generally known that the commercial existence of the East India Company was terminated in 1834,[3] when its principal remaining source of commercial profits, the monopoly of the China trade, was cut off. Consequently, the

---

[1] The figures seem to have been taken by Marx from the Parliamentary Debate, dated 5 February 1858. Hansard, Vol. 250, pp. 780–803.

[2] *The Globe and Traveller* was then a pro-Whig newspaper. See *FIWI*, p. 184.

[3] As a consequence of the Charter Act of 1833.

holders of East India stock having derived their dividends, nominally, at least, from the trade profits of the Company, a new financial arrangement with regard to them had become necessary. The payment of the dividends, till then charge-able upon the commercial revenue of the Company, was transferred to its politi-cal revenue. The proprietors of East India stocks were to be paid out of the revenues enjoyed by the East India Company in its governmental capacity, and, by act of Parliament, the Indian stock, amounting to £6,000,000 sterling, bear-ing ten per cent interest, was converted into a capital not to be liquidated except at the rate of £200 for every £100 of stock. In other words, the original East India stock of £6,000,000 sterling was converted into a capital of £12,000,000 ster-ling, bearing five per cent interest,[4] and chargeable upon the revenue derived from the taxes of the Indian people. The debt of the East India Company was thus, by a Parliamentary sleight of hand, changed into a debt of the Indian people. There exists, besides, a debt exceeding £50,000,000 sterling, contracted by the East India Company in India, and exclusively chargeable upon the State revenues of that country, such loans contracted by the Company in India itself having always been considered to lay[5] beyond the district of Parliamentary leg-islation, and regarded no more than the debts contracted by the colonial govern-ment in Canada or Australia for instance.

On the other hand, the East India Company was prohibited from con-tracting interest-bearing debts in Great Britain herself, without the especial sanc-tion of Parliament. Some years ago, when the Company set about establish-ing railways and electric telegraphs in India, it applied for the authorization of Indian Bonds in the London market, a request which was granted to the amount of £7,000,000 sterling, to be issued in Bonds bearing 4 per cent interest, and secured only on the Indian State revenues. At the commencement of the outbreak in India, this bond-debt stood at £3,894,400 sterling,[6] and the very necessity of again applying to Parliament shows the East India Company to have, during the course of the Indian insurrection, exhausted its legal powers of borrowing at home.

Now it is no secret that before recurring to this step, the East India Company had opened a loan at Calcutta, which, however, turned out a complete failure. This proves, on the one hand, that Indian capitalists are far from consi-dering the prospects of British supremacy in India in the same sanguine spirit which distinguishes the London press; and, on the other hand, exacerbates the feelings of John Bull to an uncommon pitch, since he is aware of the immense

---

[4] Here and below Marx draws on 'The Financial Obligations of the East India Com-pany', *The Economist*, No. 749, 2 January 1858. See *CW*, Vol. 15, p. 444.

[5] So printed in the *New York Daily Tribune* (*NYDT*), and so in *CW*, Vol. 15. *FIWI*, p. 102; *On Colonialism*, p. 174; and Av., p. 267 read: 'to lie'.

[6] 'Indian Loans', *The Economist*, No. 250, 9 January 1858. See *CW*, Vol. 15, p. 444 n.

hoardings of capital having gone on for the last seven years in India, whither, according to a statement recently published by Messers Haggard & Pixley, there has been shipped in 1856 and 1857, from the port of London alone, bullion to the amount of £21,000,000. The London *Times*, in a most persuasive strain, has taught its readers that

> of all the incentives to the loyalty of the natives, that of making them our creditors was the least doubtful; while on the other hand, among an impulsive, secretive and avaricious people no temptation to discontent or treachery could be stronger than that created by the idea that they were annually taxed to send dividends to wealthy claimants in other countries.[7]

The Indians, however, appear not to understand the beauty of a plan which would not only restore English supremacy at the expense of Indian capital, but at the same time, in a circuitous way, open the native hoards to British commerce. If, indeed, the Indian capitalists were as fond of British rule as every true Englishman thinks it an article of faith of[8] assert, no better opportunity could have been afforded them of exhibiting their loyalty and getting rid of their silver. The Indian capitalists shutting up their hoards, John Bull must open his mind to the dire necessity of defraying himself in the first instance, at least, the expenses of the Indian insurrection, without any support on the part of the natives. The impending loan constitutes, moreover, a precedent only, and looks like the first leaf in a book, bearing the title, *Anglo-Indian Home Debt*. It is no secret that what the East India Company wants are not eight millions, or ten millions, but twenty-five to thirty million pounds, and even these as a first installment only, not for expenses to be incurred, but for debts already due. The deficient revenue for the last three years amounted to £5,000,000; the treasure plundered by the insurgents up to the 15th October last, to £10,000,000 according to the statement of *The Phoenix*,[9] an Indian governmental paper; the loss of revenue in the north eastern provinces, consequent upon the rebellion, to £5,000,000, and the war expenses to at least £10,000,000.

It is true that successive loans by the Indian Company, in the London Money Market, would raise the value of money and prevent the increasing depreciation of capital; that is to say, the further fall in the rate of interest; but such a fall is exactly required for the revival of British industry and commerce. Any artificial check put upon the downward movement of the rate of discount is equivalent to an enhancement in the cost of production and the terms of credit, which, in its present weak state, English trade feels itself unable to bear. Hence the general cry of distress at the announcement of the Indian loan. Though the

---

[7] 'Money Market and City Intelligence', *The Times*, No. 22883, 6 January 1858. See ibid., p. 445.
[8] Misprint for 'to'.
[9] Published in Calcutta from 1856 to 1861. See *FIWI*, p. 225 and *CW*, Vol. 15, p. 765.

Parliamentary sanction adds no imperial guarantee to the loan of the Company, that guarantee, too, must be conceded, if money is not to be obtained on other terms: and despite all fine distinctions, as soon as the East India Company is supplanted by the British Government its debt will be merged into the British debt. A further increase of the large national debt seems, therefore, one of the first financial consequences of the Indian revolt.

FREDERICK ENGELS

Windham's Defeat

(*New York Daily Tribune*, February 20, 1858. Printed as a leading article.)

While during the Crimean war all England was calling for a man capable of organizing and leading her armies, and while incapables like Raglan,[1] Simpson[2] and Codrington[3] were intrusted with the office, there was a soldier in the Crimea endowed with the qualities required in a general. We mean Sir Colin Campbell, who is now daily showing in India that he understands his profession with a master's mind. In the Crimea, after having been allowed to lead his brigade at the Alma[4] where from the rigid line-tactics of the British army, he had no chance to show his capacities, he was cooped up in Balaklava and never once allowed to participate in the succeeding operations. And yet, his military talents had been clearly established in India long before, by no less an authority than the greatest general England has produced since Marlborough, by Sir Charles James Napier. But Napier was an independent man, too proud to stoop to the reigning oligarchy – and his recommendation was enough to make Campbell marked and distrusted.

Other men, however, gained distinctions and honors in that war. There was Sir William Fenwick Williams[5] of Kars, who now finds it convenient to rest on the laurels acquired by impudence, self-puffing, and by defrauding Gen. Kmetty[6]

This article was written by Engels at Marx's request. The title is given on the basis of Marx's notebook of 1858 (*FIWI*, p. 129), and Engels's letter to Marx dated 30 January 1858 (*CW*, Vol. 40, p. 257).

[1] Lord Fitzroy James Henry, first Baron Raglan (1788–1855): In the Crimean War won the battle of Alma on 20 September 1854; blamed for the failure of the mistimed attack on Malakhoff and Redan on 18 June 1855.

[2] Sir James Simpson (1792–1868): general; second in command to Sir James Napier in the Kacchi expedition of 1854; chief of the staff in Crimea in 1854 and successor to Lord Raglan in command.

[3] Sir William John Codrington (1804–1884): general; showed courage and promptitude at Alma and Inkerman; commander-in-chief at Sebastopol, 1855–56; MP in 1857.

[4] The battle of Alma took place on 20 September 1854 during the Crimean War (1853–1856). See *CW*, Vol. 15, p. 683.

[5] Sir William Fenwick Williams (1800–1883): major general in 1855, held Kars against the Russians and won the battle of Kars in 1855.

[6] Gyorgy Kmetty (Ismail Pasha) (1810–1865): Turkish general of Magyar descent; during the Crimean War, was commander of the Turkish forces on the Danube (1853–54) and in the Caucasus (1854–55).

of his well-earned fame. A baronetcy, a thousand a year, a comfortable berth at Woolwich, and a seat in Parliament, are quite sufficient to prevent him risking his reputation in India. Unlike him, 'the hero of the Redan', Gen. Windham, has set out to command a division against the Sepoys, and his very first act has settled him for ever. This same Windham, an obscure colonel of good family connections, commanded a brigade at the assault of the Redan, during which operation he behaved extremely phlegmatically, and at last, no reinforcement arriving, twice left his troops to shift for themselves, while he went to inquire about them himself. For this very questionable act, which in other services would have been inquired into by a court-martial, he was forthwith made a General, and shortly afterward called to the post of Chief of the Staff.

When Colin Campbell advanced to Lucknow, he left the old intrenchments, the camp and the town of Cawnpore, together with the bridge over the Ganges, in charge of General Windham and a force sufficient for the purpose. There were five regiments of infantry, whole or in part, many guns of position, 10 field guns and two naval guns, beside 100 horse; the whole force above 2,000. While Campbell was engaged at Lucknow, the various bodies of rebels hovering about the Doab drew together for an attack on Cawnpore. Beside a miscellaneous rabble, collected by insurgent Zemindars, the attacking force counted of drilled troops (disciplined they cannot be called), the remainder of the Dinapore Sepoys[7] and a portion of the Gwalior contingent. These latter were the only insurgent troops, the formation of which can be said to go beyond that of companies, as they had been officered by natives almost exclusively, and thus, with their field officers and captains, retained something like organized battalions. They were consequently regarded with some respect by the British. Windham had strict orders to remain on the defensive, but getting no replies to his dispatches from Campbell, the communication being interrupted, he resolved to act on his own responsibility. On the 26th November, he advanced with 1,200 infantry, 100 horse and 8 guns[8] to meet the advancing insurgents. Having easily defeated their vanguard, he saw the main column approaching and retired close to Cawnpore. Here he took up a position in front of the town, the 34th Regiment[9] on the left, the rifles (5 companies) and two companies of the 82nd on the right. The line of retreat lay through the town and there were some brick-kilns in rear of the left. Within four hundred yards from the front, and on various points still nearer to the flanks, were woods and jungle, offering excellent shelter to the advancing enemy. In fact, a worse position could not well have been chosen – the British exposed in the open plain, while the Indians could approach under shelter to within three or four hundred yards! To bring out Windham's 'heroism' in a still

---

[7] Troops led by Kunwar Singh of Jagdishpur.

[8] See Windham's letter to Campbell from Kanpur dated 30 November 1857, reproduced in Charles Ball, *History of the Indian Mutiny*, Vol. II, p. 198; Campbell, *Narrative*, pp. 248–49.

[9] Led by Lt. Colonel R. Kelly. See Ball, *History of the Indian Mutiny*, Vol. II, p. 198.

stronger light, there was a very decent position close by, with a plain in front and
rear, and with the canal as an obstacle before the front; but, of course, the worse
position was insisted on. On the 28th November,[10] the enemy opened a cannonade, bringing up his guns to the edge of the cover afforded by the jungle. Windham,
who, with the modesty inherent in a hero, calls this a 'bombardment', says his
troops stood it for five hours; but after this time, there happened something which
neither Windham, nor any man present, nor any Indian or British newspaper, has
as yet dared to relate.[11] From the moment the cannonade was turned into a
battle, all our direct sources of information cease, and we are left to draw our
own conclusions from the hesitating, prevaricating and incomplete evidence before us. Windham confines himself to the following incoherent statement:[12]

> In spite of the heavy bombardment of the enemy, my troops resisted the attack
> [rather novel to call a cannonade against field troops an *attack*[13]] for five
> hours, and still held the ground, until, I found from the number of men bayo-
> neted by the 88th that the mutineers had fully penetrated the town; *having been
> told* that they were attacking the fort, I directed Gen. Dupuis[14] to fall back. The
> whole force retired into the fort, with all our stores and guns, shortly before
> dark. Owing to the flight of the camp followers, I was unable to carry off my
> camp equipage and some of the baggage. Had not an error occurred in the
> conveyance of an order issued by me, I am of opinion that I could have held my
> ground, at all events until dark.[15]

Gen. Windham, with that instinct shown already at the Redan, moves
off to the reserve (the 88th occupying the town, as we must conclude), and finds,
not the enemy alive and fighting, but a great number of the enemy bayoneted by
the 88th. This fact leads him to the conclusion that the enemy (he does not say
whether dead or alive[16]) has fully penetrated the town! Alarming as this conclusion is both to the reader and to himself, our hero does not stop here. He is told
that the fort is attacked. A common general would have inquired into the truth of
this story, which of course turned out to be false. Not so Windham. He orders a

---

[10] So printed in the *NYDT*. The date should be 27 November – see Campbell, *Narrative*,
   pp. 248–49 and Ball, *History of the Indian Mutiny*, Vol. II, p. 98 – and is so printed in
   Av. and *CW*, Vol. 15, p. 448.
[11] Campbell, *Narrative*, pp. 248–49 provides some details.
[12] The text of Windham's letter of 30 November 1857 to the commander-in-chief is
   reproduced in Campbell, *Narrative*, pp. 248–49 and Ball, *History of the Indian
   Mutiny*, Vol. II, p. 198.
[13] Apparently an insertion by Engels, not by the editors.
[14] Major General R.A. Dupuis was second in command to Windham. In *NYDT* his name
   is spelt 'Dupries'.
[15] It seems that Engels's source of information was *The Times*, No. 22904, 30 January
   1858; cited in *CW*, Vol. 15, p. 444. *The Times* correspondent, with access to the
   commander-in-chief, seems to have extensively used Windham's letter for his report to
   The Times, though making some omissions from the text.
[16] An insertion by Engels, rather than the editors of *NYDT*. For Windham's letter of 30
   November 1857, see Campbell, *Narrative*, pp. 248–49.

retreat, though his troops could have held the position at least until dark, had not an error been committed in the conveyance of one of Windham's orders! Thus, first you have Windham's heroic conclusion, that where there are many dead Sepoys there must be many live ones; secondly, the false alarm respecting the attack on the fort; and thirdly, the error committed in the conveyance of an order; all of which mishaps combined made it possible for a very numerous rabble of natives to defeat the hero of the Redan, and to beat the indomitable British pluck of his soldiers.

Another reporter, an officer present, says:

> I do not believe any one can accurately describe the fight and retreat of this forenoon. A retreat was ordered. Her Majesty's 34th Foot being directed to fall back behind the brick kiln, neither officers nor men knew where to find it! The news flew rapidly about the cantonments that our force was worsted and on the retreat, and an overwhelming rush was made at the inner intrenchments, as resistless as the mass of water at the Falls of Niagara. Soldiers and Jacks, Europeans and natives, men, women and children, horses, camels and oxen, poured in countless numbers from 2 p.m. By nightfall the intrenched camp, with its motely assemblage of men and beasts, baggage, luggage, and ten thousand non-descript incumbrances, rivaled the chaos that existed before the fiat of creation went forth.[17]

Finally, the *Times*'s Calcutta correspondent states that evidently the British suffered on the 27th 'what almost amounts to a repulse',[18] but that from patriotic motives the Anglo-Indian press covers the disgrace with the impenetrable veil of charity. Thus[19] much, however, is also admitted, that one of Her Majesty's regiments, composed mostly of recruits, one moment got into disorder, without however giving way, and that at the fort the confusion was extreme, Windham having lost all control over his men, until in the evening of the 28th Campbell arrived and 'with a few haughty words' brought everybody to his place again.

Now, what are the evident conclusions from all these confused and prevaricating statements? No other than that, under the incapable direction of Windham, the British troops were completely, though quite unnecessarily, defeated; that when the retreat was ordered, the officers of the 34th Regiment, who had not even taken the trouble to get in any way acquainted with the ground they had fought on, could not find the place they were ordered to retreat to; that the regiment got into disorder and finally fled; that this led to a panic in the camp,

---

[17] For full text of the report by an army officer, see Campbell, *Narrative*, and Ball, *History of the Indian Mutiny*, Vol. II, p. 198.

[18] *The Times*, No. 22902, 28 January 1858. See CW, Vol. 15, p. 450 n.; Campbell, *Narrative*, p. 249. Roberts, in *Letters*, pp. 107–08, admits that 'the rebel troops from Gwalior were occupying the station, having driven our troops back twice and finally driving them in the intrenchment'.

[19] 'This' in Av., which seems more appropriate.

which broke down all the bounds of order and discipline, and occasioned the loss of the camp equipage and part of the baggage; that finally, in spite of Windham's assertion about the stores, 15,000 Minie cartridges,[20] the Paymaster's chest, and the shoes and clothing for many regiments and new levies, fell into the hands of the enemy.

English infantry, when in line or column, seldom run away. In common with the Russians, they have a natural cohesion which generally belongs to old soldiers only, and which is in part explained by the considerable admixture of old soldiers in both services, but it in part also evidently belongs to national character. This quality, which has nothing whatever to do with 'pluck', but is on the contrary rather a peculiar development of the instinct of self-preservation, is still very valuable, especially in defensive positions. It also, in common with the phlegmatic nature of Englishmen, prevents panic; but it is to be remarked that when Irish troops are once disordered and brought to panic, they are not easy to rally. Thus it happened to Windham on Nov. 27. He will figure henceforth among that not very large but distinguished list of English generals who have succeeded in making their troops run away under a panic.

On the 28th the Gwalior contingent were reinforced by a considerable body from Bithoor, and closed up to within four hundred yards of the British intrenched outposts. There was another engagement, conducted on the part of the assailants without any vigor whatever. During it an example of real pluck occurred on the part of the soldiers and officers of the 64th, which we are glad to relate, although the exploit itself was as foolish as the renowned Balaklava charge.[21] The responsibility of it, too, is shifted upon a dead man – Col. Wilson of that regiment. It appears that Wilson advanced with one hundred and eighty men[22] against four guns of the enemy, defended by far superior numbers. We are not told who they were; but the result leads to the conclusion that they were of the Gwalior troops. The British took the guns with a rush, spiked three of them, and held out for some time, when, no reinforcements arriving, they had to retreat, leaving sixty men and most of their officers on the ground. The proof of the hard fighting is in the loss. Here we have a small force, which, from the loss they suffered, must have been pretty well met, holding a battery till one-third of their numbers are down. This is hard fighting indeed, and the first instance of it we have since the storming of Delhi. The man who planned this advance, however, deserves to be tried by court-martial and shot. Windham says it was Wilson. He fell in it, and cannot reply.[23]

In the evening the whole British force was pent up in the fort, where disorder continued to reign, and the position with the bridge was in evident

[20] In Campbell, *Narrative*, p. 249: '11,000 Rounds'.
[21] Lord Ragan, the British commander-in-chief, gave the orders for a cavalry attack on the Russian batteries in the battle of Balaklava on 25 October 1854, a disastrous charge immortalized in Tennyson's verse.
[22] In Campbell, *Narrative*, p. 149: '200 or 250 men'.
[23] See Windham's letter of 30 November 1857, in Campbell, *Narrative*, pp. 248–49.

danger. But then Campbell arrived. He restored order, drew over fresh troops in the morning, and so far repelled the enemy as to secure the bridge and fort. Then he made all his wounded, women, children and baggage cross, and held a defensive position until all these had a fair start on the road to Allahabad. As soon as this was accomplished, he attacked the Sepoys on the 6th, and defeated them, his cavalry and artillery following them up for fourteen miles the same day. That there was little resistance offered is shown from Campbell's report; he merely describes the advance of his own troops, never mentioning any resistance or maneuvers on the part of the enemy; there was no check, and it was not a battle, but a *battue*.[24] Brigadier Hope Grant, with a light division, followed the fugitives, and caught them on the 8th in the act of passing a river; thus brought to bay, they turned round and suffered severe loss. With this event Campbell's first campaign, that of Lucknow and Cawnpore, is brought to a close, and a fresh series of operations must begin, whose first developments we may expect to hear of within a fortnight or three weeks.

---

[24] A hunt in which animals are driven to a particular place where they can be more easily killed by the huntsmen; whence wholesale slaughter.

[British Atrocities in India]

(*New York Daily Tribune*, April 5, 1858. Printed as a leading article.)

If the Sepoy rebellion in India developed all at once on the part of the Hindoo and Mohammedan barbarians a ferocious and fanatical hatred of their Christian and civilized masters, which, from the reputed mildness and ingrained habits of submission to authority on the part of these Oriental mercenaries, nobody had anticipated, it is not the less true that the same event has called out on the side of the Christians and civilized masters a display of the dark side of human nature not less unexpected and lamentable. To judge from the tone of the English press for the last few months, and the declamations of public speakers, even those of the clerical order, the English nation, from having been the patron and advocate of humanity and clemency, where the passions, the interests and alleged wrongs of others were concerned, has all at once, in its own case, been seized with a tiger-like appetite for blood.

It is very satisfactory to find that this access of revengeful fury seems at last to have reached its crisis, and that the voice of humanity, moderation and justice begins once more to be heard. A recent debate on this subject in the British House of Commons, while giving some evidence of this, affords also abundant proof that the English, in the way of suppressing Indian rebellions, have exhibited an unscrupulous ferocity, a savage antipathy hardly outdone by that of the Sepoys themselves. In fact, it turns out that the most grievous charges against the Sepoys – those by which indignation was most inflamed against them, both in India and England – were, after all, not facts, but the mere inventions of English terror and hatred.[1] The murder by the Sepoys of some of the wives and children of their English officers was passionately aggravated in the accounts sent to England by horrible details of mutilation, outrage and torture, which, after having served their own purpose of stimulating hatred and antipathy to the highest point, it is now discovered never took place. In many cases the women and

There is no direct proof that the text of this article is by Marx, though its sentiments and, perhaps, style suggest it. The editors of the *New York Daily Tribune* (NYDT) could have inserted some words or sentences of their own, since it was printed as a leading article. The article does not appear in CW, Vol. 15; *FIWI*; and *On Colonialism*. It is, however, included in Av., pp. 280–84.

[1] Sir Austen Henry (1817–1894), a radical politician and Liberal MP, held that the 'stories of horrible cruelties alleged to have been committed upon English women and children at Delhi, Cawnpore, Jhansi and elsewhere were almost without exception shameful fabrications'. *The Times*, 25 August 1858.

children were spared, and were protected and sent in perfect safety to the posts and garrisons occupied by their friends,[2] while the stories of mutilations and fiendish outrages, which had for their localities now Delhi and now Cawnpore, have, after a strict investigation made on the spot, failed to be supported by any evidence whatever.

The English, on the other hand, whether the officers and soldiers actually engaged in India in the suppression of the rebellion, or the English public at home, have not appeared disposed to make the slightest discrimination between the offense of murdering women and children and that of hostility, proved or suspected, against the English domination. Lord Canning, indeed, as the head of the Indian Government, issued instructions[3] highly honorable to his humanity, in reference to the treatment of mutineers, in which he drew a distinction – and it would seem a very plain one – between the case of the Sepoy who rose in mutiny, murdered or helped to murder the officers and set fire to the cantonments, and that of him who, after this had happened, being left without any European officer to advise or encourage him, yielded to the force of example and joined in the movement. These instructions, however, found very little response in the public sentiment either of the English in India or the English at home; in fact, they provoked a perfect howl of indignation, and it does not appear that down to this time they have had slightest effect upon the conduct of the war – if war that can properly be called, which, so far as the Sepoys are concerned, seems rather to have the character of wholesale slaughter and military execution.[4] 'Let not the people of English land', writes a subaltern officer in a published letter which was read during the course of the debate, 'be in the least alarmed at proclamations of the Governor-General, or any one else. We do not care one straw for them.'

Not only is no quarter given in action, but the whole tenor of the correspondence sent to England, and published there with applause, indicates on the part of the writers a savage passion for blood. A magistrate of Agra is described as hanging men with his own hands, and then shooting at them with his revolver. Another magistrate boasts of having already hanged ninety-five, and hopes the next day to make up the round hundred.[5] Two young officers shoot a Mohammedan apiece for scowling at them, and a Court of Inquiry justifies the act. In every village where the telegraph posts or wires are found injured, the head man is hanged. The prisoners brought into camp by the natives, at from thirty to fifty rupees a head, are hanged, shot or blown away from the guns.[6] Every Sepoy without a discharge is hung as soon as taken, and not only that, but the same

---

[2] For such incidents, see Campbell, *Narrative*, pp. 74–75.

[3] Canning's proclamation of 27 May 1857, reproduced in Ball, *History of the Indian Mutiny,* Vol. I, p. 138; Campbell, *Narrative*, pp. 74–75.

[4] Ball, *History of the Indian Mutiny*, Vol. I, p. 521: 'Every Sepoy we watch, "Shoot him" is the word.' Also see ibid., p. 525.

[5] Vibrat, *Sepoy Mutiny as seen by a Subaltern*, p. 162. Also see Roberts, *Letters*, p. 12.

[6] For such atrocities, see Kaye, *History of the Sepoy War*, Vol. II, pp. 261–71; Vol. III, pp. 88, 636. Also, Mrs Muter, *My Recollections* (London, 1911), pp. 132–33.

measure of vengeance is dealt out to every man concealing a Sepoy, or guilty of having given them food or communicated with them. It would seem, indeed, as if the halter rather than the sword had become the favorite instrument of the English officers. 'A lot more rebels' – this is an extract from an officer's letter – 'were strung up this morning. They are being thinned fast. I wish the authorities would set some more of the higher class swinging; it would do a vast deal of good.' A late dispatch of Sir Colin Campbell directs that the march of the troops must be deliberate, in order to afford time to the magistrates to visit the rebellious villages, and 'to display to the people, in an unmistakable manner, the resolution to visit punishment on all those who have, during the last few months' – done what? Committed murders, put women and children to death? Not at all – 'who have, during the last few months, *set aside their allegiance.*' Wherever a detachment of English troops appears, a bloody assize, it seems, is held, one village being laid waste after another, and the head men hung in cold blood on the sole ground, that they had 'set aside their allegiance' – in other words, have 'done something to favor, or are suspected of having done something to favor the reestablishment of the rule which the English had overthrown.'

That the halter disposes of all who escape death on the field, appears from the significant fact, referred to by one of the parties to the debate, that after a war with a numerous enemy, carried on during ten months, and in which not less than fifty different combats have occurred, the British, so far as official and non-official information goes, are not in possession of a single prisoner, taken either in conflict or after pursuit. The very last telegraphic news from India contains accounts of four actions, in which, with an English loss of only three men, 1,250 of Sepoys perished.

The programme of the Calcutta papers for the pacification of Oude is not less ferocious and bloody. Two years ago, an English force swooped suddenly down on this kingdom, deprived the King of his throne, and set up an English Commissioner in his place. The people of Oude did not relish this change of rulers, and they took advantage of the recent mutiny to attempt to throw off the English yoke. As this province has now become the seat and center of the rebellion, it is proposed to carry a war of extermination into it. The Calcutta papers recommend, in substance, that it should be made one great slaughter-house; that the Sepoys who survive the effects of shot and shell, be set upon in cold blood with the bayonet; and should any escape by taking refuge in the pestilential swamps of the country, it is hoped that the wild beasts may complete the work which their English rivals have left unfinished. A recent act of the Legislative Council at Calcutta, giving authority to brand mutineers, has given great dissatisfaction, as seeming to indicate an intention to substitute transportation in place of this wholesale slaughter.

In the debate in the House of Commons, to which we have referred, there were not wanting members to justify all these ferocities, whether already carried into act or only proposed as a rule for the future. Mr W. Vansittart hoped that the House would not be carried away by feelings of morbid sensibility for

the mutinous Sepoys, in which he was certain that the country did not participate. He had always understood that the crime of mutiny must be expiated by
death, and at the present moment he thought that penalty was required not only
by justice, but by political necessity. *All India knew that Sepoys had outraged
English women. All India knew that every man that mutinied, expressed by his
mutiny his sympathy with that outrage.* All India was looking with intense anxiety to see whether the English would or would not revenge the inexpiable insult. If
they did not, if any thought of the number of criminals, if any feeling of compas-
sion interfered with the executioner, there was an end of English character in
Indian eyes.

Several other members seemed to sympathize to a greater or less extent
with these fierce sentiments; but the feeling of the House was evidently with those
who thought that to persist in refusing all quarter and hanging all prisoners was
not only cruel but impolitic, and that the moment for clemency had arrived; that
sufficient blood had been shed, and that justice ought now to be tempered by
mercy. The President of the Board of Control freely admitted that the people of
Oude, assembled under the banners of their native prince, and fighting for the
independence of their country, ought not for a moment to be placed in the same
category with mutinous Sepoys who had murdered their officers and committed
other atrocities, and he intimated that instructions on this point had already been
sent out to India. Mr Mangles, on behalf of the Directors of the East India Company, was unwilling to admit that the annexation of Oude had anything to do
with the revolt. He took it upon himself to assert that no Asiatic since the world
began had been animated by what we call national feeling, and he thought it
quite absurd, therefore, to compare the case of the people of Oude to that of
Hungarians or Italians fighting for their nationality. At the same time he warmly
applauded the mixture of firmness and moderation on the part of Lord Canning,
which had exposed him to so much obloquy among his countrymen in India, but
which was now beginning to receive the approval it was entitled to, and which
he was happy to find so unequivocally supported by the House.

It is to be hoped that the feeling indicated by this debate will give a
check, as well in England as in India, to the blood-thirsty spirit, hateful enough
in a single tyrant, but which, when adopted by a whole nation, becomes horrible
indeed.

[Scheme for the Administration of India]

(*New York Daily Tribune*, April 26, 1858. Printed as a leading article.)

There seems to be a pretty general agreement on the part of the English public that the machinery of Indian government in England works badly, and needs to be changed; but what to substitute in place of the present system appears to be a great puzzle. The administration of Indian affairs, so far as residents in England have anything to do with it, is shared, under the existing system, between the Directors of the East India Company, chosen by the proprietors of India stock, and the Board of Control, presided over by a Cabinet Minister – two bodies which are apt to look at Indian affairs from different points of view, and whose cooperation is not always harmonious.

Lord Palmerston, in the bill which he introduced, proposed to substitute, in place of this double-headed administration, a council of eight persons, appointed by the Crown, with a ninth, a Cabinet Minister, as President. It was objected that this would operate to deprive the middle classes of England of that control over Indian affairs which they had hitherto enjoyed, or, more properly speaking, of that large share they had, through the patronage exercised by the East India Directors, in furnishing the officers, civil and military, by whom the local administration of India is conducted. It was also objected that this scheme would make the Government of India too immediately dependent upon fluctuations of English politics, with which it had no natural connection, and would leave it without those elements of stability essential to its successful working; while the additional power and patronage thus given to the Minister might even prove dangerous to English liberty. To meet these objections, the bill of the Derby Ministry proposes to increase the governing council to eighteen members, to be presided over by a Cabinet Minister, one-half of the eighteen to be appointed by the Crown, the other half to be elective. The appointments by the Crown are, however, by this bill, not to be arbitrary, but are to be made from certain specified classes of persons, with a view to the selection for that purpose of representative men. Each of the four Indian Presidencies is to furnish a member from among those persons who have been employed ten years in their respective civil services. The Indian diplomatic service is to furnish a fifth member from among those persons who, having been employed for ten years in the Indian service, have been resident for five years in a diplomatic character at the court of some

---

This article, though not in the name of Marx, seems to be from his pen. It is not attributed to Marx in *CW* or any other collection except Avineri, pp. 285–88.

native prince. The other four members, appointed by the Crown, are to be representatives respectively of the four military services – the British army in India and the armies of Bengal, Bombay and Madras; five years' Indian service in the Queen's army, and ten years' service in each of the others being a necessary qualification.

The elective members are also required to be persons who have a special qualification, either from residence in India, from having been engaged in trade with that country, or in the manufacture of goods for export thither. Four of these members are to be chosen by a constituency estimated at five thousand individuals, made up of all persons residing in England who have served ten years in India in the army, navy or civil service; of the registered proprietors of stock in Indian railways to the amount of £2,000, and of holders of India stock to the amount of £ 1,000. The qualifications of these four members is to be ten years' service in India in the army or navy, or in legal or civil employments, or fifteen years' residence employed in agriculture, manufactures or commerce. The other five elective members must either have resided in India ten years, or must have been engaged for five years in trade with India, or in the manufacture of goods for export thither. These five, it is proposed, shall be elected by the parliamentary constituencies of London, Manchester, Liverpool, Glasgow and Belfast. All the members are eventually to hold office for six years, one-third to be replaced every two years.

This complicated scheme, though elaborately contrived to meet the objections urged against Lord Palmerston's plan, does not, however, appear to meet with a very favorable reception. Upon its introduction, Mr Roebuck[1] denounced it as a sham, the electoral principle being introduced to give color to the despotic principle. Mr Bright described the provisions in relation to the elective part of the members as clap-trap, while he insisted that so far as the important point of responsibility was concerned, Lord Palmerston's proposed council of eight was to be preferred. By the press, the elective part of the scheme has been very vigorously attacked, as open in an aggravated degree to all the objections now urged to the share in the government of India enjoyed by the proprietors of Indian stock, and as involving also, in the matter of canvassing the electors, sacrifices and labors which nobody will submit to. According to *The Times*, even under the existing system, the canvass for an East India Directorship is no trifling matter. The candidate, we are told, is obliged to devote five years to the operation. A constituency must be personally visited, scattered all over the British Isles, and even over parts of the Continent. The candidate has to coax frumpish old maids, to wheedle eccentric old bachelors, and to encounter the solicitations of fathers and mothers, happy if he can persuade them to be content with a single cadetship in exchange for their vote and interest. But the new constituency, so far as four of

---

[1] John Arthur Roebuck (1801–1879): MP from Bath, 1832–37 and 1841–47, and from Sheffield, 1849–68; Chairman of the Administrative Reform Association, 1856.

the elective members are concerned, would make matters worse. In addition to a five years' canvass of the proprietors of India stock, the candidate for election would be obliged to bestow at least five years more in addressing himself to the India railway shareholders, and in seeking out wherever they could be found, whether resident in England or elsewhere, all the sailors and soldiers who had spent ten years in India. The vesting the choice of the other five elective members in the parliamentary constituency of the five cities named is objected to, not only as a selection without any reason for it, but as likely to lead to the employment of Indian patronage as a means of bribing the electors in relation to their votes for members of parliament. These attacks have evidently produced their effect, and it seems doubtful if the bill can be carried without great modification.

FREDERICK ENGELS

The Fall of Lucknow

(*New York Daily Tribune*, April 30, 1858. Printed as a leading article.)

The second critical period of the Indian insurrection has been brought to a close. The first found its center in Delhi, and was ended by the storming of that city; the second centered in Lucknow, and that place, too, has now fallen. Unless fresh insurrections break out in places hitherto quiet, the revolt must now gradually subside into its concluding, chronic period, during which the insurgents will finally take the character of dacoits or robbers, and find the inhabitants of the country as much their enemies as the British themselves.

The details of the storming of Lucknow are not yet received, but the preliminary operations and the outlines of the final engagements are known. Our readers recollect[1] that after the relief of the Residency of Lucknow, Gen. Campbell blew up that post, but left Gen. Outram with about 5,000 men in the Alumbagh, an intrenched position a few miles from the city. He himself, with the remainder of his troops, marched back to Cawnpore, where Gen. Windham had been defeated by a body of rebels; these he completely beat, and drove them across the Jumna at Calpee. He then awaited at Cawnpore the arrival of reinforcements and the heavy guns, arranged his plans of attack, gave orders for the concentration of the various columns destined to advance into Oude, and especially turned Cawnpore into an intrenched camp of strength and proportions requisite for the immediate and principal base of operations against Lucknow. When all this was completed, he had another task to perform before he thought it safe to move – a task the attempting of which at once distinguishes him from almost all preceding Indian commanders. He would have no women loitering about the camp. He had had quite enough of the 'heroines' at Lucknow, and on the march to Cawnpore; they had considered it quite natural that the movements of the army, as had always been the case in India, should be subordinate to their fancies and their comfort. No sooner had Campbell reached Cawnpore than he sent the whole interesting and troublesome community to Allahabad, out of his way; and immediately

Written by Engels at Marx's request. See Engels's letters to Jenny Marx, dated 14 April 1858, and to Marx, dated 22 April 1858, in *CW*, Vol. 40, pp. 307–38. The editors of *CW*, Vol. 15, have published it under the title given above because this accords with the entry in Marx's notebook for 1858. There is no heading in the *New York Daily Tribune* (*NYDT*).

[1] See Engels's article, 'The Relief of Lucknow', *NYDT*, 1 February 1858, in this volume.

sent for the second batch of ladies, then at Agra. Not before they had reached
Cawnpore, and not before he had seen them safely off to Allahabad did he follow
his advancing troops toward Lucknow.

The arrangements made for this campaign of Oude were on a scale
hitherto unprecedented in India. In the greatest expedition ever undertaken by the
British there,[2] the invasion of Afghanistan,[3] the troops employed never exceeded
20,000 at a time, and of these the great majority were natives. In this campaign
of Oude, the number of Europeans alone exceeded that of all the troops sent into
Afghanistan. The main army, led by Sir Colin Campbell personally, consisted of
three divisions of infantry, one of cavalry, and one of artillery and engineers.[4]
The first division of infantry under Outram, held the Alumbagh. It consisted of
five European and one native regiment. The second (four European and one
native regiment), and third (five European and one native regiment),[5] the cavalry division under Sir Hope Grant[6] (three European and four or five native
regiments) and the mass of the artillery (forty-eight field guns, siege-trains and
engineers), formed Campbell's active force, with which he advanced on the road
from Cawnpore. A brigade concentrated under Brigadier Franks at Jaunpore and
Azimghur,[7] between the Goomtee and the Ganges, was to advance along the
course of the former river to Lucknow. This brigade numbered three European
regiments and two batteries, besides native troops, and was to form Campbell's
right wing. Including it, Campbell's force in all amounted to –

	Infantry	Cavalry	Artillery and Engineers	Total
Europeans	15,000	2,000	3,000	20,000
Natives	5,000	3,000	2,000	10,000

or, in all 30,000 men; to whom must be added the 10,000 Nepaulese Ghoorkas
advancing under Jung Bahadoor from Goruckpore on Sultanpore, making the
total of the invading army 40,000 men, almost all regular troops. But this is not
all. On the south of Cawnpore, Sir H. Rose[8] was advancing with a strong column from Saugor upon Calpee and the Lower Jumna, there to intercept any

---

[2] 'here' in Av.
[3] That is, the first Anglo-Afghan War of 1839–42.
[4] The editors of CW, Vol. 15, p. 505 n., say that Engels used the material from The
    Times, Nos 22954, 22959, 22963, 30 March and 5 and 9 April 1858, for the informa-
    tion given here.
[5] Av. omits: 'third (five European and one native regiment)'.
[6] Sir James Hope Grant (1808–1875): played an important role during the rebellion of
    1857–58, with movable columns; and commanded Trans-Ghaghra force.
[7] Azamgarh, in eastern Uttar Pradesh.
[8] Hugh Henry Rose (1801–1885): ensign 1820, major general in 1854; took Rathgarh
    and Gorhakota, relieved Sagar and captured the important pass of Maltun during
    1857–58; defeated Tantia Tope, and took Kuch and Kalpi.

fugitives that might escape between the two columns of Franks[9] and Campbell. On the north-west, Brigadier Chamberlain crossed toward the end of February the upper Ganges, entering the Rohilcund, situated north-north-west of Oude, and, as was correctly anticipated, the chief point of retreat of the insurgent army. The garrisons of the towns surrounding Oude must also be included in the force directly or indirectly employed against that kingdom, so that the whole of this force is certainly from 70,000 to 80,000 combatants, of which, according to the official statements, at least 28,000 are British. In this is not included the mass of Sir John Lawrence's force, which occupies at Delhi a sort of flank position, and which consists of 5,500 Europeans at Meerut and Delhi, and some 20,000 or 30,000 natives of the Punjaub.

The concentration of this immense force is the result partly of Gen. Campbell's combinations, but partly also of the suppression of the revolt in various parts of Hindostan, in consequence of which the troops naturally concentrated toward the scene of action. No doubt Campbell would have ventured to act with a smaller force; but while he was waiting for this, fresh resources were thrown, by circumstances, on his hands; and he was not the man to refuse to avail himself of them, even against so contemptible an enemy as he knew he would meet at Lucknow. And it must not be forgotten that, imposing as these numbers look, they still were spread over a space as large as France; and that at the decisive point at Lucknow he could only appear with about 20,000 Europeans, 10,000 Hindoos,[10] and 10,000 Ghoorkas the value of the last, under native command, being at least doubtful. This force, in its European components alone, was certainly more than enough to insure a speedy victory, but still its strength was not out of proportion to its task; and very likely Campbell desired to show the Oudians, for once, a more formidable army of white faces than any people in India had ever seen before, as a sequel to an insurrection which had been based on the small number and wide dispersion of the Europeans over the country.

The force in Oude consisted of the remnants of most of the mutinous Bengal regiments and of native levies from the country itself. Of the former, there cannot have been more than 35,000 or 40,000 at the very outside. The sword, desertion and demoralization must have reduced this force, originally 80,000 strong, at least one-half; and what was left was disorganized, disheartened, badly appointed, and totally unfit to take the field. The new levies are variously stated at from 100,000 to 150,000 men; but what their numbers may have been is unimportant. Their arms were but in part firearms, of inferior construction; most of them carried arms for close encounter only – the kind of fighting they were least likely to meet with. The greater part of this force was at Lucknow, engaging

---

[9] Sir Thomas Harte Franks (1808–1862): brigadier in command of the 4th infantry division; defeated Mohammad Husain Nazim, but failed before Dohrighat in 1858.

[10] 'Hindoos', we may recall, stands for 'Indians', which word could not be used in the United States, 'Indians' being there taken to stand for indigenous Americans.

Sir J. Outram's troops; but two columns were acting in the direction of Allahabad and Jaunpore.

The concentric movement upon Lucknow began about the middle of February. From the 15th to the 26th the main army and its immense train (60,000 camp followers alone) marched from Cawnpore upon the capital of Oude, meeting with no resistance. The enemy, in the meantime, attacked Outram's position, without a chance of success, on February 21 and 24. On the 19th Franks advanced upon Sultanpore, defeated both columns of the insurgents in one day, and pursued them as well as the want of cavalry permitted. The two defeated columns having united, he beat them again on the 23rd, with the loss of 20 guns and all their camp and baggage. Gen. Hope Grant, commanding the advanced guard of the main army, had also, during its forced march, detached himself from it, and making a point to the left had, on the 23rd and 24th, destroyed two forts on the road from Lucknow to Rohilcund.

On March 2 the main army was concentrated before the southern side of Lucknow. This side is protected by the canal, which had to be passed by Campbell in his previous attack on the city; behind this canal strong intrenchments had been thrown up. On the 3rd, the British occupied the Dilkhoosha Park, with the storming of which the first attack had also commenced. On the 4th, Brig. Franks joined the main army, and now formed its right flank, his right supported by the River Goomtee. Meantime, batteries against the enemy's intrenchments were erected, and two floating bridges were constructed below the town, across the Goomtee; and as soon as these were ready, Sir J. Outram, with his division of infantry, 1,400 horse and 30 guns, moved across to take position on the left, or north-eastern bank. From here he could enfilade a great part of the enemy's line along the canal, and many of the intrenched palaces to its rear; he also cut off the enemy's communications with the whole north-eastern part of Oude. He met with considerable resistance on the 6th and 7th, but drove the enemy before him. On the 8th, he was again attacked, but with no better success. In the meantime, the batteries on the right bank had opened their fire; Outram's batteries, along the river-bank, took the position of the insurgents in flank and rear; and on the 9th the 2nd Division, under Sir E. Lugard[11] stormed the Martiniere, which, as our readers may recollect,[12] is a college and park situated on the north side of the canal, at its junction with the Goomtee, and opposite the Dilkhoosha. On the 10th, the Bank-House was breached and stormed, Outram advancing further up the river, and enfilading with his guns every successive position of the insurgents. On the 11th, two Highland regiments (42nd and 93rd) stormed the Queen's Palace, and Outram attacked and carried the stone bridges leading from the left bank of the river into the town. He then passed his troops across and joined in the

---

[11] Sir Edward Lugard (1810–1898): English general, chief of staff during the Anglo-Persian War of 1856–57; took part in suppressing the rebellion of 1857–58. See *CW*, Vol. 15, p. 718.

[12] See article in *NYDT*, 'The Relief of Lucknow', 1 February 1858, in this volume.

attack against the next building in front. On March 13, another fortified building, the Imambarrah, was attacked, a sap being resorted to in order to construct the batteries under shelter; and on the following day, the breach being completed, this building was stormed. The enemy, flying to the Kaiserbagh, or King's Palace, was so hotly pursued that the British entered the place at the heels of the fugitives. A violent struggle ensued, but by 3 o'clock in the afternoon the palace was in the possession of the British. This seems to have brought matters to a crisis; at least, all spirit of resistance seems to have ceased, and Campbell at once took measures for the pursuit and interception of the fugitives. Brigadier Campbell, with one brigade of cavalry and some horse artillery, was sent to pursue them, while Grant took the other brigade round to Seetapore, on the road from Lucknow to Rohilcund, in order to intercept them. While thus the portion of the garrison which took to flight was provided for, the infantry and artillery advanced further into the city, to clear it from those who still held out. From the 15th to the 19th, the fighting must have been mainly in the narrow streets of the town, the line of palaces and parks along the river having been previously carried; but on the 19th, the whole of the town was in Campbell's possession. About 50,000 insurgents are said to have fled, partly to Rohilcund, partly toward the Doab and Bundelcund. In this latter direction they had a chance of escaping, as Gen. Rose, with his column, was still sixty miles at least from the Jumna, and was said to have 30,000 insurgents in front of him. In the direction of Rohilcund there was also a chance of their being able to concentrate again; Campbell would not be in a position to follow them very fast, while of the whereabouts of Chamberlain we know nothing, and the province is large enough to afford them shelter for a short time. The next feature of the insurrection, therefore, will most likely be the formation of two insurgent armies in Bundelcund and Rohilcund, the latter of which, however, may soon be destroyed by concentric marches of the Lucknow and Delhi armies.

The operations of Sir C. Campbell in this campaign, as far as we can now judge, were characterized by his usual prudence and vigour. The dispositions for his concentric march on Lucknow were excellent, and the arrangements for an attack appear to have taken advantage of every circumstance. The conduct of the insurgents, on the other hand, was as contemptible, if not more so, than before. The sight of the redcoats struck them everywhere with panic. Frank's column defeated twenty times its numbers, with scarcely a man lost; and though the telegrams talk of 'stout resistance' and 'hard fighting',[13] as usual, the losses of the British appear, where they are mentioned, so ridiculously small that we fear there was no more heroism needed and no more laurels to be gathered this time at Lucknow than when the British got there before.

---

[13] 'The Siege of Lucknow', *The Times*, No. 22966, 13 April 1858. See *CW*, Vol. 15, p. 509 n.(a).

FREDERICK ENGELS

[How Lucknow Was Taken]

(*New York Daily Tribune*, May 25, 1858. Printed as a leading article.)

At last we are in possession of detailed accounts of the attack and fall of Lucknow. The principal sources of information, in a military point of view, the dispatches of Sir Colin Campbell, have not yet, indeed, been published; but the correspondence of the British press, and especially the letters of Mr Russell in the London *Times*,[1] the chief portions of which have been laid before our readers, are quite sufficient to give a general insight into the proceedings of the attacking party.

The conclusions we drew from the telegraphic news, as to the ignorance and cowardice, displayed in the defence, are more than confirmed by the detailed accounts. The works erected by the Hindoos,[2] formidable in appearance, were in reality of no greater consequence than the fiery dragons and grimacing faces painted by Chinese 'braves' on their shields or on the walls of their cities. Every single work exhibited an apparently impregnable front, nothing but loopholed and embrasured walls and parapets, difficulties of access of every possible description, cannon and small arms bristling every-where. But the flanks and rear of every position were completely neglected, a mutual support of the various works was never thought of, and even the ground between the works, as well as in front of them, had never been cleared, so that both front and flank attacks could be prepared without the knowledge of the defence, and could approach under perfect shelter to within a few yards from the parapet. It was just such a conglomeration of intrenchments as might be expected from a body of private sappers deprived of their officers, and serving in an army where ignorance and indiscipline reigned supreme. The intrenchments of Lucknow are but a translation of the whole method of Sepoy warfare into baked clay walls and earthen parapets. The mechanical portion of European tactics had been partially impressed upon their minds; they knew the manual and platoon drill well enough;

The editors of *CW*, Vol. 15, pp. 527–32, and *FIWI*, pp. 143–49, have printed this article under the title 'Details of the Attack on Lucknow'. We have followed the heading given by Avineri.

[1] A reference to 'The Fall of Lucknow', *The Times*, No. 22986, 6 May 1858. Reference from *CW*, Vol. 15, p. 527 n.
[2] It is likely that Engels's original text had 'Indians' here, which the *New York Daily Tribune* (NYDT) editors converted into 'Hindoos' to avoid confusion with American Indians, generally referred to in the US as Indians.

they could also build a battery and loophole a wall; but how to combine the movements of companies and battalions in the defence of a position, or how to combine batteries and loopholed houses and walls, so as to form an intrenched camp capable of resistance – of this they were utterly ignorant. Thus, they weakened the solid masonry walls of their palaces by over-loopholing them, heaped tier upon tier of loopholes and embrasures, placed parapeted batteries on their roofs, and all this to no purpose whatever, because it could all be turned in the easiest possible manner. In the same way, knowing their tactical inferiority, they tried to make up for it by cramming every post as full of men as possible, to no other purpose than to give terrible effect to the British artillery and to render impossible all orderly and systematic defence as soon as the attacking columns fell upon this motley host from an unexpected direction. And when the British, by some accidental circumstance, were compelled to attack even the formidable front of the works, their construction was so faulty that they could be approached, breached and stormed almost without any risk. At the Imambarra[3] this was the case. Within a few yards from the building stood a pucka (sun-baked clay)[4] wall. Up to this the British made a short sap (proof enough that the embrasures and loopholes on the higher part of the building had no plunging fire upon the ground immediately in front); and used this very wall as a breaching battery, prepared for them by the Hindoos themselves! They brought up two 68-pounders (naval guns) behind this wall. The lightest 68-pounder in the British service weighs 87 cwt., without the carriage; but supposing even that an 8-inch gun for hollow shot only is alluded to, the lightest gun of that class weighs 50 cwt., and with the carriage at least three tuns. That such guns could be[5] *brought* up at all in such proximity to a palace several stories high, with a battery on the roof, shows a contempt of commanding positions and an ignorance of military engineering which no private sapper in any civilized army could be capable of.

Thus much for the science against which the British had to contend. As to courage and obstinacy, they were equally absent from the defense.[6] From the Martiniere to the Mousabagh,[7] on the part of the natives, there was but one grand and unanimous act of bolting, as soon as a column advanced to the attack. There is nothing in the whole series of engagements that can compare even with the massacre (for fight it can scarcely be called) in the Secundrabagh[8] during Campbell's relief of the Residency. No sooner do the attacking parties advance, than there is a general helter-skelter to the rear, and where there are but a few

---

[3] The Asafi Imambara constructed by Asaf-ud Daulah, the nawab of Awadh (d. 1798).

[4] 'Pucka' means construction of kiln-baked bricks, not sun-baked.

[5] The line 'and with the carriage . . . could be' does not appear in Av.

[6] So printed in *NYDT*.

[7] Musabagh, a large palace with gardens and enclosures in the midst of open country filled with trees (Russell, *My Diary in India in the Year 1858–59*, London, 1859, p. 207). It was constructed by Asaf-ud Daulah. See Abdul Halim Sharar, *Guzishta Lakhnau* (Lucknow, 1965), p. 36.

[8] Sikandarbagh.

narrow exits so as to bring the crowded rabble to a stop, they fall pell-mell, and without any resistance, under the volleys and bayonets of the advancing British. The 'British bayonet' has done more execution in any one of these onslaughts on panic-stricken natives than in all the wars of the English in Europe and America put together. In the East, such bayonet-battles, where one party only is active and the other abjectly passive, are a regular occurrence in warfare; the Burmese stockades in every case furnished an example. According to Mr Russell's account, the chief loss suffered by the British was caused by Hindoos cut off from retreat, and barricaded in the rooms of the palaces, whence they fired from the windows upon the officers in the courtyards and gardens.

In storming the Imambarra and the Kaiserbagh, the bolting of the Hindoos was so rapid, that the place was not taken, but simply marched into. The interesting scene, however, was now only commencing; for, as Mr Russell blandly observes, the conquest of the Kaiserbagh on that day was so unexpected that there was no time to guard against indiscriminate plunder. A merry scene it must have been for a true, liberty-loving John Bull to see his British grenadiers helping themselves freely to the jewels, costly arms, clothes, and all the toggery[9] of his Majesty of Oude. The Sikhs, Ghoorkas and camp followers were quite ready to imitate the example, and a scene of plunder and destruction followed which evidently surpassed even the descriptive talent of Mr Russell. Every fresh step in advance was accompanied with plunder and devastation. The Kaiserbagh had fallen on the 14th[10] and half an hour after, discipline was at an end, and the officers had lost all command over their men. On the 17th, Gen. Campbell was obliged to establish patrols to check plundering, and to remain in inactivity 'until the present license ceases'. The troops were evidently completely out of hand. On the 18th, we hear that there is a cessation of the *grosser* sort of plunder, but devastation is still going on freely.[11] In the city, however, while the vanguard were fighting against the natives' fire from the houses, the rear-guard plundered and destroyed to their hearts' content. In the evening, there is another proclamation against plundering; strong parties of every regiment to go out and fetch in their own men, and to keep their camp followers at home; nobody to leave the camp except on duty. On the 20th, a recapitulation of the same orders. On the same day, two British 'officers and gentlemen', Lieuts Cape and Thackwell, 'went into the city *looting*, and were murdered in a house'; and on the 26th, matters were still so bad that the most stringent orders were issued for the suppression of plunder and outrage; hourly roll-calls were instituted; all soldiers strictly forbidden to enter the city; camp followers, if found armed in the city, to be hanged; soldiers not to wear arms except on duty, and all non-combatants to be disarmed. To give due weight to these orders, a number of triangles for flogging were erected 'at proper places'.

[9] Clothes, garments (*OED*).
[10] Russell, *My Diary*, pp. 189–91.
[11] See ibid., p. 206, for details.

This is indeed a pretty state of things in a civilized army in the nineteenth century; and if any other troops in the world had committed one-tenth of these excesses, how would the indignant British press brand them with infamy! But these are the deeds of the British army, and therefore we are told that such things are but the normal consequence of war. British officers and gentlemen are perfectly welcomed to appropriate to themselves any silver spoons, jewelled bracelets, and other little memorials they may find about the scene of their glory; and if Campbell is compelled to disarm his own army in the midst of war, in order to stop wholesale robbery and violence, there may have been military reasons for the step; but surely nobody will begrudge these poor fellows a week's holiday and a little frolic after so many fatigues and privations.

The fact is, there is no army in Europe or America with so much brutality as the British. Plundering, violence, massacre – things that everywhere else are strictly and completely banished – are a time-honored privilege, a vested right of the British soldier. The infamies committed for days together, after the storming of Badajoz and San Sebastian, in the Peninsular war, are without a parallel in the annals of any other nation since the beginning of the French Revolution; and the medieval usage, proscribed everywhere else, of giving up to plunder a town taken by assault, is still the rule with the British. At Delhi imperious military considerations enforced an exception; but the army, though bought off by extra pay, grumbled, and now at Lucknow they have made up for what they missed at Delhi. For twelve days and nights there was no British army at Lucknow – nothing but a lawless, drunken, brutal rabble, dissolved into bands of robbers, far more lawless, violent and greedy than the Sepoys who had just been driven out of the place. The sack of Lucknow in 1858 will remain an everlasting disgrace to the British military service.

If the reckless soldiery, in their civilizing and humanizing progress through India, could rob the natives of their personal property only, the British Government steps in immediately afterward and strips them of their real estate as well. Talk of the First French Revolution confiscating the lands of the nobles and the church! Talk of Louis Napoleon confiscating the property of the Orleans family! Here comes Lord Canning, a British nobleman, mild in language, manners and feelings, and confiscates, by order of his superior, Viscount Palmerston, the lands of a whole people, every rood, perch and acre, over an extent of ten thousand square miles.[12] A very nice bit of *loot* indeed for John Bull! And no sooner has Lord Ellenborough, in the name of the new Government, disapproved of this hitherto unexampled measure, then up rise *The Times* and a host of minor British

---

[12] This refers to Canning's Proclamation of 3 March 1858 ordering confiscation of properties of the rebel *ta'luqadars* and promising rewards to the loyal ones. Later on, to win the *ta'luqadars* to the side of the government, they were promised inviolability of their possessions. Marx criticized the Proclamation in his articles 'The Annexation of Oudh' and 'Lord Canning's Proclamation and Land Tenure in India'. The Proclamation is reproduced in Ball, *History of the Indian Mutiny*, Vol. II, pp. 276–77; and Campbell, *Narrative*, p. 413.

papers to defend this wholesale robbery, and break a lance for the right of John Bull to confiscate everything he likes. But then, John is an exceptional being, and what is virtue in him, according to *The Times*, would be infamy in others.

Meanwhile – thanks to the complete dissolution of the British army for the purpose of plunder – the insurgents escaped, unpursued, into the open country. They concentrate in Rohilcund, while a portion carry on petty warfare in Oude, and other fugitives have taken the direction of Bundlecund. At the same time, the hot weather and the rains are fast approaching; and it is not to be expected that the season will be so uncommonly favorable to European constitutions as last year. Then, the mass of the European troops were more or less acclimated; this year, most of them are newly arrived. There is no doubt that a campaign in June, July and August will cost the British an immense number of lives, and what with the garrisons that have to be left in every conquered city, the active army will melt down very rapidly. Already are we informed that reinforcements of 1,000 men per month will scarcely keep up the army at its effective strength; and as to garrisons, Lucknow alone requires at least 8,000 men, over one-third of Campbell's army. The force organizing for the campaign of Rohilcund will scarcely be stronger than this garrison of Lucknow. We are also informed that among the British officers the opinion is gaining ground that the guerrilla warfare which is sure to succeed the dispersion of the larger bodies of insurgents, will be far more harassing and destructive of life to the British than the present war with its battles and sieges. And, lastly, the Sikhs are beginning to talk in a way which bodes no good to the English. They feel that without their assistance the British would scarcely have been able to hold India, and that, had they joined the insurrection, Hindoostan would certainly have been lost to England, at least, for a time. They say this loudly, and exaggerate it in their Eastern way. To them the English no longer appear as that superior race which beat them at Moodka, Ferozepore and Aliwal. From such a conviction to open hostility there is but a step with Eastern nations; a spark may kindle the blaze.

Altogether, the taking of Lucknow has no more put down the Indian insurrection than the taking of Delhi. This summer's campaign may produce such events that the British will have, next winter, to go substantially over the same ground again, and perhaps even to reconquer the Punjaub. But in the best of cases, a long and harassing guerrilla warfare is before them – not an enviable thing for Europeans under an Indian sun.

The Annexation of Oude

(*New York Daily Tribune*, May 28, 1858. Printed as a leading article.)

About eighteen months ago, at Canton, the British Government propounded the novel doctrine in the law of nations that a State may commit hostilities on a large scale against a province of another State without either declaring war or establishing a state of war against that other State.[1] Now the same British Government, in the person of the Governor-General of India, Lord Canning, has made another forward move in its task of upsetting the existing law of nations. It has proclaimed that 'the proprietary right in the soil of the Province of Oude is confiscated to the British Government, which will dispose of that right in such manner as it may see fitting.'[2]

When, after the fall of Warsaw in 1831, the Russian Emperor confiscated the 'proprietary right in the soil' hitherto held by numerous Polish nobles,[3] there was one unanimous outburst of indignation in the British press and Parliament. When, after the battle of Novara,[4] the Austrian Government did not confiscate, but merely sequestered, the estates of such Lombard noblemen as had taken an active part in the war of independence, that unanimous outburst of British indignation was repeated. And when after the 2d December, 1851, Louis Napoleon confiscated the estates of the Orleans family, which, by the common law of France, ought to have been united to the public domain on the accession of Louis Philippe, but which had escaped that fate by a legal quibble, then British indignation knew no bounds, and the London *Times* declared that by this act the very foundations of social order were upset, and that civil society could no longer exist. All this honest indignation has now been practically illustrated. England, by one stroke of the pen, has confiscated not only the estates of a few noblemen, or of a royal family, but the whole length and breadth of a kingdom nearly as large as Ireland, 'the inheritance of a whole people', as Lord Ellenborough himself terms it.[5]

This title is given in accordance with the entry made in Marx's notebook on 14 May 1858: *India* (Politics) *Annexation of Oude*. See *CW*, Vol. 15, p. 692; *FIWI*, n. 87.

[1] Here Marx alludes to the incidents leading to the Second Opium War. See Dona Torr, *Marx on China* (Bombay, 1952), pp. 19–25 and notes.
[2] Lord Canning's Proclamation, reproduced in Campbell, *Narrative*, p. 413.
[3] After the Polish rebellion against Czarist Russian occupation, 1830–31.
[4] The battle of Novara was fought between the Piedmontese and Austrian troops in March 1849.
[5] Lord Ellenborough's speech in the House of Lords on 7 May 1858, *The Times*, No. 22988, 8 May 1858. Reference in *CW*, Vol. 15, 534 n.

But let us hear what pretexts – grounds we cannot call them – Lord Canning, in the name of the British Government, sets forth for this unheard-of proceeding: First, 'The army is in possession of Lucknow.' Second, 'The resistance, begun by a mutinous soldiery, has found support from the inhabitants of the city and of the province at large.'[6] Third, 'They have been guilty of a great crime, and have subjected themselves to a just retribution.' In plain English: Because the British army have got hold of Lucknow, the Government has the right to confiscate all the land in Oude which they have not yet got hold of. Because the native soldiers in British pay have mutinied, the natives of Oude, who were subjected to the British rule by force, have not the right to rise for their national independence. In short, the people of Oude have rebelled against the legitimate authority of the British Government, and the British Government now distinctly declares that rebellion is a sufficient ground for confiscation. Leaving, therefore, out of the question all the circumlocution of Lord Canning, the whole question turns upon the point that he assumes the British rule in Oude to have been legitimately established.

Now, British rule in Oude was established in the following manner: When, in 1856, Lord Dalhousie thought the moment for action had arrived, he concentrated an army at Cawnpore which, the King of Oude[7] was told, was to serve as a corps of observation against Nepaul. This army suddenly invaded the country, took possession of Lucknow, and took the King prisoner. He was urged to cede the country to the British, but in vain. He was then carried off to Calcutta, and the country was annexed to the territories of the East India Company. This treacherous invasion was based upon article 6 of the treaty of 1801, concluded by Lord Wellesley.[8] This treaty was the natural consequence of that concluded in 1798 by Sir John Shore. According to the usual policy followed by the Anglo-Indian Government in their intercourse with native princes, this first treaty of 1798 was a treaty of offensive and defensive alliance on both sides. It secured to the East India Company a yearly subsidy of 76 lacs of rupees ($3,800,000);[9] but by article 12 and 13 the King was obliged to reduce the taxation of the country. As a matter of course, these two conditions, in open contradiction to each other, could not be fulfilled by the King at the same time. This result, looked for by the East India Company, gave rise to fresh complications, resulting in the treaty of 1801, by which a cession of territory had to make up for the alleged infractions of the former treaty; a cession of territory which, by the way, was at the time denounced in Parliament as a downright robbery, and would have brought Lord Wellesley before a Committee of Inquiry, but for the political influence then held by his family.

[6] Canning's Proclamation, 3 March 1858.
[7] Wajid Ali Shah, the last king of Awadh.
[8] The Treaty between the East India Company and the Nawab of Awadh concluded on 10 November 1801. See, Aitchison, *Collection of Treaties*, Vol. II (reprint, Delhi, 1983), pp. 130–33.
[9] Ibid., pp. 128–29. A US dollar is here assumed to be worth Rs 2.

In consideration of this cession of territory, the East India Company, by article 3, undertook to defend the King's remaining territories against all foreign and domestic enemies; and by article 6 guaranteed the possession of these territories to him and his heirs and successors for ever. But this same article 6 contained also a pit-fall for the King, viz.: The King engaged that he would establish such a system of administration, to be carried into effect by his own officers, as should be conducive to the prosperity of his subjects, and be calculated to secure the lives and property of the inhabitants. Now, supposing the King of Oude had broken this treaty; had not, by his government, secured the lives and property of the inhabitants (say by blowing them from the cannon's mouth, and confiscating the whole of their lands), what remedy remained to the East India Company? The King was, by the treaty, acknowledged as an independent sovereign, a free agent, one of the contracting parties. The East India Company, on declaring the treaty broken and thereby annulled, could have but two modes of action: either by negotiation, backed by pressure, they might have come to a new arrangement, or else they might have declared war against the King. But to invade his territory without declaration of war, to take him prisoner unawares, dethrone him and annex his territory, was an infraction not only of the treaty, but of every principle of the law of nations.

That the annexation of Oude was not a sudden resolution of the British Government is proved by a curious fact. No sooner was Lord Palmerston, in 1830, Foreign Secretary, than he sent an order to the then Governor-General to annex Oude. The subordinate at that time declined to carry out the suggestion. The affair, however, came to the knowledge of the King of Oude,[10] who availed himself of some pretext to send an embassy to London. In spite of all obstacles, the embassy succeeded in acquainting William IV, who was ignorant of the whole proceeding, with the danger which menaced their country. The result was a violent scene between William IV and Palmerston, ending in a strict injunction to the latter never to repeat such *coups d'etat* on pain of instant dismissal. It is important to recollect that the actual annexation of Oude and the confiscation of all the landed property of the country took place when Palmerston was again in power. The papers relating to this first attempt at annexing Oude, in 1831, were moved for, a few weeks ago, in the House of Commons, when Mr Baillie, Secretary of the Board of Control, declared that these papers had disappeared.

Again, in 1837, when Palmerston for the second time, was Foreign Secretary, and Lord Auckland Governor-General of India, the King of Oude was compelled to make a fresh treaty with the East India Company. This treaty takes up article 6 of the one of 1801, because 'it provides no remedy for the obligation contained in it' (to govern the country well); and it expressly provides, therefore, by article 7,

[10] Naseeruddin Haider (reigned as king, 1827–37).

that the King of Oude shall immediately take into consideration, in concert with the British Resident, the best means of remedying the defects in the police,[11] and in the judicial and revenue administrations of his dominions; and that if his Majesty should neglect to attend to the advice and counsel of the British Government,[12] and if gross and systematic oppression, anarchy and misrule should prevail[13] within the Oude dominions, such as seriously to endanger the public tranquility, the British Government reserves to itself the right of appointing its own officers to the management of whatsoever portions of the Oude territory, either to a small or great extent, in which such misrule[14] shall have occurred, for so long a period as it may deem necessary; the surplus receipts in such case, after defraying all charges, to be paid into the King's Treasury, and a true and faithful account rendered to his Majesty of the receipts and expenditure.[15]

By article 8, the treaty further provides:

That in case the Governor-General of India in Council should be compelled to resort to the exercise of the authority vested in him by article 7,[16] he will endeavor so far as possible to maintain, with such improvements as they may admit of,[17] the native institutions and forms of administration within the assumed territories, so as to facilitate the restoration of these[18] territories to the Sovereign of Oude, when the proper period for such restoration shall arrive.

This treaty professes to be concluded between the Governor-General of British India in Council, on one hand, and the King of Oude, on the other. It was, as such, duly ratified by both parties, and the ratifications were duly exchanged. But when it was submitted to the Board[19] of Directors of the East India Company, it was annulled (April 10, 1838), as an infraction of the friendly relations between the Company and the King of Oude, and an encroachment, on the part of the Governor-General, on the rights of that potentate. Palmerston had not asked the Company's leave to conclude the treaty, and he took no notice of their annulling resolution. Nor was the King of Oude informed that the treaty had ever been cancelled. This was proved by Lord Dalhousie himself (minute Jan. 5, 1856):

It is very probable that the King, in the course of the discussion which will take place with the Resident, may refer to the treaty negotiated with his predecessor

---

[11] In the original, the treaty inserts the word 'existing' here (Aitchison, *Collection of Treaties*, Vol. II, p. 140).

[12] The words 'or its local representative' are here added in the original treaty (ibid.).

[13] The words 'which God forbid' added in the original treaty are omitted here.

[14] In the original treaty the following words are added here: 'as that above alluded to'.

[15] The original treaty adds here 'of the territory so assumed'.

[16] Here the words 'of this treaty' are added in the original treaty.

[17] The words from 'with such improvements' to 'admit of' are placed within brackets in the original treaty.

[18] 'those' in the original treaty.

[19] Correctly, 'Court'.

in 1837; the Resident is aware that the treaty was not continued in force, having been annulled by the Court of Directors as soon as it was received in England. The Resident is further aware that, although the King of Oude was informed at the time that certain aggravating provisions of the treaty of 1837, respecting an increased military force, would not be carried into effect, *the entire abrogation of it was never communicated to his Majesty*. The effect of this reserve and want of full communication is felt to be embarrassing to-day. It is the more embarrassing that the canceled instrument was still included in a volume of treaties which was published in 1845,[20] by the authority of Government.

In the same minute, sec. 17, it is said:

> If the King should allude to the treaty of 1837, and should ask why, if further measures are necessary in relation to the administration of Oude, the large powers which are given to the British Government by the said treaty should not now be put in force, his Majesty must be informed that the treaty has had no existence since it was communicated to the Court of Directors, by whom it was wholly annulled. His Majesty will be reminded that the Court of Lucknow was informed at the time that certain articles of the treaty of 1837, by which the payment of an additional military force was imposed upon the King, were to be set aside. It must be presumed that it was not thought necessary at that time to make any communication to his Majesty regarding those articles of the treaty which were not of immediate operation, and that the subsequent communication was inadvertently neglected.

But not only was this treaty inserted in the official collection of 1845, it was also officially adverted to as a subsisting treaty in Lord Auckland's notification to the King of Oude, dated July 8, 1839; in Lord Hardinge's (then Governor-General) remonstrance to the same King, of November 23, 1847; and in Col. Sleeman's (Resident at Lucknow) communication to Lord Dalhousie himself, of the 10th December, 1851. Now, why was Lord Dalhousie so eager to deny the validity of a treaty which all his predecessors, and even his own agents, had acknowledged to be in force in their communications with the King of Oude? Solely because, by this treaty, whatever pretext the King might give for interference, that interference was limited to an assumption of government by British officers in the name of the King of Oude, who was to receive the surplus revenue. That was the very opposite of what was wanted. Nothing short of annexation would do. This denying the validity of treaties which had formed the acknowledged base of intercourse for twenty years; this seizing violently upon independent territories in open infraction even of the acknowledged treaties; this final confiscation of every acre of land in the whole country; all these treacherous and brutal modes of proceeding of the British toward the natives of India are now beginning to avenge themselves, not only in India, but in England.

[20] So in *NYDT*. Av. reads 1854.

[Lord Canning's Proclamation and Land Tenure in India]

(*New York Daily Tribune*, June 7, 1858. Printed as a leading article.)

Lord Canning's proclamation in relation to Oude, some important documents in reference to which we published on Saturday,[1] has revived the discussion as to the land tenures of India – a subject upon which there have been great disputes and differences of opinion in times past, and misapprehensions in reference to which have led, so it is alleged, to very serious practical mistakes in the administration of those parts of India directly under British rule. The great point in this controversy is, what is the exact position which the zamindars, talookdars[2] or sirdars, so called, hold in the economical system of India? Are they properly to be considered as landed proprietors or as mere tax-gatherers?

It is agreed that in India, as in most Asiatic countries, the ultimate property in the soil rests[3] with the Government; but while one party to this controversy insists that the Government is to be looked upon as a soil [*rect.* sole] proprietor, letting out the land on shares to the cultivators, the other side maintains that in substance the land in India is just as much private property as in any other country whatever – this alleged property in the Government being nothing more than the derivation of title from the sovereign, theoretically acknowledged in all countries, the codes of which are based on the feudal law and substantially acknowledged in all countries whatever in the power of the Government to levy taxes on the land to the extent of the needs of the Government, quite independent of all considerations, except as mere matter of policy, of the convenience of the owners.

Admitting however, that the lands of India are private property, held by as good and strong a private title as land elsewhere, who shall be regarded as the real owners? There are two parties for whom this claim has been set up. One of these parties is the class known as zemindars and talookadars,[4] who have been

---

Marx presumably refers to this article in his letter dated 31 May 1858 to Engels. See *CW*, Vol. 40, p. 317.

[1] The words 'some important documents . . . on Saturday' are insertions by the editors of *NYDT* and allude to the 'Annexation of Oude' by Marx published in the *NYDT*, 25 May 1858.

[2] So printed in *NYDT*.

[3] In Av. 'vests', with a *sic* and the subsequent word 'with' omitted.

[4] So spelt here.

considered to occupy a position similar to that of the landed nobility and gentry of Europe; to be, indeed, the real owners of the land, subject to a certain assessment due to the Government, and, as owners, to have the right of displacing at pleasure the actual cultivators, who, in this view of the case, are regarded as standing in the position of mere tenants at will, liable to any payment in the way of rent which the zemindars may see fit to impose. The view of the case which naturally fell in with English ideas, as to the importance and necessity of a landed gentry as the main pillar of the social fabric, was made the foundation of the famous landed settlement of Bengal seventy years ago[5] under the Governor-Generalship of Lord Cornwallis – a settlement which still remains in force, but which, as it is maintained by many, wrought great injustice alike to the Government and to the actual cultivators. A more thorough study of the institutions of Hindostan, together with the inconveniences, both social and political, resulting from the Bengal settlement, has given currency to the opinion that by the original Hindoo institutions, the property of the land was in the village corporations, in which resided the power of allotting it out to individuals for cultivation while the zamindars and talookdars were in their origin nothing but officers of the Government, appointed to look after, to collect, and to pay over to the prince the assessment due from the village.

This view had influenced to a considerable degree the settlement of the landed tenures and revenue made of late years in the Indian provinces, of which the direct administration has been assumed by the English. The exclusive proprietary rights claimed by the talookdars and zamindars have been regarded as originating in usurpations at once against the Government and the cultivators, and every effort has been made to get rid of them as an incubus on the real cultivators of the soil and the general improvement of the country. As, however, these middlemen, whatever the origin of their rights might be, could claim prescription in their favor, it was impossible not to recognize their claims as to a certain extent legal, however inconvenient, arbitrary and oppressive to the people. In Oude, under the feeble reign of the native princes, these feudal landholders had gone very far in curtailing alike the claims of the Government and the rights of the cultivators; and when, upon the recent annexation of that kingdom, this matter came under revision, the Commissioners charged with making the settlement soon got into a very acrimonious controversy with them as to the real extent of their rights. Hence resulted a state of discontent on their part which led them to make common cause with the revolted sepoys.

By those who incline to the policy above indicated – that of a system of village settlement – looking at the actual cultivators as invested with a proprietary right in the land, superior to that of the middlemen, through whom the Government receives its share of the landed produce – the proclamation of Lord Canning is defended as an advantage taken of the position in which the great body of the zemindars and talookdars of Oude had placed themselves, to open a

---

[5] The Permanent Settlement, 1793. The scheme was proposed in 1789.

door for the introduction of much more extensive reforms than otherwise would
have been practicable – the proprietary right confiscated by that proclamation
being merely the zemindaree or talookadaree right, and affecting only a very
small part of the population, and that by no means the actual cultivators.

Independently of any question of justice and humanity, the view taken
on the other hand by the Derby Ministry of Lord Canning's proclamation, corres-
ponds sufficiently well with the general principles which the Tory, or Conservative party maintain on the sacredness of vested rights and the importance of
upholding an aristocratic landed interest. In speaking of the landed interest at
home, they always refer rather to the landlords and rent-receivers than to the
rent-payers and to the actual cultivators; and it is, therefore, not surprising that
they should regard the interests of the zemindars and talookdars, however few
their actual number, as equivalent to the interests of the great body of the people.

Here indeed is one of the greatest inconveniences and difficulties in the
Government of India from England, that views of Indian question are liable to be
influenced by purely English prejudices or sentiments, applied to a state of society and a condition of things to which they have in fact very little real pertinency.
The defense which Lord Canning makes in his dispatch, published to-day, of the
policy of his proclamation against the objections of Sir James Outram, the Commissioner of Oude, is very plausible, though it appears that he so far yielded to
the representations of the Commissioner as to insert into the proclamation the
mollifying[6] sentence, not contained in the original draft sent to England, and on
which Lord Ellenborough's dispatch was based.[7]

Lord Canning's opinion as to the light in which the conduct of landholders
of Oude in joining in the rebellion ought to be viewed does not appear to differ
much from that of Sir James Outram and Lord Ellenborough. He argues that
they stand in a very different position not only from the mutinous Sepoys, but
from that of the inhabitants of rebellious districts in which the British rule had
been longer established. He admits that they are entitled to be treated as persons
having provocation for the course they took; but at the same time insists that they
must be made to understand that rebellion cannot be resorted to without involving serious consequences to themselves. We shall soon learn what the effect of the
issue of the proclamation has been, and whether Lord Canning or Sir James
Outram was nearer right in his anticipation of its results.

---

[6] Misprinted 'modifying' in Av.
[7] Russell (*My Diary*, p. 216) says that James Outram was understood to have obtained
permission from Lord Canning to modify the menaces of the Proclamation, and to
offer considerable concessions to the rebels in Oude.

FREDERICK ENGELS

[After the Fall of Lucknow]

(*New York Daily Tribune*, June 15, 1858. Printed as a leading article.)

In spite of the great military operations of the English in the capture first
of Delhi and then of Lucknow, the successive headquarters of the Sepoy rebellion, the pacification of India is yet very far from being accomplished. Indeed, it
may be almost said that the real difficulty of the case is but just beginning to
show itself. So long as the rebellious Sepoys kept together in large masses, so
long as it was a question of sieges and pitched battles on a great scale, the vast
superiority of the English troops for such operations gave them every advantage.
But with the new character which the war is now taking on, this advantage is
likely to be in a great measure lost. The capture of Lucknow does not carry with
it the submission of Oude; nor would even the submission of Oude carry with it
the pacification of India. The whole Kingdom of Oude bristles with fortresses of
greater or less pretensions; and though perhaps none would long resist a regular
attack, yet the capture of these forts one by one will not only be a very tedious
process, but it will be attended with much greater proportional loss than operations against such great cities as Delhi and Lucknow.

But it is not alone the Kingdom of Oude that requires to be conquered
and pacified. The discomfited Sepoys dislodged from Lucknow have scattered
and fled in all directions. A great body of them have taken refuge in the hill
districts of Rohilcund to the north, which still remains entirely in possession of
the rebels. Others fled into Goruckpore on the east – which district, though it had
been traversed by the British troops on their march to Lucknow, it has now
become necessary to recover a second time. Many others have succeeded in
penetrating southward into Bundelcund.

Indeed, a controversy seems to have arisen as to the best method of proceeding, and whether it would not have been better to have first subdued all the
outlying districts which might have afforded the rebels a shelter, before directing
operations against their main body collected at Lucknow. Such is said to have
been the scheme of operations preferred by the military; but it is difficult to see
how, with the limited number of troops at the disposal of the English, those
surrounding districts could have been so occupied as to exclude the fugitive Sepoys,

Written by Engels, for Marx himself was then ill and 'totally incapable of writing for
several weeks'. He stayed with Engels in Manchester from 6 to about 24 May 1858.
See *CW*, Vol. 40, pp. 315 and 618 (n. 318).

when finally dislodged from Lucknow, from entering into them, and, as in the case of Goruckpore, making their reconquest necessary.

Since the capture of Lucknow, the main body of the rebels appear to have retired upon Bareilly. It is stated that Nena[1] Sahib was there. Against this city and district, upward of a hundred miles north-west from Lucknow, it has been judged necessary to undertake a Summer campaign, and at the latest accounts Sir Colin Campbell was himself marching thither.

Meanwhile, however, a guerrilla warfare seems to be spreading in various directions. While the troops are drawn off to the North, scattered parties of rebel soldiery are crossing the Ganges into the Doab, interrupting the communication with Calcutta, and by their ravages disabling the cultivators to pay their land-tax, or at least affording them an excuse for not doing so.

Even the capture of Bareilly, so far from operating to remedy those evils, will be likely, perhaps, to increase them. It is in this desultory warfare that the advantage of the Sepoys lies. They can beat the English troops at marching to much the same extent that the English can beat them at fighting. An English column cannot move twenty miles a day; a Sepoy force can move forty, and, if hard pushed, even sixty. It is this rapidity of movement which gives to the Sepoy troops their chief value, and this, with their power of standing the climate and the comparative facility of feeding them, makes them indispensable in Indian warfare. The consumption of English troops in service, and especially in a Summer campaign, is enormous. Already, the lack of men is severely felt. It may become necessary to chase the flying rebels from one end of India to the other. For that purpose, European troops would hardly answer, while the contact of the wandering rebels with the native regiments of Bombay and Madras, which have hitherto remained faithful, might lead to new revolts.

Even without any accession of new mutineers, there are still in the field not less than a hundred and fifty thousand armed men, while the unarmed population fail to afford the English either assistance or information.

Meanwhile the deficiency of rain in Bengal threatens a famine – a calamity unknown within this century, though in former times, and even since the English occupation, the source of terrible sufferings.

---

[1] Rect. Nana.

FREDERICK ENGELS

[The British Army in India]

(*New York Daily Tribune*, June 26, 1858. Printed as a leading article.)

Our indiscreet friend, Mr William Russell, of the London *Times*, has recently been induced, by his love of the picturesque, to illustrate, for the second time, the sack of Lucknow, to a degree which other people will not think very flattering to the British character.[1] It now appears that Delhi, too, was 'looted' to a very considerable extent, and that besides the Kaiserbagh, the city of Lucknow generally contributed to reward the British soldier for his previous privations and heroic efforts. We quote from Mr Russell:

> There are companies which can boast of privates with thousands of pounds worth in their ranks. One man I heard of who complacently offered to lend an officer 'whatever sum he wanted if he wished to buy over the Captain'. Others have remitted large sums to their friends [. . .] Ere this letter reaches England, many a diamond, emerald and delicate pearl will have told its tale in a very quiet, pleasant way, of the storm and sack of the Kaiserbagh. It is as *well that the fair wearers . . . saw not how the glittering baubles were won, or the scenes in which the treasure was trove.*[2] . . . Some of these officers have made, literally, *their fortunes.* . . . There are certain small caskets in battered uniform cases which contain *estates in Scotland and Ireland*, and snug fishing and shooting boxes in every game-haunted or salmon-frequented angle of the world. . . .

This, then accounts for the inactivity of the British army after the conquest of Lucknow. The fortnight devoted to plunder was well spent. Officers and soldiers went into the town poor and debt-ridden, and came out suddenly enriched. They were no longer the same men; yet they were expected to return to their former military duty, to submission, silent obedience, fatigue, privation and battle. But this is out of the question. The army, disbanded for the purpose of

---

On 4 June 1858, Marx gave the title 'Army in India' in his notebook, and in a letter to Engels on 7 June, he acknowledged the receipt of Engels's article for the *New York Daily Tribune* (*NYDT*): 'very amusing one, too'. See *CW*, Vol. 15, p. 693, n. 562; and *CW*, Vol. 40, p. 319.

[1] The quotations here and further on are from W.H. Russell, 'Lucknow, April 5', *The Times*, No. 23009, 31 May 1858. Cf. *CW*, Vol. 15, p. 556.

[2] Meaning 'found and seized', the word 'trove' being used here as past participle of 'trover'.

plunder, is changed for ever; no word of command, no prestige of the General, can make it again what it once was. Listen again to Mr Russell:

> It is curious to observe how riches develop disease; how one's liver is affected by loot, and what tremendous ravages in one's family, among the nearest and dearest, can be caused by a few crystals of carbon. . . . The weight of the belt round the private's waist, full of rupees and gold mohurs, assures him the vision [of a comfortable independency at home] can be realized, and it is no wonder he resents the 'fall in, there, fall in'! . . . Two battles, two shares of prize-money, the plunder of two cities, and many pickings by the way, have made some of our men too rich for easy soldiering.[3] . . .

Accordingly, we hear that above 150 officers have sent in their resignations to Sir Colin Campbell – a very singular proceeding indeed in an army before the enemy, which in any other service would be followed up in twenty-four hours by cashiering and severest punishment otherwise, but which, we suppose, is considered in the British army as a very proper act for 'an officer and a gentleman' who has suddenly made his fortune. As to the private soldiers, with them the proceeding is different. Loot engenders the desire for more; and if no more Indian treasures are at hand for the purpose, why not loot those of the British Government? Accordingly, says Mr Russell: 'There has been a suspicious upsetting of two treasure tumbrils under a European guard, in which some few rupees were missing, and *paymasters exhibit a preference for natives in the discharge of the delicate duty of convoy!*'

Very good, indeed. The Hindoo or Sikh is better disciplined, less thieving, less rapacious than that incomparable model of a warrior, the British soldier! But so far we have seen the individual Briton only employed. Let us now cast a glance at the British army, 'looting' in its collective capacity:

> Every day adds to the prize property, and it is estimated that the sales will produce £600,000. *The town of Cawnpore is said to be full of the plunder of Lucknow*; and if the damage done to public buildings, the destruction of private property, the deterioration in value of houses and land, and the results of depopulation could be estimated , it would be found that the *capital of Oude has sustained a loss of five or six millions sterling.*[4]

The Calmuck hordes of Genghis Khan and Timur, falling upon a city like a swarm of locuts, and devouring everything that came in their way, must have been a blessing to a country, compared with the irruption of these Christian, civilized, chivalrous and gentle British soldiers. The former, at least, soon passed

---

[3] This description also appears in Russell, *My Diary*, pp. 194–96.

[4] We read in another source: "The loot here (Qaisarbagh) was considerable. Diamonds and emerald necklaces, pearls, jewels of every descriptions, and shawls were quickly walked off with the soldiers.' H. Grant, *Incidents in the Sepoy War* (London, 1863), p. 256.

away on their erratic course; but these methodic Englishmen bring along with them their prize-agents, who convert loot into a system, who register the plunder, sell it by auction, and keep a sharp look-out that British heroism is not defrauded of a tittle of its reward. We shall watch with curiosity the capabilities of this army, relaxed as its discipline is by the effects of wholesale plunder, at a time when the fatigues of a hot weather campaign require the greatest stringency of discipline.

The Hindoos must, however, by this time be still less fit for regular battle than they were at Lucknow, but that is not now the main question. It is far more important to know what shall be done if the insurgents, after a show of resistance, again shift the seat of war, say to Rajpootana, which is far from being subdued. Sir Colin Campbell must leave garrisons everywhere; his field army has melted down to less than one half of the force he had before Lucknow. If he is to occupy Rohilcund what disposable strength will remain for the field? The hot weather is now upon him; in June the rains must have put a stop to active campaigning, and allowed the insurgents breathing time. The loss of European soldiers through sickness will have increased every day after the middle of April, when the weather became oppressive; and the young men imported into India last winter must succumb to the climate in far greater numbers than the seasoned Indian campaigners who last Summer fought under Havelock and Wilson. Rohilcund is no more the decisive point than Lucknow was, or Delhi. The insurrection, it is true, has lost most of its capacity for pitched battles; but it is far more formidable in its present scattered form, which compels the English to ruin their army by marching and exposure. Look at the many new centres of resistance. There is Rohilcund, where the mass of the old Sepoys are collected; there is North-eastern Oude beyond the Gogra, where the Oudians have taken up position; there is Calpee, which for the present serves as a point of concentration for the insurgents of Bundlecund. We shall most likely hear in a few weeks, if not sooner, that both Bareilly and Calpee have fallen. The former will be of little importance, inasmuch as it will serve to absorb nearly all, if not the whole of Campbell's disposable forces. Calpee, menaced now by General Whitelock, who has led his column from Nagpoor to Banda, in Bundlecund, and by General Rose,[5] who approaches from Jhansi, and has defeated the advanced guard of the Calpee forces, will be a more important conquest; it will free Campbell's base of operations, Cawnpore, from the only danger menacing it, and thus perhaps enable him to recruit his field forces to some extent by troops set at liberty thereby. But it is very doubtful whether there will be enough to do more than to clear Oude.

Thus, the strongest army England ever concentrated on one point in India is again scattered in all directions, and has more work cut out than it can

---

[5] Hugh Henry Rose (1801–1885): volunteered for service in India in 1857; took Rathgarh and Garahkota, relieved Sagar, and captured the important pass of Maltun in 1858; defeated Tantia Tope and took Kuch and Kalpi.

conveniently do. The ravages of the climate during the Summer's heats and rains, must be terrible; and whatever the moral superiority of the European over the Hindoos, it is very doubtful whether the physical superiority of the Hindoos in braving the heat and rains of an Indian Summer will not again be the means of destroying the English forces. There are at present but few British troops on the road to India, and it is not intended to send out large reinforcement before July and August. Up to October and November, therefore, Campbell has but that one army, melting down rapidly as it is, to hold his own with. What if in the meantime the insurgent Hindoos succeed in raising Rajpootana and Mahratta country in rebellion? What if the Sikhs, of whom there are 80,000 in the British service, and who claim all the honor of the victories for themselves, and whose temper is not altogether favorable to the British were to rise?

Altogether, one more Winter's campaign, at least, appears to be in store for the British in India, and that cannot be carried on without another army from England.

FREDERICK ENGELS

The Indian Army

(*New York Daily Tribune*, July 21, 1858. Printed as a leading article.)

The war in India is gradually passing into that stage of desultory guerrilla warfare, to which, more than once, we have pointed as its next impending
and most dangerous phase of development. The insurgent armies, after their
successive defeats in pitched battles, and in the defence of towns and intrenched
camps, gradually dissolve into small bodies of from two to six or eight thousand
men, acting, to a certain degree, independently of each other, but always ready
to unite for a short expedition against any British detachment which may be
surprised singly. The abandonment of Bareilly without a blow, after having drawn
the active field force of Sir C. Campbell some eighty miles away from Lucknow,
was the turning point, in this respect, for the main army of the insurgents; the
abandonment of Calpee[1] had the same significance for the second great body of
natives. In either case, the last defensible central base of operations was given
up, and the warfare of an army thereby becoming impossible, the insurgents
made eccentric retreats by separating into smaller bodies. These movable columns require no large town for a central base of operations. They can find means
of existence, of re-equipment, and of recruitment in the various districts in which
they move; and a small town or a large village as a center of reorganization may
be as valuable to each of them as Delhi, Lucknow or Calpee to the larger armies.
By this change, the war loses much of its interest; the movements of the various
columns of insurgents cannot be followed up in detail and appear confused in the
accounts; the operations of the British commanders, to a great extent, escape
criticism, from the unavoidable obscurity enveloping the premises on which they
are based; success or failure remain the only criterion, and they are certainly of
all the most deceitful.

This uncertainty respecting the movements of the natives is already very
great. After the taking of Lucknow, they retreated eccentrically some south-east,
some north-east, some north-west. The latter were the stronger body, and were
followed by Campbell into Rohilcund. They had concentrated and re-formed at

---

This title conforms to Marx's entry in his notebook for 1858. See *CW*, Vol. 15, p. 693
n. *FIWI* retains the above title. In Av. it appears under the title 'Guerrilla Warfare in
India'. Also see Marx's letter to Engels dated 2 July 1858 asking for an article on India
(*CW*, Vol. 40, p. 325).

[1] Kalpi.

Bareilly; but when the British came up, they abandoned the place without resistance, and again retreated in different directions. Particulars of these different
lines of retreat are not known. We only know that a portion went toward the hills
on the frontiers of Nepaul, while one or more columns appear to have marched
in the opposite direction, toward the Ganges and the Doab (the country between
the Ganges and the Jumna). No sooner, however, had Campbell occupied Bareilly,
than the insurgents, who had retreated in an easterly direction, effected a junction with some bodies on the Oude frontier and fell upon Shahjehanpore, where
a small British garrison had been left; while further insurgent columns were
hastening in that direction. Fortunately for the garrison, Brigadier Jones[2] arrived
with reinforcements as early as the 11th of May, and defeated the natives; but
they, too, were reinforced by the columns concentrating on Shahjehanpore, and
again invested the town on the 15th. On this day, Campbell, leaving a garrison
in Bareilly, marched to its relief; but it was not before the 24th of May that he
attacked them and drove them back, the various columns of insurgents which
had cooperated in this manoeuvre again dispersing in different directions.

While Campbell was thus engaged on the frontiers of Rohilcund, Gen.
Hope Grant marched his troops backward and forward in the South of Oude,
without any result, except losses to his own force by fatigue under an Indian
summer's sun. The insurgents were too quick for him. They were everywhere but
where he happened to look for them, and when he expected to find them in front,
they had long since again gained his rear. Lower down the Ganges, Gen. Lugard[3]
was occupied with a chase after a similar shadow in the district between Dinapore,
Jugdispore and Buxar. The natives kept him constantly on the move, and, after
drawing him away from Jugdispore, all at once fell upon the garrison of that
place. Lugard returned, and a telegram reports his having gained a victory on
the 26th.[4] The identity of the tactics of these insurgents with those of the Oude
and Rohilcund columns is evident. The victory gained by Lugard will, however,
scarcely be of much importance. Such bands can afford to be beaten a good
many times before they become demoralized and weak.

Thus, by the middle of May the whole insurgent force of Northern India
had given up warfare on a large scale, with the exception of the army of Calpee.
This force, in a comparatively short time, had organized in that town a complete
centre of operations; they had provisions, powder and other stores in profusion,
plenty of guns, and even foundries and musket manufactories. Though within 25
miles of Cawnpore, Campbell had left them unmolested; he merely observed
them by a force on the Doab, or western side of the Jumna, Generals Rose and

---

[2] Sir John Jones (1811–1878): lieutenant colonel at the siege of Delhi; as Brigadier of
the Roorkee field-force acquired the name of 'Avenger'; made lieutenant general,
1877.

[3] Sir Edward Lugard (1810–1898): general; had taken part in Anglo-Persian War of
1856–57.

[4] This alludes to the defeat and death of Kunwar Singh of Jagdishpur, Arrah (Bihar).

Whitlock[5] had been on the march to Calpee for a long while; at last Rose arrived, and defeated the insurgents in a series of engagements in front of Calpee. The observing force on the other side of the Jumna, in the meantime, had shelled the town and fort, and suddenly the insurgents evacuated both, breaking up this, their last large army into independent columns. The roads taken by them are not all clear, from the accounts received; we only know that some have gone into the Doab, and others toward Gwalior.

Thus the whole district from the Himalayas to the Bihar and Vindhya Mountains, and from Gwalior and Delhi to Joruckpore[6] and Dinapore, is swarming with active insurgent bands, organized to a certain degree by the experience of a twelve months' war, and encouraged, amid a number of defeats, by the indecisive character of each, and by the small advantages gained by the British. It is true, all their strongholds and centres of operations have been taken from them; the greater portion of their stores and artillery are lost; the important towns are all in the hands of their enemies. But on the other hand, the British, in all this vast district, hold nothing but the towns, and of the open country, nothing but the spot where their movable columns happen to stand; they are compelled to chase their nimble enemies without any hope of attaining them; and they are under the necessity of entering upon their harassing mode of warfare at the very deadliest season of the year. The native Indian can stand the midday heat of his Summer with comparative comfort, while mere exposure to the rays of the sun is almost certain death to the European; he can march forty miles in such a season, where ten break down his northern opponent; to him even the hot rains and swampy jungles are comparatively innocuous, while dysentery, cholera, and ague follow every exertion made by Europeans in the rainy season or in swampy neighbourhoods. We are without detailed accounts of the sanitary conditions of the British army; but from the comparative numbers of those struck by the sun and those hit by the enemy in Gen. Rose's army, from the report that the garrison of Lucknow is sickly, that the 38th Regiment arrived last Autumn above 1,000 strong, now scarcely numbers 550, and from other indications we may draw the conclusion that the Summer's heat, during April and May, has done its work among the newly-imported men and lads who have replaced the bronzed old Indian soldiers of last year's campaign. With the men Campbell has, he cannot undertake the forced marches of Havelock nor a siege during the rainy season like that of Delhi. And although the British Government are again sending off strong reinforcements, it is doubtful whether they will be sufficient to replace the wear and tear of this Summer's campaign against an enemy who declines to fight the British except on terms most favorable to himself.

The insurgent warfare now begins to take the character of that of the Bedouins of Algeria against the French;[7] with the difference that the Hindoos are

---

[5] George Whitlock (1798–1868): joined the service of East India Company in 1818.

[6] Gorakhpur.

[7] A reference to the warfare in Algeria following the French expedition of 1830, which continued until 1857.

far from being so fanatical, and that they are not a nation of horsemen. This latter is important in a flat country of immense extent. There are plenty of Mohammedans among them who would make good irregular cavalry; still the principal cavalry nations of India have not joined the insurrection so far. The strength of their army is in the infantry, and that arm being unfit to meet the English in the field, becomes a drag in guerrilla warfare in the plain; for in such a country the sinew of desultory warfare is irregular cavalry. How far this want may be remedied during the compulsory holiday the English will have to take during the rains, we shall see. This holiday will, altogether, give the natives an opportunity of reorganizing and recruiting their forces. Beside the organization of cavalry, there are two more points of importance. As soon as the cold weather sets in, guerrilla warfare alone will not do. Centres of operation, stores, artillery, intrenched camps or towns, are required to keep the British busy until the cold season is over; otherwise the guerrilla warfare might be extinguished before the next summer gives it fresh life. Gwalior appears to be, among others, a favorable point, if the insurgents have really got hold of it. Secondly, the fate of the insurrection is dependent upon its being able to expand. If the dispersed columns cannot manage to cross from Rohilcund into Rajpootana and the Mahratta country; if the movement remains confined to the northern central district, then, no doubt, the next Winter will suffice to disperse the bands, and to turn them into dacoits, which will soon be more hateful to the inhabitants than even the pale-faced invaders.

[Taxation in India]

(*New York Daily Tribune*, July 23, 1858. Printed as a leading article.)

According to the London journals, Indian stock and railway securities have of late been distinguished by a downward movement in that market, which is far from testifying to the genuineness of the sanguine convictions which John Bull likes to exhibit in regard to the state of the Indian guerrilla war; and which, at all events, indicates a stubborn distrust in the elasticity of Indian financial resources. As to the latter, two opposite views are propounded. On the one hand, it is affirmed that taxes in India are onerous and oppressive beyond those of any country in the world; that as a rule throughout most of the presidencies, and through those presidencies most where they have been longest under British rule, the cultivators, that is, the great body of the people of India, are in a condition of unmitigated impoverishment and dejection; that, consequently, Indian revenues have been stretched to their utmost possible limit, and Indian finances are therefore past recovery. A rather discomfortable opinion this at a period when, according to Mr Gladstone,[1] for some years to come, the extraordinary Indian expenditure alone will annually amount to about £20,000,000 sterling. On the other hand, it is asserted the asseveration being made good by an array of statistical illustrations – that India is the least taxed country in the world; that, if expenditure is going on increasing, revenue may be increased too; and that it is an utter fallacy to imagine that the Indian people will not bear any new taxes. Mr Bright, who may be considered the most arduous and influential representative of the 'discomfortable' doctrine, made, on the occasion of the second reading of the new Government of India bill,[2] the following statement:

> The Indian Government had cost more to govern India than it was possible to extort from the population of India, although the Government had been by no means scrupulous either as to the taxes imposed, or as to the mode in which they had been levied. It cost more than £30,000,000 to govern India, for that was the gross revenue, and there was always a deficit, which had to be made up by loans borrowed at a high rate of interest. The Indian debt now amounted to £60,000,000, and was increasing; while the credit of the Government was

---

[1] Gladstone's speech in the House of Commons on 7 June 1858. *The Times*, No. 23014; cf. *CW*, Vol. 15, p. 575 n.

[2] A reference to the bill introduced in the Parliament by the Derby Ministry in March and adopted on 2 August 1858 as an Act. Marx analyses the Act in his Article 'The Indian Bill'.

falling, partly because they had not treated their creditors very honorably on one or two occasions, and now on account of the calamities which had recently happened in India. He had alluded to the gross revenue; but as that included the opium revenue, which was hardly a tax upon the people of India, he would take the taxation which really pressed upon them at £ 25,000,000. Now, let not this £ 25,000,000 be compared with the £ 60,000,000 that was raised in this country. Let the House recollect that in India it was possible to purchase twelve days' labor for the same amount of gold or silver that would be obtained in payment for one in England. This £25,000,000 expended in the purchase of labor in India would buy as much as an outlay of £300,000,000 would procure in England. He might be asked how much was the labor of an Indian worth? Well if the labor of an Indian was only worth 2d. a day, it was clear that we could not expect him to pay as much taxation as if it was worth 2s. . . . We had 30,000,000 of population in Great Britain and Ireland; in India there were 150,000,000 inhabitants. We raised here £60,000,000 sterling of taxes; in India, reckoning by the day's labor of the people of India, we raised £300,000,000 of revenue, or five times a greater revenue than was collected at home. Looking at the fact that the population of India was five times greater than that of the British Empire, a man might say; that the taxation per head in India and England was about the same, and that therefore there was no great hardship inflicted. But in England there was an incalculable power of machinery and steam, of means of transit, and of everything that capital and human invention could bring to aid the Industry of a people. In India there was nothing of the kind. They had scarcely a decent road throughout India.[3]

Now, it must be admitted that there is something wrong in this method of comparing Indian taxes with British taxes. There is on the one side the Indian population, five times as great as the British one, and there is on the other side the Indian taxation amounting to half the British. But, then, Mr Bright says, Indian labor is an equivalent for about one-twelfth only of British labor. Consequently £30,000,000 of taxes in India would represent £300,000,000 of taxes in Great Britain, instead of the £60,000,000 actually there raised. What then is the conclusion he ought to have arrived at? That the people of India in regard to their numerical strength pay the *same* taxation as the people in Great Britain, if allowance is made for the comparative poverty of the people in India, and £30,000,000 is supposed to weigh as heavily upon 150,000,000 Indians as £60,000,000 upon 30,000,000 Britons. Such being his supposition, it is certainly fallacious to turn round and say that a poor people cannot pay so much as a rich one, because the comparative poverty of the Indian people has already been taken into account in making out the statement that the Indian pays as much as

[3] Bright's speech in the House of Commons on 24 June 1858. *The Times*, No. 23029, 25 June 1858. Cf. *CW*, Vol. 15, p. 676 n.

the Briton. There might, in fact, another question be raised. It might be asked, whether a man who earns say 12 cents a day can be fairly expected to pay 1 cent with the same ease with which another, earning $12 a day, pays $ 1? Both would relatively contribute the same aliquot part of their income, but still the tax might bear in quite different proportions upon their respective necessities. Yet Mr Bright has not yet put the question in these terms, and, if he had, the comparison between the burden of taxation, borne by the British wages laborer on the one hand, and the British capitalist on the other, would perhaps have struck nearer home than the comparison between Indian and British taxation. Moreover, he admits himself that from the £30,000,000 of Indian taxes, the £5,000,000 constituting the opium revenue must be subtracted, since this is, properly speaking, no tax pressing upon the Indian people, but rather an export duty charged upon Chinese consumption. Then we are reminded by the apologists of the Anglo-Indian administration that £16,000,000 of Income is derived from the land revenue, or rent, which from times immemorial has belonged to the State in its capacity as supreme landlord, never constituted part of the private fortune of the cultivator and does, in fact, no more enter into taxation, properly so-called, than the rent paid by the British farmers to the British aristocracy can be said to enter British taxation. Indian taxation, according to this point of view, would stand thus:

Aggregate sum raised	£30,000,000
Deduct for opium revenue	£ 5,000,000
Deduct for rent of land	£16,000,000
Taxation proper	9,000,000

On this £9,000,000, again, it must be admitted that some important items, such as the post-office, the stamp duties, and the custom duties, bear in a very minute proportion on the mass of people. Accordingly, Mr Hendricks, in a paper recently laid before the British Statistical Society on the Finances of India,[4] tries to prove, from Parliamentary and other official documents, that of the total revenue paid by the people of India, not more than one-fifth is at present raised by taxation, i.e., from the real income of the people; that in Bengal 27 per cent only, in the Punjab 23 per cent only, in Madras 21 per cent only, in the North-Western Provinces 17 per cent only, and in Bombay 16 per cent only of the total revenue is derived from taxation proper.

The following comparative view of the average amount of taxation derived from each inhabitant of India and the United Kingdom, during the years 1855–56, is abstracted from Mr Hendricks' statement:

---

[4] *The Economist*, No. 772, 12 June 1858. Reference from *CW*, Vol. 15, p. 577 n.

Bengal, per head, revenue	£0	5	0	Taxation proper £0	1	4
North-West province		3	5	Taxation proper	0	7
Madras		4	7	Taxation proper	1	0
Bombay		8	3	Taxation proper	1	4
Punjaub		3	3	Taxation proper	0	9
United Kingdom		–	–	Taxation proper	1	10	0

For a different year the following estimate of the average paid by each individual to the national revenue is made by Gen. Briggs:[5]

In England, 1852	£1	19	4
In France	£1	12	0
In Prussia	0	19	3
In India, 1854	0	3	8–1/2

From these statements it is inferred by the apologists of the British Administration that there is not a single country in Europe, where, even if the comparative poverty of India is taken into account, the people are so lightly taxed. Thus it seems that not only opinions with respect to Indian taxation are conflicting, but that the facts from which they purport to be drawn are themselves contradictory. On the one hand, we must admit the nominal amount of Indian taxation to be relatively small; but on the other, we might heap evidence upon evidence from Parliamentary documents, as well as from the writings of the greatest authorities on Indian affairs, all proving beyond doubt that this apparently light taxation crushes the mass of the Indian people to the dust, and that its exaction necessitates a resort to such infamies as torture, for instance. But is any other proof wanted beyond the constant and rapid increase of the Indian debt and the accumulation of Indian deficits? It will certainly not be contended that the Indian Government prefers increasing debts and deficits because it shrinks from touching too roughly upon the resources of the people. It embarks in debt, because it sees no other way to make both ends meet. In 1805 the Indian debt amounted to £25,626,631; in 1829 it reached about £34,000,000; in 1850, £47,151,018; and at present it amounts to about £60,000,000.[6] By the by, we leave out of the count the East Indian debt contracted in England, which is also chargeable upon the East Indian revenue.

The annual deficit, which in 1805 amounted to about two and a half millions, had, under Lord Dallhousie's Administration, reached the average of five millions. Mr George Campbell, of the Bengal Civil Service, and of a mind strongly biased in favor of the Anglo-Indian Administration, was obliged to avow, in 1852, that:

---

[5] John Briggs (1785–1875). The figures appear to have been derived from Campbell, *Modern India*, pp. 412, 419.
[6] Ibid., pp. 412, 414, 417.

Although no Oriental conquerors have ever obtained so complete an ascendancy, so quiet, universal and undisputed possession of India as we have, yet all have enriched themselves from the revenues of the country, and many have out of their abundance laid out considerable sums on works of public improvements. . . . From doing this we are debarred. . . . The quantity of the whole burden is by no means diminished (under the English rule), yet *we have no surplus*.[7]

In estimating the burden of taxation, its nominal amount must not fall heavier into the balance than the method of raising it, and the manner of employing it. The former is detestable in India, and in the branch of the land-tax, for instance, wastes perhaps more produce than it gets. As to the application of the taxes, it will suffice to say that no part of them is returned to the people in works of public utility, more indispensable in Asiatic countries than anywhere else, and that, as Mr Bright justly remarked, nowhere so extravagant is a provision made for the governing class itself.

---

[7] The quotation is from ibid., p. 406: only the word 'accordingly' is omitted after the first word of the quotation ('Although'). Italics as well as the words enclosed within round brackets, are of Marx.

The Indian Bill

(*New York Daily Tribune*, July 24, 1858. Printed as a leading article.)

The latest Indian bill passed through its third reading in the House of Commons,[1] and since Lords swayed by Derby's influence, are not likely to show fight, the doom of the East India Company appears to be sealed. They do not die like heroes; it must be confessed; but they have bartered away their power, as they crept into it, bit by bit, in a business like way. In fact, their whole history is one of buying and selling. They commenced by buying sovereignty, and they have ended by selling it. *They have fallen*, not in a pitched battle, but under the hammer of the auctioneer, into the hands of the highest bidder. In 1693 they procured from the Crown a charter for twenty-one years by paying large sums to the Duke of Leeds and other public officers. In 1767 they prolonged their tenure of power for two years by the promise of annually paying £400,000 into the Imperial exchequer. In 1769 they struck a similar bargain for five years; but soon after, in return for the Exchequer's foregoing the stipulated annual payment and lending them £1,400,000 at 4 per cent, they alienated some parcels of sovereignty, leaving to Parliament in the first instance the nomination of the Governor General and four Councilors, altogether surrendering to the Crown the appointment of the Lord Chief Justice and his three Judges, and agreeing to the conversion of the Court of Proprietors from a democratic into an oligarchic body.[2] In 1858, after having solemnly pledged themselves to the Court of Proprietors to resist by all Constitutional 'means' the transfer to the Crown of the governing powers of the East India Company, they have accepted that principle, and agreed to a bill penal as regards the Company, but securing emolument and place to its principal Directors. If the death of a hero, as Schiller[3] says, resembles the setting of the sun, the exit of the East India Company bears more likeness to the compromise effected by a bankrupt with his creditors.

By this bill the principal functions of administration are intrusted to a Secretary of State in Council, just as at Calcutta the Governor-General in Council manages affairs. But both these functionaries – the Secretary of State in England and the Governor-General in India – are alike authorized to disregard the

---

This title is in accordance with the entry in Marx's notebook for 1858 (CW, Vol. 15, p. 694, n. 570). In Av. the title given is 'The Abolition of the East India Company'.

[1] *The Times*, No. 23036, 3 July 1858. Cf. CW, Vol. 15, p. 585 n.
[2] A reference to the provisions of the Regulating Act 1773.
[3] Schiller, *Die Rauber*, Act III, Scene II. Cf. CW, Vol. 15, p. 586 n.

advice of their assessors and to act upon their own judgement. The new bill also invests the Secretary of State with all the powers at present exercised by the President of the Board of Control, through the agency of the Secret Committee – the power, that is, in urgent cases, of dispatching orders to India without stopping to ask the advice of his Council. In constituting that Council it has been found necessary, after all, to resort to the East India Company as the only practicable source of appointments to it other than nominations by the Crown. The elective members of the Council are to be elected by the Directors of the East India Company from among their own members.

Thus, after all, the name of the East India Company is to outlive its substance. At the last hour it was confessed by the Derby Cabinet that their bill contains no clause abolishing the East India Company, as represented by a Court of Directors, but that it becomes reduced to its ancient character of a company of stockholders, distributing the dividends guaranteed by different acts of legislation. Pitt's Bill of 1784 virtually subjected their government to the sway of the Cabinet under the name of the Board of Control. The act of 1813 stripped them of their monopoly of commerce, save the trade with China. The act of 1834 destroyed their commercial character altogether, and the act of 1854 annihilated their last remnant of power, still leaving them in possession of the Indian Administration. By the rotation of history the East India Company, converted in 1612 into a joint-stock company, is again clothed in its primitive garb, only that it represents now a trading partnership without trade, and a joint-stock company which has no funds to administer, but only fixed dividends to draw.

The history of the Indian bill is marked by greater dramatic changes than any other act of modern Parliamentary legislation. When Sepoy insurrection broke out, the cry of Indian reform rang through all classes of British society. Popular imagination was heated by the torture reports; the Government interference with the native religion was loudly denounced by Indian general officers and civilians of high standing; the rapacious annexation policy of Lord Dalhousie, the mere tool of Downing Street; the fermentation recklessly created in the Asiatic mind by the piratical wars in Persia and China – wars commenced and pursued on Palmerston's private dictation – the weak measures with which he met the outbreak, sailing ships being chosen for transport in preference to steam vessels, and the circuitous navigation around the Cape of Good Hope instead of transportation over the Isthmus of Suez – all these accumulated grievances burst into the cry for Indian Reform – reform of the Company's Indian Administration, reform of the Government's Indian policy. Palmerston caught at the popular cry, but resolved upon turning it to his exclusive profit. Because both the Government and the Company had miserably broken down, the Company was to be killed in sacrifice, and the Government to be rendered omnipotent. The power of the Company was to be simply transferred to the dictator of the day, pretending to represent the Crown as against the Parliament, and to represent Parliament as against the Crown, thus absorbing the privileges of the one and the other in his single person. With the Indian army at his back, the Indian Treasury at his command, and the Indian patronage in his pocket, Palmerston's position would have become impregnable.

His bill passed triumphantly through the first reading, but his career was cut short by the famous Conspiracy bill, followed by the advent of the Tories to power.[4]

On the very first day of their official re-appearance on the Treasury benches, they declared that, out of deference for the decisive will of the Commons, they would forsake their opposition to the transfer from the Company to the Crown of the Indian Government. Lord Ellenborough's legislative abortion seemed to hasten Palmerston, when Lord John Russell, in order to force the dictator into a compromise, stepped in, and saved the Government by proposing to proceed with the Indian bill by way of Parliamentary resolution, instead of by a governmental bill. Then Lord Ellenborough's Oude dispatch, his sudden resignation, and the consequent disorganization in the Ministerial camp, were eagerly seized upon by Palmerston. The Tories were again to be planted in the cold shade of opposition, after they had employed their short lease of power in breaking down the opposition of their own party against the confiscation of the East India Company. Yet it is sufficiently known how these fine calculations were baffled. Instead of rising on the ruins of the East India Company, Palmerston has been buried beneath them. During the whole of the Indian debates, the House seemed to indulge, the peculiar satisfaction of humiliating the *Civis Romanus*.[5] All his amendments, great and small, were ignominiously lost; allusions of the most unsavory kind, relating to the Afghan war,[6] the Persian war,[7] and the Chinese war,[8] were continually flung at his head; and Mr Gladstone's clause, withdrawing from the Indian Minister the power of originating wars beyond the boundaries of India, intended as a general vote of censure on Palmerston's past foreign policy, was passed by a crushing majority, despite his furious resistance. But although the man has been thrown overboard, his principle, upon the whole, has been accepted. Although somewhat checked by the obstructive attributes of the Board of Council, which, in fact, is but the well-paid specter of the old Court of Directors, the power of the executive has, by the formal annexation of India, been raised to such a degree that, to counterpoise it, democratic weight must be thrown into the Parliamentary scale.

[4] A reference to Palmerston's Alien Bill (also called Conspiracy to Murder Bill) of 8 February 1858. It stipulated that any Englishman or foreigner living in the United Kingdom who became party to a conspiracy to murder a person in Britain or any other country, was to be tried by an English court and severely punished. By a majority of votes the House of Commons adopted John Bright's amendment and rejected the bill. Palmerston's government was thereupon compelled to resign.

[5] 'Am a Roman Citizen', an expression used by Palmerston in his speech in the House of Commons on 25 June 1858. Cf. *CW*, Vol. 15, p. 694 n.

[6] An allusion to the Afghan War, 1838–42.

[7] The Anglo-Persian War, 1856–57.

[8] The Second Opium War, 1856–60.

FREDERICK ENGELS

Transport of Troops to India

(*New York Daily Tribune*, August 13, 1858)
London, July 27, 1858

At the beginning of the Anglo-Indian war, two curious questions were mooted – the one relating to the respective superiority of steamers or sailing vessels, the other as to the use of the overland route for the transport of troops. The British Government having decided in favor of sailing vessels against steamers, and for the voyage round the Cape of Good Hope against the overland route, the House of Commons, on the motion of Sir De Lacy Evans,[1] ordered, on the 4th of February 1858, a Committee to be appointed, under the chairmanship of the veteran General, which was to inquire 'concerning the measures resorted to'.[2] The formation of this Committee was completely altered by the intervening change of Ministry, consequent upon which three Palmerstonians were substituted for Lord Stanley and Sir John Pakington.[3] The report of the Committee proving, on the whole, favorable to the late Administration, Gen. Sir De Lacy Evans had a protest printed and circulated, in which he asserts the conclusion arrived at to be at utter variance with the premises from which it pretended to be drawn, and quite inconsistent with the facts and evidence laid before them. An examination of the evidence itself must oblige all impartial persons to fully concur in this view of the case.

The decisive importance of a short line of communication between an army in the field and its base of communication needs no demonstration. During the American War of Independence the principal obstacle England had to grapple with was a sea line of 3,000 miles over which she had to convey her troops, stores and re-enforcements. From Great Britain to the mouths of the Indus and

---

Written on Marx's request, by Engels. The editors changed the title to 'How the Indian War has been Mismanaged' and published it without attribution to Engels or Marx. Here the title is given according to the entry in Marx's notebook for 1858. Cf. CW, Vol. 15, p. 694 n. 579; and CW, Vol. 40, p. 619 n. 325.

[1] Sir George de Lacy Evans (1787–1870); fought against Amir Khan and in the Napoleonic Wars and Crimean War; Liberal politician; elected MP for Westminister, 1846, 1852, 1857.
[2] General de Lacy Evans's speech in the House of Commons, 4 February 1858. *The Times*, 5 February 1858; CW, Vol. 15, p. 590 and n(a).
[3] Sir John Somerset Pakington (1799–1880): statesman, Tory turned Conservative; Secretary for War and the Colonies under Derby in 1852; Secretary for War 1867–68.

Ganges, to Calcutta, Madras, Kurrachee[4] and Bombay, the distance, according to past arrangements, may be reckoned at about 14,000 miles; but the use of steam offered the means of shortening it considerably. Hitherto on all occasions it had been the practice to effect the relief of regiments in India, by this long sea voyage in sailing vessels. This was considered a sufficient reason on the part of the late British Administration, for declaring at the beginning of the Indian troubles, that sailing vessels would still be preferred to steamers for the conveyance of troops. Up to the 10th of July, 1857, of 31 vessels taken up, nearly the whole were sailing ships. Meanwhile, public censure in England and unfavorable news from India effected so much that in the interval from the 10th of July to the 1st of December, among the 59 ships taken up for troops, 29 screw steamers were admitted. Thus a rough test was afforded of the relative qualities of steamers and sailing vessels in accomplishing the transit. According to the return furnished by the Marine Department of the East India Company, giving names of transports, and length of passages to the four principal ports of India, the following may be considered the average results as between steamers and sailing vessels.

From England to Calcutta	*Days*
From August 6 to October 21, 1857, average of steamers, omitting fractions	82
Average of 22 sailing vessels, from June 10 to August 27, 1857	116
Difference in favor of steamers	34
To Madras	
Average of 2 steamers	90
Average of 2 sailing ships	131
Difference in favor of steamers	41
To Bombay	
Average of 5 steamers	76
Average of 9 sailing ships	118
Difference in favor of steamers	42
To Kurrachee	
Average of 3 steamers	91
Average of 10 ships	128
Difference in favor of steamers	37
Average of the whole of the 19 passages by steamers to four ports of India	83
Average passages of 43 sailing ships	120
Difference between average of steam and sailing vessels	37

The same official return, dated Feb. 27, 1858, gives the following details:

	Men
To Calcutta were conveyed by steamers	6,798
By sailing ships	9,489
Total to Calcutta	16,287

---

[4] Modern Karachi, the main commercial city and port of Pakistan.

To Madras, by steamers	2,089
By sailing ships	985
Total to Madras	3,074
To Bombay, by steamers	3,906
By sailing ships	3,439
Total to Bombay	7,345
To Kurrachee, by steamers	1,351
By sailing ships	2,321
Total to Kurrachee	3,672

It appears, then, from the above that 27 steamers carried to the four ports of disembarkation in India 14,144 men, averaging, therefore, 548 men in each ship; that in 55 sailing ships were conveyed 16,234 men, averaging 289 men in each. Now, by the same official statement of averages, it appears that the 14,144 men conveyed in steamers arrived at their respective places of destination on an average of 37 days sooner than the 16,234 men embarked on sailing ships. On the part of the British Admiralty and the other ministerial departments no arguments were adduced in favor of the traditionary transport but precedent and routine, both dating from an epoch when steam navigation was utterly unknown. Lord Palmerston's principal plea, however, for the delay was expense, the cost of steamers in most of the above cases amounting to perhaps treble that of sailing ships. Apart from the fact that this great enhancement of charge for steamers must have gradually diminished after the first unusual demand, and that in so vital an emergency expense ought not to be admitted as an element of calculation, it is evident that the increased cost of transport would have been more than compensated for by the lessened chances of the insurrection.

Still more important than the question of superiority as between steamers and sailing vessels, seems the controversy respecting the voyage round the Cape on the one hand and the overland route on the other; Lord Palmerston affirming the general impracticability of the latter route. A controversy in regard to it between his Board of Control and the East India Directors, appears to have commenced contemporaneously with the first information of the Indian revolt reaching England. The question had, in fact, been solved as long ago as the beginning of this century. In the year 1801, when there were no steam navigation company's agents to aid the military arrangements, and when no railway existed, a large force under Sir David Baird[5] proceeded from India and landed at Kosseir[6] in May and June; crossed in nine days the desert of Kherie, on the Nile;

---

[5] Sir David Baird (1757–1829): ensign in 1772; captain of 73rd Highland light infantry in India under Munro in 1780; joined Colonel Baillie's force, fought against Mysore, captured by Hyder Ali; released in 1784; major general in second war against Tipu Sultan, 1798; stormed Seringapatam, 1799; commanded Indian forces in Egypt against the French 1801–02; returned to India in 1802; resigned and returned to England; served at many places in Europe.

[6] Quseir, Egyptian port on the Red Sea.

proceeded down that river, garrisoned Alexandria, and in the following year, 1802, several regiments returned to India by Suez and the Red Sea, in the month of June. That force, amounting to 5,000 men, consisted of a troop of horse-artillery, six guns and small arms, ammunition, camp equipage, baggage, and 126 chests of treasure. The troops generally were very healthy. The march across the Suez Desert, from the lake of St. Pilgrims,[7] near Grand Cairo to Suez, was performed in four days with the greatest ease, marching by night and encamping during the day. In June the ships proceeded to India, the wind at that season blowing down in Red Sea. They made a very quick passage. Again, during the late Russian war, in the summer of 1854, the 10th and 11th regiments of Dragoons (1,400 horses, 1,600 men) arrived in Egypt from India, and were forwarded thence to the Crimea. These corps, though their transfer took place during the hot months, or monsoon, and though they had to remain some time in Egypt, are known to have been remarkably healthy and efficient, and to have continued so throughout their Crimean service. In the last instance there is the experience of the actual Indian war. After the waste of nearly four months, some thousand troops were dispatched by Egypt with extraordinary advantage as to economy of time, and with perfect preservation of health. The first regiment that was conveyed by this line passed from Plymouth to Bombay in thirty-seven days. Of the first regiment sent from Malta, the first wing arrived at Bombay in sixteen and the second wing in eighteen days. An overwhelming mass of evidence, from numerous trustworthy witnesses, attest the peculiar facilities, especially in periods of emergency, afforded by the overland route transport. Col. Poeklington, Deputy Quartermaster-General, appointed in October, 1857, to direct and superintend the transit of the troops, and who, expressly prepared by order of the War Department a report for the Committee of Inquiry, states:

> The advantages of the overland route are very considerable, and the traject is most simple. A thousand men per week can be conveyed across the isthmus by the Transit administration of Egypt without interference with the ordinary passenger traffic. Between 300 and 400 men can move at a time, and perform the distance from ship to ship in 26 hours. The transit by rail is completed to within almost twenty miles of Suez. This last portion of the journey is performed by the soldiers on donkeys in about six hours. There can be no doubt as to the experiment having succeeded.

The time occupied by troops from England to India is, by the overland route, from 33 to 46 days. From Malta to India, from 16 to 18 or 20 days. Compare these periods with the 83 by steamers, or the 120 by sailing ships, on the long sea route, and the difference will appear striking. Again, during the longer route, Great Britain will have from 15,000 to 20,000 troops, in effect *hors de combat*,[8] and beyond counter orders for a period annually, of from 3 to 4

[7] The lake no longer exists, and its site cannot be traced on current maps.
[8] French: 'out of action'.

months, while, with the shorter line, it will be but for the brief period of some 14 days, during the transit from Suez to India, that the troops will be beyond reach of recall, for any unexpected European contingency.

In resorting to the overland route only 4 months after the outbreak of the Indian war, and then only for a mere handful of troops, Palmerston set at naught the general anticipation of India and Europe. The Governor-General in India assumed that the Home Government would dispatch troops by the way of Egypt. The following is a passage from the Governor-General in Council's letter to the Home Government, dated 7 August 1857: 'We are also in communication with the Peninsular and Oriental Steam Navigation Company for the conveyance from Suez of the troops that may possibly have been dispatched to India by that route.'

On the very day of the arrival at Constantinople of the news of the revolt, Lord Stratford de Redcliffe telegraphed to London to know whether he should apply to the Turkish Government to allow the British troops to pass through Egypt, on their way to India. The Sultan[9] having meanwhile offered and transmitted a firman to that effect on the 2nd of July, Palmerston replied by telegraph, that it was not his intention to send troops by that route. It being in France likewise assumed, as a matter of course, that the acceleration of the military re-enforcements must at that moment form the paramount object of British policy, Bonaparte spontaneously tendered permission for the passage over France of British troops, to enable their being embarked, if deemed desirable, at Marseilles, for Egypt. The Pasha of Egypt[10] lastly, when, at length, Mr Holton, the Superintendent of the Peninsular and Oriental Company in Egypt, was authorized to reply on the subject, answered immediately, 'It would be a satisfaction to him to give facility to the passage of not only 200 men, as in the present instance, but to that of 20,000, if necessary, and not *en bourgeois*[11] but in uniform, and with their arms, if required.'

Such were the facilities recklessly thrown away, the proper use of which might have prevented the Indian war from assuming its formidable dimensions. The motives by which Lord Palmerston was prompted in preferring sailing vessels to steamers, and a line of communication extending over 14,000 miles to one limited to 4,000 miles, belong to the mysteries of contemporaneous history.

[9] Abdul Majeed.
[10] Sayeed Pasha.
[11] In civilian clothes.

History of the Opium Trade [1]

(*New York Daily Tribune*, September 20, 1858. Printed as a leading article.)

The news of the new treaty wrung from China by the allied Plenipotentiaries has, it would appear, conjured up the same wild vistas of an immense extension of trade which danced before the eyes of the commercial mind in 1845, after the conclusion of the first Chinese war. Supposing the Petersburg wires to have spoken truth, is it quite certain that an increase of the Chinese trade must follow upon the multiplication of its emporiums? Is there any probability that the war of 1857–58 will lead to more splendid results than the war of 1841–42? So much is certain that the treaty of 1843, instead of increasing American and English exports to China proved instrumental only in precipitating and aggravating the commercial crisis of 1847. In a similar way, by raising dreams of an inexhaustible market and by fostering false speculations, the present treaty may help preparing a new crisis at the very moment when the market of the world is but slowly recovering from the recent universal shock. Beside its negative result, the first opium-war succeeded in stimulating the opium trade at the expense of legitimate commerce, and so will this second opium-war do, if England be not forced by the general pressure of the civilized world to abandon the compulsory opium cultivation in India and the armed opium propaganda to China. We forbear dwelling on the morality of that trade, described by Montgomery Martin, himself an Englishman,[1] in the following terms:

> Why, the slave trade was merciful compared with the opium trade: We did not destroy the bodies of the Africans, for it was our immediate interest to keep them alive; we did not debase their natures, corrupt their minds, nor destroy their souls. But the opium seller slays the body after he has corrupted, degraded, and annihilated the moral being of unhappy sinners, while every hour is bringing new victims to a Moloch which knows no satiety, and where the English murderer and Chinese suicide vie with each other in offerings at his shrine.

The heading of this article is provided in CW, Vol. 16, p. 13, from Marx's Notebook for 1858.

[1] Montgomery Martin (*c*. 1803–1868) was a well-known writer on India. The quotation that follows has been traced by Dona Torr, *Marx on China*, p. 117, and the editors of CW, Vol. 16, p. 14 n., to Martin's *China: Political, Commercial and Social*, II (London, 1847), p. 261.

The Chinese cannot take both goods and drug: under actual circumstances, extension of the Chinese trade resolves into extension of the opium trade; the growth of the latter is incompatible with the development of legitimate commerce – these propositions were pretty generally admitted two years ago. A Committee of the House of Commons, appointed in 1847 to take into consideration the state of British commercial intercourse with China, reported thus:

> We regret that the trade with that country has been for some time in a very unsatisfactory condition, and that the *result of our extended intercourse has by no means realized the just expectations* which had naturally been founded in a *free access to so magnificent a market.* We find that the difficulties of the trade do not arise from any want of demand in China for articles of British manufacturers, or from the increasing competition of other nations; the *payment for opium* absorbs the silver to the great inconvenience of the general traffic of the Chinese, and tea and silk must in fact pay the rest.

The Friend of China, of July 28, 1849, generalizing the same proposition, says in set terms:

> The opium trade progresses steadily. The increased consumption of teas and silk in Great Britain and the United States would merely result in the increase of the opium trade; the case of the manufacturers is hopeless.

One of the leading American merchants in China reduced, in an article inserted in Hunt's *Merchant's Magazine*, for January, 1850, the whole question of the trade with China to this point:

> Which branch of commerce is to be suppressed, the opium trade or the export trade of American or English produce?

The Chinese themselves took exactly the same view of the case. Montgomery Martin narrates:

> I inquired of the Taoutai at Shanghai which would be the best means of increasing our commerce with China, and his first answer to me, in presence of Capt. Balfour, Her Majesty's Consul, was: 'Cease to send us so much opium and we will be able to take your manufactures'.[2]

The history of general commerce during the last eight years has, in a new and striking manner, illustrated these positions; but, before analyzing the deleterious effects on legitimate commerce of the opium trade, we propose giving a short review of the rise and progress of that stupendous traffic, which, whether we regard the tragical collisions forming, so to say, the axis round which it turns, or the effects produced by it on the general relations of the Eastern and Western worlds, stands solitary on record in the annals of mankind.

[2] Ibid., p. 258.

Previous to 1767 the quantity of opium exported from India did not exceed 200 chests, the chest weighing about 133 lbs. Opium was legally admitted in China on the payment of a duty of about $3 per chest, as a medicine; the Portuguese who brought it from Turkey being its almost exclusive importers into the Celestial Empire.

In 1773, Colonel Watson and Vice-President Wheeler – persons deserving to take a place among the Hermentiers, Palmers and other poisoners of world-wide fame – suggested to the East India Company the idea of entering upon the opium traffic with China. Consequently, there was established a depot for opium in vessels anchored in a bay to the southeast of Macao. The speculation proved a failure. In 1781 the Bengal Government sent an armed vessel, laden with opium, to China; and, in 1794, the Company stationed a large opium vessel at Whampoa, the anchorage for the port of Canton. It seems that Whampoa proved a more convenient depot than Macao, because, only two years after its selection, the Chinese Government found it necessary to pass a law which threatens Chinese smugglers of opium to be beaten with a bamboo and exposed in the streets with wooden collars around their necks. About 1798, the East India Company ceased to be direct exporters of opium, but they became its producers. The opium monopoly was established in India; while the Company's own ships were hypocritically forbidden from trafficking in the drug, the licenses it granted for private ships trading to China contained a provision which attached a penalty to them if freighted with opium of other than the Company's own make.

In 1800, the import into China had reached the number of 2,000 chests. Having, during the eighteenth century, borne the aspect common to all feuds between the foreign merchant and the national custom-house, the struggle between the East India Company and the Celestial Empire assumed, since the beginning of the nineteenth century, features quite distinct and exceptional; while the Chinese Emperor, in order to check the suicide of his people, prohibited at once the import of the poison by the foreigner, and its consumption by the natives, the East India Company was rapidly converting the cultivation of opium in India, and its contraband sale to China, into integral parts of its own financial system. While the semi-barbarian stood on the principle of morality, the civilized opposed the principle of pelf. That a giant empire, containing almost one-third of the human race, vegetating to the teeth of time, insulated by the forced exclusion of general intercourse, and thus contriving to dupe itself with delusions of Celestial perfection – that such an empire should at last be overtaken by the fate on occasion of a deadly duel, in which the representative of the antiquated world appears prompted by ethical motives, while the representative of overwhelming modern society fights for the privilege of buying in the cheapest and selling in the dearest markets – this, indeed, is a sort of tragical couplet, stranger than any poet would ever have dared to fancy.

History of the Opium Trade [2]

(*New York Daily Tribune*, September 25, 1858. Printed as a leading article.)

It was the assumption of the opium monopoly in India by the British Government, which led to the proscription of the opium trade in China. The cruel punishments inflicted by the Celestial legislator[1] upon his own contumacious subjects, and the stringent prohibition established at the China custom-houses, proved alike nugatory. The next effect of the moral resistance of the Chinaman was the demoralization, by the Englishman, of the Imperial authorities, custom-house offices and mandarins generally. The corruption that ate into the heart of the Celestial bureaucracy, and destroyed the bulwark of the patriarchal constitution, was, together with the opium chests, smuggled into the Empire from the English storeships anchored at Whampoa.

Nurtured by the East India Company, vainly combatted by the Central Government at Pekin, the opium trade gradually assumed larger proportions, until it absorbed about $2,500,000 in 1816. The throwing open in that year of the Indian commerce, with the single exception of the tea trade, which still continues to be monopolized by the East India Company, gave a new and powerful stimulus to the operations of the English contrabandists. In 1820, the number of chests smuggled into China had increased to 5,147; in 1821, to 7,000, and in 1824 to 12,639. Meanwhile, the Chinese Government, at the same time that it addressed threatening remonstrances to the foreign merchants, punished the Hong merchants,[2] known as their abettors, developed an unwonted activity in its prosecution of the native opium consumers, and, at its custom-houses, put into practice more stringent measures. The final result, like that of similar exertions in 1794, was to drive the opium depots from a precarious to a more convenient basis of operations. Macao and Whampoa were abandoned for the Island of Lintin, at the entrance of the Canton River, there to become permanently established in vessels armed to the teeth, and well manned. In the same way, when the Chinese Government temporarily succeeded in stopping the operations of the old Canton houses, the trade only shifted hands, and passed to a lower class of men, prepared to carry it on at all hazards and by whatever means. Thanks to the greater facilities thus afforded, the opium trade increased during the ten years from 1824 to 1834 from 12,639 to 21,785 chests.

[1] The Qing Emperor of China.
[2] Chinese merchants' guild dealing with foreign merchants.

Like the years 1800, 1816 and 1824, the year 1834 marks an epoch in the history of the opium trade. The East India Company then lost not only its privilege of trading in Chinese tea, but had to discontinue and abstain from all commercial business whatever. It being thus transformed from a mercantile into a merely government establishment, the trade to China became completely thrown open to English private enterprise, which pushed on with such vigor that, in 1837, 39,000 chests of opium, valued at $25,000,000, were successfully smuggled into China, despite the desperate resistance of the Celestial Government. Two facts here claim our attention: First, that of every step in the progress of the export trade to China since 1816, a disproportionately large part progressively fell upon the opium-smuggling branch; and secondly, that hand in hand with the gradual extinction of the ostensible mercantile interest of the Anglo-Indian Government in the opium trade, grew the importance of its fiscal interest in that illicit traffic. In 1837 the Chinese Government had at last arrived at a point where decisive action could no longer be delayed. The continuous drain of silver, caused by the opium importations, had begun to derange the exchequer, as well as the moneyed circulation of the Celestial Empire. Heu Naetse, one of the most distinguished Chinese statesmen, proposed to legalize the opium trade and make money out of it; but after a full deliberation, in which all the high officers of the Empire shared, and which extended over a period of more than a year's duration, the Chinese Government decided that, 'On account of the injuries it inflicted on the people, the nefarious traffic should not be legalized.' As early as 1830, a duty of 25 per cent would have yielded a revenue of $3,850,000. In 1837, it would have yielded double that sum, but then the Celestial barbarian declined laying a tax sure to rise in proportion to the degradation of his people. In 1853, Hien-Fung, the present Emperor, under still more distressed circumstances, and with the full knowledge of the futility of all efforts at stopping the increasing import of opium, persevered in the stern policy of his ancestors. Let me remark, *en passant*, that by persecuting the opium consumption as a heresy the Emperor gave its traffic all the advantages of a religious propaganda. The extraordinary measures of the Chinese Government during the years 1837, 1838 and 1839, which culminated in Commissioner Lin's arrival at Canton, and the confiscation and destruction, by his orders, of the smuggled opium, afforded the pretext for the first Anglo-Chinese rebellion, the utter exhaustion of the Imperial exchequer, the successful encroachment of Russia from the North, and the gigantic dimensions assumed by the opium trade in the South. Although proscribed in the treaty with which England terminated a war, commenced and carried on in its defense, the opium trade has practically enjoyed perfect impunity since 1843. The importation was estimated, in 1856, at about $35,000,000, while, in the same year, the Anglo-Indian Government drew a revenue of $25,000,000, just the sixth part of its total State income, from the opium monopoly. The pretexts on which the second opium war has been undertaken are of too recent date to need any commentary.

We cannot leave this part of the subject without singling out one flagrant self-contradiction of the Christianity-canting and civilization-mongering British Government. In its imperial capacity it affects to be a thorough stranger to the contraband opium trade, and even to enter into treaties proscribing it. Yet, in its Indian capacity, it forces the opium cultivation upon Bengal, to the great damage of the productive resources of that country; compels one part of the Indian ryots to engage in the poppy culture; entices another part into the same by dint of money advances; keeps the wholesale manufacture of the deleterious drug a close monopoly in its hands; watches by a whole army of official spies its growth, its delivery at appointed places, its inspissation and preparation for the taste of the Chinese consumers, its formation into packages especially adapted to the conveniency of smuggling, and finally its conveyance to Calcutta, where it is put up at auction at the Government sales, and made over by the State officers to the speculators, thence to pass into the hands of the contrabandists who land it in China. The chest costing the British Government about 250 rupees is sold at the Calcutta auction mart at a price ranging from 1,210 to 1,600 rupees. But not yet satisfied with this matter of fact complicity, the same Government, to this hour, enters into express profit and loss accounts with the merchants and shippers, who embark in the hazardous operation of poisoning an empire.

The Indian finances of the British Government have, in fact, been made to depend not only on the opium trade with China, but on the contraband character of that trade. Were the Chinese Government to legalize the opium trade simultaneously with tolerating the cultivation of the poppy in China, the Anglo-Indian exchequer would experience a serious catastrophe. While openly preaching free trade in poison, it secretly defends the monopoly of its manufacture. Whenever we look closely into the nature of British free trade, monopoly is pretty generally found to lie at the bottom of its 'freedom'.

FREDERICK ENGELS

[The Revolt in India]

(*New York Daily Tribune*, October 1, 1858. Printed as a leading article.)

The campaign in India has been almost completely suspended during the hot and rainy summer months. Sir Colin Campbell having secured, by a vigorous effort in the beginning of summer, all the important positions in Oude and Rohilcund, very wisely put his troops into quarters, leaving the open country in the possession of the insurgents, and limiting his efforts to maintaining his communications. The only episode of interest which occurred during this period in Oude was the excursion of Sir Hope Grant to Shahgunge for the relief of Maun Singh,[1] a native chief, who, after a deal of tergiversation, had lately made his peace with the British, and was now blockaded by his late native allies. The excursion proved a mere military promenade, though it must have caused great loss to the British by sunstroke and cholera. The natives dispersed without showing fight, and Maun Singh joined the British. The easy success of this expedition, though it cannot be taken as an indication of an equally easy subjection of the whole of Oude, shows that the insurgents have lost heart completely. If it was the interest of the British to rest during the hot weather, it was the interest of the insurgents to disturb them as much as possible. But instead of organizing an active guerrilla warfare, intercepting the communications between the towns held by the enemy, of waylaying small parties, harassing the foragers, of rendering impassable the supply of victuals, without which no large town held by the British could live – instead of this, the natives have been satisfied with levying revenue and enjoying the leisure left to them by their opponents. Better still, they appear to have squabbled among themselves. Neither do they appear to have profited by the few quiet weeks to reorganize their forces, to refill their ammunition stores, or to replace the lost artillery. The bolt at Shahgunge shows a still

Written by Engels at Marx's request. Title as given in CW, Vol. 15. No title in the *New York Daily Tribune* (*NYDT*). In Av.: 'Internal Failure of Insurrection in Oude – Final Defeat of the Indian Revolt'.

[1] Man Singh, a brahman, was in confinement at Faizabad in 1857; released from imprisonment by the British, he helped them during 1857–58. His duplicity angered the Rebels who besieged Man Singh at Shahganj, his headquarters. He was then rescued by Hope Grant (DG, Faizabad). See Grant, *Incidents in the Sepoy War*, p. 77. Also see Sleeman, *Journey*, Vol. I, p. 63; and Gubbins, *Account of the Mutinies*, pp. 323–25.

greater want of confidence in themselves and their leaders than any previous defeat. In the meantime, a secret correspondence is carried on between the majority of the chiefs and the British Government, who have after all found it rather impracticable to pocket the whole of the soil of Oude, and are quite willing to let the former owners have it again on reasonable terms. Thus, as the final success of the British is now beyond all doubt, the insurrection in Oude bids fair to die out without passing through a period of active guerrilla warfare. As soon as the majority of the landholders come to terms with the British, the insurgent bodies will be broken up, and those who have too much to fear from the Government will turn robbers (dacoits) in the capture of whom the peasantry will gladly assist.

South-west of Oude the Jugdispore jungles appear to offer center for such dacoits. These impenetrable forests of bamboo and underwood are held by a party of insurgents under Ummer Singh,[2] who shows rather more activity and knowledge of guerrilla warfare; at all events, he attacks the British whenever he can, instead of quietly waiting for them. If, as it is feared, part of the Oude insurgents should join him before he can be expelled from his stronghold, the British may expect rather harder work they have had of late. These jungles have now for nearly eight months served as a retreat to insurgent parties, who have been able to render very insecure the Grand Trunk Road from Calcutta to Allahabad, the main communication of the British.

In Western India, the Gwalior insurgents are still followed up by Gen. Roberts and Col. Holmes. At the time of the capture of Gwalior, it was a question of much consequence, what direction the retreating army might take; for the whole of the Mahratta country and part of Rajpootana appeared ready for a rising as soon as a sufficiently strong body of regular troops arrived there to form a nucleus for the insurrection. A retreat of the Gwalior force in a south-westerly direction then seemed the most likely maneuver to realize such a result. But the insurgents, from reasons which we cannot guess at from the reports before us, have chosen a north-westerly direction. They went to Jeypore,[3] thence turning south toward Oodeypore,[4] trying to gain the road to the Mahratta country. But this roundabout marching gave Roberts an opportunity of coming up with them, and defeating them totally without any great effort. The remnants of this body, without guns, without organization and ammunition, without leaders of repute, are not the men who are likely to induce fresh risings. On the contrary, the immense quantity of plunder which they carry along with them, and which hampers all their movements, appears already to have excited the avidity of the

---

[2] Amar Singh, son of Sahibzada Singh, the famous rebel leader. The youngest brother of Kunwar Singh of Jagdishpur, he commanded the Shahabad forces after the death of Kunwar Singh; captured and imprisoned by the British at Gorakhpur, he died on 3 January 1860. See K.K. Datta, *Biography of Kunwar Singh and Amar Singh* (Patna, 1957), p. 24.

[3] Jaipur in Rajasthan.

[4] Udaipur in Rajasthan.

peasantry. Every straggling Sepoy is killed and eased of his load of gold mohurs. If it has come to that, Gen. Roberts may safely leave the final dispersion of these Sepoys to the country population. The loot of Scindhiah's treasures by his troops saves the British from a renewal of the insurrection in a quarter more dangerous than Hindostan; for a rising in the Mahratta country would put the Bombay army upon a rather severe trial.

There is a fresh mutiny in the neighbourhood of Gwalior. A small vassal of Scindhiah, Maun Singh[5] (not the Maun Singh of Oude) has joined the insurgents, and got hold of the small fortress of Paoree. This place is, however, already invested by the British, and must soon be captured. In the meantime, the conquered districts are gradually pacified. The neighbourhood of Delhi, it is said, has been so completely tranquillized by Sir J. Lawrence that a European may travel about with perfect safety, unarmed, and without an escort. The secret of the matter is, that the people of every village have been made collectively responsible for any crime or outrage committed on its ground; that a military police has been organized; and, above all, that the summary justice of the Court-Martial, so peculiarly impressive upon Orientals, is every-where in full swing. Still, this success appears to be the exception, as we do not hear anything of the kind from other districts. The complete pacification of Rohilcund and Oude, of Bundelcund and many other large provinces, must yet require a very long time and give plenty of work yet to British troops and Court-Martials.

But while the insurrection of Hindostan dwindles down to dimensions which deprive it of almost all military interest, there has occured an event far off, at the utmost frontiers of Afghanistan, which is big with the threat of future difficulties. A conspiracy to murder their officers and to rise against the British has been discovered among several Sikh regiments at Dera Ismael Khan. How far this conspiracy was ramified, we cannot tell. Perhaps it was merely a local affair, arising among a peculiar class of Sikhs; but we are not in a position to assert this. At all events, this is highly dangerous symptom. There are now nearly 100,000[6] Sikhs in the British service, and we have heard how saucy they are; they fight, they say, to-day for the British, but may fight tomorrow against them, as it may please God. Brave, passionate, fickle, they are even more subject to sudden and unexpected impulses than other Orientals. If mutiny should break out in earnest among them, then would the British indeed have hard work to keep their own. The Sikhs were always the most formidable opponents of the British among the natives of India; they have formed a comparatively powerful empire; they are of peculiar sect of Brahminism, and hate both Hindoos and Mussulmans. They have seen the British 'raj' in the utmost peril; they have contributed a great

[5] Rajput chief of Narwar, who joined Tantia Tope after having been dislodged by the British. But defecting to the British, he played a key role in the plot to capture Tantia Tope. See S.N. Sen, *Eighteen Fifty Seven* (New Delhi, 1957), p. 373; S.A.A. Rizvi, *Freedom Struggle in Uttar Pradesh*, Vol. III (Lucknow, 1957), pp. 560–61.
[6] This figure seems exaggerated.

deal to restore it, and they are even convinced that their own share of the work was the decisive one. What is more natural than that they should harbor the idea that the time has come when the British raj shall be replaced by a Sikh raj, that a Sikh Emperor is to rule India from Delhi or Calcutta? It may be that this idea is still far from being matured among the Sikhs, it may be that they are so cleverly distributed that they are balanced by Europeans, so that any rising could be easily put down; but that this idea exists among them must be clear, we presume, to everybody who has read the accounts of the behavior of the Sikhs after Delhi and Lucknow.

Still, for the present, the British have reconquered India. The great rebellion, stirred up by the mutiny of the Bengal army, is indeed, it appears, dying out. But this second conquest has not increased England's hold upon the mind of the Indian people. The cruelty of the retribution dealt out by the British troops, goaded on by exaggerated and false reports of the atrocities attributed to the natives, and the attempt at confiscating the Kingdom of Oude, both wholesale and retail, have not created any particular fondness for the victors. On the contrary, they themselves confess that among both Hindoos and Mussulmans, the hereditary hatred against the Christian intruder is more fierce than ever. Impotent as this hatred may be at present, it is not without its significance and importance, while that menacing cloud is resting over the Sikh Punjaub. And this is not all. The two great Asiatic powers, England and Russia, have by this time got hold of one point between Siberia and India, where Russian and English interests must come into direct collision. That point is Pekin. Thence westward a line will ere long be drawn across the breath of the Asiatic Continent, on which this collision of rival interests will constantly take place. Thus the time may indeed not be so very distant when 'the Sepoy and the Cossack will meet in the plains of the Oxus,' and if that meeting is to take place, the anti-British passions of 150,000[7] native Indians will be a matter of serious consideration.

[7] Rect. 150,000,000 – the usual figure of the population of India officially given out at this time.

New York Daily Tribune 1859

Great Trouble in Indian Finance

(*New York Daily Tribune*, April 30, 1859. From an Occasional Correspondent.)
London, April 8, 1859

The Indian financial crisis, which at this moment shares with the war rumors and the electioneering agitation in the privilege of absorbing public interest in England, must be considered in a double point of view. It involves both a temporary necessity and a permanent difficulty.

On the 15th of February Lord Stanley brought in a bill in the House of Commons authorizing the Government to raise a loan of £7,000,000 in England, in order to adjust the extra expenditure of the Indian administration for the current year. About six weeks later, John Bull's self-congratulations as to the small cost of the Indian rebellion were roughly interrupted by the arrival of the Overland Mail, conveying a cry of financial distress from the Government at Calcutta. On March 25, Lord Derby rose in the House of Lords to state that a further loan for India of £5,000,000, in addition to the £7,000,000 loan now before Parliament, would be required to meet the demands of the present year, and that even then, certain claims for compensation and prize money, amounting to £2,000,000 at least, would remain to be paid from some source not yet apparent. To make things pleasant, Lord Stanley had, in his first statement, only provided for the wants of the Indian Treasury at London, leaving the British Government in India to its own resources, which, from the dispatches received, he could not but know to be far from sufficient. Quite apart from the expenses of the Home Government, or the Indian administration at London, Lord Canning estimated the deficit of the Government at Calcutta, for the current year of 1859–60 at £12,000,000, after allowing an increase in the ordinary revenue of £800,000, and a decrease on military charges of £2,000,000. Such was his penury that he had stopped paying part of his civil service; such was his credit that the Government 5 per cents were quoted at 12 percent discount; and such was his distress that he could only be saved from bankruptcy by the shipment from England to India of £3,000,000 of silver within a few months. Three points thus become evident. First: Lord Stanley's original statement was a 'dodge', and, so far from embracing all the Indian liabilities, did not even touch the immediate wants of

See Marx's letter to Engels dated 1 April 1859, in *CW*, Vol. 40, pp. 410–11. Included in *CW*, Vol. 16, pp. 279–86, and in Av., but not in *On Colonialism* and *FIWI*.

the Indian Government in India. Secondly: During the whole period of the insurrection, if we except the sending from London in 1857 of £1,000,000 of silver to
India, the Calcutta Government was left to shift for itself, to provide out of its
own resources for the main part of the extraordinary war charges which, of
course, had to be disbursed in India, for the barrack accommodation of some
60,000 additional Europeans, for the restoration of the treasures plundered, and
for the replacing of all the revenues of the local Administrations which had been
swept away. Thirdly: There is, apart from the wants of the Home Government, a
deficit of £12,000,000, to be met in the present year. By operations, the questionable nature of which we forbear to dwell upon, the sum is to be reduced to
£9,000,000, of which sum £5,000,000 are to be borrowed in India and £4,000,000
in England. Of the latter, £1,000,000 in silver bullion has already been shipped
to Calcutta from London, and £2,000,000 more is to be dispatched in the shortest
possible period.

It will be seen from this succinct statement that the Indian Government
was very[1] unfairly dealt with by its English masters, who left it in the lurch, in
order to throw dust in the eyes of John Bull; but it must, on the other hand, be
admitted that the financial operations of Lord Canning surpass in awkwardness
even his military and political exploits. Up to the end of January, 1859, he had
contrived to raise the necessary means by loans in India, issued partly in Government stocks, partly in Treasury bills; but, strange to say, while his efforts had
answered during the epoch of the revolution, they failed entirely from the moment English authority was restored by the force of arms. And not only did they
fail, but there was a panic in regard to Government securities; there was an
unprecedented depreciation in all funds, with protests from the Chambers of
Commerce at Bombay and Calcutta, and, in the latter town, public meetings
composed of English and native money-mongers, denouncing the vacillation, the
arbitrary nature and the helpless imbecility of the Government measures. Now,
the loanable capital of India which up to January, 1859, had supplied the Government with funds, began to fail after that period, when the power of borrowing
seems to have been exceeded. In point of fact the aggregate loans which from
1841 to 1857 amounted to £21,000,000, absorbed in the two years of 1857 and
1858 alone about £9,000,000, equal to almost one-half of the money borrowed
during the previous sixteen years. Such a failure of resources, while accounting
for the necessity of successively screwing up the rate of interest on Government
loans from 4 to 6 percent, is, of course, far from explaining the commercial panic
in the Indian security market, and the utter inability of the Governor-General to
meet the most urgent requirements. The riddle is solved by the fact that it has
become a regular maneuver with Lord Canning, to bring out new loans at higher
rates of interest than those given on existing open loans, without any previous
notice to the public, and with the utmost uncertainty prevailing as to the further

---

[1] Omitted in Av.

financial operations contemplated. The depreciation of the funds, in consequence of these maneuvers, had been calculated at not less than £11,000,000. Pinched by the poverty of the Exchequer, frightened by the panic in the stock market, and roused by the protests on the part of the Chambers of Commerce and the Calcutta meetings, Lord Canning thought best to be a good boy and to try to come up to the desiderata of the monetary mind; but his notification of the 21st of February, 1859, shows again that the human understanding does not depend on human will. What was he required to do? Not to open simultaneously two loans on different conditions, and to tell the monetary public at once the sum required for the current year, instead of deceiving them by successive announcements, one contradictory of the other. And what does he do in his notification? In the first instance he says that there is to be raised by loan in the Indian market for the year 1859–60, £5,000,000, at 5–1/2 percent, and that 'when this amount shall have been realized, the loan of 1859–60 shall be closed, and no further loan will be opened in India during that year.' In the very same proclamation, sweeping away the entire value of the assurances just given, he proceeds: 'No loan carrying a higher rate of interest, will be opened in India in the course of the year 1859–60, unless under instructions from the Home Government.'

But that is not all. He opens, in fact, a *double loan* on different terms. While announcing that 'the issue of Treasury bills on the terms notified on Jan. 26, 1859, will be closed on April 30,' he proclaims 'that a new issue of Treasury bills will be notified from the 1st of May', bearing interest of nearly $5^{3/4}$ percent, and redeemable at the expiration of one year from the date of issue. Both loans are kept open together, while, at the same time the loan opened in January has not yet been concluded. The only financial matter which Lord Canning seems able to comprehend is that his annual salary amounts to £20,000 in name, and to about £40,000 in fact. Hence, despite the sneers of the Derby Cabinet, and his notorious incapacity, he sticks to his post from 'a feeling of duty'.

The effects of the Indian financial crisis on the English home market have already become apparent. In the first instance, the silver remittances on account of Government coming to swell the large remittances on mercantile account, and falling at an epoch when the ordinary silver supplies from Mexico are held back in consequence of the distracted condition of that country, have, of course, sent up the price of bar silver. On March 25, it has risen to the facticious price of $62^{3/4}$d. per ounce standard, causing such an influx of silver from every part of Europe that the price in London again fell to $62^{2/3}$d.; while the rate of discount at Hamburg rose from 2–1/2 to 3 percent. Consequent upon these heavy importations of silver, exchanges have turned against England, and a drain of gold bullion has set in, which for the present only relieves the London money market of the plethora, but in the long run may seriously affect it, coupled, as it will be, with large Continental loans. The depreciation, however, on the London money market, of the Indian Government stocks and guaranteed railway securities, prejudicial as it must prove to the Government and railway loans still to be brought forward in the course of this season, is certainly the most serious effect on the home market as yet resulting from the Indian financial crisis. The shares of many Indian railways, although 5 percent interest upon them is guaranteed by the Government are now at 2 or 3 percent discount.

Taking all in all, however, I regard the momentary Indian financial panic as a matter of secondary importance, if compared with the general crisis of the Indian Exchequer, which I may perhaps consider on another occasion.

London, April 12, 1859

The latest overland mail, so far from showing any abatement of the financial crisis in India, reveals a state of derangement hardly anticipated. The shifts to which the Indian Government is driven in order to meet its most urgent wants, may be best illustrated by a recent measure of the Governor of Bombay. Bombay is the market where the opium of Malwa, averaging 30,000 chests annually, finds its outlet by monthly installments of 2,000 or 3,000 chests, for which bills are drawn upon Bombay. By charging 400 rupees upon every chest imported into Bombay, the Government raises a revenue of £1,200,000 annually on Malwa opium. Now, to replenish his exhausted exchequer, and ward off immediate bankruptcy, the Bombay Governor has issued a notification, which raises the duty on each chest of Malwa opium from 400 to 500 rupees; but at the same time, he declares that this increased duty will not be levied till after the 1st of July, so that the holders of opium in Malwa have the privilege of bringing in the drug under the old duties for four months longer. Between the middle of March, when the notification was issued, and the 1st of July, there are only two months and a half during which opium can be imported, the monsoon setting in on the 15th of June. The holders of opium in Malwa will, of course, avail themselves of the interval allowed them for sending in opium at the old duty; and, consequently, during the two months and a half pour all their stock in hand into the Presidency. Since the balance of opium, of the old and new crops, remaining at Malwa amounts to 26,000 chests, and the price of Malwa opium reaches 1,250 rupees per chest, the Malwa merchants will have to draw upon the Bombay merchants for no less a sum than £3,000,000 of which more than £1,000,000 must come into the Bombay Treasury. The aim of this financial dodge is transparent. With a view to anticipate the annual revenue from the opium duty, and induce the dealers in the article to pay it at once, an enhancement of the duty is held out prospectively *in terrorem*. While it would be quite superfluous to expatiate upon the empirical character of this contrivance, which fills the Exchequer for the present by creating a corresponding void a few months hence, no more striking instance could be given of the exhaustion of ways and means, on the part of the great Mogul's successors.

Let us now turn to the general state of Indian finance, as it has grown out of the late insurrection. According to the last official accounts the net revenue derived by the British from their Indian firm amounts to £23,208,000, say,

£24,000,000. This annual revenue has never sufficed to defray the annual expenses. From 1836 to 1850 the net deficit amounted to £1,000,000 annually. Even in the year 1856, when the Exchequer was exceptionally filled by the wholesale annexations, robberies and extortions of Lord Dalhousie, the income and expense did not exactly square, but, on the contrary, a deficit of about a quarter of a million was added to the usual crop of deficits. In 1857 the deficiency was £9,000,000, in 1858 it amounted to £13,000,000, and in 1859 it is estimated by the Indian Government itself at £12,000,000. The first conclusion, then, which we arrive at is that even under ordinary circumstances, deficits were accumulating, and that under extraordinary circumstances they must assume such dimensions as to reach one-half and more of the annual income.

The question which next presents itself is, To what degree has this already-existing gap between the expenses and the income of the Indian Government been widened by recent events? The new permanent debt of India accruing from the suppression of the mutiny is calculated by the most sanguine English financiers at between forty and fifty millions sterling, while Mr Wilson[2] estimates the permanent deficit, or the annual interest for this new debt to be defrayed out of the annual revenue, at not less than three millions. However, it would be a great mistake to think that this permanent deficit of three millions is the only legacy left by the insurgents to their vanquishers. The costs of the insurrection are not only in the past tense, but are in a high degree prospective. Even in quiet times, before the outbreak of the mutiny, the military charges swallowed sixty per cent at least of the aggregate regular income, since they exceeded £12,000,000; but the state of affairs is now changed. At the beginning of the mutiny the European force in India amounted to 38,000 effective men, while the native army mustered 260,000 men. The military forces at present employed in India amount to 112,000 Europeans and 320,000 native troops including the native police. It may be justly said that these extraordinary numbers will be reduced to a more moderate standard with the disappearance of the extraordinary circumstances which swelled them to their present size. Yet the military commission appointed by the British Government has arrived at the conclusion that there will be required in India a permanent European force of 80,000 men, with a native force of 200,000 men – the military charges being thus raised to almost double their original height. During the debates on the Indian finances, in the House of Lords, on April 7, two points were admitted by all speakers of authority: on the one hand that an annual expenditure upon the revenue of India little short of twenty millions for the army alone was incompatible with a net revenue of twenty-four millions only; and, on the other hand, that it was difficult to imagine a state of things which for an indefinite series of years would render it safe for the English to leave India without a European force double its amount before the outbreak of

---

[2] James Wilson (1805–1860): politician and economist, founder of the famous journal, *Economist* (1843); financial member of the Council of India (1859), in which capacity he established a paper currency in India, and imposed the income tax.

the mutiny. But suppose even that it would do to add permanently to the European forces not more than one third of their original strength, and we get a new annual permanent deficit of four millions sterling at least. The new permanent deficit, then, derived on one hand from the consolidated debt contracted during the mutiny, and on the other hand from the permanent increase of the British forces in India, cannot, on the most moderate calculation, fall below seven millions sterling.

To this must be added two other items – the one accruing from an increase of liabilities, the other from a diminution of income. By a recent statement of the Railway Department of the Indian office at London, it results that the whole length of railways sanctioned for India is 4,817 miles, of which 559 miles only are yet opened. The whole amount of capital invested by the different railway companies amounts to £40,000,000 sterling, of which £19,000,000 are paid and £21,000,000 are still to be called in – 96 percent of the aggregate sum having been subscribed in England and 4 percent only in India. Upon this amount of £40,000,000, the Government has guaranteed 5 percent interest, so that the annual interest charged upon the revenues of India reaches £2,000,000, to be paid before the railways are in working order, and before they can yield any return. The Earl of Ellenborough estimates the loss accruing to the Indian finances from this source, for the next three years to come, at £6,000,000 sterling, and the ultimate permanent deficit upon these railways at half a million annually. Lastly, of the £24,000,000 of Indian net revenue, a sum of £3,619,000 is derived from the sale of opium to foreign countries – a source of revenue which, it is now generally admitted, must to a considerable extent be impaired by the late treaty with China. It becomes, then, evident, that apart from the extra expenditure still necessitated to complete the suppression of the mutiny, an annual permanent deficit of £8,000,000 at least, will have to be defrayed out of a net revenue of £24,000,000, which the Government may, perhaps, by the imposition of new taxes, contrive to raise to £26,000,000. The necessary result of this state of things will be to saddle the English taxpayer with the liability for the Indian debt, and, as Sir G.C. Lewis[3] declared in the House of Commons, 'to vote four or five millions annually as a subsidy for what was called a valuable dependency of the British crown'. It will be confessed that these financial fruits of the 'glorious' reconquest of India have not a charming appearance; and that John Bull pays exceedingly high protective duties for securing the monopoly of the Indian market to the Manchester free-traders.

[3] Sir George Cornwall Lewis (1806–1863): Whig; Secretary to the Treasury, 1850–52, editor and publisher of *Edinburgh Review*, 1852–55; held offices as Chancellor of Exchequer (1855–58) and Home Secretary (1859–61).

British Commerce

(*New York Daily Tribune*, August 19, 1859)

The British Board of Trade has just published returns of the exports for the first six months of the present year, while its table of the declared values of the imports embraces only the five months ending May 31.[1] On comparing the corresponding periods of 1858 and 1859, it will be found that, with some small exceptions not worth mentioning, the British imports from the United States had generally decreased, in value at least, while the British exports to this country were increasing in quantity as well as in value. To illustrate this fact, we have extracted the following tabular statement from the official returns:

British Exports to the United States for the six months ending June 30

Articles	Quantities		Declared value	
	1858	1859	1858	1859
			£	£
Cottons, yards	60,150,771	110,360,198	1,031,724	1,924,951
H'ware & Cut., cwts	35,349	78,432	242,914	534,107
Linens, yards	17,379,691	31,170,751	515,416	961,956
Iron, Pig, tuns	22,745	39,370	68,640	111,319
Bar, Bolt and Rod	21,463	56,026	175,944	457,384
Wrought	9,153	19,368	113,436	238,903
Sheet and nails, cwts	5,293	15,522	28,709	77,840
Lead, tuns	1,214	1,980	27,754	44,626
Oil (seed), gals	411,769	930,784	50,950	111,103
Silk manufactures, lbs	47,101	134,470	51,277	144,417
Woolen cloths, p'cs	76,311	81,686	273,409	421,006
Wool's, mix, st'fs, y's	13,897,331	30,893,901	562,749	1,188,859
Do., worsted st'fs, p's	185,129	489,171	229,981	758,914
Earth'ware & porce'n	–	–	168,927	279,407
H'dashery & millin'y	–	–	456,364	861,921
Tin plates	–	–	397,027	607,011

Published in *NYDT* as a leading article, without ascription to Marx. In part published in Av. See *CW*, Vol. 16, pp. 478–81.

[1] 'Accounts Relating to Trade and Navigation for the Six Months Ended June 30, 1859'; 'Real Value of the Principal Articles Imported. An Account of the Computed Real Value of the Principal Articles of Foreign and Colonial Merchandise Imported in the Five Months Ended 31st May 1859'; *The Economist*, No. 831 (Supplement), July 30, 1859. See *CW*, Vol. 16, p. 478 n.

British Imports from the United States for five months ending May 31

Articles	1858	1859
Wheat	£371,452	£7,013
Wheat and Corn Flour	693,847	14,666
Cotton (raw)	11,631,523	10,486,418

The returns of the British exports show, generally, an increase not only on 1858, but also on 1857, as will be seen from the following statement:[2]

British Exports for the six months ending June 30

Declared value

1857	1858	1859
£60,826,381	£53,467,804	£63,003,159

On closer examination, however, it becomes evident that not only the total increase in the value of the exports of 1859 over those of 1857 is due to the extension of the commerce with India, but that there would have been a falling off of more than £2,000,000 in the general British export trade of 1859 – as compared with that of 1857 – if India had not made up more than the deficit. On the market of the world, therefore, all traces of the crisis of 1857 have not yet altogether disappeared. The most important and surprising feature of the Board of Trade Returns is, undoubtedly, the rapid development of the British export trade to the East Indies. Let us first by official figures, illustrate the fact:

Exports to British East Indies, 6 months ending June 30

	1856	1857	1858	1859
Beer and Ale	£210,431	£130,213	£474,438	£569,398
Cottons, Calicoes, & c	2,554,976	3,116,869	4,523,849	6,094,433
Cotton Yarn	579,807	540,576	967,332	1,280,435
Earthenware and Porcelain	30,374	23,521	43,975	43,195
Haberdashery and Millinery	39,854	70,502	77,319	105,723
Hardwares and Cutlery	84,758	101,083	139,813	153,423
Saddlery and Harness	12,339	15,587	35,947	19,498
Machinery—steam-engines	[37,503	54,074	59,104	100,803][3]
other sorts	156,028	313,461	170,959	179,255
Iron—bar, bolt, and rod				
(exclusive of railway iron)	506,201	228,838	166,321	172,725
Railway iron	–	272,812	475,413	578,749
Iron—wrought (exclusive of				
railway iron)	266,355	217,484	192,711	242,213
Copper—unwrought	62,928	34,139	9,018	51,699
Sheets and Nails	144,218	228,325	318,381	205,213
Salt	23,995	31,119	21,849	4,468
Stationery	66,495	79,968	86,425	89,711
Woolen Cloths	96,045	166,509	202,076	174,826
Total	£4,872,307	£5,625,080	£7,964,930	£10,065,767

---

[2] 'The Board of Trade Returns for the Half-Year Ending June 30, 1859', *The Economist*, No. 831, July 30, 1859. See *CW*, Vol. 16, p. 479 n.

[3] The figures in square brackets are missing in the *New York Daily Tribune* and are given in *CW*, Vol. 16, p. 48 according to *The Economist*, No. 831, July 30, 1859.

Recollecting the fact that for about 16 years – from 1840 to 1856 – the British export trade to India was generally stationary, although there was sometimes a small rise beyond, sometimes a perceptible fall below the average figure of £8,000,000 – one is rather startled to see this stationary trade doubled in the short interval of two years, and that sudden progress, too, taking place at the epoch of an atrocious servile war. The question whether this expansion of commerce is due to only temporary circumstances or to a bonafide development of Indian demand, derives its peculiar interest from the present conjuncture of Indian finances which forces the British Government to ask Parliament for leave to contract a new Indian loan in London, and which, simultaneously, induces even the London *Times* to moot the question whether, after all, England had not better confine herself to the three old provinces and restore the rest of the Peninsula to its native rulers.[4]

With the scanty materials before us, it would be impossible to arrive at a categorical judgment as to the real character of the sudden expansion of the British export trade to India, but all the data known incline us to the opinion that transitory circumstances have, so to say, swelled that trade beyond its organic dimensions. In the first instance, we are unable to discover any peculiar movement in the British imports from India which might have led to the increase of exports to that country. There has been an increase in some articles, but it is almost balanced by a decrease in others; and, altogether, the vacillations of the Indian exports are too feeble to account one way or the other for the sudden changes in the imports thither. The civil war may, however, have helped the English to explore countries formerly little known, and the soldier may thus have cleared the way for the merchant. Besides, an excessive import and accumulation of silver has of late years been going on in India, and even the Hindoo, somewhat vivified by the scenes of excitement just passed through, may have encroached upon his hoarding mania, and, to some degree, taken to spending silver instead of burying it. Still, we are not warranted in laying too great stress upon such hypotheses, especially as, on the other side, the positive fact stares us in the face of an extraordinary Government expenditure to the annual amount of about £14,000,000. This state of things, while it sufficiently accounts for the sudden growth of the English export trade to India, can hardly be thought to prognosticate a long continuance of this new movement. The most lasting effect will probably be the complete destruction of Indian native industry, since, as the reader will have seen from the last tabular statement, the surplus of British exports to India is principally due to the intrusion of British cottons and cotton-yarns. Overtrading on the part of Manchester may, to some degree, also have contributed to swell the figures of the British export table.

[4] *The Times*, No. 23375, August 3, 1859 (leading article); *CW*, Vol. 16, p. 481 n.

Trade with China

(*New York Daily Tribune*, October 10, 1859. 'Correspondence, London, September 20, 1859'. Unsigned.)
[Excerpt]

In the second article, on the same subject, *The Economist* [September 17, 1859] dwells on the importance, direct and indirect, of the English trade to China. In the year 1858, the British exports to China had risen to £2,876,000, while the value of the British imports from China had averaged upward of £9,000,000 for each of the last three years. . . . England, therefore, independently of the balance due by herself to China, has also to pay to that country large sums in respect to gold imported [by England] from Australia and cotton from America [which themselves owe sums to China]. Now this balance due to China by England, Australia and the United States is, to a great extent, transferred from China to India, as a set-off against the amount due by China to India, on account of opium and cotton. Be it remarked, *en passant*, that the imports from China to India have never yet reached the amount of £1,000,000 sterling, while the exports to China from India realize the sum of nearly £10,000,000.

(*New York Daily Tribune*, December 3, 1859. Unsigned article, 'Trade with China'.)
[Excerpt]

It is this same combination of husbandry with manufacturing industry, which, for a long time, withstood and still checks, the export of British wares to East India; but there that combination was based upon a peculiar constitution of the landed property, which the British, in their position as supreme landlords of the country, had it in their power to undermine, and thus forcibly convert part of the Hindoo self-sustaining communities into mere farms, producing opium, cotton, indigo, hemp, and other raw materials, in exchange for British stuffs. In China the English have not wielded this power, nor are they likely ever to do so.

New York Daily Tribune 1860

British Commerce

(*New York Daily Tribune*, July 16, 1860. Unsigned leading article.)
[Excerpt]

The Board of Trade Returns for the five months ending May 31, 1860, which have just been issued at London, show but a trifling change in the movement of British exports, if compared with the exports during the first five months of 1859.

From £52,337,268, to which they had amounted in 1859, they rose to £52,783,535 in 1860 – this small surplus being altogether due to an increase in the month of May last.

The first feature that strikes us on comparing the respective exports during the five months of 1860 and 1859, is a considerable decline in the British export trade to the British East Indies, as will be seen from the following statement:

Principal British Articles Exported to the East Indies in the Five Months Ending May 31

	Quantities		Value	
	1859	*1860*	*1859*	*1860*
Beer and ale, barrels	168,355	166,461	£507,308	£491,609
Cottons, yards	396,022,733	311,163,765	4,884,982	3,977,289
Cotton yarn, lbs	17,411,542	15,044,812	1,002,439	903,516
Iron (bar, bolt, rod), tuns	16,851	12,194	127,678	90,954
Iron (cast), tuns	12,138	4,108	132,946	42,912
Iron (wrought), tuns	11,823	10,554	188,126	195,659
Sheets and rails	31,582	79,117	169,072	437,170
Earthen ware and porcelain	–	–	£34,530	£24,039
Haberdashery and millinery	–	–	83,832	42,126
Leather – saddlery and harness	–	–	16,780	15,600
Machinery – steam engines	–	–	73,087	100,846
Other kinds	–	–	165,899	196,928
Tin plates	–	–	19,127	6,441
Total			£7,405,806	£6,525,089
Decrease[1]	–	–	–	£876,717

Not included in *Old Colonialism* or in Avineri. See CW, Vol. 17, pp. 406–08.

[1] While the totals given for the third and fourth columns conform to the actual totals of the items under the respective columns, the figure for the 'Decrease' should be £880,717, not £876,717.

From the table it appears that the aggregate decrease in the main exports to the East Indies amounts to about one million sterling; that it is heaviest in the leading articles (cotton and cotton yarns); and that the only exception consists of commodities immediately with railway building. It ought, moreover, to be kept in view that the commercial news received by the last Overland Mail is highly unfavorable and points to an overcharged market; so that, consequently, the value of the exports as declared in England, and as estimated on a range of prices far beyond the average, will by no means be realized in India. Now, there can be no doubt that the Indian trade has been overdone. The artificial demand raised by the Government during the Indian rebellion; the stimulus given to commercial activity by the subsiding of the revolutionary disturbances, and the contraction of most of the other markets of the world, consequent upon the general crisis of 1857–58, all these circumstances concurred to swell the bulk of the Indian trade beyond its natural capacities. Still, according to all past experience, the new-fangled prosperity market might have borne the bombardment by cotton goods for some years longer, but for the sage interference of the British Government. Mr. Wilson,[2] it seems, was expressly dispatched to Calcutta for the purpose of convulsing the Anglo-Indian trade, by the joint operation of clumsy fiscal measures in the interior, and of burdensome customs duties levied on imports from abroad. Has ever, in the whole history of commerce, such a spectacle been witnessed as that of the United Kingdom allowing its most important colonial market to be crippled by the spontaneous acts of its own Government, at the very same time that it cringes before the French Emperor, and bears with his political encroachments, on the pretext of a factitious alleviation in the French customs duties?

---

[2] James Wilson (1805–1860), having been Financial Secretary to the Treasury, 1853–58, served as Finance Member, Viceroy's Colonial in India, 1859–60.

Army in India, Commerce

(*New York Daily Tribune*, August 11, 1860)
[Excerpt]

You are aware that the present Parliamentary session stands unrivalled by a startling succession of Government failures. Apart from Mr Galdstone's abortion of protective duties, not one single important measure has been carried. But while the Government were withdrawing bill after bill, they had contrived to smuggle through the second reading a little resolution,[1] consisting of one single little clause, which, if carried, would have brought about the greatest constitutional change witnessed in England ever since 689. That resolution simply proposed the abolition of the local English army in India, its absorption into the British army, and consequently the transfer of its supreme command from the Governor-General at Calcutta to the London Horse Guards, alias the Duke of Cambridge. Quite apart from the other serious consequences such a change must be fraught with, it would put part of the army out of the control of Parliament, and, on the grandest scale, add to the Royal patronage. It seems that some members of the Indian Council, who unanimously objected to the Government project, but, by virtue of the Indian Act of 1858, can occupy no seats in the House of Commons, whispered their protests into the ears of some M.P.s, and so it came that when the Government already considered their dodge to be safe, a sudden Parliamentary *emeute*,[2] led by Mr. Horsman,[3] broke through their intrigue in the very nick of time. It is a truly ludicrous spectacle, this perplexity of a Cabinet unexpectedly found out, and the bewilderment of a House of Commons fretting at the snares laid to its own profound ignorance.

The declared value of the exports for last month shows the progress of the downward movement of British commerce. [As] I have singled out in a previous letter,[4] compared with the exports of June, 1859, there is a falling off nearly a million and a half sterling for June, 1860.

From 'Syria, Parliamentary Affairs, Army in India, Commerce'. Unsigned article. Not included in *On Colonialism*, and only part on Syria reproduced in Avineri. See *CW*, Vol. 17, pp. 432–33.

[1] Moved in the House of Commons on 12 June 1860 (*CW*, Vol. 17, p. 432 n.).
[2] 'Popular rising'.
[3] Edward Horsman's speech in the House of Commons on 26 July 1860 (*CW*, Vol. 17, p. 432 n.). Horsman (1807–1876), a Liberal MP, had served as Chief Secretary for Ireland, 1855–57.
[4] *NYDT*, 16 July 1860.

The returns for the month of June in the last three years are as follows:

1858	1859	1860
£10,241,433	£10,665,891	£9,236,454

For the half year ending with the 30th June, the declared value of the exports is less by a million than in the same six months of last year:

1858	1859	1860
£53,467,804	£63,003,159	£62,019,989

The falling off of the last month is distributed over the cotton, cotton yarn, linen, hardware, and cutlery, iron and worsted trade. Even in the exports of manufactured woolen goods, the trade in which has hitherto shown a steadily increasing prosperity, this month excepted, 'woolen and worsted yarn' shows a decline. The export of cotton goods for the *six months* to British India has declined from £6,094,430, in the first half of 1859, to £4,738,440 in the first half of 1860, or by £1,360,000 worth of goods.[5]

With regard to the imports the most striking feature is the huge bulk of the cotton arrivals. In June, 1860, 2,102,048 cwts. have been received, as against 1,655,306 cwts. in the June of last year, and 1,339,108 cwts. in June, 1858. The increase for the six months is no less than three millions of hundred weights; so that the half year receipts are greater by more than 60 per cent. The cotton imported in the month of May, 1860, is worth more by £1,800,000 than the import in 1859. No less than six millions and a half sterling have been spent in raw cotton in the first five months of 1860, beyond what was so spent in the same period of the previous year.

If the rapid decrease in the export of cotton goods and yarns be compared with the still more decided increase in the cotton imports, it will be understood that some crisis is approaching, the more so since the new arrivals of the raw material fall upon unusually replete cotton stores.

---

[5] The difference actually amounts to £1,355,990.

The New Sardinian, French and Indian Loans

(*New York Daily Tribune*, August 28, 1860)
London, August 14, 1860
[Excerpt]

In yesterday's [13 August 1860] sitting of the House of Commons, before a House hardly large enough to make up a quorum, Sir Charles Wood,[1] that true pattern of the genuine Whig place-hunter, carried a resolution empowering him to contract a new loan of Three Millions Sterling on behalf of the Indian Treasury. According to his statement, the Indian deficit was in 1858–59 (the financial year always beginning with and ending in April) £14,187,000, in 1859–60 £9,981,000, and is estimated for 1860–61 at £7,400,000. Part of that deficit he promised to cover from the yield of Mr Wilson's[2] newly-introduced taxes – a very questionable prospect, after all – while the other part was to be provided for by the new loan of three millions. The public debt, which in 1856–57, the year before the Rebellion, amounted to £59,442,000, had now increased to £97,851,000. At a still more rapid rate the interest on the debt had grown. From £2,525,000 in 1856–57 it had risen to £4,461,000 in 1859–60. Although the revenue had been forcibly expanded by the imposition of new taxes, still it could not keep pace with the expenditure which, even according to Mr Charles Wood's own statement, was increasing in every direction, save that of Public Works. To make up for an outlay of three millions on fortified barracks, there has been put during the present, and will be put during the following year, 'almost a perfect stop to public works and public buildings of a civic character.' This 'perfect stop' Sir Charles seemed to consider one of the beauties of the system. Instead of 40,000, as in 1856–57, there are now kept 80,000 European soldiers in India; and, instead of a native army of hardly 200,000, one of above 300,000 men.

Not included in *On Colonialism* or in Avineri. See *CW*, Vol. 17, p. 456.

[1] Then, Secretary of State for India. He held this office from 1859 to 1866.
[2] James Wilson (1805–1860), Financial Secretary to the Treasury, 1853–58; Finance Member, Viceroy's Council, 1859–60.

British Commerce

(*New York Daily Tribune*, September 29, 1860)
London, September 8, 1860
[Excerpt]

The *Tribune* was the first paper which called attention to the serious decline of the British export trade to the East Indies, a decline most conspicuous in the great staple articles, viz.: cotton goods and cotton yarns.[1] The reaction hence arising has begun to be felt in Lancashire and Yorkshire, at the very moment when the home market is contracting in consequence of a harvest which is full five weeks later than that of last year, and, despite the improving prospects since Thursday, the 30th of August, will, at all events, fall below an average yield. The British Chambers of Commerce have, consequently, taken the alarm, and assailed the central government with protests against the New Indian Customs' Act, by which the duty upon the staple imports from Great Britain was increased from 5 to 10 per cent.; that is to say, at a rate of 100 per cent. The English press, which, till then, had cautiously abstained from touching this point, has thus at last been compelled to break through its reserve. The London *Economist* treats us to the 'Trade of India', and 'The Cause of its Depression.'[2] Apart from the circumstance of *The Economist* being considered the first English authority in matters of this kind, its articles on India derive peculiar interest from their connexion with the writing-desk of Mr. Wilson, the present Indian Chancellor of the Exchequer.[3] The first part of the article, an attempt at disengaging the late Indian customs legislation from all responsibility for the present contraction of the Indian market, is best answered by the necessity to which the Governor-General at Calcutta has been put, of convening, at Calcutta, a committee, to consist of representatives of the Revenue Boards of Calcutta, Bombay, and Madras, and their respective Chambers of Commerce, and to be charged with the task of revising and readjusting the tariff lately introduced. That tariff, as I stated when first introducing this subject to your readers,[4] did not create the Indian commercial crisis, whose outbreak it, however, accelerated by its sudden introduction at a time when the Indian commerce was already bloated to a size beyond its

---

Not included in *On Colonialism* or in Avineri. See CW, Vol. 17, pp. 479–81.

[1] *NYDT*, 16 July 1860.
[2] 'The Trade of India. The Cause of Its Depression', *The Economist*, No. 889, 8 September 1860, pp. 977, 978. (Reference traced in CW, Vol. 17, p. 479 n.)
[3] The allusion must be to the close connection between the *Economist*, and Wilson, the latter having actually established that weekly paper in 1843.
[4] *NYDT*, 16 July 1860.

natural capacity. The glut of British commodities in the Indian market and of Indian commodities in the English market is avowed by *The Economist*.

'We believe', he says, 'it will be admitted on all hands that the enormous profits made in the Indian trade during a portion of last year, led to a sudden and large increase of supplies to the market, more than was required for any consumption, as far as this country was concerned, and to a very extensive speculative trade by the native capitalists for the supply of the markets in the interior from the seaports. For example, the exports of cotton piece goods to British India amounted [...] in 1859 to the value of £12,043,000 against £9,299,000 in 1858 and £5,714,000 in 1857; and of yarns the exports were in 1859 £2,546,000 against £1,969,000 in 1858, and £1,147,000 in 1857. For a long time goods were taken off as rapidly as they arrived, and as long as prices continued to rise, there was no lack of speculative Mahajuns[5] to make purchases and to consign to the markets of the interior; and there is no doubt, from the best information we can obtain, that *large stocks of goods accumulated at all the markets in the North-West*. Upon this point the testimony of Mirzapur, Allahabad, Lucknow, Agra, Delhi, Amritsar and Lahore is uniform.'[6]

The Economist then proceeds to detail some circumstances which contributed to consolidate in a certain sense the glut in the Indian markets. The main cause – the continuance of large supplies from England – he does not even allude to. In the first instance, then, the Autumn crops of 1859 throughout northern India, consequent upon the drouth[7] generally prevailing, fell much below an average, and were affected both as to quality and quantity. Hence a high range of the prices of provisions through the Winter and Spring, which, later on in the season, was still more enhanced by famine prospects. Furthermore, with scarcity and high prices, there was raging the disease.

'Throughout the whole of the North-West, the cholera prevailed to so alarming an extent among the densely-peopled cities, that the ordinary business of life was in many cases suspended, and the population fled as from an invading enemy.'

But, worst of all

'Upper India was threatened, for a month or six weeks before the departure of the last mail, with a misfortune most appalling. The rains, upon which alone the Autumn crops depend, usually fall by the middle or at latest the end of June. This year, up to the middle of July, not a drop of rain had fallen. From the north-west frontier down to Lower Bengal, from the Khyber pass to Benares, including the great Doabs of the Sutlej, the Jumna, and the Ganges, all was one arid, hard and immovable surface of parched earth. It was only in the few exceptional places which were moistened by the rivers passing through them, or by the

[5] *Mahajans*, indigenous bankers and money-lenders.
[6] *The Economist*, No. 889, 8 September 1860, p. 978; Marx's italics (CW, Vol. 17, p. 480 n.).
[7] US spelling for 'drought'.

tributaries of the great irrigation works, the Jumna and Ganges canals, that any cultivation was possible. The prospect of a famine equal to that of 1837 and 1838 created on all hands the greatest apprehension. Prices rose still more. Cattle were dying in numbers or being drawn to the hills in place of tilling the soil, and the people are described as being on the borders of starvation.'

The worst apprehensions, however, have been set to rest, according to the telegraphic accounts received and published at Calcutta during the eight days previous to the departure of the last mail, which left on the 27th of July. Rains had at last fallen copiously, and in proper time to avert a famine, if not to secure a good crop.

The details given by *The Economist* go far to prove that for the next future there exists not the least prospect of a revival in the Indian trade, which had already fallen off about £2,000,000 for the first half year of 1860 as compared with the first half year of 1859.

New York Daily Tribune 1861

The British Cotton Trade

(*New York Daily Tribune*, October 14, 1861)
London, September 21, 1861
[Excerpt]

From the outbreak of the American war[1] the prices of cotton were steadily rising, but the ruinous disproportion between the prices of the raw material and the prices of yarns and cloth was not declared until the last weeks of August. Till then, any serious decline in the prices of cotton manufactures, which might have been anticipated from the considerable decrease of the American demand, had been balanced by an accumulation of stocks in first hands, and by speculative consignments to China and India. Those Asiatic markets, however, were soon overdone.

'Stocks', says *The Calcutta Price Current of* 7 August 1861, 'are accumulating, the arrivals since our last being no less than 24,000,000 yards of plain cottons. Home advices show a continuation of shipments in excess of our requirements, and so long as this is the case, improvement cannot be looked for … The Bombay market, also, has been greatly over-supplied.'

Some other circumstances contributed to contract the Indian market. The late famine in the north-western provinces has been succeeded by the ravages of the cholera, while throughout Lower Bengal an excessive fall of rain, laying the country under water, seriously damaged the rice crops. In letters from Calcutta, which reached England last week, sales were reported giving a net return of 9¼d. per pound for 40s twist, which cannot be bought at Manchester for less than 11-3/8 d., while sales of 40-inch shirtings, compared with present rates at Manchester, yield losses at 7½d., 9d., and 12d. per piece. In the China market, prices were also forced down by the accumulation of the stocks imported. Under these circumstances, the demand for the British cotton manufactures decreasing, their prices can, of course, not keep pace with the progressive rise in the price of the raw material; but, on the contrary, the spinning, weaving, and printing of cotton must, in many instances, cease to pay the costs of production. Take, as an example, the following case, stated by one of the greatest Manchester manufacturers, in reference to coarse spinning:

Included in *On Colonialism* but not in Avineri. See *CW*, Vol. 19, pp. 18–20.

[1] The American Civil War (1861–65) broke out in April 1861.

	Per lb.	Margin	Cost of Spinning Per lb.
17 September 1860			
Cost of cotton...	6¼ d.	4d.	3d.
16s warp sold for...	10¼ d.	—	—
	Profit, 1d. per lb.		
17 September 1861			
Cost of cotton...	9 d.	2d.	3½ d.
16s warp sold for ...	11 d.	—	—
	Loss, 1½ d. per lb.		

The consumption of Indian cotton is rapidly growing, and with a further rise in prices, the Indian supply will come forward at increasing ratios; but still it remains impossible to change, at a few months' notice, all the conditions of production and turn the current of commerce. England pays now, in fact, the penalty for her protracted misrule of that vast Indian Empire. The two main obstacles she has now to grapple with in her attempts at supplanting American cotton by Indian cotton, is the want of means of communication and transport throughout India, and the miserable state of the Indian peasant, disabling him from improving favorable circumstances. Both these difficulties the English have themselves to thank for. English modern industry, in general, relied upon two pivots equally monstrous. The one was the *potato* as the only means of feeding Ireland and a great part of the English working class. This pivot was swept away by the potato disease and the subsequent Irish catastrophe.[2] A larger basis for the reproduction and maintenance of the toiling millions had then to be adopted.[3] The second pivot of English industry was the slave-grown cotton of the United States. The present American crisis forces them to enlarge their field of supply and emancipate cotton from slave-breeding and slave-consuming oligarchies. As long as the English cotton manufactures depended on slave-grown cotton, it could be truthfully asserted that they rested on a twofold slavery, the indirect slavery of the white men in England and the direct slavery of the black men on the other side of the Atlantic.

[2] The Irish famine of 1845–46, which killed over a million people (Karl Marx, *Capital*, I, London, 1887, p. 726).

[3] Marx presumably has in mind here the repeal of the Corn Laws in 1846, which enabled cheap corn to be imported into England.

The Intervention in Mexico

(*New York Daily Tribune*, November 23, 1861)
London, November 8, 1861
[Excerpt]

The military expedition of Palmerston's [against Mexico] carried out by a coalition with two other European powers, is started during the prorogation [of Parliament], without the sanction and against the will of the British Parliament. The first extra-Parliamentary war of Palmerstone's was the Afghan war softened and justified by the production of *forged papers*.[1] Another war of that sort was his Persian War of 1856–57.[2] He defended it at the time on the plea that 'the principle of the previous sanction of the House did not apply to *Asiatic* wars.'[3] It seems that it does neither apply to *American* wars. With the control over foreign wars, Parliament will lose all control over the national exchequer, and Parliamentary government turn to a mere farce.

Included in neither *On Colonialism* nor Avineri. See *CW*, Vol. 19, p. 78.

[1] The official 'blue-book', *Correspondence Relating to Persia and Afghanistan* (London, 1839). The fact that this collection was deliberately garbled by the omission of important passages from the letters of the British agent Burnes was exposed by J.W. Kaye in his *History of the War in Afghanistan* (London, 1851). See V.A. Smith, *Oxford History of India*, 2nd edn (London, 1922), pp. 674–75, 688–89. The first Afghan War took place in 1839–42, and ended with a British withdrawal.

[2] On the outbreak and conclusion of this war, Marx wrote two articles, 'War against Persia' and 'The Persian Treaty', published in *NYDT*, 14 February and 24 June 1857 (not included in this volume, but see *On Colonialism*, pp. 97–100, 126–29).

[3] A quotation from Palmerstone's speech in the House of Commons, 16 July 1857 (*CW*, Vol. 19, p. 78).

Appendices

Unsigned Articles in the *New York Daily Tribune*, 1853–58, not established to be by Karl Marx

Parliamentary Debate on India

(*New York Daily Tribune*, June 25, 1853. Printed as a leading article.)

Napoleon said: 'War is the SCIENCE OF BARBARIANS.' By means of that science, England has subjugated over one hundred millions of people or nearly all the East Indian Empire, and now must subjugate the rest. Certain employments – all, in a word, dissociated from Church and State – are deemed beneath the notice of noble families in England, or those founded in scientific barbarism. Hence, the majority of the representatives of the noble families are scientific barbarians; and the wars of the White and Red Roses,[1] of Scotland and Ireland, having ceased, they must find employment in attacking distant nations. Even peaceably disposed, calico-derived Sir Robert Peel[2] died, leaving two of his sons scientific barbarians, in the Army and Navy, and the third a hereditary land-monopolist with the scientifically barbarous title of a baronet;[3] and the daughter married to a scientific barbarian, with coats-of-arms, and other awkward devices. That is about the extent of the most liberal men of the scientifically barbarous families of England. Gen. Gough,[4] who barely escaped the doom of a Fili-buster in India, was elevated to a peerage for his scientific barbarism, and the funds provided by Parliament, wrung proportionally out of the carcase of Ireland

Published in *New York Daily Tribune* without attribution to Marx. The repeated use of the words 'scientific barbarian' (also 'scientifically barbarous') is most unlike Marx's prose. The article does not appear in *CW*, Vol. 12; and *On Colonialism*. It is included only in Av. Avineri (p. 81 n.) suggests that the article 'shows many signs of editorial changes at the hands of *NYDT* editors'. So much labour on the part of the editors with an article seems rather unlikely. Bayard Taylor might well have been the author: see note 12 below.

[1] The 'War of Roses' occurred in the fifteenth century in England, involving baronial families in much mutual slaughter.
[2] Sir Robert Peel (1788–1850): statesman, Tory MP for Cashel; formed a ministry in August 1841; aspired to ensure for British trade the first position in the world. His father, Sir Robert Peel, first baronet (1750–1830), succeeded his father, Robert Peel, in calico-printing industry in Lancashire, and enlarged the business by making use of the new inventions of Arkwright and Hargreaves. Hence the designation here of 'calico-derived' for Sir Robert Peel, the Prime Minister.
[3] The son who went into the navy was Sir William Peel (1824–1858), while Sir Robert Peel (1822–1895) succeeded to the baronetcy.
[4] Sir Hugh Gough (1779–1869): appointed commander-in chief in India in 1843; made Baron Gough at the conclusion of the First Sikh War in 1845 having won the battles of Mudki in 1845, Feroz Shah in 1845 and Sobraon in 1846; created Viscount after the Second Sikh War, 1845–49; made General in 1854 and Field Marshal in 1862.

where he lives. Lloyd Jones,[5] a money-changer, being rich enough to sit among the scientific barbarians, was lately elevated to the peerage with the understanding that he was to give over following his trade, it not being scientifically barbarous. As work, even at this day, is so despised by the scientific barbarians, that not even the greatest bill broker in Europe can sit in their company, the contempt in which it was held in past centuries can hardly be measured. England, therefore, under scientific barbarians, has been two thousand years in making the progress, which the State of New York alone will have achieved in three hundred years. The London *Times*, about a year since, estimated the wealth of this State alone as nearly equal to that of England.

As all falsehood must come to an end, and scientific barbarism, added to remorseless trade, must extinguish any State crucified between two such thieves, it is not surprising that India should have arrived at a point of wretchedness that even Government cannot blink: hence, we have a five hours' speech from Sir Charles Wood on Indian Reform.

That any reform can take place in India under the combined tortures of the Trade of War and the War of Trade is not to be looked for, and hence the ministerial speech amounts to nothing. Speeches of equal pretence, if not of equal length, were made when Ireland was shrieking to the God of the poor and needy, under the pangs of social and national death. We have no disposition to blow the flames of public crimination or wrath, but the policy of the English Government in regard to other nations in order to obtain markets and provide for privileged orders, being, without figure of speech, infernal, we shall dwell somewhat on the state of India.

It is never asserted that India primarily injured England, or that the wars against her were undertaken for the purposes of civilization. The object was confessedly plunder by means of murder, in every respect as hideous as the Slave trade when carried on with the full sanctions and copartnership of Bishops and other persons not so near the throne of grace. Conquest, against such an almost innumerous mass of human beings, was carried on under circumstances of such diffusive horror and suffering as fully to employ the genius of Burke[6] in depleting them. So far from showing the progress of Christianity, they differed in no degree from the wars of the Greeks and Romans in scientific barbarism. That such unutterable woes should be wrought upon myriads because the sons of the English aristocracy were too proud to become carpenters, carriers, shoemakers, brick-

---

[5] Probably a reference to Samuel Jones Lloyd (1796–1883): banker (London and Westminster Bank, founded in 1834); a major influence behind the Bank Act of 1844; received peerage in 1860.

[6] Edmund Burke (1729–1797): famous orator and statesman; an active member of the committee which investigated the affairs of the East India Company; wrote the 'Ninth Report' on the trade of Bengal, and the system pursued by Warren Hastings, and the 'Eleventh Report' on the system of presents; drafted the government's East India Bill, 1783; continued his attack on Warren Hastings in 1785; delivered a nine days' speech for the impeachment of Warren Hastings in reply to the defence in 1794.

layers, and farmers, earning their living at home in an honorable way, but must extend scientific barbarism to the verge of hell itself, is as awful as it is apparently incredible. But in a country where the laboring man forms a caste – honorable work is shrunk from as the sting of a serpent – and the void of error so created must be filled up with crime. 'Thou shalt earn thy bread by the sweat of thy brow.' From this, Privilege habitually attempts to escape, and sneaking behind the barriers of custom, falters not at the infliction of all agonies on the poor, ignorant and helpless. 'Those who ought to be the Vanderbilts of England', says the London *Daily News*,

> would shrink from employing their wealth in the magnificent manner adopted by their American friend. They would dread the effect of making any unusual display which would assuredly subject them to the reproach of being millionaires and parvenus. Here is the great difference between the two countries. In England a man is too apt to be ashamed of having made his own fortune, unless he has done so in one of the few roads which the aristocrats condescend to travel by – the church, the bar or the army. And if he is vulgar enough not to be ashamed himself, his wife and children make amends by sedulously avoiding everything which can put other people in mind of their origin. It was thought something superhumanly heroic of Sir Robert Peel to confess that he was the son of a cotton-spinner, although everyone knew it.

Such a state of things at home in England is necessarily balanced by the following condition of things abroad in India. 'Look,' says the same authority,

> at India. The whole wealth of the country is absorbed and the development of its industry is checked by a Government which hangs like an incubus over it and paralyses its free motions. Its capacities for wealth are enormous, but no one makes use of them. Its population is stationary or degenerating. It can with difficulty pay up the revenue which its masters exact from it. It is becoming bankrupt, and will be perhaps chargeable to the mother country. Its hundred millions of inhabitants vegetate in poverty, their ideas limited to the narrowest of all spheres. While hundreds of thousands of migrants are pouring annually into America and becoming absorbed into the population of that country, adding to its wealth and their own, India is a sealed territory to nearly all except those who have friends in Leadenhall Street or Cannon Row.[7] What can a man do in a country like India but vegetate among the oppressed, or live the life of a sybarite among the oppressors. Is it wonderful that at the first shriek of the railway whistle, the Lotus-eating lords of the land should rush away up the country, far away from a sound which everywhere is connected with energy, wealth, activity, freedom, progress?

---

[7] Streets in London on which the offices of the East India Company and the Board of Control were respectively situated.

Notwithstanding this real picture, Sir Charles Wood attempts in a white-washing speech of five hours, to apologize away the policy of the East India Company, while in regard to his reforms the *London Times* concludes its comments thereon in these words:

> For puppet kings and rajahs he would give us buckram directors, without patronage, without power, without certainty of tenure, simply waiting for the signal of their final destruction. This may do in India, where millions feed on rice, but we more than doubt its adaptation to the mind of this country, or to the actual exigencies of the case.

Lord William Bentinck[8] characterizes the English policy in India (of which, as Governor-General, he was certainly a judge) as the reverse of the Mahomedan; as 'cold, selfish and unfeeling – the iron hand of power on the one side, monopoly and exclusion on the other.'

According to Colonel Sykes,[9] the outlay during three Presidencies, with a population of seventy millions, up to 1851 was, for public works, only £93,000! Incredible as it may seem, the little State of Rhode Island has expended, until very recently, if not up to this moment, as much in Internal Improvements as the East India Company for the whole Empire! The revenues of that country, an Anglo-Indian officer assured us, were diminished of late years in the proportion of seven to five. The debt now amounts to £51,000,000. The poison or opium revenue, amounting to £3,000,000, is near its termination – with a crisis involved.

The rent of the land according to Lord Cornwallis[10] belongs to the State; this decision was come to forty years ago. Mr Mill[11] repeated this doctrine to the Commons Committee of 1831, adding that 'a country wherein the whole rent is paid to the State, is in a most happy condition, seeing that such rent would suffice for all the wants of the Government, and the people would then be untaxed.' Mr Mill, on being pressed admitted

> the difficulty of any European collector, with an imperfect knowledge of the natives, their language, and circumstances; with a swarm of ill paid and corrupt servants; with perhaps 10,000 square miles of country to look after, and 150,000 tenants to settle with individually; *but he had no doubt means would*

---

[8] William Cavendish Bentinck (1774–1839): Governor General of India, 1828–33.

[9] William Henry Sykes (1790–1872): entered the service of the East India Company in 1803 and saw a good deal of active service; appointed statistical reporter to the Bombay government in 1824; author of several reports.

[10] Charles Cornwallis (1738–1805); first Marquis and second Earl Cornwallis; Governor General of India (1786–93 and 1805), died and buried at Ghazipur, Uttar Pradesh (India).

[11] James Mill (1773–1836): utilitarian philosopher; published *History of India* in 1818; entered service of East India Company in 1819, rising to the post of 'Examiner of the India Correspondence' in 1830.

be found of limiting the demand to the rent, and then the prosperity of the country would be as fully secured as it can be, and if the land-tax were limited to the rent only, then the revenue system of India is the best in the world.

Mr Mill is a political economist of the English school, but on this occasion he did not define the right of the scientific barbarian to steal the rent at all. That is a question to be decided in the English books of political economy, which illuminate our Democratic party.[12] The people of India, notwithstanding the combined efforts of the scientific barbarians and economists, flee often *en masse* into the dominions of the 'effete' native princes. They do so, says Dickinson,[13] because they do not feel themselves degraded as they do under British rule,[14] for it is not the arbitrary power of a national sovereign, but subjugation to a foreign one, which destroys national power and extinguishes national spirit, and with this the mainspring of whatever is laudable both in public and private life. 'But,' continues the same author,

> we make them feel the rule of the stranger to their heart's core; we set a barrier of privilege between the natives and their foreign masters; the lowest European officer in a black or red coat is above every native gentlemen, though the latter may be a descendant of a line of princes, and is often a man of the most chivalrous feelings and the highest accomplishments; nevertheless, we treat them as an inferior race of beings, and we are making them so; our monopoly of every high office[15] is systematically degrading the people of India; the deterioration of native character under our rule is manifest to every one; and Sir Thomas Munro[16] went so far as to say, 'it would be more desirable that we should be expelled from the country altogether, than the result of our system of Government should be such an abasement of a whole people.' Here are samples of the blessings of the British rule.[17]

The manner in which the East Indians are not allowed to have machinery to work up their cotton, which is sent in ox-carts sometimes eight hundred miles over wet lands, to be shipped to the Ganges, thence round the Cape of

---

[12] That is, the Democratic Pary of the United States. Since this article was published as an editorial, the editors probably felt entitled to make the writer sound as if he was an American. Such references may also point to Bayard Taylor, an American, to have been the author of this piece.

[13] See Dickinson, 'The Government of India under a Bureaucracy', No. VI of *India Reform*, pp. 111–12. From the words 'because they do not feel' onwards, Dickinson has been quoted *verbatim*.

[14] Misprint in Av. ('role').

[15] The words 'from generation to generation' of Dickinson's text ('The Government of India under a Bureaucracy', *India Reform*, p. 112) are omitted here.

[16] Thomas Munro (1761–1827): served against Hyder Ali, 1780–84; assisted in forming the civil administration of Barahmahal, 1792–99; introduced and developed the *ryotwari* system in Madras Presidency as Governor of Madras, 1819–27.

[17] Dickinson, 'Government of India under a Bureaucracy', *India Reform*, p. 112.

Good Hope to England, to be there fabricated and then returned to the natives, at whatever per cent above ninety such an operation costs, is worthy of the attention of the Memphis Convention[18] and a parallel could be drawn between it and the action of the same monopolists toward our southern plantations – with the difference, however, that the East Indian is too feeble to resist, and we[19] are too stupid – too much in love with the doctrines of Mr Mill in regard to Free Trade.

In order to plunder more efficaciously, the Indian Government has set aside the right of the native princes to adopt heirs – a right guaranteed to them by an early act of Parliament, and sanctioned by various Governors-General. The cool manner in which Mr Macaulay, in his Article on Warren Hastings, speaks of the systematic depredations of English adventurers in India in order to acquire fortunes, thus fitting them to intermarry with the English nobility, will bear comparison with the richest slang of highwaymen and cutthroats and when we find that the most voluminous author on India, Rickarts,[20] asserts that 'during sixty years a handful of Englishmen have plundered India of a thousand millions sterling', we ask ourselves – what is the influence of the Christian religion on a nation which can applaud such things, which can lift such thieves to the highest places of hereditary honor, place them nearest the person of anointed and Sacred Majesty, give them the preference on all public occasion to genius and worth, clothe them with titles such as the Jews gave their Jehovah, make them privileged landowners, fountains of patronage, mirrors of morals and manners, models for aspiring ambition?

One country – Ireland – has been saved from revolting almost to her last man, by the emigration to this country;[21] emigration, likewise, hither, says the London *Times*, 'has prevented cannon from being planted in the streets of London'; but the Indian Empire is too far off for our succor. There it lies, cursed with complete and universal poverty; 'for the ryot or native cultivator is already reduced to hopeless beggary, and the native gentleman is fast following in his steps.'

Such are the results of the British Monopoly system, joined with the science of barbarians.

---

[18] Memphis, 35.08 N., 90.01 W., is a major river port on the Mississipi river, USA; the Convention here referred to must have been concerned with navigation rates.

[19] That is, Americans.

[20] Author not traceable.

[21] That is, the United States.

[Debate on the Indian Revolt]

(*New York Daily Tribune*, Tuesday, August 11, 1857. Printed as a leading article.)

An important debate has taken place in the British House of Commons on the insurrection in India, in which Mr Disraeli[1] led off with raising the questions, Was it a mere military mutiny, or was it a national revolt? Is the conduct of the troops the consequence of a sudden impulse, or is it the result of an organized conspiracy? He was inclined to look upon the soldiers not as the avengers of professional grievances, but as the exponents of general discontent. According to his view of the case, the policy of the Indian Government had of late years undergone a change which had alienated and offended every powerful interest in the country. The English power in India was not based, so he urged, on conquest. The English had never conquered India; they had only availed themselves of the quarrels, civil and religious, between the native populations and the native princes, to raise themselves, few and weak as they were, to a controlling position. It was not their own strength that had made them rulers of India, only their skill and art in playing off one part of the native population against the other. And it was upon this principle that, until within the last ten years, the whole administration of affairs on the part of the English had been conducted. That administration had been based upon the principle, not of setting aside, but of upholding the religions, the laws, the distribution of property, and all existing privileges, exactly as they were when the English placed themselves at the head of affairs. The allowing the existence of quasi-independent States, with armies of their own, was a part of this system. A faithful observance of the treaties entered into with those States, the rigid maintenance of the laws and customs of the people, above all, a scrupulous adhesion to the guarantees given to the landed proprietors and the priesthoods of the popular religions, formed the cornerstone on which the edifice of English power in India had been erected.

This article is not admitted to any collection of Marx's writings and overlaps in content with the article published in the *New York Daily Tribune (NYDT)* on 14 August 1857 under the title 'The Indian Question', which is definitely the work of Marx.

[1] Benjamin Disraeli (1804–1881): statesman and man of letters; MP for Buckinghamshire, 1847–76; became Chancellor of Exchequer and leader of the House of Commons under Lord Derby's second government, 1858–59; became Prime Minister in 1868. Here Marx refers to Disraeli's speech in the House of Commons on 27 July 1857. Cf. *CW*, Vol. 15, p. 309 n. (a).

But within ten years past, according to Mr Disraeli, a new system had been adopted, exactly the reverse of the old one. The object seemed to have been, not to maintain Indian nationality, but to destroy it. These assaults upon the nationality of India he discussed under three heads: First, the absorption of native principalities; second, the disturbance of the settlement of property; third, tampering with religion. Under the first head, Mr Disraeli specified the annexation to the territories of Sattara and Berar on the ground that there were not legal heirs – the Government refusing to recognize the custom of adoption universally prevalent in India – and the annexation of Oude and several smaller territories on other pretexts, generally the misgovernment of the reigning princes. These proceedings had given a shock of alarm to the two hundred princes still existing in India with a population of sixty million under their control.

Under the second head were specified the refusal of the Government to recognize the principle of inheritance by adoption in case of succession to private estates; the steps recently taken to get rid of exemptions from the land tax under which many estates were claimed to be held; and the changing from perpetual pensions into mere annuities the amounts which had been assigned to the former rulers when the English obtained the sovereignty of certain portions of India.

With respect to interference with the religious prejudices of the Hindoos, Mr Disraeli has no objection to the missionary system as such. He could not join the charge that the missionary enterprise has caused the present troubles. Missionaries were no novelty in India. So long as the missionaries were mere missionaries, and nothing more, they occasioned no jealousy on the part of the natives. What he complained of was that the missionaries have been taken, or seemed to have been taken, under the patronage of the Government, and that the system of public education introduced into India has been employed for proselytizing purposes. He thought the introduction of the Bible into the Indian schools, and the attempt at female education in India, very bad things; but what he principally complained of was, the law providing that no man should lose his property on account of a change in his religion, and the law allowing Hindoo widows to marry a second time.

The speech of Mr Disraeli, an elaborate and carefully prepared lecture on Indian affairs – and very artfully addressed from beginning to end to the ideas, feelings and sympathies of the Conservative section of the House – seems to have taken the Government orators rather by surprise. The President of the Board of Control and the Chairman of the Court of Directors replied to it, but in a rather rambling and inefficient manner. Considerable complaint was made that in such moment of difficulty and anxiety – and when the practical question, as Mr Disraeli seemed to admit at the conclusion of his speech, was not how the difficulty was got into, but how to get out of it – so many topics of complaint should have been introduced.

The answer put into Mr Disraeli's view of the origin of the Bengal mutiny was, that no connection was shown between that mutiny and the causes to which it was ascribed. It was confined entirely to the soldiers. The Indian princes had taken no part in it; on the contrary, several of them had volunteered their aid to put it down. The proprietors had taken no part in it. The priesthood had taken no part in it. It was, so far as appeared, a simply military revolt. But upon the matter of the alleged recent change in the policy of the Indian Admin-istration, Mr Disraeli was not very distinctly met. Such a change of policy was neither admitted nor denied, and as to the specifications, a disposition was evinced to discuss them rather as isolated facts, each standing upon its own merits, than as part of a system.

In the matter of interferences with the religious prejudices of the natives, the President of the Board of Control seemed determined not to be outdone by Mr Disraeli. He, too, was willing to tolerate missionaries; but the practice on the part of military and civil servants of the Company, in acting the part of mission-aries, by distributing tracts and otherwise, he thought very objectionable, and seemed to intimate that the Government had no objection to a stop being put to it. We are inclined to suspect, however, that this is a matter with which neither Government nor opposition will choose to meddle. It may be dangerous interfer-ing with the religious ideas of the Hindoos; but the English people also have religious ideas, and to meddle with them might prove still more dangerous.

[Sepoy Revolt in India]

(*New York Daily Tribune*, September 1, 1857. Printed as a leading article.)

One beneficial result at least is sure to follow upon the Sepoy revolt in India. That dependency, its population, its government, and its history since it has been under English rule, have become all at once, for the first time, an object of deep interest to the English people. The English newspapers teem with articles upon the subject, and whatever knowledge of India exists, instead of being locked up in books read only by a studious few or confined as heretofore to a few old Indian residents, to a few officials, or a few curious and inquiring persons, is likely now to be generally diffused, and not only generally diffused, but sifted too. For India has hitherto been mostly looked at and described, even by the few who had had any knowledge of it, very much through English glasses. Even the policy of the Anglo-Indian Administration, instead of being based upon a comprehensive and statesmanlike view of things as they actually exist in India, has been very extensively modified by Whig and Tory ideas and theories much more applicable to the condition of British than of Indian society.

India, it is to be remarked, has been the spoil of conquerors and has been governed by intruders from the very earliest period to which its history can be traced back. Such appears to be its normal condition, growing out of its geographical position. The rich district of the Punjaub or Five Rivers, the immensely fertile valley and delta of the Ganges, even the Plateaus of Southern India, are all tropical countries, with a climate favorable indeed to agricultural abundance and the wealth thence arising, but unfavorable to human energy and courage. North of these fertile and thence populous regions, the Himalayas, the *region of cold,* as the word signifies, rise by a rapid and almost precipitous ascent to a height of upward of ten thousand feet, and then by successive terraces to still greater heights till the highest peaks attain the greatest elevation in the known world. The valleys of these mountains, and the elevated plateaus of which they serve as buttresses, have always cherished hardy and warlike races, who at all times, even down to the present, have descended into the tropical regions as plunderers, and from time to time in the character of conquerors and founders of empires. We have no written records or historical narrative of that event, but it is proved by a great variety of circumstances, and beyond all question, that the three higher castes of the Hindoos – the priests, the warriors and the cultivators – belonged to a race which intruded itself into India from the north, bringing with it a new language, a new

The article is not included in CW, Vol. 15; *On Colonialism*; and Av.

religion, and new social institutions; and the evident relationship of the Sanscrit to the Latin, the Greek, the German and the Slavonic tongues, proves these intruders and conquerors to have sprung from the same root with the existing dominant races of Europe. While these foreign intruders made themselves, as princes, soldiers, priests and landholders, the masters of the country, the original populations, pressed more and more toward the southern extremity of the peninsula, were included in the inferior caste of Sudras, handicraftsmen and artisans, wholly excluded from political or intellectual influence, and restricted exclusively to industrious labor as the servants of the higher classes.

After the country had been thus ruled, nobody knows for how many ages, but not without violent internal commotions and bloody religious quarrels, which ended in the expulsion of the Budhists – who seem to have been a sort of Brahminicial rationalists from India, and the complete triumph of the orthodox creed, not, however, without incorporating into itself, as generally happens in such cases, many of the ideas and superstitions of the rival faith; somewhat more than a thousand years ago, India became exposed to a new invasion by armies and nations from the North, who had, by this time, adopted the Mohammedan faith. These invasions and conquests, pushed through a series of centuries, extended gradually over Hindostan, till, at the time when India became known to Europeans, the Mohammedan rule had established itself in nearly all parts of the peninsula, though the subjection of the more mountainous and barren districts was always very imperfect.

These Mohammedan invaders and conquerors, it is to be observed, did not, any more than their Brahminical predecessors, affect at all to humor the religious ideas, or to adopt the social system, of the conquered people. The Mohammedan conquerors, on the other hand, steadily disregarded every prejudice of the Hindoos conflicted with their wishes or their interests. They did not hesitate to resort to violence and persecution for the propagation of the Mohammedan faith – in its simplicity the most perfect counterpart that can be conceived to the complicated and elaborate system of the Brahmins – and, though a considerable proportion of the existing Mohammedan population of India are doubtless the descendants of the invaders, it is certain, nevertheless, that considerable numbers of the native population were led or forced to embrace the faith of their rulers.

In process of time, and before the English stepped in as the rulers of India, the Mohammedan Empire had fallen to pieces, as indeed it often had done before, by internal dissensions, which had split it up into a number of rival States anxious to purchase the aid and intervention of Europeans, even at a very dear price to themselves. Not only that, but a considerable part of the country had reverted again to the rule of princes of the older race. It is to be observed, however, that in this revolt against the Mohammedans the old ruling Hindoo castes, the Brahmins and the Kshatriyas had no share. It is even alleged that the Kshatriyas or Warrior caste has become extinct, though the Rajpoots and the inhabitants of some other wild and desolate regions set up a claim to belong to it. The great internal revolution in Central India against Mohammedan rule was effected by the Mahrattas, who and their princes belong to the inferior caste of Sudras, not reckoned by the Hindoo creed among the regenerated, and by the ancient Hindoo law liable to be put to death, should they have the presumption to attempt to read the Vedas. A similar revolution was accomplished in the Punjaub by the Seiks,[1] a new sect by which Mohammedan and Hindoo ideas were combined, but in which the Mohammedan element predominated, since the Hindoo institution of castes was wholly rejected.

The English first entered India exclusively as merchants. They had factories in which to store their goods, and in the disturbed state of the country they obtained liberty to fortify these factories and to maintain soldiers to guard them. As security for money advanced to native princes, they received the collectorship of the taxes, some-what equivalent to the landlordship of certain neighbouring districts. From thus acting as auxiliaries and stewards to their Mohammedan patrons, they gradually, as happens so often in private life, all the world over, became themselves the masters. Such was the commencement of the English territorial aggrandizement, which, once commenced, went on at a rapid pace. The chief obstacle which the English encountered was not from the natives, but from the French, who had begun to play the same game; and it was only after a desperate struggle of twenty years that the French were obliged to succumb, and to leave the conquest of India to the English. This event took place at the same time with the expulsion of the French from the American continent, and while by the American Revolution, Britain was losing her empire in the West, at the same time, by the progress of the Company's arms in India, she was gaining a new empire in the East. From that time, her progress has been most rapid. Mohammedan, Mahratta, Rajpoot and Seik, successively felt the weight of her arm, and submitted to her authority, till within less than a hundred years from her first territorial acquisitions she has become master not only of all India, but of several important adjacent districts; while her empire, till shaken by the pending military revolt was not only more extensive but also more firm and solid, and her authority far more complete, that any thing hither to known in India.

That the present revolt will be speedily crushed, at a greater or less expense of time, blood and treasure, cannot, we think, admit of a doubt; nor does it seem less certain that this suppression will be followed by very great changes in the methods of Indian administration. As happened in the Canadian rebellion, the immediate object in view – if indeed, the mutinous Sepoys had any object beyond plunder and the gratification of personal antipathies toward their officers – may fail to be accomplished, and yet very permanent results may be achieved. The Sepoys have doubtless been guilty of many cruelties, which will, we fear, be hardly less cruelly revenged; but in drawing and fixing attention upon India, and in forcing a critical examination of the whole practice and theory of the English rule, they have certainly rendered a great service at once to India and to England.

---

[1] So printed in *NYDT*.

[Plans for English Colonization in India]

(*New York Daily Tribune*, April 3, 1858. Printed as a leading article.)

The question of the colonization of India has been raised in the British House of Commons, on a motion which, after considerable debate, was adopted, for the appointment of a Select Committee, to take into consideration the prospects and feasibility of that operation. It was assumed by Mr Ewart,[1] who made the motion for the Committee, that in what are known as the hill countries, embracing all the northern portion of India, and the lines of the Eastern and Western Ghauts, there must be many districts highly favorable to the European constitution, and affording tracts of land open to colonization and cultivation by European labor, or, at least, under European superintendence. It was assumed that the establishment of European settlements in these districts, somewhat on the plan of the Roman colonies, might add greatly to the military hold of England on India, furnishing a force at hand ready to pour down from the hills whenever their services might be required, and, when not employed in military service, able to support themselves by agricultural labor. The introduction of railroads into India – an experiment which was going on successfully, and which, contrary to expectation, was eagerly availed of by the Hindoo population – would, it was suggested, afford facilities for the establishment of such colonies and means of communication between them hitherto unknown. Nor would they be of benefit merely in military point of view. These colonies would naturally become the sites of churches, schools and libraries, whence the knowledge of the English language and the ideas of European civilization might be diffused among the natives. The occupation of the Himalaya districts by European colonies might also afford a barrier against Russian invasion, and might lead to a trade and intercourse with Central Asia, from which England was now entirely excluded.

These suggestions, however, as to the feasibility of European colonization in India – though no opposition was made to[2] the appointment of the Committee – did not receive much indorsement from those members of the House connected with the East India Company or the Board of Control. At the same time they took occasion expressly to disclaim any inclination on the part of the

---

There does not seem to be any proof that this article was written by Marx. It also lacks touches of his characteristic style. Only Avineri has treated this as being from Marx's pen; it has not been admitted in Marx and Engels, *Collected Works*.

[1] William Ewart (1798–1869): politician, MP from various places since 1828; the longest tenure being from Dumfries Burghs (1841–68); Free Trader.
[2] 'in' in Av.

Company or the Indian authorities to discourage or put any obstacles in the way of the settlement of Europeans in India. The idea of such a policy had come down from the time when the Company was a purely commercial association, which monopolized the trade of India and China, and, like all similar bodies, regarded interlopers with great jealousy. But since 1813, when the Company lost the monopoly of the India trade, and more especially since 1834, when it had ceased to trade at all, every motive of interest had induced the Indian authorities to encourage the settlement of Europeans in India, and the extension of agriculture and manufactures, as leading directly to an increase of revenue. Neither was it true, as was so often asserted, that there was anything in the land tax that operated to discourage settlement and cultivation. The old system of raising the assessment on the land in proportion to the crop had been abandoned, the assessment being fixed at a moderate rate for a period of thirty years. Jungle land might be obtained in perpetuity by those wishing to cultivate it at a yearly rent not exceeding half a dollar the acre. The land, however, in India did not belong to the Government, the greater proportion of it being as much private property as the land in England, many of the natives holding their estates by titles six or seven hundred years old. It was only in certain districts where were large tracts of waste land, in which no individual had an interest, that the Government had any power to make land grants.

As to settlement among the hills, as a pecuniary operation, the inducements would be small. Colonists would find there a rugged and barren country, which no amount of cultivation would render productive. In those rough districts, cultivation was carried on by terraces, and it was rarely that a square plot of more than a hundred yards could be thus obtained. One peculiarity of the Himalaya Mountains was that valleys were scarcely to be found in them. The country consisted of hills rising over hills. The consequence was, that very small portions of the land were available for cultivation, and over almost every acre of such land proprietary rights already existed.

Even as to climate, the lower range of hills was as pestilential as the plains. There was a point in the elevation of the country called fever range, below which a European could only reside at the risk of life. Unfortunately, above that range the country became so rugged and precipitate, that it was impossible to construct roads, while, as already stated, the amount of land capable of cultivation was very limited. Even in the hill districts all reports concur in stating that the European race does not prolong itself beyond the third generation.

If these statements are to be taken as correct, the prospect of planting a European settlement in the Himalaya range of mountains would not seem very promising.

[The Future of Landed Property in Oude]

(*New York Daily Tribune*, May 24, 1858. Printed as a leading article.)

The proclamation of Lord Canning[1] with respect to the treatment to be extended to the landholders of India, which appeared in Saturday's paper, has been productive of remarkable results, if not in India – where its effect is yet unknown – at least in England. This proclamation it seems was prepared in anticipation of the occupancy of Lucknow, and ten days or a fortnight before its issue, a copy of it was forwarded to the British Government, accompanied by a copy of the instructions intended to be given to the Chief Commissioner of Oude, as to the manner in which he was to act under it, with respect to different classes of persons. These instructions – though considered as a practical measure, the character of the proclamation must mainly depend upon them – have not been made public. It is worthy of notice, however, as bearing upon this point, that the clause of the proclamation which holds out a promise of lenient treatment to such of the landholders of Oude as came forward promptly and assisted in the restoration of order – and which probably embodies the substance of those[2] instructions – was not contained in the original draft of the proclamation as forwarded to the Government; a change which Lord Derby described as having materially modified its character and as relieving it, to a certain extent, from the objections which the Government had taken to it as it was transmitted to them. What these objections were will appear from Lord Ellenborough's letter, sent through the recent Committee of the Court of Directors of the East India Company, which we publish to-day, and which was submitted to Parliament upon a call by Mr Bright, upon the Ministers to know if they had sanctioned the proclamation or concurred in it. In the debate that ensued, the Ministers denied any intention or wish to force Lord Canning to resign. They called attention to the fact that the Governor-General was not required to withdraw the proclamation, only to mitigate in practise its stringent severity. Nevertheless, it is abundantly apparent, both from the terms of the dispatch and the sentiments expressed by Derby and Ellenborough in the House of Lords, that the Ministry were directly at issue with the Governor-General, both as to the justice and the policy of his conduct in this matter.

The ground is taken in this dispatch that the war in Oude cannot be regarded as a military mutiny, but ought rather to be considered as a legitimate

This article is included as one by Marx only in Av.

[1] 3 March 1858. See Campbell, *Narrative*, p. 417.
[2] 'these' in Av.

resistance made by the people of that province, in behalf of their sovereign and themselves, to what they had good reason to regard as an unprovoked and unjustifiable invasion of their rights. It is further set forth that, instead of attempting to subdue the rebellion by subjecting the inhabitants to a penalty more sweeping and more severe than any recorded in history, not merely justice but policy demanded the extension of clemency to the great body of the people, as the only means of securing that willing obedience without which the maintenance of British authority in India is neither possible nor desirable.

Such being the style and tenor of this document, the dispatch itself, and especially the publication of it, were regarded, notwithstanding the disclaimer of the Ministry, in the light of an assault upon the Governor-General with the design to force his resignation. In fact, all things considered, there appears no ground for supposing, however a literal construction of the proclamation might seem to imply it, that Lord Canning intended a general confiscation of the landed property of Oude, or anything more than to signify to the landholders in an emphatic manner that the only chance of saving their property was instant submission to British authority and an exhibition of zeal for the reestablishment of British rule. Indeed, the latest telegraphic news from India announces that an amnesty had been offered in Oude to those who return to their allegiance, mutineers excepted.

In the debates which grew out of the submission to Parliament of Lord Ellenborough's dispatch, the Ministers, and especially Lord Ellenborough himself, wished to present the point at issue as a question between the principle of clemency and the principle of confiscation. The other side, however, declined to entertain that question, or to go at all into the merits or demerits of the proclamation, on the ground that till they had Lord Canning's statement of his policy and intention in its issue, they were not in a position to discuss that question. In conformity with this view of the case, Mr Cardwell[3] in the House of Commons gave notice of a motion – and notice of a similar motion was given in the House of Lords by Lord Shaftesbury[4] expressly waiving the expression of any opinion as to the policy of Lord Canning's proclamation for want of sufficient information to form one, but censuring the publication of the dispatch as calculated to weaken the authority of the Governor-General, and to encourage further resistance on the part of those still in arms against British authority. The motion in the Commons stood for Thursday the 13th of May; that in the Lords for Friday. On the Wednesday preceding, Lord Ellenborough, seeing how things were like to go, made an attempt to save the Ministry by taking upon himself the sole responsibility, both of writing the dispatch and of its publication. The dispatch he vindicated as a message of peace to the people of India, and its publication as a necessary means of compelling those in office to act in the spirit of Government; but both the dispatch itself and its publication were, he declared, his individual acts,

---

[3] Edward Cardwell (1813–1886): statesman; MP for Oxford city in 1852.
[4] Antony Ashley Cooper, seventh Earl of Shaftesbury (1801–1885): MP, 1826–51; held minor offices.

upon which his colleagues in the Ministry had not been consulted, and for which they ought not to be held responsible. After having thus endeavored to free his colleagues from the odium of this unfortunate affair, he announced that he had tendered his resignation of the place he held in the Ministry, and that it had been accepted.

Whether this movement on the part of Lord Ellenborough will save the Derby Ministry, remains to be seen.

Supplement

Letters of Marx and Engels, 1852–62:
Excerpts Relating to India

Note: All the letters of Marx and Engels (and one of Jenny Marx to Engels), extracts from which are given below, were written in German. The English translations were made by Peter and Betty Ross for the English edition of the *Collected Works* of Karl Marx and Frederick Engels, Volumes 39, 40 and 41 (Moscow, 1983–85). Where the originals contained English words and phrases, these have been reproduced here in small capitals. Where such intrusion of English extends to a sentence or a passage of some length, this is indicated in footnotes, while the original English text appears in normal print. French words and phrases used in the original are either directly rendered in English or are given in italics with English renderings provided in footnotes. In the rather rare case where a word in the translation by P. and B. Ross has been replaced by another, the latter is marked by an asterisk. All notes are by the editor.

The reader is reminded that the correspondence published here is restricted to 1852–62, this being the period during which Marx wrote for the *New York Daily Tribune*.

1. Engels to Marx, 20 April 1852

[Extract. *CW*, Vol. 39, pp. 82–83.]

In considering the present state of commerce, particularly as regards India, there is one point that should not be overlooked. Despite 3 years of colossal and ever-increasing imports of English industrial goods into India, the news from there has for some time been moderately good again, stocks are gradually being sold and are fetching higher prices. The reason for this can only be that, in the provinces most lately conquered by the English, Sind, the Punjab, etc., etc., where native handicrafts have hitherto almost exclusively predominated, these are now finally being crushed by English competition, either because the manufacturers here [in England] have only recently come round to producing materials suitable for these markets, or because the NATIVES have finally sacrificed their preference for local cloths in favour of the cheaper price of the English materials usually exported to India. The last Indian crisis of 1847 and the concomitant sharp DEPRECIATION of English products in India may have contributed greatly to this; and it is already clear from old Gülich that even the parts of India occupied by the English in his day had not for a long time completely abandoned their traditional domestic manufactures.[1] This is the only explanation for the fact that the 1847 affair has not long since recurred in more acute form in Calcutta and Bombay. But all this will be changed once the 3,000,000 bales of cotton from the last crop have come on to the market, been processed and consigned as finished goods, predominantly to India. The cotton industry is now so flourishing that, despite this season's crop, which is 300,000 bales more than that of 1848/49, cotton prices are rising both here and in America, that American manufacturers have already bought 250,000 bales more than last year (when they used in all only 418,000 bales), and that manufacturers here are already beginning to maintain that even a crop of 3 million bales would be insufficient for their needs. Up till now, America has exported 174,000 bales more to England, 56,000 more to France and 27,000 more to the rest of the Continent than she did last year. (Each season runs from 1 Sept. to 7 April.)[2] And given prosperity of this order, it is of course easy to explain how Louis Napoleon can prepare at leisure for his *bas-empire* [Second Empire]; the surplus of direct cotton imports into France between 1850 and 1852 now amounts to 110,000 bales (302,000 against 192,000), i.e. more than 33 per cent.

According to all the rules the crisis should come this year and will,

---

[1] G. Gülich, *Geschichtliche Darstellung des Handels, der Gewerbe und des Ackerbaus der bedeutendsten handeltreibenden Staaten unserer Zeit*, Bd. 3, S. 263–64. Reference traced in *CW*, Vol. 39, p. 82 n.

[2] Engels may have used the article 'Commerical Intelligence. New York, 7 April' in *The Times*, 20 April 1852, but the figures given by him somewhat differ from those in the newspaper – Note by editors of *CW*, Vol. 39, p. 82 n.

indeed, probably do so; but if one takes into consideration the present quite unexpected resilience of the Indian market, the confusion created by California and Australia, the cheapness of most raw materials, which also means cheap industrial manufactures, and the absence of any heavy speculation, one is almost tempted to forecast that the present period of prosperity will be of exceptionally long duration. At any rate it may well be that the thing will last until the spring. But WITHIN SIX MONTHS MORE OR LESS: it is, after all, safest to stick to the old rule.

2. Marx to Adolf Cluss,[3] 22 April 1852

[Extract. *CW*, Vol. 39, p. 84.]

The thriving state of the cotton industry is due chiefly to the Indian market, whence there has been good news for some time past – despite continuing colossal imports from England. This may be explained by the fact that in the territories most lately conquered by the English, Sind, the Punjab, etc., where native handicrafts have hitherto almost exclusively predominated, these are now finally being crushed by English competition. The last Indian crisis of 1847 and the concomitant sharp DEPRECIATION of English products in India may have contributed to this. This unexpected resilience of the Indian market, California, Australia, as well as the cheapness of most raw materials in the absence of any heavy speculation, gives reason to suppose that the period of prosperity will be of exceptionally long duration. It may well be that the thing will last until the spring, etc., etc., etc.

3. Marx to Joseph Weydemeyer,[4] 30 April 1852

[Extract. *CW*, Vol. 39, p. 96.]

Big business and industry are now doing better than ever in England and hence on the Continent. As a result of the exceptional circumstances – California, Australia, England's commercial penetration of the Punjab, Sind and other only recently conquered parts of India, it may well be that the crisis will be postponed

---

[3] Adolph Cluss (1825–1905): member of the Communist League; migrated to the USA in 1848, where he conducted Communist propaganda; left politics after the 1850s to become a noted architect.

[4] Joseph Weydemeyer (1818–1866): German Communist revolutionary; migrated to the USA in 1851; a friend of Marx and committed to spreading Marxism in the USA.

until 1853. But then its eruption will be appalling. And until that time there can be no thought of revolutionary convulsions.

4. Engels to Marx, 24 August 1852

[Extract. CW, Vol. 39, p. 165.]

The minor PANIC in the money market appears to be over, CONSOLS and RAILWAY SHARES are again rising merrily, MONEY IS EASIER, speculation is still pretty evenly distributed over CORN, COTTON, STEAM BOATS, MINING OPERATIONS, etc., etc. But cotton has already become a very risky proposition; despite what is so far a very promising crop, prices are rising continuously, merely as a result of high consumption and the possibility of a brief cotton shortage before fresh imports can arrive. Anyway I don't believe that the crisis will this time be preceded by a regular *rage* for speculation; if circumstances are favourable in other respects, a few mails bringing bad news from India, a PANIC in New York, etc., will very soon prove that many a virtuous citizen has been up to all kinds of sharp practice on the quiet. And these crucial ill-tidings from overstocked markets must surely come soon. Massive shipments continue to leave for China and India, and yet the advices are nothing out of the ordinary; indeed, Calcutta is DECIDEDLY OVERSTOCKED, and here and there NATIVE DEALERS are going bankrupt. I don't believe that PROSPERITY will continue beyond October or November – even Peter Ermen[5] is becoming worried.

At all events, whether a revolution is immediately produced – immediately, i.e. in 6–8 months – very largely depends on the intensity of crisis. The poor harvest in France makes it look as though something is going to happen there; but if the crisis becomes chronic and the harvest turns out after all a little better than expected, we might even have to wait until 1854. I admit that I should like another year in which to swot, having still a good deal of stuff to get through.

5. Engels to Marx, 29 November 1852

[Extract. CW, Vol. 39, p. 253.]

Fortunately the only circumstance which might have brought overproduction in the cotton industry to a premature end has now been eliminated; the new crop will be *far in excess of 3 million bales*, i.e. the biggest there has ever

---

[5] Partner in the Manchester firm of Ermen and Engels, in which Engels himself worked.

been, and cotton is again going down; so there'll be no shortage of raw material. Only let the corn harvest fail next year and we shall see a merry dance. But unless it does so, it is difficult to say whether anything decisive will happen as early as next year, given the abnormal conditions, given the mushroom growth of the markets in Australia and California where, as there are hardly any women and children, one individual consumes perhaps four times as much as elsewhere and gold is freely squandered in the towns, given the new market which the Calcutta houses are already exploiting in Burma, given the way Bombay and Karachi are expanding their trade with North-East India[6] and the adjacent territories (particularly so in the case of the latter), etc.

6. Engels to Marx, before 28 May 1853

[Extract. CW, Vol. 39, pp. 326–28.]

Yesterday I read the book on Arabian inscriptions which I told you about.[7] The thing is not without interest, repulsive though it is to find the parson and biblical apologist for ever peeping through. His greatest triumph is to show that *Gibbon* made some mistakes in the field of ancient geography, from which he also concludes that Gibbon's theology was deplorable. The thing is called *The Historical Geography of Arabia*, by the Reverend Charles Forster. The best things to emerge from it are:

(1) The supposed genealogy of Noah, Abraham, etc., to be found in Genesis is a fairly accurate enumeration of the Beduin tribes of the time, according to the degree of their dialectal relationships, etc. As we all know, Beduin tribes continue to this day to call themselves Beni Saled, Yusuf, etc., i.e. sons of so and so. This nomenclature, which owes its origins to the early patriarchal mode of existence, ultimately leads up to this type of genealogy. The enumeration in Genesis is *plus ou moins* [plus or minus] confirmed by ancient geographers, while more recent travellers have shown that most of the old names still exist, though in dialectally altered form. But from this it emerges that the Jews themselves were no more than a small Beduin tribe like the others, which was brought into conflict with the other Beduins by local conditions, agriculture, etc.

(2) As for the great Arab invasion, you will remember our discussion when we concluded that, like the Mongols, the Beduins carried out periodic invasions and that the Assyrian and Babylonian Empires were founded by Beduin tribes on the very same spot, as, later, the Caliphate of Baghdad.

[6] Engels probably intended to write 'North-West India'.
[7] Charles Forster, *The Historical Geography of Arabia, or the Patriarchal Evidences of Revealed Religion*, 2 volumes (London, 1844).

The founders of the Babylonian Empire, the Chaldeans, still exist under the same name, Beni Chaled, and in the same locality. The rapid construction of large cities, such as Nineveh and Babylon, happened in just the same way as the creation in India only 300 years ago of similar giant cities, Agra, Delhi, Lahore, Multan, by the Afghan and/or Tartar invasions. In this way the Mohammedan invasion loses much of its distinctive character.

(3) In the South-West, where the Arabs settled, they appear to have been a civilized people like the Egyptians, Assyrians, etc., as is evident from their buildings. This also explains many things about the Mohammedan invasion. So far as the religious sphere* is concerned, the ancient inscriptions in the South, in which the ancient Arab national tradition of monotheism (as with the American Indians) still predominates, a tradition of which the Hebrew is only a *small part*, would seem to indicate that Mohammed's religious revolution, like *every* religious movement, was *formally a reaction*, a would-be return to what was old and simple.

It is now quite clear to me that the Jews' so-called Holy Writ is nothing more than a record of ancient Arab religious and tribal traditions, modified by the Jews' early separation from their tribally related but nomadic neighbours. The circumstance of Palestine's being surrounded on the Arabian side by nothing but desert, i.e. the land of the Beduins, explains its separate development. But the ancient Arabian inscriptions and traditions and the Koran, as well as the ease with which all genealogies, etc., can now be unravelled show that the main content was Arab, or rather, generally Semitic, as in our case the [Scandinavian] *Edda* and the German heroic saga.

7. Marx to Engels, 2 June 1853

[Extract. CW, Vol. 39, pp. 332–34.]

As regards the Hebrews and Arabs, I found your letter most interesting. It can, by the by, be shown that 1. in the case of all eastern tribes there has been, since the dawn of history, a *general* relationship between the SETTLEMENT of one section and the continued nomadism of the others. 2. In Mohammed's time the trade route from Europe to Asia underwent considerable modification, and the cities of Arabia, which had had a large share of the trade with India, etc., suffered a commercial decline – a fact which at all events contributed to the process. 3. So far as religion is concerned, the question may be reduced to a general and hence easily answerable one: Why does the history of the East *appear* as a history of religions?

On the subject of the growth of eastern cities one could hardly find anything more brilliant, comprehensive or striking than *Voyages contenant la descripiton des états du Grand Mogol, etc.* by old François Bernier (for 9 years Aurangzeb's physician). He provides in addition a very nice account of military organization and the manner in which these large armies fed themselves, etc. Concerning both these he remarks *inter alia*:

> The main body consists of cavalry, the infantry not being so numerous as is commonly supposed[8] unless we suppose that with the fighting men they confound servants, sutlers, tradesmen, and all those individuals belonging to bazars, or markets, who accompany the troops. Including these followers, I can well conceive that the army immediately about the King's person, particularly when it is known that he intends to absent himself for some time from the capital may amount to 2-, or even 300,000 infantry. This will not be deemed an extravagant computation, if we bear in mind the immense quantity of tents, kitchens, baggage, furniture, and even women, usually attendant on the army. For the conveyance of all these are again required many elephants, camels, oxen, horses and porters. It should be borne in mind that from the nature and government of this country, where the King is *the sole and only proprietor of all the land in the Empire* [Marx's italics], a capital city such as Delhi or Agra, derives its chief support from the presence of the army and the population is reduced to the necessity of following the Mogul [emperor], whenever be undertakes a journey of long continuance. These cities resemble any place rather than Paris; *they might fitly be compared to a camp* [Marx's italics] if the lodgings and accommodations were not a little superior to those found in the tents of armies.[9]

In reference to the Grand Mogul's march on Kashmir, with an army 400,000 strong, he writes:

> It is no doubt difficult to conceive how so vast a number both of men and animals can be maintained in the field. The best solution of the difficulty will be found in the sobriety of the Indians and simple nature of their diet. Of the great number of troopers not a tenth, not even a twentieth part, eat animal food; they are satisfied with their 'kichery' [*khichri*], a mess of rice and other vegetables, over which when cooked they pour boiled butter [ghee]. It should be considered too that camels endure fatigue, hunger and thirst in a surprising degree, live upon a little, and eat any kind of food. At the end of every march, they are left to browse in the fields, where everything serves for fodder. It is important likewise to observe that the same merchants who supply the bazars in Delhi are compelled to furnish them in the camp, and so also the petty merchants, etc. . . As regards forage, the poor people rove about from village to village, and what they succeed in purchasing, they endeavour to sell in the army at an advanced

---

[8] From this point Marx quotes Bernier in French.

[9] For the text quoted by Marx in French, we have inserted the translation of the corresponding passage (with some modification) by A. Constable, revised by V.A. Smith, *Travels in the Mogul Empire* by François Bernier (London, 1916), pp. 219–20. Marx slightly abridges Bernier's French text.

price. It is a common practice with them to clear, with a sort of trowel, whole fields of a peculiar kind of grass, which having beaten and washed, they depose of in the camp at a price sometimes very high and sometimes inadequately low.[10]

Bernier rightly sees all the manifestations of the East – he mentions Turkey, Persia and Hindustan – as having a common basis, namely the *absence of private landed property*. This is the real *clef* [key] even to the eastern heaven.

8. Engels to Marx, 6 June 1853

[Extract. CW, Vol. 39, pp. 339–42.]

The absence of landed property is indeed the key to the whole of the East. Therein lies its political and religious history. But how to explain the fact that orientals never reached the stage of landed property, not even the feudal kind? This is, I think, largely due to the climate, combined with the nature of the land, more especially the great stretches of desert extending from the Sahara right across Arabia, Persia, India and Tartary to the highest of the Asiatic up-lands. Here artificial irrigation is the first prerequisite for agriculture, and this is the responsibility either of the communes, the provinces or the central govern-ment. In the East, the government has always consisted of 3 departments only: Finance (pillage at home), War (pillage at home and abroad), and *travaux publics*,[11] provision for reproduction. The British government in India has put a somewhat narrower interpretation on nos. 1 and 2 while completely neglecting no. 3, so that Indian agriculture is going to wrack and ruin. Free competition is proving an absolute fiasco there. The fact that the land was made fertile by artificial means and immediately ceased to be so when the conduits fell into disrepair, explains the otherwise curious circumstance that vast expanses are now arid wastes which once were magnificently cultivated (Palmyra, Petra, the ruins in the Yemen, any number of localities in Egypt, Persia, Hindustan); it explains the fact that one single war of devastation could depopulate and entirely strip a country of its civilization for centuries to come. This, I believe, also accounts for the destruction of southern Arabian trade before Mohammed's time, a circumstance very rightly regarded by you as one of the mainsprings of the Mohammedan revolution. I am not sufficiently well acquainted with the history of trade during the first six centuries AD to be able to judge to what extent general material conditions in the world made the trade route via Persia to the Black Sea and to Syria and Asia Minor via the Persian Gulf preferable to the Red Sea route.

---

[10] This passage is given by Marx in French. We have replaced it with Constable's trans-lation, ibid., pp. 381–82, modified a little to suit Marx's abridgement of the original.
[11] 'Public works'.

But one significant factor, at any rate, must have been the relative safety of the caravans in the well-ordered Persian Empire under the Sassanids, whereas between 200 and 600 AD the Yemen was almost continuously being subjugated, overrun and pillaged by the Abyssinians. By the seventh century the cities of southern Arabia, still flourishing in Roman times, had become a veritable wilderness of ruins; in the course of 500 years what were purely mythical, legendary traditions regarding their origin had been appropriated by the neighbouring Beduins (cf. the Koran and the Arab historian Novairi), and the alphabet in which the local inscriptions had been written was almost wholly unknown although *there was no other*, so that *de facto writing* had fallen into oblivion. Things of this kind presuppose, not only a SUPERSEDING, probably due to general trading conditions, but outright violent destruction such as could only be explained by the Ethiopian invasion. The expulsion of the Abyssinians did not take place until about 40 years before Mohammed, and was plainly the first act of the Arabs' awakening national consciousness, which was further aroused by Persian invasions from the North penetrating almost as far as Mecca. I shall not be tackling the history of Mohammed himself for a few days yet; so far it seems to me to have the character of a Beduin reaction against the settled, albeit decadent urban fellaheen[12] whose religion by then was also much debased, combining as it did a degenerate form of nature worship with a degenerate form of Judaism and Christianity.

Old Bernier's stuff is really very fine. It's a real pleasure to get back to something written by a sensible, lucid old Frenchman who constantly hits the nail on the head *sans avoir l'air de s'en apercevoir.*[13]

Since I am in any case tied up with the eastern mummery for some weeks, I have made use of the opportunity to learn Persian. I am put off Arabic, partly by my inborn hatred of Semitic languages, partly by the impossibility of getting anywhere, without considerable expenditure of time, in so extensive a language – one which has 4,000 roots and goes back over 2,000-3,000 years. By comparison, Persian is absolute child's play. Were it not for that impossible* Arabic alphabet in which every half dozen letters look like every other half dozen and the vowels are not written, I would undertake to learn the entire grammar within 48 hours. This for the better encouragement of Pieper[14] should he feel the urge to imitate me in this poor joke. I have set myself a maximum of three weeks for Persian, so if he stakes two months on it he'll best me anyway. What a pity Weitling[15] can't speak Persian; he would then have his *langue*

---

[12] Plural of Arabic *fellah* or *fallah*, tiller of the soil, peasant; here used by Engels in the obvious sense of settled population since he speaks of 'urban fellaheen'.

[13] 'Without appearing to be aware of it'.

[14] Wilhelm Pieper (*c.* 1826–1899): German philologist and journalist; a Communist earlier in life; friend of Marx (1850–53) in London.

[15] Wilhelm Weitling (1808–1871): early leader of the German working class, emigrated to the USA in 1849.

universelle toute trouvée[16] since it is, to my knowledge, the only language where 'me' and 'to me' are never at odds, the dative and accusative always being the same.

It is, by the way, rather pleasing to read dissolute old Hafiz in the original language, which sounds quite passable and, in his grammar, old Sir William Jones[17] likes to cite as examples dubious Persian jokes, subsequently translated into Greek verse in his *Commentariis poeseos asiaticae*, because even in Latin they seem to him too obscene. These commentaries, Jones' *Works,* Vol. II, *De poesi erotica*, will amuse you. Persian prose, on the other hand, is deadly dull. E.g. the Rauzat-us-safa by the noble Mirkhond, who recounts the Persian epic in very flowery but vacuous language.[18] Of Alexander the Great, he says that the name Iskander, in the Ionian language, is Akshid Rus (like Iskander, a corrupt version of Alexandros); it means much the same as *filusuf*, which derives from *fila*, love, and *sufa*, wisdom, 'Iskander' thus being synonymous with 'friend of wisdom'.

Of a RETIRED king he says: 'He beat the drum of abdication with the drumsticks of retirement', as will old Willich,[19] should he involve himself any more deeply in the literary fray. Willich will also suffer the same fate as King Afrasiab of Turan when deserted by his troops and of whom Mirkhond says: 'He gnawed the nails of horror with the teeth of desperation until the blood of vanquished consciousness welled forth from the finger-tips of shame'.

9. Marx to Engels, 14 June 1853

[Extract. *CW*, Vol. 39, pp. 346–48.]

The *Tribune*, needless to say, is puffing Carey's book[20] for all it's worth. Both, indeed, have this in common, that, in the guise of Sismondian-philanthropic-socialist anti-industrialism, they represent the protectionist, i.e.

---

[16] 'Universal language ready-made'.

[17] Sir William Jones (1746–1794): Orientalist; founder of Asiatic Society of Bengal; scholar of Persian and Sanskrit.

[18] Mir Khwand (1433–1498) completed his history of the world, *Rauzatu-s Safa*, at Herat (Afghanistan) in or after 1469. It obtained exceptional popularity. Engels could have perused any of the editions lithographed at Bombay in 1845, 1848 and 1850. See C.A. Storey, *Persian Literature: A Bio-bibliographical Survey*, Vol. I (London, 1935), pp. 92–101.

[19] August Willich (1810–1878): officer in the Prussian army, resigned, espoused Communist views, but split with Marx and Engels to form a separate group in 1850. Engels's reference to his retirement may be an allusion to this action of his. Willich emigrated to the USA in 1853 and fought on the Federal side in the Civil War.

[20] H. Ch. Carey, *The Slave Trade, Domestic and Foreign: Why it Exists and how it may be Extinguished* (Philadelphia, 1853).

industrial, bourgeoisie of America. That is also the key to the mystery why the *Tribune*, despite all its 'isms' and socialist flourishes, manages to be the 'LEADING JOURNAL' in the United States.

Your article on Switzerland was, of course, a direct swipe at the *Tribune'* 'LEADERS' (anti-centralization, etc.) and *their* man Carey. I continued this clandestine campaign in my first article on India, in which England's destruction of native industries is described as *revolutionary*. This they will find very SHOCKING. Incidentally the whole administration of India by the British was detestable and still remains so today.

The stationary nature of this part of Asia, despite all the aimless activity on the political surface, can be completely explained by two mutually supporting circumstances: 1. The PUBLIC WORKS system of the central government and, 2. Alongside this, the entire Empire which, apart from a few large cities, is an agglomeration of VILLAGES, each with its own distinct organization and each forming its own small world. A parliamentary report described these VILLAGES as follows:[21]

> A village, geographically considered, is a tract of country comprising some 100 or 1000 acres of arable and waste lands: politically viewed, it resembles a corporation or township. Every village is, and appears always to have been, in fact, a separate community or republic. Officials: 1. The *Potail*, Goud, Mundil etc. as he is termed in different languages, is the head inhabitant, who has generally the superintendence of the affairs of the village, settles the disputes of the inhabitants, attends to the police, and performs the duty of collecting the revenue within the village … 2. The *Curnum*, Shanboag, or Putwaree, is the register. 3. The *Taliary* or *Sthulwar* and 4. The *Totie*, are severally the watchmen of the village and of the crops. 5. The *Neerguntee* distributes the water of the streams or reservoirs in just proportion to the several fields. 6. The *Joshee*, or astrologer, announces the seed-times and harvests, and the lucky or unlucky days or hours for all the operation of farming. 7. the *smith*, and 8. The *carpenter* frame the rude instruments of husbandry, and the ruder dwellings of the farmer. 9. The *potter* fabricates the only utensils of the village. 10. The waterman keeps clean the few garments … 11. The *barber*, 12. *the silversmith*, who often combines the function of village *poet* and *schoolmaster*. Then the *Brahmin*, for worship. Under this simple form of municipal government the inhabitants of the country have lived from time immemorial. The boundaries of the villages have been but seldom altered; and although the villages themselves have been sometimes injured, and even desolated by war, famine and disease; the same name, the same limits, the same interests, and even the same families, have continued for ages. The inhabitants give themselves no trouble about the breaking up and division of kingdoms, while the village remains entire, they care not

---

[21] Marx quotes the original English from the *Fifth Report of the Select Committee on the Affairs of the East India Company* (London, 1812), p. 82.

to what power it is transferred, or to what sovereign it devolves. Its internal economy remains unchanged.

The post of Potail is mostly hereditary. In some of these COMMUNITIES the LANDS of the VILLAGE [are] CULTIVATED IN COMMON, in most of them EACH OCCUPANT TILLS HIS OWN FIELD. Within the same, slavery and the caste system. WASTE LANDS FOR COMMON PASTURE. Home-weaving and spinning by wives and daughters. These idyllic republics, of which only the VILLAGE boundaries are jealously guarded against neighbouring VILLAGES, continue to exist in well-nigh PERFECT form in the NORTH-WESTERN PARTS OF India only recently occupied by the English. No more solid basis for Asiatic despotism and stagnation is, I think, conceivable. And however much the English may have Irelandized the country, the breaking up of the archetypal forms was the *conditio sine qua non*[22] for Europeanization. The TAX-GATHERER alone could not have brought this about. Another essential factor was the destruction of the ancient industries, which robbed these villages of their SELF-SUPPORTING character.

In Bali, an island off the east coast of Java, this Hindu organization [is] still intact, alongside Hindu religion, its traces, like those of Hindu influence, discernible all over Java. So far as the *property question* is concerned, this is a great *bone of contention* among English writers on India. In the broken mountainous terrain south of the Kistna, however, there appears to have been property in land. In Java, on the other hand, as noted in the *History of Java* by a former *English* governor, Sir Stamford Raffles,[23] the sovereign [was] absolute LANDLORD throughout the country 'WHERE RENT TO ANY CONSIDERABLE AMOUNT WAS ATTAINABLE'. At all events, the Mohammedans seem to have been the first in the whole of Asia to have established the principle of 'no property in land'.

Regarding the above-mentioned VILLAGES, I should note that they already feature in the Manu, according to which the whole organization rests on them. 10 are administered by a senior COLLECTOR, then 100, then 1,000.[24]

[22] 'Indispensable condition'.
[23] Sir Thomas Stamford Raffles (1781–1826): Lieutenant-Governor of Java (1811–15) when the English held the island after having seized it from the Dutch; published *History of Java* in 1817 – this being the work Marx refers to here.
[24] *Manusmriti*, VII, 115–17; *The Laws of Manu*, translated by G. Bühler (Oxford, 1886), p. 234.

10. Marx to Adolf Cluss, 18 October 1853

[Extract. *CW*, Vol. 39, p. 390.]

Dana[25] copied my stuff [on China] almost word for word, watering down this and that and, with rare tact, *deleting* anything of an audacious nature NEVER MIND IT IS A BUSINESS OF HIS NOT OF MINE. In one of my Indian articles he also amended the bit where I speak of cholera as 'THE INDIAN'S REVENGE UPON THE WESTERN WORLD' to 'INDIA'S RAVAGES' which is nonsense. *En passant* Freiligrath[26] solicited that 'revenge' for a poem about cholera upon which he is still at work.

Again, in another of my articles on India, dealing with the princes there, he transmogrified 'THE SKELETON OF ETIQUETTE' into 'THE SECLUSION (PITIFUL!) OF ETIQUETTE'. NEVER MIND! Provided he pays.

11. Marx to Lassalle,[27] 23 January 1855

[Extract. *CW*, Vol. 39, p. 514.]

In general, it would appear that, relatively speaking, Europe's importance as a market for English goods is steadily diminishing; since in 1854, 60 per cent of total exports (I mean total exports of *British products*, disregarding re-exports) were absorbed by the United States, Australia and India alone, a figure which does not include Britain's colonies outside Europe (excepting India).

I have jotted down the above information to provide a very general answer to your questions. I shall see what I can find in the way of definite statistical material in my note-books. As already mentioned, books will no doubt *only* begin coming out *now...*

---

[25] Charles Anderson Dana (1819–1897): American journalist, radical and Abolitionist; editor-in-chief, *NYDT*, 1849–62.

[26] Ferdinand Freiligrath (1810–1876): German poet and Communist; later in life withdrew from the movement.

[27] Ferdinand Lassalle (1825–1864): German working class leader, with whom Marx and Engels cooperated despite differences.

12. Marx to Engels, 31 January 1855

[Extract. *CW*, Vol. 39, p. 517.]

Main items [of British Coalition Government's activities] in the spring and summer session [1854]:

1. *India Bill:* Ministry wishes to extend EAST INDIA COMPANY CHARTER (EXPIRING ON APRIL, 1854) by 20 years. Is compelled to drop this, its bill remaining in force *only provisionally* and for so long as it pleases Parliament. Apart from laying down that APPOINTMENTS IN THE CIVIL SERVICE AND SCIENTIFIC MILITARY SERVICES are to be subject to open competition, this Act confines itself to the following: Sir Charles Wood (President of the BOARD OF CONTROL) is to receive £5,000 instead of £1,200 as previously, 18 DIRECTORS instead of 24. Instead of all being nominated by the COURT OF PROPRIETORS, now 12 to be nominated by the latter and 6 by the Ministry. Salary of DIRECTORS to be once more *increased* from £300 to £500, those of the CHAIRMAN and DEPUTY CHAIRMAN to £1,000. GOVERNOR-GENERALSHIP of India to be separated from the GOVERNORSHIP of Bengal. New PRESIDENCY ON THE INDUS. Thus, instead of the inexpensive and, as practice has shown, efficient SIMPLE COMMISSIONERS, new GOVERNORS, PRESIDENTS with LUXURIOUS COUNCILS NEW SINECURES. A few quite insignificant little reforms in the Indian judiciary.

13. Engels to Marx, not before 27 September 1856

[Extract. *CW*, Vol. 40, p. 74.]

Another thing which considerably restrains speculators over here [Manchester] is the high price of all raw materials, particularly silk, cotton and wool, where it is far from SAFE to do anything at all. When the CRASH comes, however, there'll be a rude awakening for the English. I should like to know how many of the Continent's speculative shares have found their way to England – vast numbers, I imagine. This time there'll be a *dies irae*[28] such as has never been seen before; the whole of Europe's industry in ruins, all markets over-stocked (already nothing more is being shipped to India), all the propertied classes in the soup, complete bankruptcy of the bourgeoisie, war and profligacy to the nth degree. I, too, believe that it will all come to pass in 1857, and when I heard that you were again buying furniture, I promptly declared the thing to be a dead certainty and offered to take bets on it.

---

[28] 'The Day of Wrath'.

14. Marx to Engels, 14 July 1857

[Extract. *CW*, Vol. 40, p. 146.]

The Indian revolt has placed me in something of a quandary. As far as the *Tribune* is concerned, I am EXPECTED TO HAVE SOME SUPERIOR VIEW OF MILITARY AFFAIRS. If you can supply me with a few general axioms, I can easily combine them with the stuff I've already got together to make a readable article. The situation of the insurgents in Delhi and the MOVES of the British are the only points on which a few military generalities are needed. All the rest is MATTER OF FACT.

14-A. Jenny Marx[29] to Engels, about 14 August 1857

[Extract. *CW*, Vol. 40, p. 565.]

Jones[30] has lost his wife and is now happy as a sandboy; he hails all INDIANS as Kossuths and applauds the INDIAN PATRIOTS.

15. Marx to Engels, 15 August 1857

As to the Delhi affair, it seems to me that the English ought to begin their retreat as soon as the RAINY SEASON HAS SET IN in real earnest. Being obliged for the present to hold the fort for you as the *Tribune's* military correspondent, I have taken it upon myself to put this forward. NB, ON THE SUPPOSITION that the REPORTS to date have been true. It's possible that I shall make an ass of myself. But in that case one can always get out of it with a little dialectic. I have, of course, so worded my proposition as to be right either way. The persistent rumours about the fall of Delhi are being circulated throughout India by the government in Calcutta, no less, and are intended, as I see from the Indian papers, as the chief means of preventing unrest in the Madras and Bombay PRESIDENCIES. For your diversion I enclose herewith a plan of Delhi *which, however, you must let me have back.*

---

[29] Jenny Marx (1814–1881): wife of Karl Marx. The Rebellion of 1857 had broken out in India in May 1857.

[30] Ernest Charles Jones (1819–1869): Chartist leader, poet and novelist; twice jailed for sedition (1848–50); edited *The People's Paper*; friend of Karl Marx. Louis Kossuth (1802–94) had been the leading spirit behind the Hungarian revolution of 1848–49.

16. Engels to Marx, 24 September 1857

[Extract. *CW*, Vol. 40, pp. 182–85.]

Your wishes concerning India coincided with an idea I had that you might perhaps like to have my views on the business. At the same time I took the opportunity of going over the contents of the latest MAIL map in hand and VOICICE QUIEN RESULTE.[31]

The situation of the English in the middle and upper reaches of the Ganges is so incongruous that militarily speaking the only right course would be to effect a junction between Havelock's column and the one from Delhi, if possible at Agra, after each had done everything possible to evacuate the detached or invested garrisons in the area; to man, besides Agra, only the neighbouring stations *south* of the Ganges, especially Gwalior (on account of the Central Indian princes) and to hold the stations lower down the Ganges – Allahabad, Benares, Dinapur – with the existing garrisons and reinforcements from Calcutta; meanwhile to escort women and non-combatants down river, so that the troops again become mobile; and to employ mobile columns to instil respect in the region and to obtain supplies. If Agra cannot be held, there must be a withdrawal to Cawnpore or Allahabad; the latter *to be held at all costs* since it is the key to the territory between the Ganges and the Jumna.

If *Agra* can be held and the Bombay army remains available, the armies of Bombay and Madras must hold the peninsula proper up to the latitude of Ahmedabad and Calcutta and send out columns to establish communications with the north – the Bombay army via Indor and Gwalior to Agra, the Madras army via Saugor and Gwalior to Agra, and via Jubbulpore to Allahabad. The other lines of communication would then run to Agra from the Punjab, assuming it is held, and from Calcutta via Dinapur and Allahabad, so that there would be 4 lines of communication and, excluding the Punjab, 3 lines of withdrawal, to Calcutta, Bombay and Madras. Concentrating the troops arriving from the south at Agra would, therefore, serve the dual purpose of keeping the Central Indian princes in check and subduing the insurgent districts astride the line of march.

If Agra cannot be held, the Madras army must first establish communications with Allahabad and then make for Agra with the Allahabad troops, while the Bombay army makes for Gwalior.

The Madras army would seem to have been recruited exclusively from the ragtag and bobtail and to that extent is reliable. In Bombay they have 150 or more Hindus to a battalion and these are dangerous in that they may disaffect the rest. If the Bombay army revolts, all military calculations will temporarily cease to apply, and then nothing is more certain that there'll be one colossal MASSACRE from Kashmir to Cape Comorin. If the situation in Bombay is such that

[31] 'Here is the result'.

in future also the army cannot be used against the insurgents, then at least the Madras columns, which will by now have pushed on beyond Nagpur, will have to be reinforced and communications established as speedily as possible with Allahabad or Benares.

The absurdity of the position in which the English have now been placed by the total absence of any real supreme command is demonstrated mainly by 2 complementary circumstances, namely, 1. That they permit themselves to be invested when dispersed over a host of small, far flung stations while 2. They tie down their one and only mobile column in front of Delhi where not only can it do nothing but is actually going to pot. The English general who ordered the march on Delhi deserves to be cashiered and hanged, for he must have known what we have only just learned, viz. that the British had strengthened the old fortifications to the point where the place could only be taken by a systematic siege, for which a minimum of 15–20,000 men would be required, and far more if it was *well* defended. Now that they are there they will have *to stick it out for political reasons;* a withdrawal would be a defeat and will nevertheless be difficult to avoid. [Italics by Marx]

Havelock's troops have worked wonders. 126 miles in 8 days including 6 to 8 engagements[32] in that climate and at this time of year is truly super-human. But they're also quite played out; he, too, will probably have to let himself be invested after exhausting himself still further by excursions over a narrow radius round Cawnpore. Or he will have to return to Allahabad.

The actual route of reconquest will run up the valley of the Ganges. Bengal proper will be easier to hold since the population has so greatly degenerated; the really dangerous region begins at Dinapur. Hence the positions at Dinapur, Benares, Mirzapur and particularly Allahabad are of the utmost importance; from Allahabad, it would first be necessary to take the Doab (between the Ganges and the Jumna) and the cities on these two rivers, then Oudh, then the rest. The lines from Madras and Bombay to Agra and Allahabad can only be secondary lines of operations.

The main thing, as always, is concentration. The reinforcements sent up the Ganges are scattered all over the place and so far not one man has reached Allahabad. Unavoidable, perhaps, if these stations were to be made secure and then again, perhaps not. At all events, the number of stations to be held must be reduced to a minimum and forces must be concentrated for the field. If C. Campbell, about whom we know nothing save that he is a brave man, wants to distinguish himself as a general, he must create a mobile army, *coûte que coûte,*[33] whether or not Delhi is abandoned. And where, *summa summarum,* there are 25–30,000 European soldiers, no situation is so desperate that 5,000 at least cannot be mustered for a campaign, their losses being made good by the garrisons withdrawn from the stations. Only *then* will Campbell be able to see how he

[32] Figures '6 to 8' inserted by Marx.
[33] 'Cost what it may.'

stands and what kind of enemy is actually confronting him. THE ODDS ARE, HOW-EVER, that LIKE A FOOL he will *se blottir devant*[34] Delhi and watch his men go to pot AT THE RATE OF 100 A DAY, in which case it will be all the more 'brave' simply to stay there until everyone has cheerfully met his doom. Now as in the past brave stupidity is the order of the day.

Concentration of forces for the fighting in the north, vigorous support from Madras and, if possible, from Bombay, that's all. Even if the Mahratta princes on the Nerbudda defect it can do little harm save by way of an example, for their troops are already with the insurgents. Certainly the very most that can be done is to hold out until the first reinforcements arrive from Europe at the end of October. But if a few more Bombay regiments revolt, that will be the end of strategy and tactics; it's there that the decision lies.

17. Marx to Engels, 20 October 1857

[Extract. CW, Vol. 40, pp. 192–93.]

What do you think of the English in India? As usual the chaps are lucky even in adversity. I now have a pretty detailed list of their troops shipments since 18 June, along with the dates on which, by the government's reckoning, they *ought* to arrive and the *locus* of arrival. The following is a resume:[35]

Day of	Arrival	Total	Calcutta	Ceylon	Bombay	Karachi	Madras
September	20	214	214				
October	2	300	300				
	15	1,906	124	1,782			
	17	288	288				
	20	4,235	3,845	390			
	30	2,028	479	1,549			
October		8,757	5,036	3,721			
November	1	3,495	1,234	1,629		632	
	5	879	879				
	10	2,700	904	340	400	1,056	
	12	1,633	1,633				
	15	2,610	2,132	478			
	19	234				234	
	20	1,216		278	938		
	24	406		406			
	25	1,276					1,276
	30	666		462	204		
November		15,115	6,782	3,593	1,542	1,922	1,276

[34] 'Squat down before'.
[35] This table, slightly abridged, was included in Marx's article 'The Revolt in India', *New York Daily Tribune*, 14 November 1857.

Day of	Arrival	Total	Calcutta	Ceylon	Bombay	Karachi	Madras
December	1	354			354		
	5	459			201		258
	10	1,758		607		1,151	
	14	1,057			1,057		
	15	948			647	301	
	20	693	185		300	208	
	25	624				624	
December		5,893	185	607	2,559	2,284	258
January	1	340			340		
	5	220					220
	15	140					140
	20	220					220
January		920			340		580
September–January		30,899	12,217	7,921	4,431[36]	4,206	2,114
Troops Despatched by Overland Mail							
October	2	235	Engineers	117		118	
	12	221	Artillerymen				
	14	244	Engineers	122		122	
October		700		460[37]		240	

The 30,899 men are composed of:

Infantry: 24,739

Artillery: 2,334

Cavalry: 3,826

Of the ARTILLERY, only 100 men arrive at Calcutta in November. The actual ARRIVALS commence on 15 October. The first cavalry arrives on 10 November.

18. Engels to Marx, 29 October 1857

[Extract. CW, Vol. 40, p. 197.]

The Sepoys must have defended the ENCEINTE of Delhi very badly; the real joke was the house-to-house fighting when, presumably, the NATIVE TROOPS were sent in first. So the actual siege – what came afterwards could hardly be described as such – lasted from the 5th to the 14th [September], long enough for breaches to be made in the unprotected wall by heavy guns firing at a range of

---

[36] The correct total should be 4,441.

[37] The total does not match with the actual total of the two figures in the column, which is 239 only.

300–400 yards. These were already in position by the 5th or 6th. The cannon on the walls do not appear to have been effectively manned, otherwise the English wouldn't have been able to make so swift an approach.

19. Marx to Engels, 31 October 1857

[Extract. *CW*, Vol. 40, pp. 197–98.]

Have received two letters from Dana. Says first, that '*Army*'[38] arrived in good time. Secondly, that, because of the COMMERCIAL CRISIS, notice has been given to all European correspondents except for myself and Bayard Taylor;[39] I, however, am to confine myself STRICTLY TO 1 ARTICLE PER WEEK – lately I had been trying to break through this limitation – and for the time being write exclusively about the INDIAN WAR AND THE FINANCIAL CRISIS.

As soon as the next mail arrives from India, you must write to me at some length about the Delhi affair or rather, IF POSSIBLE, do the whole article since this time it has to be purely technical.

20. Marx to Engels, 13 November 1857

[Extract. *CW*, Vol. 40, p. 199.]

Meanwhile I haven't written a word about India. I have got to have some accurate military stuff on the subject, EVENTS having to some extent discredited myself and the *Tribune*.[40]

---

[38] Presumably, the piece published as a leading article in *NYDT*, 13 October 1857. For this Marx had used Engels's letter of 24 September 1857 (No. 16 above).

[39] Bayard Taylor (1825–1878): American traveller and journalist, correspondent of *NYDT*.

[40] This must be a reference to the British capture of Delhi in September 1857 despite Marx's predictions in *NYDT* that this would not be possible. On 16 November, Engels wrote an article on the 'British Capture of Delhi', which appeared in *NYDT*, 5 December 1857.

21. Engels to Marx, 15 November 1857

[Extract. *CW*, Vol. 40, pp. 201–02.]

The peculiarly favourable advices from Madras and Bombay (sales with profit, which has not been the case since 1847) have revived the Indian trade. Everyone who possibly can is rushing into it. To the annoyance of the other commission houses, S. Mendel, INDIAN agent, has the whole of his big WAREHOUSE lit up until 10 o'clock every night and sends out stuff for all he's worth. No DOUBT hundreds of spinners and weavers are shipping goods there on consignment. So we have a reserve crisis up our sleeve there in case this first impact proves incapable of overturning the old muck.

22. Engels to Marx, 9 December 1857

[Extract. *CW*, Vol. 40, p. 219.]

Someone told me he knew of 5 or 6 Indian houses [at Manchester] whose stocks are such that they *cannot fail* to go to the wall in the very near future.

23. Engels to Marx, 31 December 1857

[Extract. *CW*, Vol. 40, pp. 234–35.]

In future, let me know as early as possible what your intentions are as to military articles; just now 24 hours makes quite a difference to me.

(1) In any case, detailed information is so frightfully scarce, what there is being based almost wholly on telegraphic despatches from Cawnpore to Calcutta, that it's virtually impossible to write a critical analysis. The only points I can think of are these: It is 40 MILES from Cawnpore to Lucknow (Alam Bagh) – Havelock's forced marches show that in India 15 miles a day over a protracted period is a very long march. Accordingly, with only 2–3 marches ahead of him, Colin [Campbell] ought to have arrived at Alam Bagh no later than the 3rd day after his departure from Cawnpore, WITH PLENTY OF DAYLIGHT STILL LEFT TO ATTACK AT ONCE. It is by these standards that Colin's march must be judged; I can no longer recall the dates.

(2) He had, after all, some 7,000 men (far more had been counted on, so

between Calcutta and Cawnpore the march must have gone atrociously badly and a great many men been lost) and if he beat the Oudhi with approximately 7,000 men (including the garrisons of Alam Bagh and Lucknow), it was no great feat. An army of 5–7,000 Englishmen has always been thought fully sufficient to go anywhere and do anything in the open field in India. That stamps the opponents at once. A further consideration is that the Oudhi, although the most warlike race of the Ganges valley, were greatly inferior to the Sepoys as regards discipline, cohesion, weapons, etc., etc., precisely because they had never come under direct European organization. Hence the main battle took the form of a running fight, that is to say a skirmishing engagement in which the Oudhians were pushed back from post to post. Now it is true the British are, with the Russians, the worst light infantry in Europe, but they have learnt something in the Crimea, and at all events they had this great advantage over the Oudhians that their line of skirmishers was properly and regularly supported by pickets and lines the whole under one individual commander and cooperating towards a single end; while their opponents in the normal Asiatic manner, dispersed in irregular clusters, everyone pressing to the front, thus offering a sixfold aim to the British, having no regular supports or reserves and each cluster commanded by its own clannish chief, acting independently of every other clan. For it must be repeated, up to now we have not heard in a single instance that any insurrectionary army in India had been properly constituted under a recognized chief.[41] No other indication as to the nature of the fighting is given in the despatches nor, for that matter, any description of the terrain or particulars about the employment of troops, so that it's absolutely impossible for me to say anything further (let alone from memory).

24. Marx to Engels, 7 January 1858

[Extract. *CW*, Vol. 40, p. 242.]

I received your article[42] at 5' o'clock on Tuesday afternoon. It is HIGHLY AMUSING and will delight the Yankees. The news from India, by the by, is no longer quite so favourable to the worthy English. POOR Havelock!

---

[41] In this paragraph, the text from 'An army of 5–7,000' to 'at once', and then, again, from 'a running fight' to 'a recognized chief', was written in English by Engels.

[42] This refers to Engels's article on the siege and storming of Lucknow, which appeared in *NYDT*, 30 January 1758, as a leading article.

25. Marx to Engels, 11 January 1858

[Extract. CW, Vol. 40, p. 244.]

Affairs in India – with Windham for HERO – are again taking an interesting TURN. If we have fuller particulars this week, by Wednesday or thereabouts, I shall have to send off something on the subject to the *Tribune*.

26. Engels to Marx, 14 January 1858

[Extract. CW, Vol. 40, p. 247.]

Herewith the article ['Relief of Lucknow'], though it has just occurred to me that by a ludicrous slip I have written Wilson throughout instead of *Inglis*; perhaps you would alter this as there's no time to do so now.[43]

The Lucknow garrison's greatest act of heroism consisted in the fact THAT THEY HAD TO FACE EVERY DAY THE 'COARSE BEEF' COOKED BY THE LADIES, 'ENTIRELY UNAIDED'. Must have been damned badly cooked. *The Daily News* has something on Windham, but not enough.

27. Marx to Engels, 16 January 1858[44]

[Extract. CW, Vol. 40, p. 249.]

Your article[45] is SPLENDID and IN STYLE and MANNER altogether reminiscent of the *Neue Rheinische Zeitung*[46] in its heyday. As for Windham, he may be a very bad general, but on this occasion the man was undone by what was the making of him at the Redan – unseasoned troops. I am generally of the opinion that in terms of bravery, self-reliance and STEADINESS this, the second army England has committed to India (and of which not a man will return), will not be able to hold a candle to the first, which seems to have dwindled away almost

---

[43] The text as printed in *NYDT*, 1 February 1858, shows that Marx corrected the slip before sending the article to *NYDT*.

[44] Marx dated it 14 January, but this was a slip for 16 January (CW, Vol. 39, p. 612 n. 266).

[45] 'The Relief of Lucknow', *NYDT*, 1 February 1858.

[46] A daily newspaper published from Cologne (Germany) and edited by Karl Marx during the 1848–49 Revolution. Engels was also on the editorial staff of the journal and contributed articles, often on military matters.

entirely. As regards the effect of the climate on the troops, while temporarily in charge of the military DEPARTMENT I showed in various articles by exact calculations that mortality was DISPROPORTIONATELY higher than stated in the official English despatches. In view of the DRAIN OF MEN and BULLION which she will cost the English, India is now our best ally.

28. Marx to Engels, 8 August 1858

[Extract. CW, Vol. 40, p. 336.]

In Central India, or so it seems to me, the fall of Gwalior settles the matter. The Indian papers[47] are all very hostile to Campbell and critical of his 'tactics'.

29. Marx to Engels, 9 April 1859

[Extract. CW, Vol. 40, pp. 412–13.]

The financial muddle in India must be seen as the real result of the Indian Mutiny. A GENERAL financial BREAKDOWN seems inevitable unless those classes are taxed which to date have been England's most solid supporters. However, even that will be of no substantial help. The joke is that John Bull will now have to pay out annually between 4 and 5 million [pounds] cash in India in order to keep the wheels turning, and will in this nice roundabout way restore his national debt to the proper progressive RATIO. It must certainly be admitted that the Indian market is being paid a damned high price for Manchester cottons. According to the report of the Military Commission 80,000 EUROPEANS as well as some 200,000 to 260,000 NATIVES will have to be maintained in India for years to come. This cost ABOUT £20 million and the total NET REVENUE amounts to no more than £25 million. Moreover, the mutiny has added a PERMANENT DEBT of £50 million or, according to [James] Wilson's calculations, a permanent annual deficit of 3 million. In addition, there is the GUARANTEE of £2 million per annum to the RAILWAYS until they are running and, indefinitely, a smaller sum if their NET REVENUE falls short of 5 per cent. So far (apart from the short stretch of railway that has been completed) India has got nothing out of the thing save the privilege of paying English capitalists 5 per cent for their capital. But John Bull has cheated himself,

---

[47] That is, British-owned papers published in India: Marx is probably referring to quotations from these papers in the *Times* and other London papers.

or rather has been cheated by his capitalists. India's payments are merely nominal, whereas those of John Bull are real. E.g. a substantial part of Stanley's LOAN[48] was simply to be used for paying 5 per cent to English capitalists, even in respect of railways the building of which has not yet begun. Finally, the revenue from opium, amounting hitherto to £4 million per annum, is under serious threat as a result of the Chinese treaty. Whatever happens the monopoly is bound to collapse and in China itself the cultivation of opium will soon be in full swing. Revenue was derived from opium precisely because it was an article of contraband. To my mind the present financial catastrophe in India is a more serious affair than was the war in India.

30. Engels to Marx, 26 January 1860

[Extract. CW, Vol. 41, pp. 7–8.]

In India we have the makings of a tremendous crisis. As far as the views of the local philistines on the subject are concerned, CONFER the enclosed MARKET REPORTS. Now yarn prices are mostly so high, almost higher than the peak in 1857, and yet cotton is 2–3/8 to 2–1/2 d. *cheaper*. Twenty-six new mills are under construction in Burnley alone and a proportionate number in other places. Everywhere, by degrees the workers are getting a 10 per cent rise in wages and will shortly receive even more. In my view, the practice of operating on fictitious capital is again just as RIFE in Indian business as it was in 1846/47, and most people are buying only because they *have* to, and cannot stop. But even if that were not so, the increase in production alone will bring about a colossal COLLAPSE this autumn or in the spring of 1861 at the latest.

31. Marx to Lassalle, 11 June 1861

[Extract. CW, Vol. 41, pp. 293–94.]

Many thanks for your book.[49] . . . It is an important work in every respect. However, I cannot send you a criticism, assessment, etc., until I have read right through the whole thing. Merely *en passant*, then: in *India*, adoption is the prevailing form. *English* law has taken a course diametrically opposed to

---

[48] Loan raised when Edward Henry Stanley (1826–1893) was the Secretary of State for India, 1858–59.

[49] Ferdinand Lassalle, *Das System der erworbenen Rechte* (Leipzig, 1861).

that of French law. Complete testamentary freedom (whereby no Englishman or Yankee is compelled to leave his family a farthing) dates back to the bourgeois revolution of 1688 and evolved in the same measure as bourgeois property developed in England.

32. Marx to Engels, 6 March 1862

[Extract. *CW*, Vol. 41, pp. 348–49.]

In consequence of the American crisis [the outbreak of the Civil War], the BOARD OF TRADE report for 1861 shows a considerable change in the ranking order of the various markets for English exports. *India* leads with £17,923,767 (including Ceylon and Singapore. India alone, £16,412,090).

Out of the total exports of £125,115,133 (1861), £42,260,970 go to English 'POSSESSIONS' and 'COLONIES'. If one adds to that what England exports to other parts of Asia, Africa and America, there remains at most 23 to 24 per cent for export to the countries of Europe. Should Russia continue to advance in Asia at the same rapid pace as during the past 10 years until all her EFFORTS are concentrated on India, it will be the end of John Bull's world market, a demise that will be hastened by the United State's protective tariff policy, which that country will certainly be in no hurry to relinquish, if only out of REVENGE against John. Moreover John Bull is discovering to his horror that his main colonies in North America and Australia are becoming protectionist to the same extent as he himself is becoming a FREE-TRADER. The complacent, brutal stupidity with which John has acclaimed Pam's [Palmerston's] 'SPIRITED POLICY' in Asia and America, will one day cost him damned dear.

References to India in Other Writings of Karl Marx and Frederick Engels

Compiled by Irfan Habib[1]

The material from Karl Marx's *Tribune* articles (including those of Engels) and from the Marx–Engels correspondence for the period 1852–62, published in the present volume, undoubtedly comprise the bulk of what Marx and Engels wrote on India, but important passages relating to India occur elsewhere in their writings from a fairly early date. A list, chronologically arranged, is provided below to assist the reader in consulting this material. References traced in Marx–Engels letters from outside the period 1852–62, are brought together at the end.

Note: In the works of Marx and Engels, the words 'East India' and 'East Indies' generally refer to India, based on the British (often commercial) usage of the time.

1. The earliest work where references to India occur is the major joint work of Marx and Engels, *The German Ideology*, written in 1845–46, though published only posthumously in 1932. The following references to India are taken from the translation in *Collected Works*, Vol. 5 (Moscow, 1976):

p. 51: Machine invented in England deprives workers of bread in India and China.

p. 55: Crude division of labour in India produces the caste system, not *vice versa*.

Those who have access to the English translation (same translators) of this work published from Moscow, 1964, will find these references on pages 60 and 51 respectively (the different sequence is due to the MS materials being differently arranged).

2. Karl Marx, *The Poverty of Philosophy* (1847); translation in *Collected Works*, Vol. 6 (Moscow, 1976).

p. 160: Millions of workers perish in East Indies owing to growth of English cotton industry.

---

[1] The compiler wishes to acknowledge the use of material derived from 'Reading Marx on India', Aligarh Historians Society, Communication No. 5 (1983). While preparing this list, the compiler has had access to the following volumes of Marx and Engels, *Collected Works*: 1–26, 28–32 and 38–43. [Of these, only such have been listed in the Bibliography as were found to contain some material directly relevant to India, including the articles and letters published in the present volume. — Ed.]

p. 185: Increase of circulation of commodities after the opening of the Cape of Good Hope route to the East Indies.

p. 187: Thanks to machinery, the spinner is placed in England, the weaver in East Indies.

These pages correspond to pages 113, 163 and 156 of the separate edition of *The Poverty of Philosophy* (Moscow, n.d.) (1955?).

3. Frederick Engels, 'Principles of Communism', 1847; translation in *Collected Works*, Vol. 6.

p. 345: India, having made no progress for thousands of years now 'revolutionized' by cheaper English commodities, ruining its manufactory workers.

4. Frederick Engels, Lecture, London, 30 November 1847; translation in *Collected Works*, Vol. 6.

p. 628: East Indies had remained in the same state of development for centuries. Now the English came with their manufactures destroying the Indians' livelihoods. Old aristocracy ruined; internal struggles, 'as here', begin. Closer to 'civilization'.

5. Karl Marx, Speech on the Question of Free Trade, 9 January 1848: quotation from Dr Browning's speech in House of Commons, 1835, describing the distress among Indian spinners and weavers caused by competition from British manufactures. *CW*, Vol. 6, pp. 460–61; also Karl Marx, *Poverty of Philosophy* (Moscow, n.d.) (1955?), pp. 245–48.

6. Karl Marx, 'The State of Trade', *Neue Rheinische Zeitung*, No. 239, 7 March 1849, *CW*, Vol. 9 (Moscow, 1977), pp. 3–4: Canton, Bombay, Calcutta overflowing with unsaleable British goods. British victories in the Punjab, 'which ensured peace in Hindustan', have played a part in reviving British commercial spirit; but this too would not last.

7. Karl Marx, *Grundrisse*, 'Economic Manuscripts' of 1857–58, available in two translations: (i) Martin Nicolaus (tr.), *Grundrisse: Foundations of the Critique of Political Economy* (Harmondsworth, 1973); and (ii) Ernst Wangerman's translation in Marx and Engels, *Collected Works*, Vols. 28 and 29 (Moscow, 1986 and 1987). Page references are to the Nicolaus translation, with the *Collected Works* volumes and pages indicated within brackets.

pp. 472–73 (*CW*, 28, pp. 400–01): Despotic forms in the Community, found in a few clans of India.

pp. 473–75 (*CW*, 29, pp. 401–03): Labour on communal basis required for irrigation works in Asia.

pp. 486–87 (*CW*, 28, p. 410): Asiatic form of community survives longest.

p. 493 (*CW*, 28, p. 417): Slavery and serfdom in Asiatic community.

p. 528 (*CW*, 28, p. 452): Surplus through herded forced labour in India, etc.

p. 769 (*CW*, 29, p. 152): Use of mass labour in India for works of religious ostentation.

p. 812 (*CW*, 29, p. 192): Indian currency system.

p. 851 (*CW*, 29, p. 227): Usurer appropriates both profit and wages in India.

pp. 858–59 (*CW*, 29, p. 233): Trade has little dissolving effect on Indian community.

p. 862 (*CW*, 29, p. 236): High rate of interest on unproductive borrowing in India; India on silver standard.

p. 882 (*CW*, 29, p. 253): Most diverse forms of economic communities found in India.

8. Karl Marx, *A Contribution to the Critique of Political Economy* (1859), translated by S.W. Ryazanskaya, edited by Maurice Dobb (Moscow, 1970/1978). (Same translation reprinted in *CW*, Vol. 9, Moscow, 1987, pp. 257–417.)

p. 33 n.: In Indian communal property, original forms found elsewhere can be identified.

p. 75: Indian demand for silver.

pp. 130, 134–35: Indian commerce and hoarding.

p. 140: British Government's purchase of opium in India.

p. 202: English mode of production imposed on India 'to some extent'.

8A. Original draft (MS) of above work, translation in *CW*, Vol. 29 (Moscow, 1987), pp. 430–507.

pp. 435–36, 446, 448: Silver movements from America to India in early modern times.

p. 460: Gold–silver ratio in India.

p. 464: Division of labour in 'self-supporting' Indian communities.

9. Frederick Engels, Articles in the *New American Cyclopaedia*, Vols I–IV (1858–59); reprinted in Marx and Engels, *CW*, Vol. 18 (Moscow, 1982).

'Afghanistan', Vol. I (1858), *CW*, 18, pp. 40–48.

'Artillery', Vol. II (1858): Indians and fire arms, *CW*, 18, pp. 188–90.

'Burmah', Vol. III (1859), *CW*, 18, pp. 280–90.

'Cavalry', Vol. IV (1859): Failure of Sepoy cavalry (Mutineers) to break up regular European cavalry, *CW*, 18, p. 311.

MS summary of John W. Kaye, *History of War in Afghanistan*, *CW*, 18, pp. 379–90.

10. Karl Marx, 'On the Cotton Crisis', *Die Press* (Vienna), No. 38, 8 February 1868, translated in *CW*, 19, pp. 160–62: Chamber of Commerce, Manchester, demands removal of administrative obstacles to cultivation of

cotton in India and lifting of duty of 10 per cent on English cotton yarns and textile fabrics imported into India. Bazley, M.P., complained that under this protectionist duty machinery was being exported to Bombay and Calcutta, and factories had been erected there to compete with British cotton manufactures.

11. Karl Marx, *Capital*, Vol. I (1867), translated by Samuel Moore and Edward Aveling, edited by Frederick Engels (Swan Sonnenschein, Lowrey & Co., London), 1887. This standard translation was reprinted photographically with some supplementary material by Dona Torr (London, 1938). There have been other editions of this translation, notably, the Moscow edition (Progress Publishers) of 1978, which, unfortunately, did not indicate the page numbers of the original 1887 edition. Below we give the pages of the 1887 edition (= Dona Torr's edition) with those of the Moscow edition within brackets.

p. 9 (49): Social division of labour without commodity production in primitive Indian community.

pp. 59–60 (91): Absence of exchange within ancient Indian community; its subsequent development.

p. 107 (131): Conversion of surplus use-value into money by hoarding in India.

p. 111 n. (134 n.): Silver hoarding and silver imports into India.

p. 118 (140): State taxes, chiefly rents in kind, in Asia.

p. 318 and n. (311 and n.): Waste of quantities of cotton in India, where, with communities destroyed, labour is not available at crucial times.

p. 325 (316): Cooperation in Indian communities, based on common ownership of means of production and on tribal ties.

p. 331–32 (321–22): Indian weaver's craft and hereditary skill.

p. 346 (333): Relative density of population (in terms of labour supply) low in India, owing to backwardness of means of communication.

p. 346 n. (333 n.): Extension of cotton cultivation and famines.

pp. 350–52 (337–38): Indian village community, its internal structure and relationship with external economy.

p. 377 (360): Paper-making in India, representing antique form of production.

pp. 431–32 (406): Acute effect of growth of English cotton industry on India: bones of cotton-weavers bleach the plains of India.

p. 443 n. (416 n.): India ruined by English power-loom.

p. 453 (424): India compelled to produce raw materials for Britain.

p. 461 (431): Extinction of Indian handloom weavers.

p. 523 n. (481–82 n.): Regulation of water supply as basis of power of state over disconnected producing organisms in India.

p. 610 (560–61): Production and reproduction on progressively increasing scale go on in India without capitalist accumulation.

p. 775 (703): Conquest and looting of East Indies among chief momenta of primitive accumulation.

p. 777 (704–05): Methods of primitive accumulation by East India Company and its servants in India.

p. 777 n. (705 n.): Orissa famine of 1866.

12. Karl Marx, *Capital*, Vols II and III, posthumously published under editorship of Frederick Engels (1885 and 1894), translated into English by Ernest Untermann (1909, 1919), and reprinted in India by Saraswati Library, Calcutta, in 1945 and 1946. The Untermann translation has been superseded by the translations issued from Moscow, of Vol. II in 1957 and of Vol. III in 1959. These were reprinted (with different pagination) by Progress Publishers (Moscow, 1978). In the following references, the pages given are those of the Moscow 1957 edition for Vol. II and Moscow 1959 edition for Vol. III. The corresponding pages of the Moscow 1978 reprint follow within brackets.

Vol. II

p. 34 (36): Capitalist production [in Europe] first spreads commodity production in India, China, etc., and then proceeds to destroy all previous forms of commodity production, based on either the self-employed producer or the conversion of surplus alone into commodities.

p. 110 (113): Indian peasant and commodity production.

p. 134 n. (137 n.): Book-keeper in Indian village community.

pp. 140–41 n. (144 n.): Exports and famines in India.

pp. 236–37 (240–41): Peasant and cattle in India. (Correct 'Manara-Dharma-Sestra' to 'Manava-Dharma-Sastra'.)

p. 252 (255–56): Commerce and credit mechanism between England and India.

pp. 317–18 (320–22): Mechanism of export of cotton goods from England to India.

Vol. III

p. 71 (71): Improved communication between India and England reduced time of circulation and increased profits.

pp. 148–49 (151): Rate of profit higher in an Asian country.

p. 211 (213): Indian ryot an independent producer.

p. 328 and n. (334 and n.): Disruption of Indian village communities by the English and their economic experiments.

p. 403 (410–11): Swindling in East Indian and Chinese markets.

pp. 539–40 (551–52): Drain of silver to India.

p. 546 (559): Rate of exchange with Asia.

p. 553 (565): Silver export to Asia.

pp. 563–71 (576–84): Rate of exchange with India, export of capital for railways to India, bills on India, English imports from India without payment, the tribute.

p. 577 (590): Indian tribute, £5 million.

pp. 578–79 (591–92): Silver flow, and rate of exchange with India.

pp. 583–84 (596): Usury in Asian forms.

p. 584 (596): Rate of interest in India.

p. 602 (616): Legal concept of private landed property exported to Asia.

pp. 709–10 (726): Products of Indian peasants sold without reference to price of production.

p. 767 (787): Domestic handicrafts and manufacturing labour pre-requisites of Indian village community.

pp. 771–72 (791): Surplus labour in Indian community; overlordship of state: taxes and rents coincide.

pp. 776–77 (796): Form of rent in kind exploited by the English in India.

p. 855 (877): Surplus in Indian village community.

13. Karl Marx, 'Economic Manuscript of 1861–63', portion preceding the text containing *Theories of Surplus Value* (see No. 14 below), *CW*, Vol. 30, pp. 1–347.

p. 343: Despite general superfluity of labour in India, impossibility of procuring sufficient hands to clean the cotton during the season, thereby causing much waste and reducing the available supply for England. *The Bengal Hurkaru*, 1861, quoted for this.

p. 343: Dr Forbes' churka [spinning wheel] invented to increase output of spun yarn in India, quoting paper read before Society of Arts in 1861.

14. Karl Marx, *Theories of Surplus Value*. This work really consists of Marx's economic manuscript of 1862–63, which was his draft for what was to be the final volume of *Capital*. An English translation in three parts was published from Moscow, 1963, 1968 and 1971; and there was a reprint of all the three parts by Progress Publishers (Moscow, 1975). The same translation of the work has also been used in *CW*, Vols 30–32 (Moscow, 1988–89), beginning at p. 348 in *CW*, Vol. 30, but the references below are to the Moscow reprint of 1975, which is, perhaps, the more easily available of all the editions, and has a more convenient arrangement.

Part I

p. 376: Higher rate of interest and profit in East Indies.

Part II

p. 16: High rate of profit in India with low productivity of labour.

p. 241: Main product for determining agricultural rent.

p. 407: In India high rate of surplus value, owing to low wages.

p. 482: Raw materials for England produced by Indian ryots.

Part III

p. 188: Indian worker, working with advances from capitalist, surrenders surplus produce to capitalist.

p. 416: Indian peasants as hereditary occupiers and labouring cultivators (Richard Jones).

p. 435: Indian artisans in villages maintained by villages, but town artisans linked to presence of customers, and not dependent on locales of fixed capital (Richard Jones); Indian cities like army camps (Bernier).

15. Frederick Engels, 'Fighting in France', *Pall Mall Gazette*, London, 11 November 1870: English in stamping out Sepoy Mutiny violated the norms of war by shooting down prisoners of war (*CW*, Vol. 22, Moscow, 1986, pp. 165–66).

16. Karl Marx, Drafts of Letters to Vera Zasulich (1881), published in *CW*, Vol. 24 (Moscow, 1989), pp. 346–69.

p. 351: Rural commerce in East Indies in final stage of the archaic formation.

p. 359: *Contra* Maine, Indian communities not destroyed by spontaneous operation of economic laws.

p. 368: The English ruined Indian agriculture and intensified severity of famines.

Note: For another translation of these drafts, see Teodor Shanin (ed.), *Late Marx and the Russian Road*, London, 1984, pp. 99–123.

17. Karl Marx, MS Notes on India:

(i) *Notes on Indian History (664–1858)*, translated by published by Foreign Languages Publishing House, Moscow, n.d. These notes are stated to have been written by Marx 'in the last years of his life' and are drawn from Mountstuart Elphinstone, *History of India*, 1841 (new edition, London, 1874), and Robert Sewell, *Analytical History of India* (1870).

(ii) Notes from M.M. Kovalevsky, *System of Communal Landed Property* (1870), John Budd Phear, *Aryan Village in India and Ceylon* (1880), and H.S. Maine, *Lectures on the Early History of Institutions* (1875), published in Lawrence Krader (ed.), *The Ethnological Notebooks of Karl Marx* (Assen, 1972). For reference to this work see R.A.L.H. Gunawardana, *Indian Historical Review*, II (2), 1976, pp. 386–87. Marx's comment in his notes on Kovalevsky's use of 'feudalism' for Indian agrarian society is quoted by E. Hobsbawm, Introduction to Marx, *Pre-Capitalist Economic Formations* [part of *Grundrisse*] (London, 1964), and Gunawardana, *Indian Historical Review*, II (2), p. 386, both from a paper by two Soviet scholars published in 1960, which presumably drew on these notebooks.

(iii) In his notes on the history of Ireland (1860), Marx comments that Lord Cornwallis, as a governor[-general] for India, became further qualified for destroying a nation's rights (Marx and Engels, *CW*, Vol. 21, 1985, p. 259).

18. Frederick Engels, *Anti-Dühring* (1878); translation published in *Collected Works*, Vol. 25 (Moscow, 1987), pp. 1–309.

p. 137: Break-up of Indian primitive community.

p. 150: Primitive aristocracy in Punjab based on common ownership of soil.

p. 163: Cultivation originally carried on by tribal and village communities, from India to Ireland.

pp. 166–68: Emergence of despotism out of communities in India and Persia; communities serve as basis for Oriental despotism, from India to Russia.

p. 294: Products not transformed into commodities in ancient Indian communities.

p. 300: Personification of natural forces in Indian Vedas.

19. Frederick Engels, *The Origin of the Family, Private Property and the State* (1884), English translation (Moscow, 1948).

p. 38: Pastoralism among Aryans.

p. 43: System of relationships among tribes in India.

pp. 59–60: Group-marriage survival in a tribe of Oudh.

pp. 73–74: Sexual freedom for girls before marriage among aboriginal tribes.

p. 86: Household community with common tillage.

pp. 86–87: Polyandry in India and Tibet.

p. 226: Aryans and pastoralism.

Note: In *CW*, 26 (Moscow, 1990), where the work occupies pp. 129–276, the above references occur, in the same order, on pp. 137, 140, 151, 159–60, 168, 169 and 259.

20. Frederick Engels, Preface to the English edition of *The Condition of the Working Class in England* (1892), published in Marx and Engels, *On Britain* (Moscow, 1953), pp. 17–32.

There is a reference here (*On Britain*, p. 18) to the development of colonial markets at an increasing rate so as to absorb English manufactures, whereby millions of hand-weavers in India were crushed by the Lancashire power-loom.

21. Letters of Marx and Engels

Note: In the list below all letters from the *Tribune* period, 1852–62, are omitted, since relevant extracts from these have already been given in the Supplement in this volume.

Engels to Marx, 30 July, 1 September and 23 September 1851 (*CW*, Vol. 38, Moscow, 1982, pp. 395, 450, 461): India overstocked with English cotton goods.

Engels to H. Engels, 2 November 1864 (*CW*, Vol. 42, Moscow, 1987, p. 10): Moderate pace of deliveries of cotton from India.

Engels to Marx, 12 April 1865 (*CW*, 42, p. 141): Bills drawn from India against white cotton may result in some firms coming to grief.

Engels to Marx, 25 May 1866 (*CW*, 42, p. 279): Colossal losses on cotton imported from India.

Engels to Marx, 29 January and 13 March 1867 (*CW*, 42, pp. 345, 349): Glut of markets in India, China, etc., for British cotton goods, being aggravated.

Marx to Engels, 14 March [November in original] 1868 (*CW*, 42, p. 547): Asian or Indian property forms also the original ones in Europe.

Marx to Engels, 9 December 1868 (*CW*, 43, p. 179): Mystery where England obtained cotton from during American Civil War, beyond 'all the imports from India, etc.'

Engels to Marx, 11 December 1868 (*CW*, 43, p. 181): Crisis in Lancashire owing to overproduction. Spinners and manufacturers have been 'consigning goods unsaleable here to India and China'. But those markets being overloaded, firms failing right and left.

Marx to L. Kugelmann, 17 February 1870 (Karl Marx, *Letters to Dr Kugelmann*, English translation, London, 1935(?), p. 99; *CW*, 43, p. 434): Communal property, of Indian origin.

Marx to L. Kugelmann, 13 December 1870 (Marx, *Letters to Dr Kugelmann*, p. 115): English war atrocities in India.

Marx to N.F. Danielson, 10 April 1879 (Marx and Engels, *Selected Correspondence*, Moscow, 1956, pp. 381–82): Stocks of cotton goods exported from Britain accumulating unsold in India.

Marx to Danielson, 19 February 1881 (*Selected Correspondence*, Moscow, pp. 408–09): Heavy drain of wealth from India to England, famines, Hindu–Muslim conspiracy against the English taking shape, hence 'serious complications, if not, a general outbreak' in store.

Engels to Karl Kautsky, 12 September 1882 (*Selected Correspondence*, Moscow, pp. 422–23): India likely to make a revolution on its own.

Engels to C. Schmidt, 27 October 1890 (*Selected Correspondence*, Moscow, p. 502): Colonial conquest originally achieved for obtaining imports from India; but later the need for exports to India and other colonial countries helped create modern large-scale industry [in England].

Engels to Danielson, 18 June 1892 (*Selected Correspondence*, Moscow, p. 528): Without tariff protection, Russia would have been reduced to the status of India, a country subject economically to Britain. [This letter needs to be read along with Engels's subsequent letter to Danielson, 22 September 1892, which is included in Marx and Engels, *Selected Correspondence, 1846–1895*, translated and edited by Dona Torr, Calcutta, 1945, pp. 437–40, and which comments in detail on the economic development of Russia with the aid of protection.]

Bibliography

Note: Works listed under 'References to India in Other Writings of Karl Marx and Frederick Engels', preceding this Bibliography, are not repeated here, unless they have also been referred to elsewhere in this volume. The volumes of *CW*, however, form an exception: all volumes, wherever cited, are listed.

Ahmad, Aijaz, *In Theory: Classes, Nations, Literatures* (Delhi, 1994).
—— (ed.), *Karl Marx and Frederick Engels, On the National and Colonial Questions* (New Delhi, 2001).
Aitchison, C.U., *A Collection of Treaties, Engagements and Sunnuds Relating to India and the Neighbouring Countries*, Vol. II (reprint, Delhi, 1983).
Avineri, Shlomo (ed.). See under Marx, Karl [and Frederick Engels].
Ball, Charles, *The History of Indian Mutiny* (London, n.d.; reprint, New Delhi, 1981).
Banerjee, A.C. (ed.), *Indian Constitutional Documents*, Vol. I (Calcutta, 1948).
Baran, Paul, and Paul Sweezy, *Monopoly Capital* (Penguin, 1973).
Barpujari, H.K., *Assam in the Days of the Company, 1826–1856* (Calcutta, 1980).
Berberoglu, Berch (ed.), *India, National Liberation and Class Struggle, A Collection of Classic Marxist Writings* (Meerut, 1986).
Bernier, François, *Travels in the Mogul Empire, AD 1656–1668*, translated by A. Constable, edited by V.A. Smith (Oxford, 1916).
British Parliamentary Papers, Colonies: East India, 1852–53, Vol. 14 (Shanon, Ireland, 1970).
Bühler, G. (transl.), *Manusmriti, The Laws of Manu* (Oxford, 1886).
Campbell, George, *Narrative of the Indian Revolt* (London, 1858).
——, *Modern India: Sketch of the System of Civil Government* (London, 1892).
Carey, H.Ch., *The Slave Trade, Domestic and Foreign: Why it Exists and How it may be Extinguished* (Philadelphia, 1853).
Chandra, Bipan, *The Rise and Growth of Economic Nationalism in India* (New Delhi, 1966).
Chapman, John, *The Cotton and Commerce of India, Considered in Relation to Interests of Great Britain; with Remarks on Railway Communication in the Bombay Presidency* (London, 1851).
Chattopadhyaya, Harprasad, *The Sepoy Mutiny, 1858: A Social Study and Analysis* (Calcutta, 1957).

Child, Josiah, *A New Discourse of Trade* (London, 1668; fourth edition, 1693).

———, *A Treatise Wherein is Demonstrated, I, that East India Trade is the Most National of all Foreign Trade . . .* (London, 1681).

Crouzet, François (ed.), *Capital Formation in the Industrial Revolution* (London, 1972).

Dangerfield, George, *Bengal Mutiny* (London, 1933).

Datta, K.K., *Biography of Kunwar Singh and Amar Singh* (Patna, 1957).

Davids, Rhys (transl.), *Questions of King Milinda*, 2 vols (London, 1890, 1894).

Deane, Phyllis, and W.A. Cole, *British Economic Growth, 1688–1959* (Cambridge, 1962).

Dickinson, John, *India Reform* (London, 1853).

Dobb, Maurice, *Studies in the Development of Capitalism* (London, 1946).

Dutt, R.P., *India Today* (Bombay, 1952).

Dutt, Romesh C., *Economic History of India under Early British Rule* (*Economic History of India*, Vol. I), (first published, London, 1901; sixth edition, London [n.d.]).

———, *The Economic History of India in the Victorian Age* (*Economic History of India*, Vol. II) (first published, 1903; seventh edition, London, 1950).

Ellison, Thomas, *The Cotton Trade of Great Britain* (first edition, 1886; reprint, London, 1968).

Elphinstone, Mountstuart, *History of India* (London, 1841; new edition, 1874).

[Engels, Frederick], *Revolution and Counter-Revolution or Germany in 1848–49*, articles written in *NYDT* in the name of Karl Marx, collected in a volume, with the latter described as the author, by Eleanor Marx–Aveling (London, 1896). In the ninth edition (London, 1937), the first printing is assigned to 1891, though Eleanor Marx–Aveling's Note as editor in this edition is itself dated April 1896.

Engels, Frederick, *Anti-Dühring*, English translation (Moscow, 1947).

———, *Origin of the Family, Private Property and the State*, English translation (Moscow, 1948).

Forrest, G.W., *History of the Indian Mutiny*, Vol. I (London, 1904).

Forrest, G.W. (ed.) *Selections from the Letters, Despatches and other State Papers Preserved in the Military Department of the Government of India 1857–58*, Vol. II (Calcutta, 1902).

Forster, Charles, *The Historical Geography of Arabia, on the Patriarchal Evidence of Revealed Religion*, 2 vols (London, 1844).

Goethe, Johann Wolfgang von, *Reineke Fox, West-Eastern Divan, and Achillied*, translated by Alexander Rogers (London, 1890).

Government, H.M., *Correspondence relating to Persia and Afghanistan* (London, 1851).

Grant, Hope, *Incidents in the Sepoy War, 1857–58* (Edinburgh, 1873).

Gubbins, Martin Richard, *An Account of the Mutinies in Oudh* (London, 1859; reprint, Delhi, 1978).

Habib, Irfan, *Agrarian System of Mughal India* (second edition, New Delhi, 1999).

Haidar, Kamaluddin, *Tawarikh-i Awadh* (Urdu), Vol. I (Lucknow, 1896).

Hansard, *Parliamentary Debates*, Vols 249, 250.

Hansen, A.H., *Fiscal Policy and Business Cycles* (London, 1941).

Hegel, G.W. Friedrich, *The Philosophy of History*, translated by J. Sibree (New York, 1956).

Hilton, Edward H., *The Mutiny Records: Oudh and Lucknow (1856–57)* (reprint, Lahore, 1975).

Hobsbawm, Eric, *Industry and Empire* (Penguin, 1960).

Hunter, W.W., *Statistical Account of Bengal*, IX (London, 1875).

———, *A History of Orissa*, Vol. I (Calcutta, 1956).

Innes, Mecleod, *Lucknow and Oude in the Mutiny* (London, 1896).

Jomo, K.S. (ed.), *The Pioneers of Development Economics* (New Delhi, 2005).

———, *Globalization under Hegemony*, Delhi (forthcoming).

Joshi, P.C. (ed.), *Rebellion 1857* (New Delhi, 1957).

Joshi, P.C., and K. Damodaran, *Marx Comes to India* (Delhi, 1975).

Kalecki, M., *Selected Essays on the Dynamics of the Capitalist Economy* (Cambridge, 1971).

Karat, Prakash (ed.), *A World to Win* (New Delhi, 1999).

Kaye, John William, *A History of the Sepoy War in India, 1857–1858*, Vol. I (London, 1875); Vol. II (London, 1881); Vol. III (London, 1881).

Kosambi, D.D., *An Introduction to the Study of Indian History* (Bombay, 1956).

Krader, Lawrence (ed.) *The Ethnological Notebooks of Karl Marx* (Assen, 1972).

Kumar, Dharma, *Land and Caste in South India* (Cambridge, 1965).

Kumar, Dharma, and Meghnad Desai (eds), *Cambridge Economic History of India*, Vol. II (Cambridge, 1982).

Lee, Sydney (ed.), *The Concise Dictionary of National Biography*, Part 1 (to 1900) (London, 1953).

Lalji, *Mirat-ul auza*, MS, Maulana Azad Library, Aligarh.

Lenin, V.I., *Imperialism, the Highest Stage of Capitalism*, English translation (Moscow, 1982).

———, *Selected Works*, 3 vols, Vol. I (Moscow, 1977); Vol. III (Moscow, 1975).

Luxemburg, Rosa, *The Accumulation of Capital*, translated by A. Schwarzchild (London, 1951).

Maine, Henry Sumner, *Lectures on the Early History of Institutions* (London, 1875).

Martin, Montgomery, *China, Political, Commercial and Social, in an Official Report to H.M. Government* (London, 1847).

[Marx, Karl], *Palmerston and Russia* (London, 1853).

Marx, Karl, *The Eastern Question, A Reprint of Letters Written in 1853–56, Dealing with the Events of the Crimean War*, edited by Eleanor and Edward Aveling (London, 1897).

———, *A Contribution to the Critique of Political Economy* (Moscow, 1970; reprint, 1978).

———, *Articles on India*, with Introduction by R.P. Dutt (Bombay, 1943).

———, *Capital*, Vol. I (the Moore–Aveling translation, edited by Frederick Engels) (London, 1887); edited by Dona Torr (with page-to-page correspondence) (London, 1938).

———, *Capital*, I, translated by E. and C. Paul, 2 parts (London, 1930).

———, *Capital*, Vol. I (Moscow, 1974); Vol. II (Moscow, 1957); Vol. III (Moscow, 1959).

———, *Grundrisse*, translated by Martin Nicolaus (London, 1973).

———, *Letters to Kugelmann* (London, n.d.; 1935?).

———, *Marx on China, 1853–1860,* edited by Dona Torr (Bombay, 1952).

———, *Notes on Indian History (1664–1858)* (Moscow, n.d).

———, *Pre-Capitalist Economic Formations*, edited by E.J. Hobsbawm (London, 1964).

———, *The Poverty of Philosophy* (Moscow, n.d).

———, *Theories of Surplus Value*, Vol. III (Moscow, 1971).

Marx, Karl [and Frederick Engels], *On Colonialism and Modernization*, edited by Shlomo Avineri (New York, 1969).

Marx, Karl, and Frederick Engels, *Selected Correspondence, 1846–1895*, edited by Dona Torr (Calcutta, 1945).

———, *Selected Correspondence* (Moscow, 1956).

———, *On Britain* (Moscow, 1953).

———, *On Colonialism* (Moscow, fourth edition, 1976).

———, *The First Indian War of Independence, 1857–1859* (Moscow, 1959).

———, *The German Ideology*, English translation (Moscow, 1964).

———, *Collected Works*, Vol. 2 (Moscow, 1975); Vol. 5 (Moscow, 1976); Vol. 6 (Moscow, 1976); Vol. 9 (Moscow, 1977); Vol. 11 (Moscow, 1979); Vol. 12 (Moscow, 1979); Vol. 13 (Moscow, 1980); Vol. 14 (Moscow, 1980); Vol. 15 (Moscow, 1983); Vol. 16 (Moscow, 1980); Vol. 17 (Moscow, 1981); Vol. 18 (Moscow, 1982); Vol. 19 (Moscow, 1984); Vol. 21 (Moscow, 1985); Vol. 22 (Moscow, 1986); Vol. 24 (Moscow, 1989); Vol. 25 (Moscow, 1987); Vol. 28 (Moscow, 1986); Vol. 29 (Moscow, 1987); Vol. 30 (Moscow, 1988); Vol. 31 (Moscow, 1988); Vol. 32 (Moscow, 1989); Vol. 38 (Moscow, 1982); Vol. 39 (Moscow, 1983); Vol. 40 (Moscow, 1983); Vol. 41 (Moscow, 1985); Vol. 42 (Moscow, 1987); Vol. 43 (Moscow, 1988).

———, *The Eastern Question: A Reprint of Letters dealing with the Events of the Crimean War,* compiled by Eleanor Marx–Aveling and Edward Aveling (London, 1897).

McLellan, David, *Karl Marx: A Biography* (London, 1973).

Mill, James, *The History of British India*, Vol. V (London, 1840).

Morgan, L.H., *Ancient Society, or Researches in the Line of Progress from Savagery through Barbarism to Civilization* (London, 1877).

Mun, Thomas, *A Discourse of Trade, from England unto the East Indies* (London, 1621).

Murray, Hugh, and James Wilson, *Historical and Descriptive Account of British India*, Vol. II (Edinburgh, 1832).

Muter, Mrs D.D., *My Recollections of the Sepoy Revolt (1857–58)* (London, 1911).

Naoroji, Dadabhai, *Poverty and Un-British Rule in India* (originally published in London, 1901; Indian edition, Delhi, 1962).

Natarajan, S., *A History of Press in India* (Bombay, 1962).

Nicolaievsky, Boris, and Otto Menchen-Helfen, *Karl Marx: Man and Fighter* (London, 1936).

Panikkar, K.N., T.J. Byres and Utsa Patnaik (eds), *The Making of History* (New Delhi, 2000).

Patel, Surendra J., *Agricultural Labourers of India and Pakistan* (Bombay, 1952).

Patnaik, Prabhat, *Accumulation and Stability under Capitalism* (Oxford, 1997).

Pavlov, V.I., *Historical Premises for India's Transition to Capitalism* (Moscow, 1978).

[Pollexfen, John], *England and India Inconsistent in Their Manufactures* (London, 1697).

Raffles, Thomas Stamford, *The History of Java*, Vol. I (London, 1817).

Rizvi, S.A.A., *Freedom Struggle in Uttar Pradesh*, Vol. III (Lucknow, 1957).

Roberts, Fred, *Letters Written during the Indian Mutiny* (London, 1924).

Roberts, Fred [Field-Marshal Earl Roberts of Kandahar], *Forty-One Years in India*, Vol. I (London, 1897).

Russell, W.H., *My Diary in India in the Year 1858–59*, 2 vols (London, 1860).

Said, Edward, *Orientalism*, second edition (London, 1995).

Sartre, Jean–Paul, *Search for a Method* (New York, 1968).

Saul, S.B., *Studies in British Overseas Trade* (Liverpool, 1970).

Schumpeter, Joseph, *Ten Great Economists* (London, 1966).

Select Committee of Parliament, *The Fifth Report from the Select Committee on the Affairs of the East India Company, 1812*, photo-offset edition, Irish University Press, Colonies: East India, Vol. 3 (Shanon, 1969).

Sen, S.N., *Eighteen Fifty Seven* (New Delhi, 1957).

Sewell, Robert, *An Analytical History of India* (London, 1870).

Sharar, Abdul Halim, *Guzishta Lakhnau* (Urdu) (Lucknow, 1965).

Shaw, A.G.L. (ed.), *Great Britain and the Colonies, 1815–1865* (London, 1970).

Sleeman, William, *Journey through the Kingdom of Oude in 1849–50* (reprint, Lucknow, 1989).

Smith, V.A., *Oxford History of India*, second edition (London, 1922).

Soltykoff, Prince Alexei Dimitrivich, *Lettres sur l'Inde* (Paris, 1848).

Spear, P., *Twilight of the Mughals* (Delhi, 1969).

Stokes, Eric, *The Peasant and the Raj* (Cambridge, 1978).

Storey, C.A., *Persian Literature: A Biobibliographical Survey*, Vol. I, Part 1 (London, 1927–39).

Sweezy, Paul M., *The Theory of Capitalist Development* (London, 1946).

Tarbuck, K.J. (ed.), *Imperialism and the Accumulation of Capital* (London, 1972).

Vibart, Edward, *Sepoy Mutiny as seen by a Subaltern* (London, 1898).

Wedderburn, William, *Allan Octavian Hume, Father of the Indian National Congress* (London, 1913).

Wilberforce, G. Reginal, *An Unrecorded Chapter of the Indian Mutiny* (London, 1894; reprint, Delhi, 1976).

Wilks, Mark, *Historical Sketches of South India*, I, edited by Murray Hammick (London, 1810; Mysore, 1930).

Wilson, H.H., *A Glossary of Judicial and Revenue and Revenue Terms . . . of British India* (London, 1875; reprint, Delhi, 1968).

Wittfogel, Karl A., *Oriental Despotism* (New Haven, 1957).

Index